Jane Comyns Carr

with Nick Witherick

# speakout

## Upper Intermediate
## Teacher's Resource Book

# TEACHER'S RESOURCE BOOK CONTENTS

# STUDENTS' BOOK CONTENTS

| LISTENING/DVD | SPEAKING | WRITING |
|---|---|---|
| listen to a radio programme about speed flatmating | ask personal questions; talk about the kind of people you get on with | write an informal email; learn to check your work for accuracy |
| listen to people describing how certain activities make them feel | talk about experiences | |
| listen to a phone enquiry about a language course | role play making phone enquiries; learn to manage enquiries | |
| **BBC Off the Hook:** watch and listen to a drama about starting university | describe a first encounter | write a summary of a first encounter story |
| | talk about charities and social issues | |
| listen to opinions about surveillance | discuss surveillance society; role play a meeting to discuss crime-cutting plans | write a letter of complaint; learn to use formal written language |
| listen to informal discussions | discuss different issues; learn to support your viewpoint | |
| **BBC The Happiness Formula:** watch an extract from a documentary about happiness in the West | discuss ingredients of happiness; carry out a happiness survey | write tips for being happy for a website |
| | talk about playing games and sports; discuss bad habits and how to prevent them | write an opinion essay about leisure time; learn to use linkers in an opinion essay |
| listen to a radio programme about niche travel | talk about holidays; plan and present a niche holiday | |
| listen to descriptions of two TV game shows | talk about game shows; learn to use mirror questions; describe a procedure | |
| **BBC 50 Things To Do Before You Die:** watch an extract from a programme about great experiences | recommend an experience you have had | write a true story |
| | tell a personal annecdote | write a story; learn to use adverbs in stories |
| listen to a radio programme about very short stories | talk about wishes and regrets | |
| listen to people recommending books | talk about reading habits; learn to summarise a plot; talk about a favourite book | |
| **BBC Tess of the D'Urbervilles:** watch an extract from a drama about a girl in 19th Century rural England | describe a favourite scene in a TV programme or film | write a description of a favourite scene |
| | talk about the effects of inventions | |
| listen to a programme about advertising | discuss advertising tactics | write a report; learn to make written comparisons |
| listen to people brainstorming | brainstorm ideas on a 'how to' topic; learn to show reservations | |
| **BBC Genius:** watch an extract from a programme about funny ideas | present a 'genius' business idea | write a product leaflet for a 'genius' idea |

COMMUNICATION BANK PAGE 158          AUDIO SCRIPTS PAGE 164

| LISTENING/DVD | SPEAKING | WRITING |
|---|---|---|
| | talk about different ages; discuss similarities and differences between generations | |
| listen to a radio programme about writing letters to your future self | talk about your future hopes and plans | write a letter to your future self; learn to use linkers of purpose |
| listen to a radio phone-in programme about life's milestones | role play a radio phone-in; learn to ask for clarification | |
| **BBC** How to Live to 101: watch an extract from a documentary about people who live to a very old age | plan and take part in a debate | write a forum comment giving your opinion |
| | talk about TV watching habits | |
| listen to an expert talking about hoax photographs | discuss answers to a quiz; discuss celebrities and the media | write a discursive essay; learn to use linkers of contrast |
| listen to people talking about recent news stories | talk about the press; discuss 'top five' lists; learn to make guesses | |
| **BBC** The Funny Side of the News: watch and understand a programme about live news | retell a recent news story | write a news article |
| | discuss difficult decisions | |
| listen to people talking about their attitudes to time; listen to a radio programme about people's daily rhythms | talk about your attitude to time | write an informal article; learn to use an informal style in an article |
| listen to someone talking through an awkward situation. | talk about how to handle awkward situations; role play an awkward situation; learn to soften a message | |
| **BBC** The Human Animal: watch an extract from a programme about body language | describe a family or cultural ritual | write about a family ritual |
| | discuss how good a witness you are; talk about what you would do in difficult situations | |
| listen to people talking about getting tricked | speculate about how scams work | write an advice leaflet to help visitors to your city; learn to avoid repetition |
| listen to someone reporting an incident | role play reporting an incident; learn to rephrase | |
| **BBC** 999: watch an extract from a documentary about a sea rescue | discuss items to take on a life raft | write a story about a lucky escape |
| listen to a film review on a radio programme | talk about films | write a film review; learn to write more descriptively |
| | talk about popular culture and arts experiences | |
| listen to tours of two different places | learn to express estimates; role play showing a visitor around part of your town | |
| **BBC** The One Show: watch an extract from a programme about a famous graffiti artist | choose a new articstic project for your town | write a description of a favourite work of art or building |

COMMUNICATION BANK PAGE 158          AUDIO SCRIPTS PAGE 164

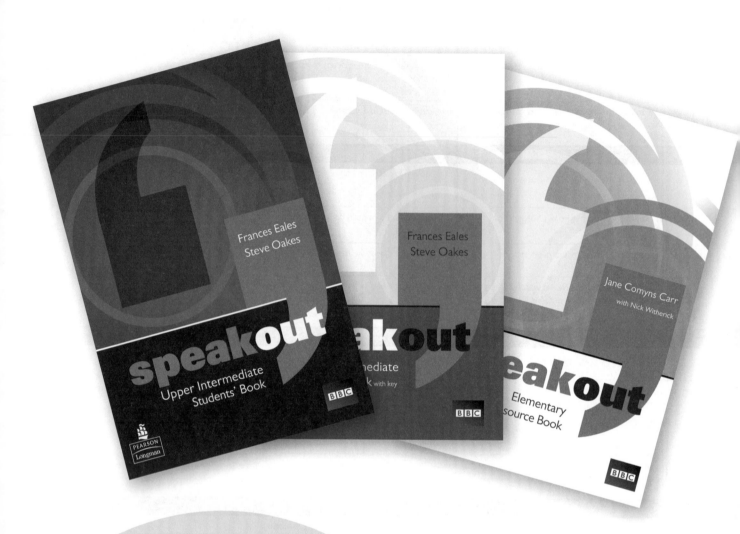

Before we started writing *Speakout*, we did a lot of research to find out more about the issues that teachers and students face and how these can be addressed in a textbook for the 21st century. The issues that came up again and again were motivation, authentic content and the need for structured speaking and listening strategies.

As English teachers, we know how motivating it can be to bring the real world into the classroom by using authentic materials. We also know how time consuming and difficult it can be to find authentic content that is truly engaging, at the right level and appropriate for our students. With access to the entire archive of the BBC, we have selected some stunning video content to motivate and engage students. We have also created tasks that will encourage interaction with the materials while providing the right amount of scaffolding.

We realise that the real world is not just made up of actors, presenters and comedians, and 'real' English does not just consist of people reading from scripts. This is why *Speakout* brings real people into the classroom. The Video podcasts show people giving their opinions about the topics in the book and illustrate some of the strategies that will help our students become more effective communicators.

*Speakout* maximises opportunities for students to speak and systematically asks them to notice and employ strategies that will give them the confidence to communicate fluently and the competence to listen actively. While the main focus is on speaking and listening, we have also developed a systematic approach to reading and writing. For us, these skills are absolutely essential for language learners in the digital age.

To sum up, we have tried to write a course that teachers will really enjoy using; a course that is authentic but manageable, systematic but not repetitive – a course that not only brings the real world into the classroom, but also sends our students into the real world with the confidence to truly 'speak out'!

From left to right: Frances Eales, JJ Wilson, Antonia Clare and Steve Oakes

# OVERVIEW OF THE COMPONENTS

## STUDENTS' BOOK

- Between 90 and 120 hours of teaching material
- Language Bank with reference material and extra practice
- Vocabulary bank to expand vocabulary
- Audioscripts of the class audio

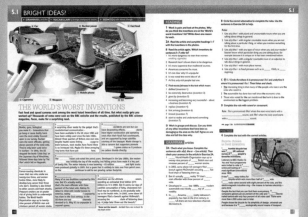

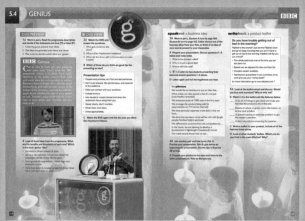

## CLASS AUDIO CDs

- Audio material for use in class
- Test audio for the Mid-course and End of Course Tests

## DVD & ACTIVE BOOK

- DVD content
- Digital Students' Book
- Audio, video and Video podcasts

## WORKBOOK

- Grammar and vocabulary
- Functional language
- Speaking and listening strategies
- Reading, writing and listening
- Regular review and self-study tests

## AUDIO CD

- Audio material including listening, pronunciation and functional practice

## MYSPEAKOUTLAB

- Interactive Workbook with hints and tips
- Unit tests and Progress Tests
- Mid-course and End of Course Tests
- Video podcasts with interactive worksheets

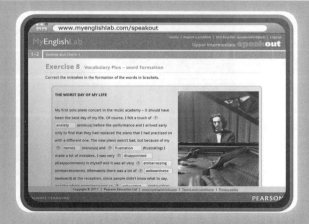

# TEACHER'S RESOURCE BOOK

- Teaching notes
- Integrated key and audioscript
- Five photocopiable activities for every unit
- Mid-course and End of Course Test

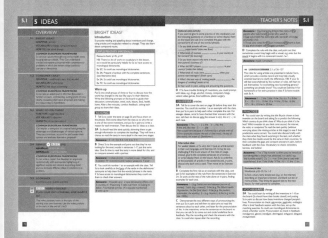

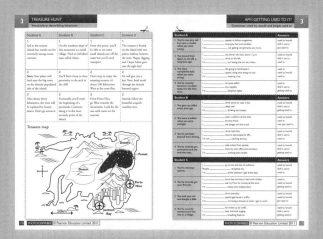

# SPEAKOUT ACTIVE TEACH

- Integrated audio and video content
- Video podcasts
- Test master containing all course tests
- Answer reveal feature
- Grammar and vocabulary review games
- A host of useful tools
- Large extra resources section

# SPEAKOUT WEBSITE

- Information about the course
- Sample materials from the course
- Teaching tips
- Placement test
- A range of useful resources
- Video podcasts

# A UNIT OF THE STUDENTS' BOOK

## UNIT OVERVIEW

Every unit of Speakout starts with an Overview, which lists the topics covered. This is followed by two main input lessons which cover grammar, vocabulary and the four skills. Lesson three covers functional language and focuses on important speaking and listening strategies. Lesson four is built around a clip from a BBC programme and consolidates language and skills work. Each unit culminates with a Lookback page, which provides communicative practice of the key language.

## INPUT LESSON 1

Lesson one introduces the topic of the unit and presents the key language needed to understand and talk about it. The lesson combines grammar and vocabulary with a focus on skills work.

> The target language and the CEF objectives are listed to clearly show the objectives of the lesson.

> Each input lesson has either a focus on listening or a focus on reading.

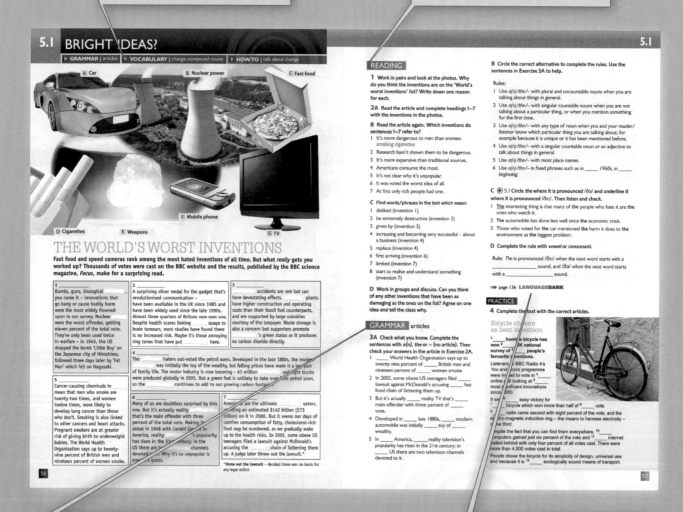

> Clear grammar presentations are followed by written and oral practice as well as pronunciation work.

> Every grammar section includes a reference to the Language bank with explanations and further practice.

# INPUT LESSON 2

Lesson two continues to focus on grammar and vocabulary while extending and expanding the topic area. By the end of the second lesson students will have worked on all four skill areas.

All lessons include a focus on speaking where the emphasis is on communication and fluency building.

Lexical sets are introduced in context. Practice of new words often includes pronunciation work.

---

## 5.2

### GRAMMAR conditionals

**3A** Match sentences 1–4 with conditional forms a)–d).

1 If you price your product just above the competition's price, you'll end up with a bigger share of the market.
2 If something costs more, it's better.
3 If I were to introduce a new lipstick on the market, should I price mine above or below the competition?
4 If a watch showed 8.20, it wouldn't sell as well.

a) Zero conditional: *if* + present simple, present simple
b) First conditional: *if* + present simple, *will/can/could/may/might/should* + infinitive
c) Second conditional (A): *if* + past simple, *would/should/could/might* + infinitive
d) Second conditional (B): *if* + *were to* + infinitive, *would/should/could/might* + infinitive

**B** Work in pairs and complete the rules.

Rules:
1 a) Use the _____ conditional to talk about hypothetical present or future events or situations.
   b) Use the _____ conditional to talk about something that is likely to happen in the future as a result of an action or situation.
   c) Use the _____ conditional to talk about something that is always or generally true as a result of an action or situation.
2 In formal English, *if* + _____ + infinitive can be used for hypothetical situations.

**C** Look at examples a)–c) and find three conjunctions which mean *if and only if*, and one which means *if not*.

a) Yes, it's fine to look at <u>as long as</u> you don't eat it.
b) Each machine would probably sell two hundred cans a day <u>unless</u> the market was saturated.
c) People will pay more <u>providing/provided</u> the difference is small.

**4A** ▶ 5.4 Listen and write sentences 1–5 in your notebook.

**B** Underline the two main stresses in each sentence, one in each clause. Listen again and check. Then listen and repeat.
➡ page 136 LANGUAGE**BANK**

60

### PRACTICE

**5A** Underline the correct alternatives in the text.

If you wanted a new product to reach the maximum number of people for the minimum cost, what ¹*would/will* you do? The answer is launch a viral advert – a video that people can email so that it spreads like a virus and gives your product free publicity. It works like this: your company makes a video and then, ²*providing/unless* this viral advert reaches a 'susceptible' user (one who likes the idea), that user ³*will/would* send the advert to others, thus 'infecting them'. ⁴*As long as/Unless* each 'infected' user shares the idea with more than one other user, the number of users ⁵*grows/would grow*. So, ⁶*provided/unless* an advert is novel or entertaining enough, it ⁷*will spread/spread* across the Web like a virus at no extra cost to the advertiser. If you ⁸*send/were to send* out a viral advert that didn't catch on, it would go nowhere – people would simply delete it. ⁹*Unless/As long as* adverts are funny, smart or edgy, they ¹⁰*won't/will* have any effect.

**B** Work in pairs and discuss. Have you ever sent or received a viral advert? What's your favourite/least favourite TV or internet advert at the moment?

### SPEAKING

**6A** Read the guidelines on creating a viral advert. What product is being advertised in the example?

## How to create a viral advert

STEP 1: Make a video of a person or animal in an odd place, for example a businessman trapped on the branch of a tree, using both hands to balance.

STEP 2: Introduce a problem, e.g. a mosquito attacks him but he can't swat it as he can't let go of the tree.

STEP 3: Bring in an unexpected solution, e.g. a gorilla swings in on a vine, lands on the same branch and hands the businessman a spray.

**B** Choose a product from the photos and create your own thirty-second viral advert, following the guidelines above.

**C** Work in groups and take turns. Describe your viral advert but don't say what product you chose. Can the other students guess?

### VOCABULARY advertising

**7A** Complete questions 1–10 with a word from the box.

commercials   pop-ups   brands
endorse/promote   campaigns
logos   influence   slogans   cold calls
advertise   makes   jingle

1 Are there too many TV _____ in programme breaks?
2 'Just do it!' and 'The world's local bank' are memorable _____. What others do you know?
3 What are the most popular _____ of car in your country? What's your favourite?
4 Which are the most popular sports equipment _____ in your country?
5 Do you think celebrities should _____ a particular product?
6 What does an image of an apple with a bite taken out of it mean to you? What other _____ do you know?
7 What type of advertisement would _____ you to try a new food or drink product?
8 Do you ever find yourself singing a particular _____ for a product or a radio station?
9 Can you recall any particularly successful advertising _____?
10 If you wanted to sell a product, where would you _____?
11 How do you feel about website _____? Do they work?
12 What do you say when someone _____ you in the evenings?

**B** Work in pairs and answer the questions in Exercise 7A.
➡ page 152 VOCABULARY**BANK**

### WRITING a report

**8A** What influences you when you buy a new gadget? Write a list of factors and put them in order of importance.
*I always go for the latest model because it makes me look trendy.*

**B** Work in groups and compare your ideas.

**9A** Look at the chart below which shows the results of a survey on why men, women and teenagers choose a particular smartphone. What is the most and least important factor for each group of people?

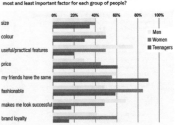

**B** Read the report written by a student on the survey results and answer the questions.

1 Which factors are mentioned?
2 The student has made one factual error. What is it?
3 What is the purpose of each of the first three paragraphs in the report?

The bar chart shows the results of a survey of students and employees in our language school in relation to their reasons for buying a particular mobile phone.

First of all, comparing the results for men and women, it can be seen that some factors affect both groups more or less equally. For example, there is no difference in how much size and colour influence their choice of phone, and the results for 'my friends have the same one' show only a slight variation.

There are, however, significant differences in the results for other factors. The usefulness or practicality of a phone's features is far more important for men than for women, as is the price and how much it makes the owner look successful. On the other hand, women place greater importance on brand loyalty.

The results for teenagers showed an interesting contrast to those for men and women. First of all ...

### LEARN TO make written comparisons

**10** Read the report again and complete tasks 1–3.

1 Circle three phrases for saying that two things are the same or nearly the same.
2 Underline four phrases for talking about differences.
3 Put a box around four linking phrases

**11A** Work in pairs. Look at the chart and make notes on five points you could make about teenagers.

**B** Complete the report by continuing the last paragraph. Write 100–150 words. Include at least six of the phrases in Exercise 10.

61

---

Grammar and vocabulary sections often include a listening element to reinforce the new language.

Every pair of input lessons includes at least one writing section with focus on a variety of different genres.

Lexical sets are often expanded in the Vocabulary bank at the back of the Students' Book.

# A UNIT OF THE STUDENTS' BOOK

## FUNCTIONAL LESSON

The third lesson in each unit focuses on a particular function, situation or transaction as well as introducing important speaking and listening strategies.

The target language and the CEF objectives are listed to clearly show the objectives of the lesson.

The functional language is learnt in context, often by listening to the language in use.

Students learn important speaking and listening strategies which can be transferred to many situations.

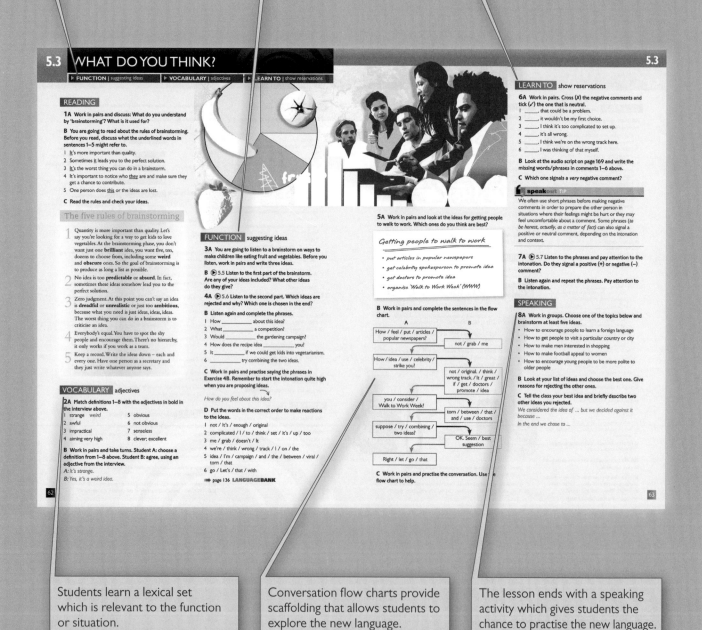

Students learn a lexical set which is relevant to the function or situation.

Conversation flow charts provide scaffolding that allows students to explore the new language.

The lesson ends with a speaking activity which gives students the chance to practise the new language.

# DVD LESSON

The fourth lesson in each unit is based around an extract from a real BBC programme. This acts as a springboard into freer communicative speaking and writing activities.

A preview section gets students thinking about the topic of the extract and introduces key language.

A series of different tasks helps students to understand and enjoy the programme.

The Speakout task builds on the topic of the extract and provides extended speaking practice.

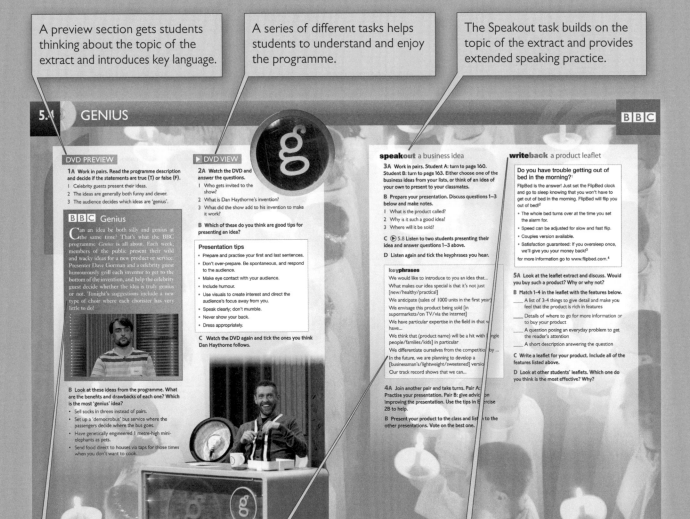

A TV listing about the programme sets the context and helps students prepare to watch the clip.

The key phrases box helps students to notice the key language for the speaking task and builds confidence.

The Writeback task further extends the topic and provides communicative writing practice.

# LOOKBACK PAGE

Each unit ends with a Lookback page, which provides further practice and review of the key language covered in the unit. The review exercises are a mixture of communicative activities and games. Further practice and review exercises can be found in the Workbook. The Lookback page also introduces the Video podcast, which features a range of real people talking about one of the topics in the unit.

## WORKBOOK

The Workbook contains a wide variety of practice and review exercises and covers all of the language areas studied in the unit. It also contains regular review sections as well as self-study tests to help students consolidate what they have learnt.

> The Workbook features extensive practice of vocabulary, grammar, reading, writing and listening.

> A variety of language practice activities consolidate the areas covered in the Students' Book.

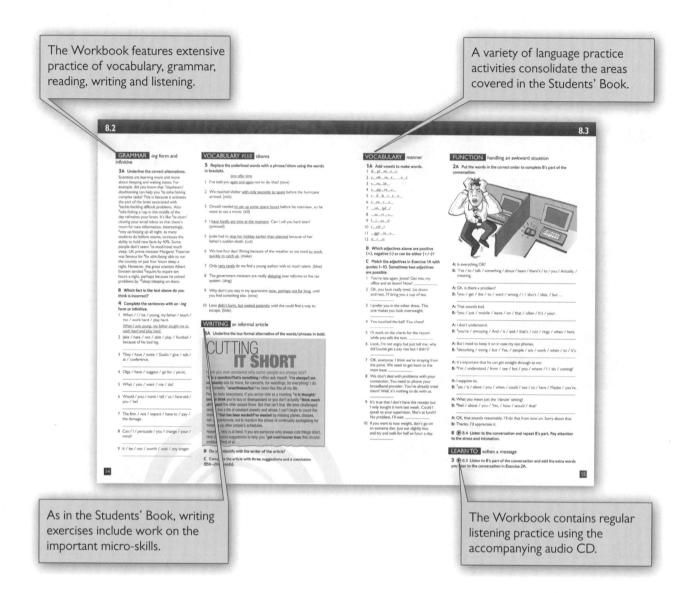

> As in the Students' Book, writing exercises include work on the important micro-skills.

> The Workbook contains regular listening practice using the accompanying audio CD.

## MYSPEAKOUTLAB

MySpeakoutLab provides a fully blended and personalised learning environment that benefits both teachers and students. It offers:

- an interactive Workbook with hints, tips and automatic grade book.
- professionally written Unit Tests, Progress Tests, Mid-course and End of Course tests that can be assigned at the touch of a button.
- interactive Video podcast worksheets with an integrated video player so students can watch while they do the exercises.

# ACTIVETEACH

Speakout ActiveTeach contains everything you need to make the course come alive in your classroom.
It includes integrated whiteboard software which enables you to add notes and embed files.
It is also possible to save all of your work with the relevant page from the Students' Book.

An answer reveal function lets you show the answers to an exercise at the touch of a button.

All audio and video content is fully integrated and includes subtitles as well as printable scripts.

Shortcuts to the relevant pages of the Language bank and the Vocabulary bank make navigation easy.

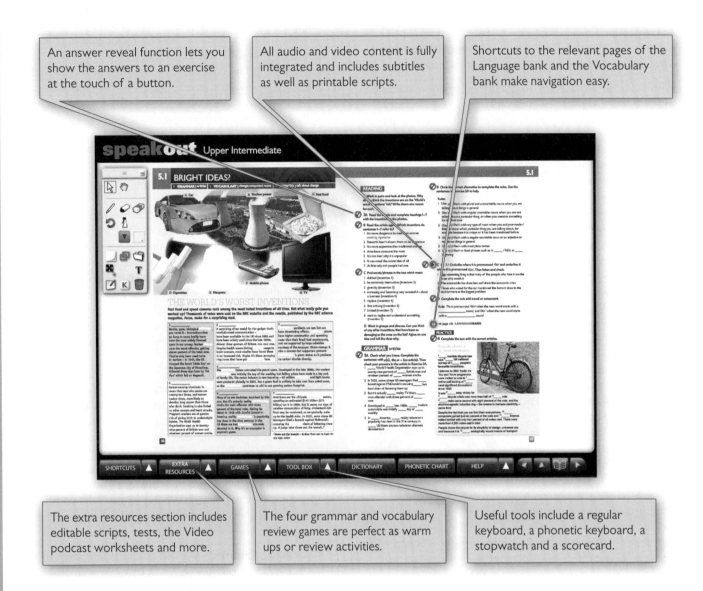

The extra resources section includes editable scripts, tests, the Video podcast worksheets and more.

The four grammar and vocabulary review games are perfect as warm ups or review activities.

Useful tools include a regular keyboard, a phonetic keyboard, a stopwatch and a scorecard.

# WEBSITE

The Speakout website will offer information about the course as well as a bank of useful resources including:

• introductory videos by the authors of the course.
• sample materials.
• teaching tips.
• placement test.
• CEF mapping documents.
• Video podcasts for all published levels.

**speakout** is designed to satisfy both students and teachers on a number of different levels. It offers engaging topics with authentic BBC material to really bring them to life. At the same time it offers a robust and comprehensive focus on grammar, vocabulary, functions and pronunciation. As the name of the course might suggest, speaking activities are prominent, but that is not at the expense of the other core skills, which are developed systematically throughout.

With this balanced approach to topics, language development and skills work, our aim has been to create a course book full of 'lessons that really work' in practice. Below we will briefly explain our approach in each of these areas.

## TOPICS AND CONTENT

In *Speakout* we have tried to choose topics that are relevant to students' lives. Where a topic area is covered in other ELT courses we have endeavoured to find a fresh angle on it. It is clear to us that authenticity is important to learners, and many texts come from the BBC's rich resources (audio, visual and print) as well as other real-world sources. At lower levels, we have sometimes adapted materials by adjusting the language to make it more manageable for students while trying to keep the tone as authentic as possible. We have also attempted to match the authentic feel of a text with an authentic interaction. Every unit contains a variety of rich and authentic input material including BBC Video podcasts (filmed on location in London, England) and DVD material, featuring some of the best the BBC has to offer.

## GRAMMAR

Knowing how to recognise and use grammatical structures is central to our ability to communicate with each other. Although at first students can often get by with words and phrases, they increasingly need grammar to make themselves understood. Students also need to understand sentence formation when reading and listening and to be able to produce accurate grammar in professional and exam situations. We share students' belief that learning grammar is a core feature of learning a language and believe that a guided discovery approach, where students are challenged to notice new forms works best. At the same time learning is scaffolded so that students are supported at all times in a systematic way. Clear grammar presentations are followed by written and oral practice. There is also the chance to notice and practise pronunciation where appropriate.

In *Speakout* you will find:

- **Grammar in context** – We want to be sure that the grammar focus is clear and memorable for students. Grammar is almost always taken from the listening or reading texts, so that learners can see the language in action, and understand how and when it is used.

- **Noticing** – We involve students in the discovery of language patterns by asking them to identify aspects of meaning and form, and complete rules or tables.

- **Clear language reference** – As well as a summary of rules within the unit, there is also a Language bank which serves as a clear learning reference for the future

- **Focus on use** – We ensure that there is plenty of practice, both form and meaning-based, in the Language bank to give students confidence in manipulating the new language. On the main input page we include personalised practice, which is designed to be genuinely communicative and to offer students the opportunity to say something about themselves or the topic. There is also regular recycling of new language in the Lookback review pages, and again the focus here is on moving learners towards communicative use of the language.

## VOCABULARY

Developing a wide range of vocabulary is key to increasing communicative effectiveness; developing a knowledge of high-frequency collocations and fixed and semi-fixed phrases is key to increasing spoken fluency. An extensive understanding of words and phrases helps learners become more confident when reading and listening, and developing a range of vocabulary is important for effective writing. Equally vital is learner-training, equipping students with the skills to record, memorise and recall vocabulary for use.

In *Speakout* this is reflected in:

- **A prominent focus on vocabulary** – We include vocabulary in almost all lessons whether in a lexical set linked to a particular topic, as preparation for a speaking activity or to aid comprehension of a DVD clip or a listening or reading text. Where we want students to use the language actively, we encourage them to use the vocabulary to talk about their own lives or opinions. At lower levels, the Photo bank also extends the vocabulary taught in the lessons, using memorable photographs and graphics to support students' understanding.

- **Focus on 'chunks'** – As well as lexical sets, we also regularly focus on how words fit together with other words, often getting students to notice how words are used in a text and to focus on high-frequency 'chunks' such as verb-noun collocations or whole phrases.

- **Focus on vocabulary systems** – We give regular attention to word-building skills, a valuable tool in expanding vocabulary. At higher levels, the Vocabulary plus sections deal with systems such as affixation, multi-word verbs and compound words in greater depth.

- **Recycling and learner training** – Practice exercises ensure that vocabulary is encountered on a number of occasions: within the lessons, on the Lookback page, in subsequent lessons and in the Photo bank/Vocabulary bank at the back of the book. One of the main focuses of the Speakout tips – which look at all areas of language learning – is to highlight vocabulary learning strategies, aiming to build good study skills that will enable students to gain and retain new language.

## FUNCTIONAL LANGUAGE

One thing that both teachers and learners appreciate is the need to manage communication in a wide variety of encounters, and to know what's appropriate to say in given situations. These can be transactional exchanges, where the main focus is on getting something done (buying something in a shop or phoning to make an enquiry), or interactional exchanges, where the main focus is on socialising with others (talking about the weekend, or responding appropriately to good news). As one learner commented to us, 'Grammar rules aren't enough – I need to know what to say.' Although it is possible to categorise 'functions' under 'lexical phrases', we believe it is useful for learners to focus on functional phrases separately from vocabulary or grammar.

The third lesson in every unit of *Speakout* looks at one such situation, and focuses on the functional language needed. Learners hear or see the language used in context and then practise it in mini-situations, in both a written and a spoken context. Each of these lessons also includes a Learn to section, which highlights and practises a useful strategy for dealing with both transactional and interactional exchanges, for example asking for clarification, showing interest, etc. Learners will find themselves not just more confident users of the language, but also more active listeners.

## SPEAKING

The dynamism of most lessons depends on the success of the speaking tasks, whether the task is a short oral practice of new language, a discussion comparing information or opinions, a personal response to a reading text or a presentation where a student might speak uninterrupted for a minute or more. Students develop fluency when they are motivated to speak. For this to happen, engaging topics and tasks are essential, as is the sequencing of stages and task design. For longer tasks, students often need to prepare their ideas and language in a structured way. This all-important rehearsal time leads to more motivation and confidence as well as greater accuracy, fluency and complexity. Also, where appropriate, students need to hear a model before they speak, in order to have a realistic goal.

There are several strands to speaking in *Speakout*:

- **Communicative practice** – After introducing any new language (vocabulary, grammar or function) there are many opportunities in *Speakout* for students to use it in a variety of activities which focus on communication as well as accuracy. These include personalised exchanges, dialogues, flow-charts and role-plays.

- **Focus on fluency** – In every unit of *Speakout* we include opportunities for students to respond spontaneously. They might be asked to respond to a series of questions, to a DVD, a Video podcast or a text, or to take part in conversations, discussions and role-plays. These activities involve a variety of interactional formations such as pairs and groups.

- **Speaking strategies and sub-skills** – In the third lesson of each unit, students are encouraged to notice in a systematic way features which will help them improve their speaking. These include, for example, ways to manage a phone conversation, the use of mirror questions to ask for clarification, sentence starters to introduce an opinion and intonation to correct mistakes.

- **Extended speaking tasks** – In the *Speakout* DVD lesson, as well as in other speaking tasks throughout the course, students are encouraged to attempt more adventurous and extended use of language in tasks such as problem solving, developing a project or telling a story. These tasks go beyond discussion; they include rehearsal time, useful language and a concrete outcome.

## LISTENING

For most users of English (or any language, for that matter), listening is the most frequently used skill. A learner who can speak well but not understand at least as well is unlikely to be a competent communicator or user of the language. We feel that listening can be developed effectively through well-structured materials. As with speaking, the choice of interesting topics and texts works hand in hand with carefully considered sequencing and task design.  At the same time, listening texts can act as a springboard to stimulate discussion in class.

There are several strands to listening in *Speakout*:

- **Focus on authentic recordings** – In *Speakout*, we believe that it is motivating for all levels of learner to try to access and cope with authentic material. Each unit includes a DVD extract from a BBC documentary, drama or light entertainment programme as well as a podcast filmed on location with real people giving their opinions. At the higher levels you will also find unscripted audio texts and BBC radio extracts. All are invaluable in the way they expose learners to real language in use as well as different varieties of English. Where recordings, particularly at lower levels, are scripted, they aim to reflect the patterns of natural speech.

- **Focus on sub-skills and strategies** – Tasks across the recordings in each unit are designed with a number of sub-skills and strategies in mind. These include: listening for global meaning and more detail; scanning for specific information; becoming sensitised to possible misunderstandings; and noticing nuances of intonation and expression. We also help learners to listen actively by using strategies such as asking for repetition and paraphrasing.

- **As a context for new language** – We see listening as a key mode of input and *Speakout* includes many listening texts which contain target grammar, vocabulary or functions in their natural contexts. Learners are encouraged to notice this new language and how and where it occurs, often by using the audio scripts as a resource.

- **As a model for speaking** – In the third and fourth lessons of each unit the recordings serve as models for speaking tasks. These models reveal the ways in which speakers use specific language to structure their discourse, for example with regard to turn-taking, hesitating and checking for understanding. These recordings also serve as a goal for the learners' speaking.

## READING

Reading is a priority for many students, whether it's for study, work or pleasure, and can be practised alone, anywhere and at any time. Learners who read regularly tend to have a richer, more varied vocabulary, and are often better writers, which in turn supports their oral communication skills. Nowadays, the Internet has given students access to an extraordinary range of English language reading material, and the availability of English language newspapers, books and magazines is greater than ever before. The language learner who develops skill and confidence in reading in the classroom will be more motivated to read outside the classroom. Within the classroom reading texts can also introduce stimulating topics and act as springboards for class discussion.

There are several strands to reading in *Speakout*:

* **Focus on authentic texts** – As with *Speakout* listening materials, there is an emphasis on authenticity, and this is reflected in a number of ways. Many of the reading texts in *Speakout* are sourced from the BBC. Where texts have been adapted or graded, there is an attempt to maintain authenticity by remaining faithful to the text type in terms of content and style. We have chosen up-to-date, relevant texts to stimulate interest and motivate learners to read. The texts represent a variety of genres that correspond to the text types that learners will probably encounter in their everyday lives.

* **Focus on sub-skills and strategies** – In *Speakout* we strive to maintain authenticity in the way the readers interact with a text. We always give students a reason to read, and provide tasks which bring about or simulate authentic reading, including real-life tasks such as summarising, extracting specific information, reacting to an opinion or following an anecdote. We also focus on strategies for decoding texts, such as guessing the meaning of unknown vocabulary, understanding pronoun referencing and following discourse markers.

* **Noticing new language** – Noticing language in use is a key step towards the development of a rich vocabulary and greater all-round proficiency in a language, and this is most easily achieved through reading. In *Speakout*, reading texts often serve as valuable contexts for introducing grammar and vocabulary as well as discourse features.

* **As a model for writing** – In the writing sections, as well as the Writeback sections of the DVD spreads, the readings serve as models for students to refer to when they are writing, in terms of overall organisation as well as style and language content.

## WRITING

In recent years the growth of email and the internet has led to a shift in the nature of the writing our students need to do. Email has also led to an increased informality in written English. However, many students need to develop their formal writing for professional and exam-taking purposes. It is therefore important to focus on a range of genres, from formal text types such as essays, letters and reports to informal genres such as blog entries and personal messages.

There are four strands to writing in *Speakout*:

* **Focus on genres** – In every unit at the four higher levels there is a section that focuses on a genre of writing, emails for example. We provide a model to show the conventions of the genre and, where appropriate, we highlight fixed phrases associated with it. We usually then ask the students to produce their own piece of writing. While there is always a written product, we also focus on the process of writing, including the relevant stages such as brainstorming, planning, and checking. At Starter and Elementary, we focus on more basic writing skills, including basic written sentence patterns, linking, punctuation and text organisation, in some cases linking this focus to a specific genre.

* **Focus on sub-skills and strategies** – While dealing with the genres, we include a section which focuses on a sub-skill or strategy that is generally applicable to all writing. Sub-skills include paragraphing, organising content and using linking words and pronouns, while strategies include activities like writing a first draft quickly, keeping your reader in mind and self-editing. We present the sub-skill by asking the students to notice the feature. We then provide an opportunity for the students to practise it.

* **Writeback** – At the end of every unit, following the DVD and final speaking task, we include a Writeback task. The idea is for students to develop fluency in their writing. While we always provide a model, the task is not tied to any particular grammatical structure. Instead the emphasis is on using writing to generate ideas and personal responses.

* **Writing as a classroom activity** – We believe that writing can be very usefully employed as an aid to speaking and as a reflective technique for responding to texts – akin to the practice of writing notes in the margins of books. It also provides a change of pace and focus in lessons. Activities such as short dictations, note-taking, brainstorming on paper and group story writing are all included in *Speakout*.

## PRONUNCIATION

In recent years, attitudes towards pronunciation in many English language classrooms have moved towards a focus on intelligibility: if students' spoken language is understandable, then the pronunciation is good enough. We are aware, however, that many learners and teachers place great importance on developing pronunciation that is more than 'good enough', and that systematic attention to pronunciation in a lesson, however brief, can have a significant impact on developing learners' speech.

In *Speakout*, we have taken a practical, integrated approach to developing students' pronunciation, highlighting features that often cause problems in conjunction with a given area of grammar, particular vocabulary items and functional language. Where relevant to the level, a grammatical or functional language focus is followed by a focus on a feature of pronunciation, for example, the weak forms of auxiliary verbs or connected speech in certain functional exponents. Students are given the opportunity to listen to models of the pronunciation, notice the key feature and then practise it.

## TEACHING UPPER INTERMEDIATE LEARNERS

An upper intermediate learner represents a great achievement in having moved from being a total beginner to a competent user of the language. Students at this level probably have extensive experience learning in classroom contexts, are familiar with different procedures and activities, and often know what they like and don't like. They may have a very strong opinion about what's worth doing and how. That can work to the teacher's advantage, if the teacher is open to students' comments, suggestions and requests.

By the upper intermediate level, learners normally can communicate comfortably on a wide range of everyday topics, with relatively little of the sort of hesitation that is common at lower levels, and which can cause some listener irritation. Many students at this level can come across as impressive if they are on a topic that they have conversed about a lot, and this can be deceptive; a relaxed, smooth conversation can come to a screeching halt, or at least a significant slow-down, if the topic shifts to a specialised area or any topic that the student hasn't 'worked with' in English. A teacher needs to be aware of this, taking into account the need to challenge students and push them out of their comfort zone – and keeping in mind that their strategies for avoiding difficulty will be more sophisticated than at lower levels.

Students at this level have a great capacity and need to use the language to express themselves, to create their own meanings rather than only generate sentences that demonstrate or practise their knowledge. Lessons should be conducted with this in mind, giving space to individual expression and reducing the amount of sustained restricted practice.

Upper intermediate students also need to become more sophisticated in their use of functional language, focussing on its appropriacy in different situations. They will also be refining their use of speaking and listening strategies to increase competency in a range of contexts.

Learners at this level have made the rounds of the grammar syllabus at least once if not several times, and yet are likely still to have significant confusion with regard to certain areas; future and perfect forms and the article system are often an issue and remain so into the advanced level. As well as consolidating previous learning, upper intermediate learners will be exploring these areas in greater depth and also encountering more complex, clause and discourse level grammar, particularly in writing and reading.

As in other levels, there may be widely-ranging strengths and weaknesses across the skills and this may cause tensions in a class. Also motivations may differ, with some students needing to focus more on exam-style accuracy and on writing, and others more interested in developing fluency in speaking.

Here are our top tips for teaching at this level:

- Find out about your learners' experience studying English. What have they enjoyed most and found most useful? What sort of activities do they dislike? What do they find most challenging? Maintain a channel of communication with students over the course, and they will help you be most effective in your teaching.

- Challenge students. Don't let them cruise through a course using language they're already comfortable with, but rather push them to express themselves in greater depth and detail, and on topics that are not a comfortable part of their repertoire.

- In dealing with language errors, don't just correct, but upgrade and enrich the learners' language. Show them how more sophisticated structures and vocabulary, including lexical phrases, can help them make the 'quality step' they need to be truly above intermediate.

- Devote more time than you have at lower levels to freer activities so that students have the opportunity to both articulate more complex ideas and to build greater fluency expressing themselves.

- Be as systematic and rigorous in focusing on grammar and vocabulary as you are with lower levels. Don't be fooled by the impression an upper-intermediate group can give, particularly those one or two strong students, of knowing it all already. Post-systematic errors – where the student knows the rule but makes the error – need to be handled mindfully, as it may well be that the learner doesn't know, or has forgotten, the relevant rule.

- Encourage personalised learning out of class so that learners can focus on areas they need to strengthen.

- Encourage extensive, out-of-class reading and listening by identifying sources of texts and videos that are easy for them to access and of course likely to interest them. Along with vocabulary that is overtly taught on a course, students at this level have the capacity to make great gains in building their passive vocabulary as well as knowledge of syntax through reading and listening.

- As always, don't forget to praise your students. Praise can be a powerful motivator, and motivation is essential to making real progress in learning a language.

Antonia Clare, Frances Eales, Steve Oakes and JJ Wilson

# TEACHER'S NOTES INDEX

## OVERVIEW

## IDEAL FLATMATES

### Introduction

Ss practise finding out about people using direct and indirect questions and personality vocabulary. They also practise listening, speaking and writing about finding flatmates.

#### SUPPLEMENTARY MATERIALS

Resource bank p143 and/or p145

Ex 11: Ss bring examples of emails in English that they have written or received.

### Warm up

This activity leads into the topic and gives Ss a chance (especially if this is a new class) to get to know each other. It also gives you an opportunity to assess Ss' language skills, especially their use of the present perfect which is reviewed in 1.2. Write *Beginnings* on the board and elicit examples of times that people begin something in their lives, e.g. a school, a job, a course, a hobby, a relationship, moving to a new town, finding a new place to live, learning a new skill, starting a family, etc. Write these on the board and put Ss in small groups to discuss which of these they have done, giving specific examples. Their aim is to find out how many of the 'beginnings' all the people in their group have experienced. One person from each group feeds back to the class.

#### Teaching tip

It is often a good idea, when asking Ss to speak about personal experience, to give an example of your own first, e.g. for the above activity talk about something you have begun. This should encourage Ss to speak about themselves and demonstrate how much detail you expect them to give when they are speaking.

#### SPEAKING

**1** Ask a student to read out the questions and clarify that for number two, if Ss haven't lived with friends or on their own before, they should imagine what it would be like. Ss then discuss the questions in pairs. In feedback, choose two or three Ss to tell the class about their partners.

#### Teaching tip

In feedback encourage Ss to give a reason for their answers, e.g. *Sonia thinks it's easier to live on your own because ....* It's important at this level to challenge Ss to speak for longer turns whenever possible.

#### LISTENING

**2** Give Ss a minute or two to read the listing then discuss with the class what might happen at a speed flatmating event. If your Ss haven't heard of speed dating, encourage them to guess, feeding in information from the culture notes as appropriate.

### Culture notes

The idea of a speed dating event is for single men and women to meet a large number of new people. Participants are rotated to meet each other over a series of short 'dates', usually lasting from three to eight minutes, depending on the organisation running the event. At the end of the event, participants give the organisers a list of the people they would like to give their contact information to. If there is a match, contact information is forwarded to both people. Supporters argue that speed dating saves time, as most people quickly decide if they are romantically compatible and first impressions are often permanent.

**3A** Before you play the recording focus Ss on the questions and check the following vocabulary: *lodger* (someone who pays rent to live in a house with its owner), *budget* (an amount of money available to spend), *badge* (small piece of metal or plastic with writing and/or a picture on it, worn on clothing).

**Answers:** 1 People who have rooms to rent and people who are looking for places to live meet each other and try to match up. 2 A list of the people who are there; a badge to say who you are and whether you've got a room or are looking.

### Teaching tip

After Ss have listened to the recording, put them in pairs to compare/discuss their answers. This helps to build their confidence before giving their answers to the class. It also helps you, if they are struggling with the answers, to identify whether you need to play the recording again.

### Unit 1 Recording 1

P= Presenter    M= Matt

P:  Now you might have heard of speed dating – those events for the young, free and single who are just too busy to find the love of their lives – but what about applying the same principle to finding a lodger for your spare room? Natalie Speed went to experience 'speed flatmating'.

M: My name's Matt Hutchinson and I'm with SpareRoom.co.uk. Basically what we do is we have an evening that introduces people looking for places to live with people who've got a spare room in their house and it's just a chance for people to meet the people that are involved rather than just see the flats. It's a chance to actually see who you'd be living with because it makes such a difference. And everybody that arrives gets a list of who's here so if you're looking for a room for example, you get a list of everybody who's got a room, what their area is, what their budget is. Everybody has a badge to say who they are and whether they've got a room or are looking.

**B** Tell Ss they are going to hear four speakers at the speed flatmating event and that they only have to listen for how each speaker feels the first time, because they will listen to the recording a second time to focus on more details. Ss listen and compare their answers.

**Answers:** 2 c 3 b 4 a

**C** Check the following vocabulary: *label, choosy, spot* (identify), *brain dead, a steep learning curve*. Focus Ss on the T/F sentences and on how the first sentence has been corrected. Give them a minute or two to look at the other sentences. They may already have some ideas about which are true or false from the first time they listened. Ss listen and compare answers in pairs, before class feedback.

**Answers:** 2 F He wants someone who will be there as little as possible. 3 T 4 T 5 T 6 F She thinks it's embarrassing when she has to show someone around and they're not interested (for example because they think she's old enough to be their mother) 7 T 8 F She's already found several people.

### Unit 1 Recording 2

N=Natalie

N: You're wearing a white label. You've got a room to rent.

Man 1: We both have a room to rent.

N: Oh, I see.

Man 1: So we're seeking another person to join us.

N: Why are you looking for someone to move in?

Man 1: Our magnificent German room-mate, who was away every weekend, has moved out. So as a result we're looking for someone equally magnificent who will be there as little as possible.

N: You're looking a little bit lost and you're wearing a pink badge. What does that mean?

Man 2: That means I'm looking for a room and also I'm willing to buddy up with someone else who's looking.

N: How long have you been looking for a room?

Man 2: A couple of weeks. I'm sort of new to the game. So I'm just trying to understand what's going on and how it works. You know, it's a bit of a shock and a bit of a steep learning curve for me.

N: Do you think you're pretty good at spotting the kind of person you can get on with?

Woman 1:  Yes I think it's easy. You just know straightaway.

N: When you've done it before, when you've done it through an online service and you've presumably had people come to look at your house, how has that been?

Woman 1:  Well I must be a bit choosy I suppose, but the two best lodgers I had, I just knew immediately, as soon as I looked at them, smiled at them, I knew that they were somehow the right sort of people and that we would get along.

N: So, really it's … this kind of event's quite good for you, rather than sitting down with somebody where you know straightaway you don't want to live with them but they're in your house, you feel obliged to show them round,

Woman 1:  Yes, because that's so embarrassing, having to show someone round when they're not interested. Sometimes I open the door and because I'm older they look at me and go 'Oh god, I don't want to live with my mother.'

Woman 2:  It's two bedrooms. There's one bathroom, which is why I always ask people what time they get up in the morning. Because I do have a bad habit that I like to have half an hour bath in the morning.

Woman 3:  That's not a bad habit!

Woman 2:  Other than that I'm not largely in the house at all. I'm actually a little bit sort of brain dead from all the conversations I've had but it's been so so useful.

N: You seem to have to be quite open straightaway, I mean, I heard you talking about your bathing habits earlier.

Woman 2:  I think that's important. I mean they're going to be living with you. They're going to be in really close contact and it's best to advertise yourself as you are from the outset.

N: And have you had any firm interest yet?

Woman 2:  I have met several people that I'd like to follow it up with. Several people that I feel I could live with.

**4** Before putting students in pairs to discuss the questions, elicit one or two examples of questions related to the topics in the box and check the difference between *diet* (what food you eat/don't eat) and *be on a diet* (limit what you eat to lose weight). In feedback, ask Ss to explain why they would/wouldn't use speed flatmating and why they wouldn't ask about certain topics. Elicit some of the questions Ss thought of and have a vote on which was the best question for each topic.

If you monitor the pairwork and note down good examples of questions, you can then call on the relevant pairs to give their examples in feedback.

## GRAMMAR direct and indirect questions

**5A/B** Before completing the questions Ss could read the conversation quickly and see which topics are mentioned from the box in Ex 4 (future plans, relationships and daily habits). They then complete the sentences and check with the recording.

**Answers:** 1 are 2 with 3 made 4 long 5 if (*whether* is also possible) 6 like

**6A** Ss work on the exercise alone, then discuss their answers in pairs. At this level you may have Ss in the class who are fluent but not very accurate and *weaker* at analysing language. If so, pair them with *stronger Ss* who can help them. In feedback, ask Ss how they know if a question is indirect (there is an 'introductory phrase' before the actual question). Before moving on to Ex 6C you could elicit more information from the class about why we use indirect questions and how they are different from the direct form.

**Answers:** a) Have you any idea how long you want to stay here? / Do you mind me asking if you're in a relationship? b) What made you decide to come to the city in the first place? c) Who are you living with? d) What are you like in the mornings?

**B** As they work through this exercise, Ss should find an example from Ex 5A to support each rule. In feedback you could have the following indirect questions on the board to help you check the answers:

*Do you mind me asking if you're in a relationship?* (The question is personal – rule 1; it is also a *yes/no* question – rule 4.)

*Could you tell me where you are staying?* (The word order is not *where are you staying?* – rule 2.)

*Have you any idea how long you want to stay?* (The auxiliary *do* is not used – rule 3.)

**Answers:** 1 Indirect 2 different from 3 don't use 4 yes/no

**C** Ss should write out the full questions in their notebooks, as they will need them for marking the stress in Ex 7A. In feedback, elicit/point out that a question mark is only used when the introductory phrase is a question, e.g. *I'd be interested to know how you organise the cooking.*

**Answers:** 1 I was wondering 2 Could you tell me 3 Do you mind me asking 4 I'd be interested to know 5 Can I ask 6 Do you know

### Unit 1 Recording 4
1  I was wondering if I could see the flat.
2  Could you tell me how much the deposit is?
3  Do you mind me asking how old you are?
4  I'd be interested to know how you organise the cooking.
5  Can I ask you how noisy it is?
6  Do you know how soon the room will be available?

**7A** Do the first question as an example on the board with the class, underlining or drawing a small box over the stressed words. Play the rest of the questions, stopping after each one if necessary to give Ss time to mark the stress.

Point out to Ss that the main stressed words are always the ones that carry the message, i.e. if the other words weren't there, the message could still be understood. If Ss have difficulty hearing the stressed words, you could model the questions yourself, emphasising the stressed words a little more and/or clicking your fingers or tapping your foot on the stresses.

**Answers:** 1 wondering – see – flat 2 tell – much – deposit 3 mind – asking – old 4 interested – know – organise – cooking 5 ask – noisy 6 know – soon – room – available

**B** To show Ss the difference between low and high intonation, model question 1 starting with high, then with low intonation and elicit/point out that higher intonation sounds more interested/polite. Then play the rest of the questions again for Ss to focus on the intonation. You could also drill the questions, either after the recording or from your own model. Even at this level, Ss still need help with word order and natural intonation in oral work.

**LANGUAGEBANK** 1.1 p128–129

Depending on how well Ss have coped with the language so far, either give them time to read the notes in class and ask you any questions, or tell them to study the notes at home. Ss can do Exs A and B in class if you feel they need more practice in word order. If so, encourage Ss to make Ex A into a full dialogue by inventing their own answers to the questions. They could also act out their dialogues for the class. NB Ex C practises the two or three word questions from 'spoken grammar': in a *mixed ability class* you could move *stronger Ss* onto this, then have them demonstrate their dialogues for the rest of the class.

**Answers:** A 1 Do you mind me asking where you've been? 2 I'd be interested to know where the meeting was! 3 What was the meeting like? 4 Do you know what time it is now? 5 Why didn't you phone? 6 Are you lying to me?
B 1 Do you know if they accept credit cards here? 2 Do you mind me asking how you became a model? 3 Have you any idea where I can get a coffee at this time? 4 Would you mind telling me when the computer is available? 5 Can I ask if you're planning to get married? 6 I was wondering where you bought that briefcase.
C 2 to 3 with 4 many 5 time 6 not

## PRACTICE

**8** Ss can work on this in pairs and practise pronouncing the questions with polite intonation before feedback to the class.

**Answers:** 1 Could you tell me how much you earn each month? 2 Do you mind me asking how much time you spend on the phone and internet each day? 3 Do you think you will usually spend weekends here or will you often go away? 4 What were your last flatmates like? 5 What annoys you most about sharing a flat? 6 What kind of music do you like listening to?

**Optional extra activity**
Vary the feedback by getting Ss to 'interview' you as a potential flatmate. (You can invent some unlikely answers to liven this up!) This will also give you the opportunity to introduce the answer *I'd rather not answer that* for questions that are too personal.

## VOCABULARY personality

**9A** Introduce the idea of a flatmate finder website and ask Ss what they might find there and whether they think it's a good idea. Then give them two or three minutes to read the descriptions quickly (ignoring unfamiliar vocabulary for the moment) and choose the best flatmate for themselves.

**B** Ss may want to work alone on this for a few minutes before discussing their answers in pairs. In feedback, elicit/point out that the phrases are informal.

**Answers:** 2 out until the early hours  3 keep to myself  4 a people person  5 a geek  6 get into  7 a good laugh  8 down to earth  9 tight-fisted  10 pull their weight

> **VOCABULARYBANK** p148 Personality adjectives
> Let Ss check the personality adjectives in their dictionaries if they have difficulty in matching the words in A. In feedback, elicit the main stress in each adjective. Elicit from the group which adjectives they think the images in B represent.
>
> **Answers:** 1A 1 sympathetic  2 cautious  3 naive  4 genuine  5 witty  6 mean  7 flexible  8 eccentric  9 trustworthy  10 moody
> B A eccentric  B sympathetic  C moody

## SPEAKING

**10A** You could lead into this by answering the questions about yourself, then put Ss into pairs and tell them to be prepared to tell the class which questions they agreed on.

**B** Ss work alone to write the questions. Direct them to Exercises 5A, 5C and 8 for ideas.

**C** If there is space in the classroom, Ss should walk around and ask at least three other Ss their questions. Otherwise, they can sit in groups of four and swap partners until they've talked to the other three people in the group. In feedback ask individuals to explain who would be suited to them and why.

**Teaching tip**
While Ss are asking each other their questions, monitor and make notes of examples of good language use and problem areas (particularly with the word order and intonation in indirect questions). You can then write the examples on the board for Ss to look at and correct or make a handout for Ss to work on in the next lesson.

## WRITING an informal email

**11A** If Ss have brought emails in English they can show them to each other while discussing questions 2 and 3.

**B** Focus Ss on the questions and give them a minute or two to read the email quickly and find the answers. Tell them they will have time to read it in more detail for the next exercise. Vocabulary to check: *handy (= convenient), click with someone (= like someone and share their ideas, opinions, etc.)*.

**Answers:** 1 They're friends  2 In Swiss Cottage, in London, with Winston  3 Through a speed flatmating event.

**C** Before you direct Ss to Ex 11C, elicit what they already know about informal emails then put them in pairs to work on the exercise. Encourage Ss to circle the answers on the email itself.

**Answers:** 1 *Hi*  2 *the, best*  3 *one*  4 a) – (dashes), ! (exclamation marks)  4b) *handy, clicked, in touch*  4c) *you're, I'm, it's, you'll*  4d) *(It was) great, (I) hope, (I) must go, (I'll) be in touch soon*

## LEARN TO check for accuracy

**12** Before Ss read the email, direct them to the correction code and elicit an example of a mistake for each category. Ss correct the mistakes. In feedback elicit/point out the examples of informal phrases with words left out: *Sounds like, Have to go*. Also, ask Ss about the advantages of using a correction code (it forces them to think about the mistake).

**Answers:** 1 Sounds like you're having a good time.  2 I've never heard of speed flat mating before.  3 I like the people there very much.  4 We often practise English together.  5 He's a very sympathetic person.  6 a friend's apartment  7 Hope to hear from you again soon./Write again soon.

**13A** Encourage Ss to make notes about the four bullet points before they start writing the email. While they're writing, be available to answer Ss' queries as required.

**speakout TIP**
Ss check their emails, clarifying anything they are unsure of with you or a partner. They could also swap emails with their partner to check both for accuracy and content, i.e. is all the information asked for in the exercise included?

**B** Give Ss a few minutes to exchange emails and read the one they receive. Ss either write the reply in class, or they can write it for homework and if possible, email it back.

**Homework ideas**
1 Ss write descriptions of themselves for a flatmate finder site.
2 Ss research speed flatmating on the internet and report their findings in the next lesson.
3 Ss write the reply to the email in Ex 12A and email it to their classmate.
4 Workbook Ex 1–5, p4–5

# IT'S A FIRST

## Introduction

Ss practise speaking about how different activities make them feel, using adjectives and modifiers. They practise reading a review of a BBC TV programme and they revise and practise the present perfect and past simple in the context of discussing experiences.

### SUPPLEMENTARY MATERIALS

Resource bank p144 and/or p146

**Warm up:** prepare pieces of paper with names of activities and criteria, as described below.

**Ex 5C, Ex 10A, Ex 10B:** Ss could use monolingual dictionaries.

## Warm up

Lead into the topic via a discussion of a range of activities. Before class, write the names of twelve to fifteen activities on pieces of A4 paper, e.g. *baking a cake, riding a horse, giving a speech, changing a tyre, singing karaoke, ballroom dancing, painting a portrait, redecorating a room, sailing, putting up shelves, planting a garden, going up in a balloon,* etc. On small slips of paper, write different criteria, e.g. *indoor/outdoor, interesting/ boring, expensive/cheap, easy/difficult,* etc. Stick the prompts on the board, divide Ss into groups of three or four and give each group a 'criteria' slip. Ss discuss how to divide the activities on the board according to their criteria. In feedback, one person from each group comes up to the board and puts the activities into two groups, without saying what their group's criteria were. The rest of the class has to guess.

### VOCABULARY  feelings

**1** Give Ss a minute or two to discuss the photos and feed back briefly to the class. If you did the warm up activity, you don't need to spend long on this.

**2A** Direct Ss to the questions and tell them to write the numbers 1–5 in their notebooks. They write the name of the activity for each number as they listen. *Stronger classes* could also listen for whether each speaker's experience was positive or negative. Ss compare answers before class feedback.

**Answers:** Speakers 1, 3 and 5
Speaker 2: singing karaoke  Speaker 4: dancing

**B** Tell Ss that the sentences are from the recording and that they should read them all before trying to complete the gaps, as some are more obvious than others. Give the pairs three or four minutes to work on the exercise before playing the recording again.

**Answers:** 1 anxious  2 relieved  3 thrilled  4 fascinated
5 frustrated  6 satisfied  7 impressed  8 embarrassed
9 awkward   10 exhausted

### Unit 1 Recording 5

1    I didn't enjoy it much. For a start, I was very anxious and I think animals can sense it when you're nervous and worried. It was OK when we were going at a walk but then we went faster and I found it difficult to stay on. Actually, I was extremely relieved when the lesson finished and I could get off.
2    It was the first time I'd tried it and it was a kind of competition. So I chose a song I knew well and I really enjoyed doing it. I came second so I was really thrilled. There were about twenty people entered and I was absolutely fascinated to see how different people behaved when they got in front of the microphone.

3    It took me ages to do and I got really annoyed and frustrated at one point because I couldn't make it straight. Eventually, I put the books on it and it looked great. I felt really satisfied when I'd finished because it was the first one I'd ever put up on my own. Yeah. It was a really satisfying thing to do.
4    Most people were there for the first time and I was really impressed by how quickly they learnt the steps. But I was useless and I'm sure my partner thought so too. I was very embarrassed because I kept treading on her toes. She was very patient but you could tell she was getting annoyed. So it was a bit of a disaster, quite disappointing.
5    He should never have started it. I think he wanted to impress me because it was our first date but I found out later that he'd never changed one before. Anyway, after three hours, I suggested calling the repair company. I felt very awkward about it but I thought we'd never get home. I didn't get to bed till two in the morning and I was completely exhausted.

**C** Using *embarrassed* as an example, ask Ss where the stress is and show them how to mark it with a line under or a box/ circle over the vowel sound (*a*). Ss work in pairs identifying and marking the stress, then check with the recording. Use the recording as a model for Ss to repeat, or model the words in short phrases yourself, e.g. *I was very anxious. I felt really satisfied.*

**Answers:** 1 an<u>xi</u>ous  2 re<u>lie</u>ved  3 <u>thri</u>lled  4 <u>fa</u>scinated
5 frus<u>tra</u>ted  6 <u>sa</u>tisfied  7 im<u>pre</u>ssed  8 em<u>ba</u>rrassed
9 <u>awk</u>ward  10 ex<u>hau</u>sted

**3A** This will be revision for most Ss at this level, so they should be able to answer all the questions in pairs. However, for *weaker Ss* you may want to check the meaning of *ungradable/extreme*, i.e. an adjective which already means *very* whatever the state the adjective represents may be and therefore cannot be made stronger or weaker in meaning, e.g. *furious* means *very angry*, so you can't say *He was very furious.*

**Answers:** 1 satisfied: used for feelings/satisfying: used for something or someone that causes the feelings
2 a) tired G/exhausted U  b) excited G/thrilled U
c) interested G/fascinated U
3 fairly – G  very – G  really – B  absolutely – U
completely – U

**B** Give Ss three or four, minutes to work in pairs. As you check their answers elicit ways in which Ss could expand the two lines into mini conversations, e.g. by adding more information to the answer, or asking follow up questions:

B:   *Yeah, I'm completely fascinated by them too. I'm studying Mandarin at the moment.*

A:   *Are you? That sounds difficult!*

**Answers:** 1B: ~~very~~/completely  2 A: really/~~very~~
B: fairly/~~absolutely~~  3 A: embarrassed /~~embarrassing~~
B: ~~embarrassed~~/embarrassing!  4 A: ~~frustrated~~/frustrating
B: frustrated/~~frustrating~~

**4A** You could lead into this and provide a model for Ss by telling them about an experience of your own. Then give Ss a few minutes to make some notes.

**B** Encourage Ss to 'listen actively' while their partner talks about their experiences, i.e. by asking follow up questions and saying *Really!/Did you?/I see/How _____!* etc. Monitor the pairs and make notes of good use of the vocabulary and any problem areas for feedback.

### Homework ideas
Workbook Ex 1, p6

## READING

**5A** Tell Ss they are going to read a review of a TV programme. Lead into the text by either writing the title on the board and asking Ss to speculate about the contents of the programme, or by asking Ss about celebrities and the kinds of TV programmes that they sometimes appear on, etc. Then give Ss two or three minutes to read the text quickly and decide if the review is positive or negative.

**Answer:** The review is positive.

### Teaching tip

It's important to give Ss strict time limits if you want them to skim a text. You can reassure them that they will have a chance to read the text in detail for the next exercises.

**B** Give Ss at least five minutes to work alone answering the questions. They can compare answers in pairs before feedback to the class.

### Culture notes

*Star Wars* is a science-fiction fantasy film conceived by the film director George Lucas (who also made the *Indiana Jones* films) and starring Harrison Ford and Carrie Fisher. The original film, which is set in fictional galaxy populated by many species of alien creature and where robotic androids are common, was released in 1977. It was hugely popular and was followed by two sequels, *The Empire Strikes Back* in 1980 and the *Return of the Jedi* in 1983.

*Revolver* is the seventh album by English rock group the Beatles, released in 1966.

*Joan Bakewell* is an English intellectual who is well known as a journalist and TV presenter.

*Mamma Mia* is a very popular musical based on the songs of Swedish group Abba. It has also been made into a film.

*Arthur Smith* (born 1954) is an English comedian and writer.

**Answers:**
1 constructing flat-pack furniture, building a wall  2 They rate them out of ten and say whether they'd like to try the activity again.  3 They like the host's personality and his interaction with guests. They also like the normality of the experiences (we can relate to them).  4 The experience of watching *Mamma Mia.*  5 He enjoys exploring new things and having new experiences.  6 Viewers will see ordinary things with fresh eyes, be entertained, might be inspired and motivated to try new things.

**C** Encourage Ss to find the words in the text and try to work out their meaning before looking at the definitions. They could use monolingual dictionaries to check their answers.

**Answers:** 2 loathing  3 recurring  4 mundane  5 bonnet 6 taps into  7 tottering

### Teaching tip

Ss should use monolingual dictionaries to encourage them to think about and define meaning in English. They will also find related words and meanings, example sentences and information about the form and pronunciation of the vocabulary.

**D** Ss can work in pairs or small groups to discuss the questions. In feedback ask them to tell the class the most surprising/interesting thing they found out about their partner or someone else in their group.

## GRAMMAR present perfect and past simple

**6** For a *stronger class*, ask Ss to cover the rules and, in pairs, work through sentences 1–5, identifying the verb form and explaining why it is being used. Then they can match the sentences to the rules.

**Answers:** 1 b)  2 d)  3 e)  4 c)  5 a)

**7A** Do the first one as an example, then give Ss a minute or two to underline the rest.

**Answers:** 1 so far  2 yet  3 already  4 Three weeks ago 5 this morning  6 this morning  7 for five weeks (now) 8 for six weeks

**B** Draw three columns on the board and write *present perfect, past simple* and *both* at the top of each. Tell Ss to copy the table into their notebooks and to write the time phrases into the correct column as they go through sentences 1–8 again. Do an example, then put Ss in pairs to help each other. As you check the answers in feedback start filling in the table on the board (see answers in bold in the table below).

**Answers:** 1 *So far* + present perfect: an action that happened in a time period up to now and when it happened isn't specified.
2 *Yet* + present perfect: an action that happened (or in this case didn't happen) in a time period up to now.
3 *Already* + present perfect: an action that happened in a time period up to now and when it happened isn't specified.
4 *Three weeks ago* + past simple: an action that happened at a specified time in the past.
5 *This morning* + present perfect: an action in an unfinished period – it's still this morning.
6 *This morning* + past simple: an action in a finished period (it's now this afternoon; the period of the morning is finished).
7 *For five weeks* (now) + present perfect: a repeated action which started in the past and continues to now. NB If Ss ask whether the present perfect continuous can be used here, tell them that it can and that they will study the continuous form in the next unit.
8 *For five weeks* + past simple: a series of actions which began and finished in the past.

**C** Write the following examples on the board and ask Ss to try substituting *up to now* for each of the time phrases in bold (write these in red on the board) *No one has refused a challenge **yet**. Arthur Smith had a piano lesson **three weeks ago**.* (If it is possible to substitute *up to now* for a phrase, then it is probably usually used with the present perfect tense). The Ss can then use this idea and these examples to help them work out where the other phrases in the box should go. Give Ss two or three minutes to look at the phrases in pairs, then finish filling in the table with the class.

| Present perfect | Past simple | Both |
|---|---|---|
| so far | ago | this morning |
| yet | This time last week | for |
| already | last month | in the summer |
| up to now | last night | |
| since | earlier today | |
| lately | | |
| over the last fortnight | | |

**8** Do the first one as an example, then play the rest of the recording, stopping after each sentence for Ss to write their answers.

> **Answers:** 1 PP　2 PS　3 PS　4 PP　5 PP　6 PS　7 PP　8 PS　9 PP　10 PS

### Unit 1 Recording 7

1 I've thought about it a lot.
2 I thought about it a lot.
3 We tried to phone you.
4 We've tried to phone you.
5 She's had her first lesson today.
6 She had her first lesson today.
7 I've changed my email address.
8 I changed my email address.
9 I think he's left the building.
10 I think he left the building.

#### ➡ LANGUAGEBANK 1.2 p128–129

Ss can read the notes in class or at home, depending on how confident they are about the rules. If you feel Ss need more basic practice of the present perfect and past simple before moving on to Ex 9A, they can do Ex A. Otherwise, set Ex A and B for homework.

> **Answers:** A 1 haven't written　2 was　3 haven't seen　4 has/'s been　5 took　6 arrived　7 checked　8 saw　9 've/have stayed　10 was　11 went　12 forgot　13 got　14 called　15 've/have been/gone　16 has handed
> B 1 before　2 this morning　3 Until I took this course　4 for　5 So far　6 until　7 since　8 this month　9 yet　10 this time last week

### PRACTICE

**9A** Give Ss a few minutes to work alone on this, then check answers with the class. Vocabulary to check: *paranoid* (having an extreme and unreasonable worry about something), *hiking* (going for long energetic walks) *loads (of)* (a large amount of).

> **Answers:** 1 've always been　2 learnt　3 've just got　4 gave　5 've played　6 haven't tried yet　7 've never bought　8 've lived　9 has been　10 've never done

**B** Ss discuss the activities for a few minutes. In feedback, encourage them to use *both* and *neither*, e.g. *We'd both like to learn to play the guitar. Neither of us would like to edit a film. Sylvia has bought something online, but I haven't.*

### VOCABULARY *PLUS* word formation

**10A** Write/Display the table on the board and tell Ss to copy it into their notebooks and complete it with noun form of the adjectives in the box. Do another example if necessary. If monolingual dictionaries are available, encourage Ss to use them to check the noun forms if they are unsure.

> **Answers:**
>
> | A -ion | B -ment | + -ity/-ety | + -ness |
> |---|---|---|---|
> | frustration | embarrassment | similarity | awkwardness |
> | satisfaction | disappointment | generosity | |
> | exhaustion | | anxiety | nervousness |

**B** Using *frustration* as an example, show Ss how the main stress is indicated in a dictionary: *fru'stration*. They can then work in pairs to identify the stress on the other nouns. When you play the recording for Ss to check, stop after each noun for Ss to repeat.

> **Answers:** satis<u>fa</u>ction　ex<u>hau</u>stion　em<u>bar</u>rassment　disap<u>poi</u>ntment　ex<u>ci</u>tement　simi<u>la</u>rity　gene<u>ro</u>sity　an<u>xie</u>ty　<u>awk</u>wardness　<u>self</u>ishness　<u>ner</u>vousness

**C** Use *frustration* and *embarrassment* as examples, then give Ss a few minutes in pairs to work out the rules.

> **Answers:** 1 *-ion*, *-ity*/*-ety* – the stress is on the syllable before the suffix.　2 *-ment*, *-ness* – the stress is on the same syllable as in the adjective.

**11A** Focus Ss on the quiz and the first example. Point out that they need to be careful with form, as one or two of the nouns are plurals. Vocabulary to check: *cure* (something that makes you better if you have an illness), *intense* (very strong).

> **Answers:** 2 generous　3 similarities　4 frustrations　5 awkward　6 satisfaction　7 disappointed　8 exhaustion　9 nervous　10 anxiety

**B** Ss can work individually to complete the quiz. Tell them to think about <u>why</u> they agree or disagree as they work through the questions.

**C** Ss can work in pairs or small groups to compare and give reasons for their answers.

#### ➡ VOCABULARYBANK p148 Word formation

Give Ss time to work through Ex 2A and B before comparing their answers in pairs. Then give Ss time to complete Ex 2C before they take it in turns to ask and answer the questions.

> **Answers:** 2A present, violent, patient, accurate, democratic, decent
> B -ence: independence, silence, permanence, intelligence
> -cy: fluency, privacy, urgency
> C 1 fluency　2 accurate　3 patience　4 permanent　5 intelligence　6 private　7 absent　8 violence

#### Homework ideas

1 Workbook Ex 2–5, p6–7

2 Language bank Ex A and B p129

3 Ss write a paragraph about a celebrity they like/admire, describing their personality and saying what they've achieved. They don't mention the celebrity's name, so that at the beginning of the next lesson, the descriptions can be passed round or stuck on the walls for Ss to walk round and read and guess the celebrity.

# I'D LIKE TO ENQUIRE

## Introduction

Ss listen to and practise making polite enquiries on the phone. They also learn to recognise vocabulary commonly used in adverts.

### SUPPLEMENTARY MATERIALS

Resource bank p147

## Warm up

Lead into the topic via a brief discussion about making phone calls in English. If you have had problems understanding or being understood on the phone in another country, tell Ss about your experience then invite them to tell the class about any problems they've had. Alternatively, ask Ss why speaking on the phone in English can be difficult (you can't see the other person's gestures or expressions, you don't know how to deal with a misunderstanding, there are certain phrases commonly used which you don't know, etc.) and what they can do to make phoning in English easier.

### VOCABULARY adverts

**1A** Give Ss a couple of minutes to *scan* the adverts quickly and circle the two that interest them. They compare their answers with a partner, explaining <u>why</u> they are interested. Vocabulary to check: *flyer* (small piece of paper with information on it, often adverts given out in the street) *hotline* (special direct telephone connection).

**B** Ss should find the words/phrases in bold and try to guess their meaning before looking at the definitions.

**Answers:** 2 matinée  3 deposit (non-refundable)
4 first come first served  5 sign up  6 limited run  7 fill in
8 limited enrolment

**C** Ss discuss this in pairs. Point out that at least two of the phrases can be used in each case. You could do *a concert* as an example with the class first.

**Answers:** a concert: deposit (non-refundable), matinee, limited run  a cookery course: sign up, fill in, limited enrolment, deposit (non-refundable), first come first served  a sale in a shop: two-for-one deal, first come first served  a hotel booking: fill-in, two-for-one deal, deposit (non-refundable)

### FUNCTION polite enquiries

**2A** Give Ss time to read the questions before you play the recording. Ss discuss their answers in pairs then check with the class.

**Answers:** 1 An English language college.  2 She wants to change from a general English course (which she booked online) to a business English course.  3 She needs to go to the college to do a level test.  4 The receptionist transfers her course fee to the business course, to hold a place for her.

**B** Ss can work in pairs to help each other complete the sentences. If they find the more complex ones too challenging, you could put a 'key' word from each of these sentences on the board, to prompt them (e.g. *possible, chance, asking, could*). Play the recording, pausing after each sentence for Ss to write.

**Answers:** 1 I'd like to enquire about a course.  2 I was wondering if it would be possible for me to change to that group. (*I was wondering* is used for politeness, not *I'm wondering*).  3 Can you tell me why I have to do it in person?  4 Would there be any chance of doing the level test on the phone?  5 Do you mind me asking what it involves? (*Do you mind …? = Is it a problem …?*)  6 I'd be really grateful if you could hold a place for me till Saturday morning.  7 Would you mind putting that in an email for me?  8 Could you tell me when the school opens?

### Unit 1 Recording 9

A: Hello, English Language College. Can I help you?

B: Yes, I'd like to enquire about a course.

A: OK. Have you seen the information on our website?

B: Well, actually the situation is that I booked myself onto a course through your website yesterday and now I'd like to change.

A: Could you tell me your name?

B: Misa Radnoti.

A: And which course was it?

B: A general English course, pre-advanced.

A: Bear with me a minute. Yes, I've got it. What would you like to change to?

B: I've just noticed this morning that you have an advanced course in business English starting next week.

A: That's right.

B: I was wondering if it would be possible for me to change to that group.

A: OK, let me just check. There are still a few places in that group, but you'll have to do a level test.

B: But I've already done an online test for the other course.

A: I appreciate that, but for this course you need to do a level test in person.

B: Can you tell me why I have to do it in person?

A: It's because it's a specialised course and there's an oral component to the level test.

B: I see. Would there be any chance of doing the level test on the phone?

A: Hold on, let me check … sorry to keep you. No, I'm afraid it has to be in person.

B: I see. Do you mind me asking what it involves?

A: There's a written task that you have to do under timed conditions and preparation materials for the oral interview.

B: I see. Sorry to be difficult, it's just that I'm really busy this week and can't make it up to the school for the level test.

A: That's going to be a problem. I'm not sure what we can do about that.

B: I'd really appreciate your help.

A: Hmm … You couldn't come in on Thursday evening, could you?

B: No, I'm afraid not. But I tell you what. I could come in on Saturday to do the level test.

A: The problem is, that's leaving it very late and we might have other applicants.

B: I'd be really grateful if you could hold a place for me till Saturday morning.

A: Can you hold on a minute? I'll just see … . OK, we can do that. We'll provisionally transfer the course fee over as a deposit.

B: That's great. Oh, I've got one more question, if I'm not keeping you.

A: No, go ahead.

B: If I don't get into this group, do I lose my course fee?

A: I'm afraid we can't refund the deposit, but you could apply it to another course.

B: That's a relief. Would you mind putting that in an email for me?

A: Certainly.

B: And could you tell me when the school opens on Saturday?

B: We're open from nine. I won't be here myself, but I'll tell my colleague to expect you.

A: Thank you very much for your help.

B: You're welcome. Thank you for calling.

**C** Play the example, telling Ss to listen for what happens to the intonation at the end of the sentence. You may then prefer to play the rest of the sentences one at a time, checking the intonation pattern. The tendency is for intonation to go down and up at the end of questions and down on other types of sentence. When you play the sentences again for Ss to repeat, encourage them to start each one with fairly high intonation, which will help them to sound polite.

> ➡ **LANGUAGEBANK** 1.3, p128–129
>
> Give Ss a few minutes to study the tables showing the forms that the polite enquiries have in common. Check by asking, e.g. *Which phrases use an -ing form? Which use an infinitive? Which use if or a wh- question word?*
> Ss practise these forms in the next exercise (Ex 3) in the lesson, so they could do Ex A from the **Language bank** for homework.
>
> > **Answers:** B: Hi, I'm phoning to find **out** about a DVD I ordered. The reference number **is** 3714.
> > A: OK. **Is there** a problem?
> > B: Yes, it hasn't arrived yet and I ordered it a month **ago**. Could you tell me **when** I can expect it?
> > A: Bear **with** with me a moment. I'm afraid we have no information **about** the arrival date.
> > B: And you don't know when it **will** be in?
> > A: It's coming from the US so I'm **afraid** not. Do you want to cancel?
> > B: No, but I'd **be** grateful if you could look into it.
> > A: No problem **at all**.
> > B: And would there be any **chance** of phoning me when it arrives?
> > A: Sure … let me just **check** if we have your phone number

**3A** Do the first one as an example, then give Ss three or four minutes to write out the enquiries, then compare answers in pairs. As you check the answers with the class, you could drill the enquiries, paying attention to Ss' intonation.

> **Answers:** 1 Could you tell me which one I need to catch to get there by noon? 2 I was wondering if it is possible (for me) to use your two-for-one deal a Friday night? 3 I'd like to enquire about your policy for returned tickets. 4 Would there be any chance of (getting/having) a window seat? 5 Would you mind telling me about withdrawal charges? 6 Do you mind me asking how much experience your student hairdressers have? 7 I'd be grateful if you could/would explain that again, from the bit about downloading the software. 8 Can you tell me where exactly the cheaper apartment would be?

**B** Elicit examples of situations for the first enquiry (a train, bus, car, boat or plane journey) then put Ss in pairs to discuss the rest.

> **Suggested answers:** 1 catching a train or a bus/coach 2 buying tickets for a journey, in a restaurant 3 a theatrical performance or a concert 4 a plane ticket, a train reservation 5 a bank account a hairdresser's 7 technical support for a computer 8 renting or buying an apartment

**LEARN TO** manage enquiries

**4A** Elicit from/remind Ss that in the original phone conversation they listened to, the caller asked the receptionist a few 'difficult' questions, which he couldn't answer straightaway. Direct them to the phrases and give them time to decide if the speaker is the receptionist or the caller and mark them R or C.

**B**

> **Answers:** 1 R 2 R 3 C 4 C 5 R 6 C

**C** Once Ss have found the phrases they could practise saying them as preparation for the next stage.

> **Possible answers:** 1 Sorry to be difficult, it's just that … /I've got one more question, if I'm not keeping you. 2 Bear with me a minute.

**5** Tell Ss not to write out the conversation, but to use the chart to help them speak. Encourage Ss to try to look at the prompts, then look up to speak, rather than 'reading' from the page, which will make them sound unnatural. For a *weaker class* you could go through the flow chart with the whole class first, eliciting examples at each step. When they have finished, tell Ss to reverse roles and practise the conversation again. Monitor the pair work and note down examples of good language use and problems for feedback and correction.

**SPEAKING**

**6A/B** Make sure you give Ss enough time to read their instructions carefully and prepare notes to help them in the conversation. Circulate while Ss are preparing and provide help if required. While Ss are talking, monitor and make notes for feedback. You could invite one or two pairs to act out their conversations for the class. NB If you don't have time for Ss to do both situations in class, you could use the second one for homework (see below).

**speakout** TIP

Before directing Ss to the tip, ask them what advice they would give someone who is nervous about making phone enquiries in English.

> **Homework ideas**
> 1 Workbook Ex 1–4B, p8
> 2 Language bank Ex A, p129
> 3 Ss arrange to phone each other after class and practise the conversation for situation 2 in Ex 6B.
> 4 If you are in an English-speaking environment, Ss find adverts in the local newspaper and underline examples of the vocabulary from Ex 1. They could also choose one advert to phone and make an enquiry about, then report back to the class in the next lesson.

# OFF THE HOOK

## Introduction

Ss watch an extract from *Off the Hook*, a BBC comedy about a group of students at a British university. Ss then learn and practise how to talk about a first encounter and write a summary of a story.

### SUPPLEMENTARY MATERIALS

Bring in some UK university undergraduate brochures or show Ss the websites so they can get an idea of what UK universities are like

Ex 3: For *weaker classes* prepare three or four true false questions to check that Ss understand the programme information.

## Warm up

Either: tell Ss to cover the texts and use the photo to lead into the topic. Ask questions, e.g. *Where are the people? How old do you think they are? What are they doing there? Do you think they all know each other? Would you like to be in this situation?*

Or: introduce the idea of a 'fresh start' and elicit from the class a) some reasons why people might want to make a fresh start (e.g. something has happened in their life to make them unhappy, they have done something wrong, etc.) and b) some ways of making a fresh start (e.g. moving to a new city or a new country, changing your appearance, etc.)

### ▶ DVD PREVIEW

**1** If you feel your Ss don't have the experience to answer these questions, give them these alternatives: *What would it be like to leave home for a long period of time? What would be positive/negative about it? Do you know anyone who wants to make, or has made a fresh start?* Elicit some examples of new situations, e.g. a course, a job, a flat share, meeting a boyfriend's/girlfriend's parents or friends, etc. Ss discuss the statements in pairs. In feedback, they can tell the class which statements they both agreed with. Ss could also talk about people they know who would agree with the statements, e.g. *My sister enjoys social situations where she doesn't know anyone – she's very self confident!*

**2A/B** Give Ss time to look at the photos and read the programme information. Vocabulary to check: *campus*, (the buildings of a university and the land that surrounds them), *encounter* (meeting), *foil* (to prevent something from being successful).

**Answers:** The photos show students on a university campus. The programme is set in a British university and it is about a young man who wants to reinvent himself and make a fresh start as he starts a new life away from home.

### Culture notes

Full-time university students in Britain typically attend universities a long way from their family homes. For this reason most universities provide or help to organize rented accommodation for many of their students. A *campus* university is situated on one site, with student accommodation, teaching and research facilities and leisure activities all together. A *collegiate* university (such as Oxford, Cambridge, Durham or London) is made up of number of different colleges to which the students belong and in which they may live, at least in their first year.

### ▶ DVD VIEW

**4A** Give Ss a moment or two to look at the questions and point out that some refer to more than one person. Play the DVD. You could tell Ss to say *Stop!* When they see the answer to the first couple of questions, then play the rest of the extract uninterrupted. Ss discuss answers in pairs.
In feedback with the class, check that Ss understand the reason for Danny's embarrassment (the inhaler for his asthma). You could also ask for Ss' reactions to the characters and the situation in the extract.

**Answers:** 2 M/D   3 D (*Oh, you saw that. Good, I was worried that not everyone had seen.*)   4 M (by kissing Danny and wanting to stay and make his bed, then by reminding him about his inhaler)/S (*I couldn't let you go off to uni all by yourself, could I?*)   5 D/B/T   6 D

**B** Ss should spend a few minutes reading through the sentences and trying to predict some of the missing words, before you play the DVD again. You may need to play the DVD a third time for Ss to confirm their answers. In feedback you could discuss with Ss the humour in the extract, particularly Danny's sarcasm (saying the opposite of what he means).

**Answers:** 1 up your bed   2 sure I'm OK   3 worried   4 brave   5 mum   6 believe   7 place   8 lectures   9 queue   10 dressed

**C** Ss could work in small groups to discuss these questions.

### DVD 1 Off The Hook

M = Mum   D = Danny   B = Becky
HO = Housing Officer   S = Shane

M: I can't believe my little honey bear's leaving me. I mean, how are you gonna cope all alone?

D: I'll be OK mum. And I will call you later, OK?

M: Do your coat up at least.

D: Mum, please, just don't.

M: Why don't you just let me come up and make up your bed?

D: Yeah, or maybe you should just stay for the first night and make sure I'm OK.

M: Can I?

D: No, absolutely not. No, come on I've got to go.

M: One more kissy.

D: OK, quickly.

M: I love you.

D: I love you too.

M: Dan, Dan! Wait! You forgot your inhaler!

B: Inhaler boy.

D: Oh, you saw that. Good, I was worried that not everyone had seen.

B: I thought you were brave. I wouldn't let my mum within a mile of the place

D: So, is this your first time away from home?

B: No, I took a gap year. I just spent the summer teaching in Africa, great experience though, such amazing landscapes and people. Have you done any travelling?

D: What me? Yeah. Loads. Like school trips and stuff. I spent the summer in Wales, actually. Yeah, such amazing hills. And sheep. See, I'm a photographer so I was there taking pictures. I'm Danny by the way.

B: I'm Becky.

S: Incoming!

D: Ow! Shane, what are you doing here?

S: I made it man! Can you believe it, there was one space left on Moral Philosophy with Comparative Philology. I don't know what it is, man, but it's only four hours of lectures a week! You know, I couldn't let you go off to uni all by yourself, could I? So, here we go man, three whole years, ooh! Oh, it's gonna be full-on fun-tastic!

D: Shane, this is Becky. Becky, Shane. He's a friend from school.

S: Woah.

HO: Hey guys, how's it going? Listen, sorry but if you're not in the queue could you just, maybe, go to the back?

S: Right, chill out granddad. What you dressed like that for charity or something?

HO: Go to the back.

D: What?

HO: Both of you. Go to the back.

D: But I didn't say anything.

HO: To the back now.

S: Just like back at school, innit?

D: Brilliant.

T: Hey, I'm Todd.

B: I'm Becky.

## speakout a first encounter

**5A** Elicit from Ss a list of reasons why someone might feel embarrassed on his/her first day at work and write these on the board. Tell Ss to listen to the story and see if any of their reasons are mentioned.

> **Answer:** He went to his boss' office with no shoes on: he'd taken them off because they were uncomfortable.

**B** Give Ss a few minutes to look through the *Key phrases* before playing the recording again. Vocabulary to check: *out of my depth* (not having the knowledge, skills, etc. to deal with a particular situation), *eventually* (in the end). Once you have checked the answers, drill the phrases and prompt Ss to substitute different alternatives from the box.

> **Answers:** I've had some very embarrassing experiences in my life; It started as a typical first day; I was feeling (kind of) nervous; I spent the whole time looking at …; By this time I was feeling …

## Unit 1 Recording 11

A: Well, I've had some very embarrassing experiences in my life but one of the worst was my very first day at work. I was a trainee solicitor in a law firm and there were fourteen of us trainees there and everyone was on their best behaviour. Everyone was dressed nicely and the guys had polished their shoes and done their hair you know wanting to make a good first impression and …

B: Yeah, I know what you mean. How old were you?

A: Only twenty-three, so I was one of the youngest in the group. Anyway, it started as a typical first day, you know a bit like the first day at school – everyone's not quite being themselves but, you know trying their hardest and you go and get your cup of tea or coffee and you try not to spill it or drop your biscuit on the floor.

B: Yeah.

A: And I remember I was feeling kind of – kind of nervous maybe a tiny bit shy and then having to pretend to be confident as if to say you know 'I'm very professional.' I spent the whole time looking at the others and wondering how experienced they were and …

B: I know the feeling.

A: And then I had to go to my desk and wait for some work to be given to me and, it was a quiet department so I was waiting and waiting and my shoes were new and were hurting so I kicked them off under the table and then another hour went by and by this time I was feeling a bit panicky because I didn't have anything to do – I hoped someone would give me some proper work to do – then the head partner rang me up and told me to come to his office because he'd got some work for me so I grabbed my pen and pad and I went racing round there. And as I walked into his office, he looked me up and down and saw that I wasn't wearing any shoes – I must have seemed ridiculously casual. It was so embarrassing, thankfully there were no holes in my socks because they were new, too. So I just spent the whole time in his office thinking – 'are you gonna say anything, are you gonna tell me off?'

B: Did he say anything?

A: Just before he sent me away he stopped me and he wanted to know why I didn't have any shoes on and I didn't have a good answer for that. I just said I wanted to feel more comfortable. I thought – I'm never going to fit in at this law firm.

B: And how did he react?

A: He smiled so I think he thought it was pretty funny, but ever since then I've always made sure I keep my shoes on!

**6A** Ss think about which situations they've been in and choose two or three that they have something to say about. They can then talk to a partner and help each other to decide on their best ones.

**B** Ss work alone preparing what to say. Emphasise that they should only make notes, not write full sentences and encourage them to use some of the *Key phrases*. Circulate and provide help if required. Before putting Ss in pairs to talk about their situations, you could focus on the listener's role and encourage Ss to 'listen actively' by saying, e.g. *Yeah/ Really?/ How …! / I know what you mean/What did … say/do?* Ss could look at examples of these in the audio script, or listen to the recording again and identify them.

**C** While each student is talking, their partner needs to make a few notes so they can write a summary of it in the *Writeback* stage. Monitor and make notes of good examples of language use and problem areas.

## writeback a summary

**7A** Tell Ss they are going to read a summary of the story about a first day at work. Give them a few minutes to read the summary and discuss in pairs what the two differences are.

> **Answers:** He wasn't reading a report at his desk, he was waiting to be given some work; he told his boss that he wasn't wearing shoes because he wanted to be comfortable, not that he'd forgotten to put them on.

**B** Elicit/Point out that the example summary has two paragraphs, one containing the background to the situation and one describing what happened. Ss can follow this model.

**C** Remind Ss about the correction code they used on p10. While they are checking each other's work, be available to deal with any queries about grammar, etc. Once Ss have checked each other's summaries for factual accuracy, you could pass them round or stick them on the wall for the rest of the class to read. You could have a class vote on the funniest/strangest/ most embarrassing situation.

> **Homework ideas**
> DVD extract: Ss write an email to a friend from the point of view of Danny/Danny's mum/Shane/Becky, describing what happened on Danny's first day at university.

# LOOKBACK

## Introduction

The aim of these activities is to provide revision and further practice of the language from the unit. You can also use them to assess Ss' ability to use the language, in which case you need to monitor but avoid helping them. You may feel that you don't need or have time to do all the activities. If so, you could allocate the activities that would be most beneficial for your Ss, or get individual Ss to decide which activities they'd like to do (both in class or for homework).

### DIRECT AND INDIRECT QUESTIONS

**1A** For *weaker classes*, you could choose one of the topics in the box and elicit a set of example questions, e.g. for 'transport '– *Do you like driving? What's going up in a hot-air balloon like? How often do you fly/travel by plane? Have you ever driven a really powerful sports car? Would you like to travel in space? Why do you not like public transport?*

Write these up on the board and then give the Ss some time to generate their own set of questions, either individually or in pairs.

**B** Tell Ss to imagine that they are going to interview a famous or important person (e.g. a politician, musician, actor, sportsperson) and ask this person their questions. This gives them a reason for making the questions polite and indirect.

**C** If Ss have written questions for a famous person, they need to tell their partner who it is and what topic they've chosen, so the partner can think about how that person would respond. After asking and answering the questions, Ss can tell the class about their partner's answers.

### PERSONALITY

**2A** Ss work alone rewriting the sentences, then compare answers in pairs. They could also discuss people they know who match the descriptions.

**Answers:** 2 He's a people person. 3 She's particular about keeping fit. 4 She's down to earth. 5 He's a good laugh. 6 She isn't tight-fisted. 7 He pulls his weight. 8 I do my best work in the early hours.

**B** After Ss have discussed this in pairs, they can compare and justify their ideas in feedback and try to agree as a class on the qualities for each type of person.

### FEELINGS

**3A** Ss work alone then compare answers.

**Answers:** 1 exhausted 2 embarrassed 3 thrilled 4 relieved

**B** Tell Ss that they can use three of the five adverbs before each of the adjectives. Give them a few minutes to discuss which adverbs <u>don't</u> belong in front of each adjective, then check with the class. Encourage Ss to add more lines to the conversations while they are practising, e.g. with follow up questions. The extra lines can be added anywhere in the conversation, not just at the end. Ss act out their conversations for the class and are awarded points for the most convincing additions and best performance.

**Answers:** 1 absolutely/completely/really exhausted 2 really/very/fairly embarrassed 3 absolutely/really/completely thrilled 4 really/very/fairly relieved

### PRESENT PERFECT AND PAST SIMPLE

**4A** With a *weaker class*, you could elicit/check the rules of use for the present perfect and past simple before giving Ss a few minutes to work on the exercise. With a *stronger class*, you could set up the exercise as a race. Ss work in pairs on the sentences and put up their hands (or make a pre-arranged 'buzzer' sound) when they have finished. If their sentences are not all correct, the next pair to finish have the chance to win, etc.

**Answers:** 1 've improved 2 haven't been 3 've never met 4 played, 've started 5 've seen 6 didn't eat

**B** Ss work in pairs and find out how many of the sentences are true for each of them. Then tell them to change the rest of the sentences to make them true. Ss report back to the class on their partner's new sentences.

### POLITE ENQUIRIES

**5A** You could set this up as a team competition. Tell Ss to close their books and divide the class into teams of four or five. Write/Display the first sentence on the board and give the teams a chance to confer on the answer (remind them about the need for polite intonation). When a team is ready they put up their hands and nominate one student to give the answer. You award points for accuracy and good pronunciation.

**Answers:** 1 I'd like to enquire about train times to Vienna. 2 Can you tell me which train I need to take to get to Vienna by 3p.m.? 3 Can I ask how far it is from the Western to the Southern train station? 4 Do you mind me asking where I can get information on local transport in Vienna? 5 I was wondering if I need to book a seat on the train? 6 Could you tell me if/whether I can book on the phone? 7 I was wondering if you could book it for me? 8 I'd be grateful if you could send me an email confirmation.

**B** Give pairs a few minutes to prepare the role-play. The tourist information needs to think of answers to the questions and the customer can rehearse the questions, saying them to themselves. After the first conversation, Ss could reverse roles and enquire about a flight, changing the questions as necessary.

## OVERVIEW

## COMIC RELIEF

### Introduction

Ss practise reading and speaking about Comic Relief and social issues, using the present perfect simple and continuous and related vocabulary. They also learn about verbs and nouns with the same form.

### SUPPLEMENTARY MATERIALS

Resource bank p148 and/or p151

Ex 2C: Ss could use monolingual dictionaries

Ex 5: bring in/download a photo of the fair trade label

Ex 7: bring in news headlines and photos/articles related to social issues

### Warm up

Lead into the topic via a discussion of charities. Elicit some names of charities (e.g. Oxfam, Amnesty International, World Wildlife Fund, the Red Cross) and examples of what they do. Then elicit on the board examples of things people can do for charity, e.g. *do a sponsored walk or run, give money to people collecting in the street, give used clothes to a charity shop, organise an event to raise funds, work as a volunteer.* Then write *Have you ever…?* in front of the list above and put Ss into small groups to discuss what they've done/would like to do. This will also allow you to assess how well Ss are using the present perfect.

### READING

**1**  Focus Ss on the photos and either discuss the questions as a class or put Ss in pairs to do so.

**2A**  Give Ss a minute or two to read through the questions, then tell them to find the answers in the two articles. You could also point out that questions 1–4 refer to the first article and question 5 refers to the second. Vocabulary to check in the first article: *vulnerable* (easily hurt emotionally or phys*ically), fundraising campaign* (a series of actions to collect money for a specific purpose), *telethon* (a special TV programme which lasts many hours and in which famous people provide entertainment and ask people to give money to charity).

**Answers:** 1 It's a charity that helps people all over the world.  2 ordinary people and celebrities  3 People do silly things to raise money and there's a telethon on the BBC.  4 every two years  5a) wearing pyjamas to work, sitting in a bath of jelly, wearing red noses b) a sponsored silence c) a twenty-four-hour dance marathon

**B**  Ss should be prepared to give reasons for their answers in feedback to the class. They could also think of some more examples of funny things people could do to raise money.

**C**  Work through the questions for guessing the meaning of *eye-opening* with the class. Explain to the Ss that they may need to look for contextual clues in the sentences before or after the one the word is in, e.g. *I've been working here for a year and it's the first time I've spoken to some of my colleagues* suggests that the experience was surprising or revealing.

You may also want to use *jelly* as a second example, as its meaning is not obvious, e.g. *1 it's a noun; 2 you can sit in it, so it must be a liquid or semi liquid, it's green (and cold), you can eat it and it tastes good; 3 Is there a similar word in your language?* (There might, for example, be a word similar to *gelatine* in the students' language(s).)

Give Ss time to work through the other words, making notes about the meaning as they go along. Once they have compared answers with a partner, they could check their definitions in a monolingual dictionary.

**Answers:** 1 hooting (n) – ( a car) making a loud noise 2 corridors (n pl) – long narrow passages between two rows of rooms 3 (adj) unaccustomed – unusual 4 marathon (n)– (an event) lasting a long time that needs energy/determination 5 worn out (adj) – very tired 6 donations (n pl) – money that people give (e.g. to a charity) to help others

### speakout TIP

Discuss this briefly with the class, asking who relies on a dictionary, who tries to guess meanings, etc. For those who don't like the 'ambiguity' of having to guess the meaning, you could suggest they mark the words they've tried to guess, then check them in a monolingual dictionary once they've read the whole text.

### GRAMMAR present perfect simple and continuous

**3A** Ask Ss to cover the articles while they complete the sentences. For *stronger classes*, you could tell the pairs to think about why the simple or continuous is used in each case and if there are any examples where both are possible.

**Answers:** 1 've been working ('ve worked is also possible) 2 has been raising (has raised is also possible) 3 has raised 4 've had 5 've been dancing 6 've closed

**B** Ss discuss the rules in pairs. Monitor their discussions closely: if they are struggling, you may want to direct them to the examples in the **Language bank** during feedback.
To summarise, you could ask Ss: *Which form focuses on the completion of the activity? Which form focuses on the duration or repetition of the activity?*

**Answers:** 1 1, 2 2a) 4 2b) 6 2c) 3 3a) 1, 2, 5 3b) 5

**4A** Point out that Ss are going to hear three pairs of questions and answers. If necessary, stop the recording after each question or answer, to give Ss time to write.

### Unit 2 Recording 1

1
A: How long have you been working here?
B: I've been here for over ten months now.
2
A: How many chocolates have you eaten?
B: I've only had three!
3
A: What have you been doing? You're filthy!
B: I've been running.

**B** Put Ss in pairs and encourage them to read out the questions and answers to each other, so they can work out the stresses and weak forms.

**Teaching tip**

*Weak forms* are the 'unstressed' vowel sounds. Demonstrate for Ss that the auxiliary verbs in the examples are 'squashed' between the main stressed words and the resulting vowel sound is extremely short. You could use circles on the board, e.g. for *How long have you been working here?* draw oOoooOoO. (The big circles represent *long, work* and *here*.)

To help Ss to produce the examples with a natural rhythm, drill only the stressed words first, then 'fill in' the unstressed words:
*long – work – here?*
*How long have you been working here?*

**LANGUAGEBANK** 2.1 p130–131

Read through these rules and examples before going on to Ex 5 and 6. You may also want Ss to do Ex 2.1A (and/or 2.1B) to give them more basic practice in choosing between the present perfect simple and continuous.

**Answers:** A 1 've been looking/'ve just bought 2 've done/'ve been running 3 've been trying/'ve decided 4 's hurt/'s been fighting 5 've eaten/'ve been eating
B 1 have you been teaching? 2 a) have you been collecting? b) have you collected? 3 have you thought that? 4 a) have you been saving? b) have you saved? 5 have you had it? 6 have you known her?

### PRACTICE

**5** Find out what Ss know about Fairtrade. If you have brought a Fairtrade label, put it on the board to prompt Ss. Tell them that the text is about someone who works with Fairtrade. Give Ss time to complete the gaps, then compare answers in pairs. Vocabulary to check: *recruit* (to find new people to work in a company).

**Answers:** 2 've visited 3 've been living 4 've met 5 've known 6 's been growing 7 's been following 8 's recently recruited 9 've doubled 10 's become

**Culture notes**
Fairtrade is a charitable organisation that aims to help producers in developing markets to get a fair price for their goods.

**6A** Give Ss a few minutes to complete the questions alone. If your Ss are all from the same country, you could change 5 with the following prompts: *you/always/live/ at the same address?* or *you/always/have/the same hairstyle?*

**Answers:** 1 Have you been working 2 have you known 3 have you been doing 4 have you seen 5 Has your country always had 6 have you been coming 7 have you drunk 8 have you been working

**B** Before Ss start the activity, you could ask them to practise saying the questions to themselves at natural speed. Ss can ask and answer in pairs, or stand up and walk round the class, asking different people their questions. In feedback, ask Ss about any surprising answers to their questions.

## Teaching tip

If you have room for Ss to stand up and walk round the class for a personalised question/answer activity like the one above, it has a number of benefits:

– Ss can practise with more than one partner (they can ask all their questions, or you can direct them to move to a new partner after a certain number of questions, or every two or three minutes).

– It provides variety of interaction in the lesson.

– It can help to 're-energise' a class that has been sitting still for a while.

## VOCABULARY social issues

**7A** Bring in some news articles with photos and/or headlines related to some of the social issues and have a brief discussion with Ss about which stories they've heard about. Put Ss in pairs to categorise the words. You may want to check the meaning and pronunciation of the following before Ss start: *drought* (long period when there is no rain), *famine* (people having little or no food), *debt* (owing money to somebody), *obesity* (being too fat in a way that is dangerous to your health).

**Possible answers:** money – poverty, homelessness, debt  health –drunkenness and drug abuse, obesity, lack of drinking water, famine  the environment – pollution, drought, lack of drinking water, famine  the family – domestic violence, divorce, debt

**B** If your Ss are from the same country, tell them to try to come to an agreement about the issues that are not a major problem. Otherwise, make sure that Ss are partnered with someone from a different country.

## SPEAKING

**8A** If your Ss are not from the same country, they could work alone and make notes on the questions to start with, then move into pairs or small groups.

**B** Put the Ss into small groups to discuss their views. Monitor the discussions and make notes of good language use and any problems, for praise and correction later. In feedback, Ss report to the class on their discussions and decide on the main problem and the best suggestion for solving it.

> ➡ **VOCABULARYBANK** p149 Issues
>
> Give the Ss plenty of time to match the images with the natural disasters in Ex 1 before feeding back with the answers as a class (make sure you check the pronunciation and word stress). Ss complete the collocations and write the nouns in Ex 2A and B using dictionaries to help them if necessary.
>
> **Answers:** 1 1 A  2 F  3 D  4 G  5 C  6 B  7 E  8 H
> 2A 1 domestic  2 ethical  3 rural  4 political  5 economic
> 6 urban  7 global  8 industrial
> B domestic  this country;  economic  economics;
> ethical  ethics;  global  world;  industrial  industry;
> rural  country(side)

## VOCABULARY *PLUS* verbs/nouns with the same form

**9A** Look at the example with the class, then give Ss a few minutes to complete the conversations. Play the recording, stopping after each conversation for Ss to confirm their answers. Vocabulary to check: *launch (*to start or set in motion).

**Answers:** 2 sponsor/sponsors  3 increase/increased
4 appeal/appealing  5 record/record  6 export/export
7 project/project  8 permit/permitted

**B** Ss can work in pairs to label the words (N) or (V).

**C** Remind Ss to mark the stress by underlining or putting a box over the stressed syllable. Point out that only two of the words have the same stress in the noun and verb forms.

**Answers:** 2A <u>spon</u>sor V/<u>spon</u>sors N  3 in<u>crease</u> N/
in<u>creased</u> V  4 ap<u>peal</u> N/ap<u>pealing</u> V  5 re<u>cord</u> V/<u>record</u> N
6 ex<u>port</u> V/<u>exports</u> N  7 <u>project</u> N/B pro<u>ject</u> V
8 <u>permit</u> N/per<u>mitted</u> V

### speakout TIP

Read through the tip with the class, then get them to mark and practise the pairs of words with a partner. You could also ask Ss which word from Ex 9A is an exception to the rule of the noun usually being stressed on the first syllable (*appeal*).

**10A** Emphasise that Ss should not show their quiz questions to each other. Give them a few minutes to mark the stress on the words and practise saying their questions to themselves.

**Answers:** Student A:  im<u>ports</u>  <u>present</u>  sus<u>pect</u>  <u>desert</u>
<u>research</u>
Student B:  re<u>corded</u>  <u>exports</u>  pro<u>duce</u>  <u>suspects</u>  <u>record</u>

**B** Ss work in pairs asking and answering the quiz questions. Remind them to make a note of their partner's answers.

**C** Give Ss a few minutes to check the quiz answers on p162 and feed back to their partners. Conduct a brief feedback on which answers Ss found most interesting/surprising.

> ➡ **VOCABULARYBANK** p149 Verbs/Nouns with the same form
>
> Encourage the Ss to work through the exercise the first time without using their dictionaries. They should check their answers in pairs before using a dictionary. They can work with a different partner to take it in turns to ask and answer the questions.
>
> **Answers:** A 2 test  3 shout  4 queue  5 guess  6 cure
> 7 fine  8 tip  9 lie  10 hurry

## Homework ideas

1 Workbook Ex 3, 1–5B, p9–10

2 Ss visit the Comic Relief website and report back on something interesting they found out.

3 Ss write about a charity that they feel is worthwhile. They could give a short talk about it in the next lesson.

4 Ss write five quiz questions for a partner using the vocabulary and ideas from the unit so far.

# WE'RE BEING WATCHED

## Introduction

Ss practise listening and speaking about surveillance, using the passive and related vocabulary. They also learn to use formal written language and write a letter of complaint.

### SUPPLEMENTARY MATERIALS

Resource bank p149 and/or p150

Ex 7A: be prepared to talk about an official complaint that you, or someone you know made.

## Warm up

Ask Ss to close their books and write the title *We're being watched* on the board. Put Ss in pairs and give them a minute or two to discuss what they think the title means. In feedback, you may want to pre-teach *surveillance* and *CCTV (closed circuit television) camera*.

### VOCABULARY surveillance

**1A** Direct Ss to the photo and ask them which type of technology from the box they can see. Discuss the question briefly with the class.

**B** Give Ss a moment or two to look at the types of technology and check *number plate* and *microchip*.
Put Ss in pairs and tell them to match the quotes without using dictionaries. Reassure them that they will look at the phrases in bold in the next exercise.

**Answers:** 1 street level cameras  2 speed cameras
3 CCTV cameras  4 phone cameras  5 microchips
6 number plate recognition

**C** Before Ss look at the meanings here, remind them about the three questions they can use to help them guess the meaning of new words (on p20) and give them a few minutes alone to try to guess the meanings of the phrases in bold. Then, with a partner, they can compare ideas and match meanings 1–8.

**Answers:** 2 a deterrent to crime  3 handed over
4 accountable for  5 law-abiding citizens  6 an invasion of privacy  7 monitor, keep track of  8 a surveillance society

### Optional extra activity

To help Ss to remember the phrases, give each pair a set of sixteen slips of paper with the phrases cut in half, e.g.:

| | |
|---|---|
| *an invasion / of privacy* | *a deterrent / to crime* |
| *law-abiding / citizens* | *accountable / for* |
| *keep track / of* | *hand sth / over* |
| *log / information* | *a surveillance / society* |

First they match the halves, then they 'test' each other by turning over one slip of paper in each pair and trying to remember the complete phrase.

**D** You could elicit one or two more example questions before putting Ss into pairs. Encourage Ss, while discussing the statements, to think about people they know who have relevant experiences, or stories in the news about surveillance. Conduct a brief class feedback.

### LISTENING

**2A** Suggest that Ss copy the table into their notebooks, giving themselves space to write the type of technology in the first column. Play the recording, telling them to listen only for the type of technology.

**Answers:** 1 street level cameras  2 speed cameras and number plate recognition  3 microchips  4 CCTV cameras  5 phone cameras

**B** You could pause the recording after each speaker to give Ss time to make notes. Ss compare answers in pairs, identifying anything they are unsure of. You can then assess whether you need to play the recording again.

**Answers:**

| Speaker | For (✓) or against (✗) the idea | Reasons |
|---|---|---|
| 1 street level cameras | ✓ | Good to see places before you go on holiday, e.g. hotels, cities. If you want to look at a person's house, you can drive or walk past it. |
| 2 speed cameras and number plate recognition | ✗ | The government use them to make money. They don't work as a deterrent (accidents have gone up). He hates being watched. |
| 3 microchips | ✗ | It's an invasion of privacy, e.g. people knowing what he eats. He doesn't want companies to send him adverts or junk mail. |
| 4 CCTV cameras | ✓ | CCTV cameras helped the police to find two men who robbed him. They help solve more crimes. Law-abiding citizens have nothing to worry about. |
| 5 phone cameras | ✓ | It means that in public everyone has to behave better, for example the police, in case the pictures are published. |

### Unit 2 Recording 3

1   I really can't see the problem. The first thing I did when it all began was I tried to find my house on the website but they hadn't brought the camera van down our road yet, so I was quite disappointed. For me, it's great because it means I can go and look at things like hotels or even cities before I go on holiday … and anyway if someone wanted to look at my house they could just drive past it or walk past it, so I can't see the problem.
2   It's obvious, isn't it? I mean, they're nothing to do with safety. They're just used by the government to make money. I mean, look at the statistics. In the last year, in my area four cameras have been placed along one stretch of road and you know what, the number of accidents has doubled. So they obviously don't work as a deterrent. And now your car number plate can be logged so that they can keep track of you wherever you go. I hate it – I hate being watched like that. It's just another example of our surveillance society.

**3** The way I see it, it's an invasion of privacy. It means whenever I go to the supermarket, it's recorded on a chip somewhere and they can find out exactly what I've bought. Why should people have the right to know what kind of food I eat? Or get my details and then send me junk mail? I certainly don't want to be sent adverts from companies I don't know. And this is just the start … I expect next thing you know, the technology will be used to tell us what we can and can't eat.

**4** Me, I'm glad they're there. A few months ago I was robbed by two men at a bus stop not far from where I live but thanks to CCTV, the people who did it were all arrested. It was a bad experience but at least they didn't get away with it. And you see it in the news all the time – that more crimes are being solved because of CCTV cameras. I think we should have more of them. Most people are law-abiding anyway so they've got no need to worry.

**5** I actually think it's an important development. There was a case recently, where there was this big demonstration and lots of people took photos and these were sent to the media. So it means that demonstrators and the police – everyone – has to be more careful because their photos might be sent to the newspapers or posted online. So in general, yeah, I feel it's a good thing.

## GRAMMAR the passive

**3A** Do the first sentence as an example, underlining *'re* and *used*. Ss can work on the rest of the sentences in pairs. For a *stronger class,* tell them to think about why the passive is being used in each case. In feedback, check the form of the passive: *be* + past participle. Point out that *be* can be used in different tenses, with modal verbs and in the *-ing* and infinitive forms. If your Ss would benefit from seeing more examples at this stage, direct them to the table in the **Language bank** on p130.

**Answers:** 2 More crimes <u>are being solved</u> because of CCTV cameras. 3 A few months ago I <u>was robbed</u> by two men but thanks to CCTV, the people who did it <u>were</u> all arrested. 4 In my area, four cameras <u>have been placed</u> along one stretch of road. 5 They technology <u>will be used</u> to tell us what we can and can't eat. 6 Everyone has to be more careful because their photos <u>might be sent</u> to the newspapers. 7 I hate <u>being watched</u> like that. 8 I certainly don't want <u>to be sent</u> adverts from companies I don't know.

**B** Encourage Ss to look back at the sentences in Ex 3A as they complete the rules.

**Answers:** 1 affected by the action. 2 a) is obvious b) is unknown c) isn't important 3 the beginning

**C** As there are several examples of each rule, you may prefer to ask Ss how many of the sentences exemplify each rule.

**Answers:**
1 all the examples
2 a) 2 b) 4, 5, 6, 7 c) 2, 4, 5, 6, 7
3 1, 2, 5, 7, 8

**4** Remind Ss that the words carrying the important information in the sentence are usually stressed and do the first phrase with the class as an example.

**Answers:** 1 They're just <u>used</u> by the <u>government</u> 2 I <u>hate</u> being <u>watched</u> like that. 3 I don't <u>want</u> to be sent <u>adverts</u> 4 I was <u>robbed</u> by two men 5 Crimes are being <u>solved</u> 6 their <u>photos</u> might be <u>sent</u> to the <u>newspapers</u>.

### ➡ LANGUAGEBANK 2.2 p130–131

Depending on how confident Ss seem with the passive, they can look at this in class or at home. If you feel they need more basic practice before moving on to Ex 5, they could do Ex A and/or Ex B. Ex B is a short text about the use of Google street view in finding a missing child, so might be more appropriate to use in the lesson. You could set Ex A for homework, asking Ss to expand each sentence into a two- or three-line dialogue.

**Answers:** A 1 My cat's being operated on this afternoon. 2 He'll be caught sooner or later. 3 Kim was burnt badly in the fire. 4 They don't mind being woken up in the middle of the night. 5 Someone could get hurt if you don't take care. 6 I've been asked to give a speech to the whole school. 7 She's expected to be at her desk by 9a.m. every day. 8 Employees' emails are sometimes monitored by their supervisor.
B 2 was found 3 was discovered 4 put 5 has been arrested 6 is believed 7 being separated 8 might be given

## PRACTICE

**5A** Do the first sentence as an example with the class, pointing out to Ss that they need to think carefully about the form of *be*. Vocabulary to check: *filter, screening, database, infiltrate.*

**Answers:** 1 are always filtered/can be kept 2 being told 3 are probably being filmed 4 will be placed/can be reminded 5 may be used 6 were lost 7 have been caught 8 have often been infiltrated/has been stolen

**B** Ss can spend a few moments alone thinking about which statements they find disturbing and why, before discussing their ides with a partner. Monitor the discussions and make a note of good use of the passive, as well as any problems, for praise and correction in feedback.

## SPEAKING

**6A** Focus Ss on the headline and the first sentence of the article, explaining that a *surge* is a sudden increase. Direct them to the questions and point out that in question 2 they need to think of a reaction for each of the four groups. Conduct a brief class feedback.

**B** You may want to run this activity with only two or three of the groups from Ex 6A, e.g. the police and parents, or the police, local residents and teenagers. Put Ss into pairs or small groups by type (i.e. all local residents together) to prepare the points they want to make. Circulate and help as required.

**C** You could set up this role-play in different ways:

1 All Ss together as a class, with people of the same 'type' (police, resident, etc.) sitting together. In this case you need to ensure that all Ss have a chance to get involved, so you may need to moderate the discussion or appoint a student to do so. To avoid interrupting the discussion by calling out names, you can throw a small ball to the person you want to speak next.

2 Ss work in small groups, each with one representative from each 'type' (police, resident, etc.) In this case, after the role-play ask each group what the outcome of their meeting was. Monitor the role-play(s) and make a note of good language use and problem areas for feedback.

### WRITING a letter of complaint

**7A** Start by eliciting some examples of things people might make an official complaint about, e.g. the food/service in a restaurant; the room/cleanliness/service in a hotel; an item they bought; the maintenance of a road/park/service by the local council. You could give an example of your own and encourage Ss to ask you questions about it. If Ss have no experience of complaining themselves, they can think about people they know, e.g. friends/family members/neighbours.

**B** Focus Ss on the questions and tell them to be prepared to explain their answers to someone who hasn't read the letter. This will stop them reading out sections of the letter verbatim and encourage them to summarise simply. Vocabulary to check: *password* (a secret group of letters or numbers that you put into a computer so that you can use a program), *violation* (an action that breaks an agreement or law*), *blur* (to make something difficult to see).

> **Answers:** 1 His local council 2 Because he and his car can be identified in some of the council's CCTV images that have been posted on the internet. 3 He wants the council to remove the images and, in future to protect images with a password and blur them so that people cannot be recognised.

**C** Before Ss look at topics a)–f), they can go through the letter in pairs and decide on the purpose of each paragraph.

> **Answers:** b) 5 c) 1 d) 6 e) 4 f) 2

### LEARN TO use formal written language

**8A** Before Ss match the phrases, they could look through the letter and put a tick (✓) in the margin next to any phrases they think would be useful for formal letter writing. They should not underline the phrases (see Ex 8B). They compare their ideas with a partner, then work together to match phrases 1–7.

> **Answers:** 1 Please contact me within ten days of the date of this letter to confirm that these steps have been taken. 2 In order to resolve this matter, I am requesting that you 3 I am writing with regard to 4 Yours faithfully, 5 Thank you for your prompt attention to this matter. 6 in the enclosed document 7 I have already pursued this matter

**B** Find the first example of the passive with the class, then put Ss into pairs.

> **Answers:** cannot be kept  can be identified  were (recently) posted  are detailed  are pass-worded  are used  have been taken
> It is common to find the passive in more formal text types. It creates a distance between the agent and the action, which makes the style less personal.

### speakout TIP

You may need to check that Ss understand *concise* (short, with no unnecessary words), *constructive* (intended to be helpful) and *considerate* (thinking about other people and avoiding upsetting them) before asking them to look at the letter again.

Ss may disagree as to whether the letter is *considerate*, but it is polite and one could argue that this is all that is necessary for an organisation like a local council.

**9A** Once Ss have chosen the situation and planned their letter, they can show their plan to a partner and give each other advice on what to add/change. Alternatively, you could give Ss the option of working in pairs, choosing the same situation so that they can discuss and plan it together.

**B** Before Ss start writing, remind them about the formal language phrases they looked at and the use of the passive. While Ss are writing, be available to answer queries, but avoid correcting at this stage.

**C** Circulate and help as required while Ss are checking their work, prompting them to correct their mistakes for themselves as much as possible, e.g. by saying things like: *Check the tense here. Look at the word order in this sentence. Is this formal enough?*

**D** So that Ss see more than one other letter, you could put them up on the walls for Ss to walk around and read.

> **Homework ideas**
> 1 Workbook Ex 1–5, p11–12
> 2 Ss write a newspaper article about the 'meeting' they had about surveillance in Ex 6C, describing what happened and what the outcome was.
> 3 Ss look at the letters page of a UK newspaper (these can be found online, e.g. at thepaperboy.com (correct at the time of going to press)) and check whether the letters follow the four Cs. They can bring the letters to show each other in the next lesson.

# JUST WHAT I WAS THINKING!

## Introduction

Ss practise listening to and giving opinions. They also learn to support their viewpoint and to incorporate 'opinion' adjectives.

### SUPPLEMENTARY MATERIALS

Resource bank p152

## Warm up

Lead into the idea of giving opinions via the following activity: *Don't say yes or no!* Demonstrate by putting a topic, e.g. *homework* on the board and telling Ss to avoid saying *yes* or *no* when they answer your questions. Ask one or two Ss a question, e.g. *Do think it's a good idea to do homework? Do you think you get enough homework?* If they answer *yes* or *no*, award yourself a point. If they answer *It depends/I'm not sure/ I suppose so*, etc. award the class a point. Once Ss have got the idea, put them in pairs and put another topic on the board, e.g. *exams* or *learning English*.

### SPEAKING

**1** Focus Ss on the photos and discuss briefly with the class what they can see in each one. Give Ss a few minutes to read the extracts and the questions, then put them in pairs to discuss their ideas. Make sure that Ss make a note of their reasons in question 2, so they can compare them with the speakers in the listening Ex 2B.

> **Answers:** Matching: 1 Photo A  2 Photo C  3 Photo B
> Article 1 – The writer is against downloading music from the internet – thinks it's a crime.
> Article 2 – The writer is neutral about cosmetic surgery – can see how some people might want it.
> Article 3 – The writer is for banning cars from the city centre because it reduces pollution.

### FUNCTION opinions

**2A** Tell Ss they are going to hear three conversations about the topics they've just discussed. To help them organise their notes, suggest that they draw the following table in their notebooks, to complete while listening:

|  | Conversation 1 | Conversation 2 | Conversation 3 |
|---|---|---|---|
| Agree with man/woman |  |  |  |
| Man's opinion |  |  |  |
| Woman's opinion |  |  |  |

Play the recording and tell Ss to complete the first row of the table.

**B** Tell Ss to make short notes about the speakers' opinions and play the recording again, stopping after each conversation to give Ss time to process what they've heard. Ss discuss answers in pairs, commenting on which opinions match their own from Ex 1.

**Answers:**

|  | Conversation 1 | Conversation 2 | Conversation 3 |
|---|---|---|---|
| Man's opinion | Against cosmetic surgery: can be dangerous, e.g. face frozen after Botox. | Against downloading music for free: it's theft, how can musicians make money. Worried about being found out. | Against banning cars from city centre: buses pollute more than cars, trial showed reduction in shop sales, centre fine as it is. |
| Woman's opinion | For cosmetic surgery if it was for a health reason | For downloading music: artists make little money from CD sales – most comes from concerts. Helps newer groups get known | For banning cars: more people will come in on buses, buses will be electric in the future, centre clogged up, polluted, can't move |

### Unit 2 Recording 5

1

A:  Do you think you would ever have cosmetic surgery?

B:  Me? No I don't think so, I'm really against it actually, I think it's …

A:  Really, why?

B:  It can be quite dangerous – some of the implants you can have, um …

A:  Yes, I know what you mean.

B:  Take the case of Mike's girlfriend – she actually had some Botox injections in her forehead.

A:  Did she?

B:  Yeah and she couldn't, you know she couldn't …

A:  Couldn't move her face?

B:  Yeah, she couldn't smile or frown – her face was just frozen solid.

A:  Although if someone's really, really overweight and it becomes a health problem, do you think maybe then they should have some kind of surgery, you know, such as liposuction to get rid of fat?

B:  Oh I see, for health reasons maybe, yes, I suppose so, I mean you've got a point there, but I still don't like the sound of it. I wouldn't do it myself.

A:  I might, if it was to do with my health.

2

A:  Do you ever download music for free?

B:  You mean illegally? No, I think I'm probably one of the few people that don't do it. I've always paid whether it's the track price or the album price.

A:  Why? I mean nobody I know pays.

B:  Well the way I see it, it's just theft, isn't it? I mean …

A:  [interrupting] Oh I totally disagree.

B:  I mean, artists have copyright on their songs, so you're stealing from them. It's as simple as that.

A:  But it's a well-known fact that musicians get very little money from CD sales anyway. So they don't lose out. I mean, they want people to hear their music.

B:  Hmm. I'm not so sure about that. If people share the music without paying, how can musicians make any money?

A: Well, the famous ones, they don't need more money and for newer groups, file-sharing is the way they get known so they don't have to spend a fortune, you know, on things like record companies and managers and …
B: Yeah, but …
A: anyway, nowadays singers and groups make most of their money from concerts.
B: Hmm. I'm still not convinced. Aren't you worried about being found out? For instance, what about that woman in America? Because of the hundreds of tracks she downloaded illegally – she got fined something like two million dollars.
A: Two million dollars? Ouch!
B: Yeah, so maybe you'd better think again.
A: Hmm.
3
A: Have you seen this plan in the local paper for changes to the city centre?
B: Oh, you mean the idea to ban cars from the centre?
A: Yes and only allowing buses. What do you think of the idea?
B: Oh, I'm in favour of it. I think it'd be really good for the environment, you know for cutting down pollution.
A: Well I don't know, apparently it's been shown that buses are more polluting than cars.
B: How can they be? But even if they are at the moment, it seems to me that they're bound to get better, you know, they'll get replaced with electric buses or something like that.
A: Maybe.
B: Does that mean you're against it?
A: Yes, on balance, I think I am. I mean, according to the article, when they did a trial in another town there was a reduction in shop sales – apparently almost ten percent.
B: That doesn't sound right, if more people came in on buses. I suppose the main thing is to put money into making sure you have a good public transport system.
A: Okay, I mean I agree to some extent, but actually, I think the town centre works perfectly fine as it is.
B: But it's clogged up. You know, you can't move, it's polluted.
A: It's a bit clogged up but if you're patient you eventually find somewhere to park.
B: Well I just hope they decide soon.
A: Yeah.

**3A** Point out that there is only one word missing from each phrase, then put Ss into pairs.

**Answers:** 1 against 2 favour 3 way 4 so 5 see 6 point 7 some 8 totally 9 so 10 convinced

**B** Give Ss a few minutes to read through the audio script, then tell them to look through the phrases again and write S or W next to the ones they think are particularly strong or weak.

**4A** Tell Ss to underline the stressed words in the sentences in Ex 3A. You may want to take the phrases one at a time, stopping after each one for Ss to tell you where the stress is and repeat the phrase.

**Answers:** 1 I'm <u>really</u> <u>against</u> it. (s) 2 I'm in <u>favour</u> of it. (s) 3 The way <u>I</u> see it … 4 I <u>suppose</u> so. 5 I <u>know</u> what you <u>mean</u>. 6 You've <u>got</u> a <u>point</u> there, but … 7 I <u>agree</u> to <u>some</u> <u>extent</u>, but … (w) 8 I <u>totally</u> <u>disagree</u>. (s) 9 I'm not so <u>sure</u>. (w) 10 I'm <u>still</u> not <u>convinced</u>. (s)

**B** Do the first one as an example, then put Ss in pairs to work on the rest. As you go through the answers in feedback, you could get Ss to repeat the phrases.

**Answers:** Giving opinions: *I think … It seems to me that … I feel …*
Agreeing: *Exactly! That's right. I agree.*
Partially agreeing: *I take/see your point, but … Fair enough, but …*
Disagreeing: *I don't agree with you.*

**⟹ LANGUAGEBANK** 2.3 p130–131
Point out that the phrases Ss have been working on are summarised in the **Language bank** for their reference.
If you feel that Ss need some accuracy practice with the phrases before moving on to Ex 5, you could do Ex A in class. Otherwise, Ss could do it for homework.

**Answers:** A
B: Are you? I'm really against **it**.
A: Well, **the** way I see it, with uniforms everyone's the same, rich or poor
B: I take your **point**, but they can be very expensive, especially as children get bigger.
A: I know **what** you mean, but kids' clothes are expensive anyway.
B: Fair **enough**, but having uniforms deprives kids of individual expression.
A: I agree **to** some extent, but uniforms provide a sense of belonging.
B: I'm not so **sure**. Lonely kids don't feel any less lonely just because they have a uniform on.
A: Maybe not, but I'm **still** not convinced.

**5A** You could start by putting two topics on the board (banning smoking in public places and violence in films affects crime) and eliciting some examples from the class of reasons for and against them.
Ss work alone to write out the conversations in their notebooks. They should not write in the course book so they can use the prompts for oral practice in the next stage.

**Answers:**
A
A: I'm in favour of banning smoking in all public places.
B: I don't agree with you. People should be free to choose.
A: I agree to some extent, but what about the rights of other people?
B: The way I see it the freedom to choose is more important.
A: I take your point, but passive smoking can be very bad for you.
B: I suppose so, but banning it in all public places is too much!
2
A: I'm against too much violence in films because of the effect on crime.
B: I don't agree with you. Thousands of people watch films but only a few people commit crimes.
A: Okay, You've got a point there, but it seems to me that even one person is one person too many.
B: I know what you mean, but I'm still not convinced.

**B** Monitor the practice and invite one or two pairs who did well to act out their conversations for the class.

### LEARN TO support your viewpoint

**6** Tell Ss they are going to look at some examples from the conversations in Ex 2 that will help them to make their opinions stronger and more convincing. You could do an example each for a) b) and c), then give Ss a minute or two (alone or in pairs) to look at the rest. In feedback, drill the phrases in bold, making sure that Ss sound natural.

**Answers:** a) 1, 2, 4, 8  b) 3, 6  c) 5, 7

**7A** Remind Ss to cover Ex 6 before they start and point out that they need to add a capital letter if the phrase starts a new sentence. Ss should write the complete conversations in their notebooks, to give them more space. After feedback Ss could practise the conversation in pairs.

**Answers:** 1 According to this article  2 for instance jobs in management/jobs in management, for instance.  3 Take the case of my brother  4 such as cooking or listening  5 it's a well-known fact that women are  6 it's been shown that men are  7 in magazines like that  8 but apparently it's based on scientific research/but it's based on scientific research, apparently

#### speakout TIP

After Ss have read the tip, you could elicit from the class that this is something they already do in their own language. It's mainly a case of knowing <u>how</u> to do it in English.

**B** Give Ss a minute or two alone to decide whether they agree or not and to think of reasons and examples, making a few notes if necessary. Monitor the discussions and be prepared to give feedback on how well Ss used the phrases for supporting their viewpoints.

##### Optional extra activity
To give Ss more practice in using the phrases, you could give them other stereotypes to discuss, e.g. teenagers, politicians. Give them time to prepare their arguments, using at least three of the phrases. Alternatively, Ss could do some research for homework, then discuss the topic in the next lesson.

### VOCABULARY opinion adjectives

**8A** Focus Ss on the example then give them time to match the rest of the adjectives. As you check the answers, you could mark the stress on the adjectives and drill them.

**Answers:** 2 sensible  3 inevitable  4 unethical  5 illegal  6 justifiable  7 outrageous  8 inoffensive

**B** You could demonstrate this by doing a couple of examples with Ss in open pairs, across the class. Then put Ss in closed pairs and suggest they swap roles after four exchanges.

##### Teaching tip
Open vs closed pairs

An open pair is when Ss ask/answer from opposite sides of the classroom. This means that the rest of the class can hear them, so it's useful for demonstrating and setting up pair work activities, especially if you choose two stronger Ss.

A closed pair is two Ss sitting next to each other. This interaction maximises student speaking time because all the pairs are speaking simultaneously.

**C** Ss can work in pairs to make the opposites. Fast finishers can think about the opposites of those adjectives where adding or removing a prefix is not possible.

**Answers:** illegal – legal
unethical – ethical
justifiable – unjustifiable
inoffensive – offensive
other opposites: disturbing – reassuring,
sensible – stupid
inevitable – avoidable/preventable
outrageous – reasonable/fair/admirable

### SPEAKING

**9A** Once Ss have chosen their three topics, give them time to prepare their arguments in their pairs, using the questions in B to prompt them and making notes as they go along. Remind them to look back at the phrases in Ex 6, as well as the adjectives in Ex 8. Circulate and help as required.

**B** Ss can work in groups of three or five for this discussion. Split up the pairs, so that Ss have to defend their opinions on their own without their partner's support. Alternatively, you can let the Ss stay in their pairs and work in groups of four or six, the pairs presenting their case together. Monitor and make notes of good language use and problems, for praise and correction in feedback.

##### Teaching tip
To put Ss into groups efficiently, give each student a letter (e.g. for groups of four letters A–D), then put all the As, Bs, Cs, Ds etc. together.

##### Optional extra activity
Instead of putting Ss in groups, you could set up a 'discussion ladder': Ss sit in two lines facing each other and start discussing a topic with the person opposite them, then on a signal from you, one line moves up one 'step' so that Ss have new partners. This will mean that Ss will sometimes be discussing a topic they haven't prepared, but this will give them practice in more spontaneous production of language. This also provides more challenge for *stronger classes*.

##### Homework ideas
1 Workbook Ex 1–3B, p13

2 Ss watch a TV programme in English (e.g. on the internet) which features a panel discussion and listen out for the phrases they've learnt for giving and supporting opinions.

# THE HAPPINESS FORMULA

## Introduction

Ss watch an extract from *The Happiness Formula*, a BBC series in which scientists investigate what makes people happy.
Ss then learn and practise how to conduct a survey and write tips for being happy.

### SUPPLEMENTARY MATERIALS

**Ex 3B**: Ss will need to use monolingual dictionaries.

**Ex 4A**: write the 'ingredients' of happiness on ten pieces of A4 paper.

## Warm up

<u>Either</u>: write *Happiness is …* on the board and put Ss in pairs to write three endings that they both agree on. Conduct a brief feedback, so Ss can see how many ideas the class had in common.

<u>Or</u>: write *Money can't make you happy …* on the board and give Ss five minutes in pairs to think of as many ways to complete the sentence as they can. Elicit these to the board in feedback, then Ss can compare their ideas with the endings in Ex 1.

### DVD PREVIEW

**1** While Ss discuss the ways of completing the statement, encourage them to think of reasons and examples to support their opinions. Elicit some of their reasons and examples in feedback.

**2** Give Ss a minute or two to read the information and establish that the two questions the programme will answer are: *Why hasn't consumerism (the work-and-buy ethic) made people happy? How should we change our way of life?* Then put Ss in pairs to predict what the scientists might say.

### Optional extra activity

To ensure that *weaker Ss* have understood the information, give them the following true/false statements to answer:
1 People are wealthier and happier now than fifty years ago. (F)
2 Consumerism hasn't made people happy. (T)
3 Scientists think we should change our way of life. (T)

### ▶ DVD VIEW

**3A** Emphasise that Ss should only try to get a general idea of what the scientist is saying, as they will watch the extract again to find more details.

**Answers:** We should slow down and take more leisure time.

**B** Encourage Ss to use monolingual dictionaries if they are unsure of the meaning of any of these words and phrases. If you feel this will be time consuming, you could divide the list up, giving alternate pairs of Ss words 1–4 or 5–8. Then join the pairs into groups of four to exchange information. Monitor and see how well Ss are coping with explaining the connections, feeding in information from the answers below if necessary.

**Suggested answers:** 1 *consume*: use a supply of something such as energy or fuel
*purchase*: to buy something
2 *status*: someone's position in society or in a profession, especially in comparison to otherpeople
*designer label*: clothes made by fashionable companies, e.g. Armani. If you wear designer labels it shows you can afford to buy expensive clothes and this can show your status.
3 *being in the rat race*: being in the unpleasant situation experienced by people working in big cities, when they continuously compete for success and have a lot of stress in their lives
*being stuck on a treadmill*: a treadmill is a piece gym equipment with a moving surface that you walk or run on. So this means being in a boring or tiring situation because you always do the same things.
4 *adapt to*: change your ideas or behaviour in order to deal with a new situation, e.g. *He adapted to the cold weather by wearing more layers of clothing*.
*become accustomed to*: think that something is normal or natural because you have experienced it over a period of time, e.g. *He became accustomed to living alone*.
6 *increase*: grow/become larger in number or amount
*diminish*: get smaller in amount/become less
7 *assumption*: something you think is true although you cannot be certain about it.
*evidence*: facts or physical signs that help to prove something is true, e.g. *Don't make any assumptions. Let's look at the evidence*.)
8 *suspect* (adj): something that is suspect might not be good, honest, trusted or reliable. It could even be dangerous: *a suspect idea, a suspect package*. (NB stress: <u>sus</u>pect)
*unreliable*: someone or something that is unreliable cannot be depended on.

**C** Give Ss time to read the questions carefully before playing the extract again. Ss discuss their answers in pairs. If necessary, you may want to play (parts of) the extract a third time.

**Answers:** 1 Once average incomes are more than £10,000 a year, extra riches don't make a country any happier.
2 The opposite of working longer and commuting further to get richer and buy more.
3 He mentions the following: the assumption that economic growth delivers happiness and the assumption that the meaning of life is expressed through material possessions.

**D** Give Ss a few minutes to think about these questions before putting them into groups.

### DVD 2 The Happiness Formula

ME = Mark Easton     PK = Professor Kahneman     I = Interviewee
PJ = Professor Jackson
ME: We work, we buy, consume and die. We don't know why. The science of happiness says the answer is to rethink everything. The rat race: give it up. The rich: tax them. Holidays: take more. In short, transform the way we live. New York City, capital of the consumerist world where status has a designer label sewn inside, but does happiness come in a gift-wrapped box? And if it doesn't, what on earth are we all doing?
PK: It's a fundamental fact in the happiness research: the standard of living has increased dramatically and, ah, happiness has increased not at all and in some cases has diminished slightly. I mean there is a lot of evidence that, ah, being richer hasn't made us, that isn't making us happier at least in the western world, so we clearly need something else.

ME: It's a huge claim. Put simply, the science shows that once average incomes are more than ten thousand pounds a year, extra riches don't make a country any happier. We are stuck on a treadmill. In our search for happiness we work longer, commute further, to get richer, to buy more. And yet the science of happiness suggests we should do exactly the opposite.

I:   If only we could learn as a society to slow down we might all be able to become happier if we could all take more leisure together.

PJ:   The assumption that economic growth delivers happiness is suspect. The assumption that consumer goods can fulfil all these tasks for us: social, psychological tasks; a sense of the meaning of my life through material possessions is deeply suspect and if we want to make progress in human terms, if we want to approach happiness in any degree, then it is these assumptions that we have to re-examine.

ME: It is starting to happen. Politicians are realising that making people happy is as important as making people rich. The next task, though, is working out how to convince us all to change the way we live.

## speakout a happiness survey

**4A**  Give Ss a few minutes to discuss the 'ingredients' and tell them think of reasons for their choices. In feedback, ask individuals to tell the class what they had in common with their partner and how they were different.

> **Optional extra activity**
> Display the ten 'ingredients' on pieces of A4 paper on the board and invite the class to put them in order from the most to the least important. This can be done in pairs first, or as a whole class, with Ss coming up to move the cards on the board.

**B**  Tell Ss to see what they have in common with the speaker. They can tick (✓) the topics in the box that the speaker mentions and underline the ones that are most important to him.

> **Answers:** He mentions a car, friendship, money and free time. The most important are friendship, money (he agrees that he couldn't live without it) and free time.

**C**  Focus Ss on the phrases and give them time to read them through. Set the task for the listening and point out that where there are options in the phrases (e.g. *Could I/Do you mind if I*), they need to put a tick under the option they hear.

> **Answers:** Do you mind if I ask you some questions?
> What would you say is missing from your life?
> Which would you find the most difficult to live without?
> How happy would you say you are, on a scale of one to five (five being very happy)?

**5A**  You could suggest that Ss aim to include at least five of the key phrases. Also point out that they should try to make their survey different from the one they heard, e.g. they could change some of the 'ingredients' for happiness. Both Ss in the pairs should write out the survey in their notebooks because they will be talking to different people in the next stage.

**B**  Ss should aim to talk to about three other people. They can either stand up and walk round the class, or they can work in groups of four, changing pairs until they have talked to the other three people in their group.

**C**  Give Ss a few minutes to prepare to summarise their findings. You could suggest some phrases to use, e.g. *All three of the people I spoke to said … Nobody thought that …Only one person couldn't live without … It was surprising that …*

Invite a few individuals to read out their findings to the class.

## writeback tips for being happy

**6A**  Tell Ss to close their books and write *Don't read the news or watch TV* and *Get a dog or cat* on the board. Ss discuss (as a whole class or in pairs) why these two tips would make people happier. Then direct them to the texts in Ex 6A. Were their ideas the same?

**B**  Focus Ss on the example and tell them to copy the headings into their notebooks. Put Ss in pairs to work on their notes.

> **Optional extra activity**
> If any of your Ss are struggling to think of ideas, you could feed in some of the following: *learn a new skill, listen to music, take up a hobby, make some time for yourself, give yourself a 'treat', get rid of negative people, do some exercise, make a new friend, laugh, watch a funny tv programme.*

**C**  Ss work alone to write their tips. Circulate and help as required, prompting Ss to correct their own mistakes as much as possible.

**D**  Ss can pass the tips round the class, or stick them on the walls for everyone to walk round and read. Then ask individuals which tips they would try and why.

> **Homework ideas**
> 1 Ss write a report with the results of the survey they conducted in Ex 5. Suggest three paragraphs for the report:
>    1 Introduction – the aim of the survey;
>    2 More details about what the survey contained and how many people were involved;
>    3 A summary of the findings.
>
> 2 Ss write a list of tips for another topic, e.g. *How to be healthy/How to find a good job/How to make new friends.*

# LOOKBACK

## Introduction

The aim of these activities is to provide revision and further practice of the language from the unit. You can also use them to assess Ss' ability to use the language, in which case you need to monitor but avoid helping them. You may feel that you don't need or have time to do all the activities. If so, you could allocate the activities that would be most beneficial for your Ss, or get individual Ss to decide which activities they'd like to do.

### SOCIAL ISSUES

**1A** Ss can work on this in pairs, or work alone and compare answers with a partner. You could give Ss a time limit, e.g. two minutes, to introduce an element of competition.

**Answers:** 1 poverty  2 famine  3 pollution  4 drought
5 drug abuse  6 domestic violence  7 homelessness  8 debt
9 obesity  10 divorce

**B** You could set this up as a 'testing' activity: Student A closes his/her book and Student B reads out a statement – Student A thinks of the social issue it refers to. Ss swap roles after three statements. *Stronger Ss* could try writing their own statements to try out on another pair.

**Answers:** 1 pollution  2 poverty, domestic violence, obesity  3 divorce  4 drought  5 poverty, famine, homelessness  6 poverty, famine, drug abuse, domestic violence, homelessness, debt, obesity

**C** Ss could choose one or two statements that interest them to discuss.

### PRESENT PERFECT SIMPLE AND CONTINUOUS

**2A** For *weaker classes*, you may need to let Ss refer to the rules and examples in the **Language bank** on p130–131. Ss work alone, while you circulate and help as necessary. For *stronger classes*, you could either put Ss in pairs and conduct this as a race, or you could run it as a team game, with teams of four or five Ss. Tell Ss to close their books, then display the prompts on the board, one at a time. Teams confer on each question and put up their hands when they're ready to answer. They are awarded points for correct grammar and bonus points for good pronunciation.

**Answers:** 1 How long have you been learning English?
2 Your English has improved a lot. What have you been doing?
3 How many teachers have you had?
4 Who was your favourite teacher before your current one?
5 How far have you travelled to class today?
6 Have you done your homework for today?
7 How long did it take you to do it?
8 Have you studied/been studying a lot this week?
9 Have you practised/ been practising English outside the class regularly in the past year?
10 Have you ever forgotten to bring anything to class?
11 How long have you been trying to understand the present perfect?
12 Have you been spending too much time in front of your computer lately?

**B** This could be done in closed pairs, or in open pairs, to give some variety of interaction. Ss take turns to choose a question and nominate someone from the other side of the class to answer it.

### SURVEILLANCE

**3** Ss work alone or in pairs to match the items. They could then 'test' each other: Student A covers 1–6 and Student B covers a)–f), then they take turns, e.g. Student A: *children* – Student B: *They aren't legally accountable for their actions.*

**Answers:** 1 e  2 f  3 d  4 c  5 b  6 a

### THE PASSIVE

**4A** Look at the example with the class, pointing out that the agent *people* has disappeared in the passive sentence, because it's not necessary and drawing Ss' attention to the use of the *-ing* form *being* after the verb *like*. Ss work alone or in pairs to change the rest of the sentences.

**Answers:** 2 I was brought up in a house full of pets.
3 I've never been robbed.  4 I hate being given clothes as a present.  5 I'm often told I look like my father.  6 I've always wanted to be admired for my intelligence.

**B** You could start by doing an example about yourself, e.g. *I don't mind being called by my nickname* (changing one word), or *I don't like being called by my nickname at work* (adding two words). Then give Ss a few minutes to work on their sentences alone.

**C** Encourage Ss to extend their sentences into conversations, e.g.
A: *I've been robbed three times.*
B: *Really? Did you lose anything valuable?* etc.
Ss can report back to the class about what they found out.

**5A** Ss should write the questions in their notebooks rather than in the course book, so that they can use the prompts for oral practice in the next stage.

**Answers:** 1 Have you ever been bitten by an animal?
2 Would you like to be invited to dinner by a celebrity/by a celebrity to dinner?  3 Do you enjoy being photographed?
4 Do you always want to be told the truth even if it hurts?
5 What will you be remembered for after you die?

**B** Encourage Ss to extend this practice beyond the question and answer, giving reasons for their answers and asking follow up questions. Ss could also stand up and walk round the class, asking different people the questions. Conduct feedback, asking Ss what surprising/interesting things they heard.

### OPINIONS

**6A** Ss work alone or in pairs to correct the mistakes. As you go through the answers, write/display the corrected phrases on the board, e.g.
A: *I'm in favour of …*
B: *I'm not so sure. …*
A: *You've got a point there, but …*, etc.
Ss can then use these prompts for their own conversations in the next stage.

**Answers:** 1 I'm in favour of  2 I'm **not** so sure  3 You've got a point there, but  4 **Fair enough**, but  5 I agree to some extent, but  6 I'm still not **convinced**.  7 I suppose **so**

**B** Ss should spend a minute or two thinking about what to say before starting the conversation. If you have time Ss could talk about all three topics, then choose their 'best' one to perform for the class.

## OVERVIEW

### 3.1 DANGEROUS GAMES
GRAMMAR | *used to, would, be/get used to*
VOCABULARY | good and bad behaviour
HOW TO | talk about habits

**COMMON EUROPEAN FRAMEWORK**
Ss can understand articles concerned with contemporary problems in which the writers adopt a particular stance or viewpoint; can communicate fluently, accurately and effectively routine and non-routine matters.

### 3.2 FIND YOUR NICHE
GRAMMAR | future forms review
VOCABULARY | locations
HOW TO | talk about the future

**COMMON EUROPEAN FRAMEWORK**
Ss can understand recordings in standard dialect likely to be encountered in social life and identify speaker viewpoints and attitudes as well as the information content; can communicate spontaneously with good grammatical control without much sign of having to restrict what they want to say.

### 3.3 HOW DOES IT WORK?
FUNCTION | describing procedures
VOCABULARY | common actions
LEARN TO | use mirror questions

**COMMON EUROPEAN FRAMEWORK**
Ss can give a clear, detailed description of how to carry out a procedure and can pass on detailed information reliably.

### 3.4 GREAT EXPERIENCES ◉ BBC DVD
**speakout** | a recommendation
**writeabout** | an experience

**COMMON EUROPEAN FRAMEWORK**
Ss can understand the majority of TV programmes on topics of personal interest such as travel shows in standard dialect; can give clear, detailed descriptions of an experience and can fluently relate a narrative or description as a linear sequence of points; can give detailed accounts of experiences, describing feelings and reactions.

### 3.5 LOOKBACK
Communicative revision activities

### BBC VIDEO PODCAST
What's the perfect way to switch off?

This video podcasts looks at the topic of how we use our leisure time and explores the different things we might do in order to relax. Use the video podcast at the start or the end of Unit 3.

## DANGEROUS GAMES

### Introduction
Ss practise reading and speaking about habits, using *used to, would* and *be/get used to* and related vocabulary. They also learn how to use linkers in an opinion essay.

#### SUPPLEMENTARY MATERIALS
Resource bank p153 and/or p155
Ex 2A: Ss need monolingual dictionaries
Ex 8B–C: prepare copies of the opinion essay with the bold phrases blanked out.

### Warm up
Lead into the topic by getting Ss to brainstorm names of games and sports in two lists: those that can be played at home and those that can be played elsewhere. After two or three minutes, tell Ss to look at their lists and circle the games/sports that could be described as 'dangerous' and explain why.

**Teaching tip**
Brainstorming involves getting Ss to think of as many examples/ideas as they can on a chosen topic, within a short time. Ss can work as a class, calling out ideas to be written on the board, or in pairs/small groups. It can be used as a warm up for a lesson, or to lead into an activity and can help you to assess Ss' knowledge of, e.g. vocabulary related to a particular topic.

### SPEAKING
**1** Give Ss a few minutes to discuss the questions in pairs or small groups.

**Possible answers:** 2 Benefits: playing computer games can be relaxing, take your mind off other things, may help you develop quick reactions; Potential problems: you become isolated from the 'real' world, you play games instead of taking physical exercise, the game may be violent

### VOCABULARY
**2A** Focus Ss on the example and ask them to think of things that they might *take care of* or *neglect*, e.g. children, appearance, house or car, etc. Tell Ss to try to think of more examples for each item as they work through the matching exercise. Encourage them to use monolingual dictionaries to check their answers. NB You may want to show them that with phrasal verbs such as *put off*, they need to look at the entry for *put*, then find the list of related meanings and phrasal verbs. Pronunciation to check: *compliment, neglect, stubborn* (silent r), *ignore, criticise*.

**Answers:** 2 d (e.g. pay attention to/ignore advice, instructions, warnings)
3 e (e.g.compliment someone on/criticise someone for their driving, cooking, appearance)
4 a (e.g. get on with/put off housework, homework, paying bills)
5 c (e.g. give in/be stubborn during an argument, under pressure).

**B** Look at the example and point out to Ss that while some particles (e.g. *off*) are part of the verb, they should only use the ones in brackets if there is another object in the sentence.

> **Answers:** 1 get on with  2 compliments you on/criticises  3 pay attention to/ignore  4 take care of/neglect  5 be stubborn/gives in

**C** Ss can take turns to ask each other the question, then compare and discuss their answers. Ask one or two Ss to report back on their answers in feedback.

## READING

### Teaching tip

The idea of a jigsaw reading or listening is to create an 'information gap' by having Ss read or listen to different texts, then share the information they gathered in order to complete a task (e.g. answer questions). The most efficient way to organise this is to group all the A students together to read and answer questions on one text and all the B students together with the other text. Once Ss with the same text have compared the answers to their questions, you pair up one A and one B student to share their information. This can be done by giving Ss a number, e.g. in a class of eighteen Ss, give the Ss the numbers A1–A9 and B1–B9, then put all the ones (A1 and B1), twos (A2 and B2) threes (A3 and B3), etc. together to work in pairs.

**3A** Explain to Ss that they are going to read two people's views of the same situation, but they will each only read one person's view. Once Student A has found the text on p159, focus Ss on the words in the box (these are the same for A and B) and set the task. Give Ss about five minutes to read their text.

> **Answers:** Student B: Jade about herself: neglected, patient about Sam: selfish, rude
> Student A: Sam about himself: a good parent, a good friend about Jade: selfish, talkative

**B** Make sure that A students are working together on Sam's story and B students are working on Jade's.

**4A** In the same pairs, Ss discuss the questions and see how much they can remember before reading their text again to confirm or change any of their answers.

> **Answers:** 1 Sam liked Jade because she was pretty and she was a good laugh. Jade liked Sam because he was good-looking and kind.
> 2 Sam thinks he spends enough time with Jade and Joe. Jade thinks he spends too much time on the computer.
> 3 Sam likes it because it's exciting and fast-paced and he has made good friends through the game.
> 4 Sam doesn't want Jade to invite his family to the home. He prefers to see them outside the home. Jade is annoyed because he ignores his family and continues playing the game. He leaves her to talk to them.
> 5 Jade got annoyed with Sam. Jade was angry because Sam's virtual friends seem to be more important to him than she and his son are. Sam was angry because Jade 'killed' his friends in the computer game.
> 6 Jade says she will never let Joe play on the computer. Sam wants to teach Joe how to play when he's old enough.

**B** Pair A and B Ss together to tell each other their answers. Emphasise that they should <u>not</u> look at each other's texts, but find out the differences between Sam's and Jade's points of view by listening to their partner's answers (Ss may want to make notes of these next to their own answers).

**C** Ss can work in pairs or groups of four to discuss the questions. In feedback you could elicit some ideas for resolving the problem and ask the class to vote on the best one(s).

## GRAMMAR *used to, would, be/get used to*

**5** For *stronger classes* you could write/display sentences 1–5 on the board, underline the examples of *used to, would* and *be/get used to* and put Ss in pairs to discuss the differences in meaning. Then direct them to the rules on the page and give them a minute or two to decide on the correct alternatives.

> **Answers:** a) Used *used to* talk about things activities and states which **happened in past but not usually now.**
> b) Use *would* to talk about **activities** in the past which no longer happen now. (Point out that *I used to like visiting him* is possible but *I would like visiting him* is not, because *like* is a state)
> c) Use *be used to* talk about things that are **familiar to us.**
> d) Use *get used to* talk about things that **become familiar to us over a period of time.**  e) After be used to and would, use the infinitive.
> f) After *be used to* and *get used to*, use the *-ing* form or a noun.

### Teaching tip

1 Ss may assume that *used to* has a present form and say, e.g. *I use to play video games in the evening.* Point out that for present habits they need to use an adverb of frequency or *tend to: I often/tend to play video games in the evening.*

2 Ss may get confused between *would* for past habits and *would* in hypothetical statements, e.g. *During the holidays I'd play video games all day* and *I'd play video games all day if I could.* It's important to give examples in clear contexts so Ss can see the difference.

**▶ LANGUAGEBANK 3.1 p132–133**

Give Ss a few minutes to read through the rules and examples and ask you any questions. Ex A and B can be set for homework. Alternatively, you could see how well Ss do in the next stage (Ex 6) and use one or both of them in class for further practice if needed.

> **Answers:** A 1 used to  2 to get used to  3 'd/used to  4 'll get used to  5 'm not used to  6 'd/used to  7 'm not used to  8 'm used to/'ve got used to
> B 1 used to live, 'm not used to having  2 's used to staying, used to do  3 didn't used to have, 's getting used to having  4 'm not used to taking, used to drive  5 'm not used to having, 'll get used to having

## PRACTICE

**6A** Do the first one as an example, then Ss work alone on the rest.

> **Answers:** 1 When I was a kid, I'd **often quarrel** with my parents.  2 As a child, I used to **eat** too many sweets.  3 I'm not used to **getting up** early, so when I have to be somewhere in the morning, I'm often late.  4 I'm **used to** saying what I think and sometimes I upset people.  5 I was/ **got used** to my mother cooking for me when I lived at home and now I can't cook for myself.  6 I come from a big family and I don't think I'll ever get used to **living** on my own.  7 I didn't **use** to be much help around the house.  8 I **used to be** quite a lazy student when I was younger and I often put off finishing my homework.

**B** Before putting Ss into groups, you could tell them to add two more sentences about their own past habits/behaviour. Circulate and help while Ss write these sentences. Then put Ss into groups of three or four to discuss the sentences. Tell them to be prepared to report back to the class about what they have in common, e.g. *We all used to … ; Maria and Sasha used to … but Toni and I didn't; None of us is used to …*.

## SPEAKING

**7** You could start by talking about the habit which annoys you the most, as a model for Ss. Incorporate examples of *used to, would, be/get used to* and/or 'behaviour' vocabulary, e.g. *When I was at university I used to share a flat with a girl who loved cooking. The problem was, she would always leave the dirty dishes and pans in the sink for someone else to clean up. If anyone mentioned washing up, she'd say she had to get on with an assignment which was already overdue, or something like that. I even tried writing her a note about it once, but she just ignored it.* Give Ss a few minutes to think about what to say, including the names of some other habits, e.g. biting your nails, talking to yourself, taking calls on your mobile while you're out with friends, leaving the lids off things/the iron on/things lying around, etc. Put Ss in pairs to talk about the habits, monitor and make notes of good language use and problem areas for praise and correction in feedback.

> **Optional extra activity**
> Ask Ss to work in pairs and add two or more annoying habits to the list. Then ask them to put the habits in order from the most to least annoying (they need to agree on the order and be prepared to justify it). In feedback, ask different pairs to explain the way they have ordered the habits and see how similar/different their orders are.

## WRITING an opinion essay

**8A** Give Ss a few minutes to discuss the questions and make notes of their answers for feedback.

> **Possible answers:** Possible 'meaningless' activities: watching TV, DVDs, films/playing computer games/listening to music/texting/social networking/shopping
> Possible 'meaningful' activities: fitness-related: sports, gym, exercise class/talking to friends  reading/volunteering/performance-related: acting, singing, dancing

> **Optional extra activity**
> Tell Ss to close their books and give them a copy of the essay with the bold phrases blanked out. They will still be able to understand the overall meaning of the essay and decide if they agree with the writer, as in Ex 8B. Then ask Ss to think of some possible words/phrases to complete the gaps. This will help them to identify the purpose of each paragraph, as in Ex 8C. Finally, put the missing phrases on the board (in the wrong order) for them to compare with their own ideas and complete the gaps.

**B** After Ss have read the essay, put them in pairs to discuss which of the writer's points they agree/disagree with. Also ask them to comment on the style of the essay and establish that it is formal.

**C** Look at the first paragraph with the class and establish that the writer is introducing the topic and giving his/her point of view. Then give Ss a few minutes to discuss the other three paragraphs.

> **Answers:** Paragraph 1 introduces the topic and gives their point of view.
> Paragraph 2 develops one side of the argument giving examples of meaningless activities.
> Paragraph 3 develops another side of the argument, giving examples of meaningful activities.
> Paragraph 4 gives a conclusion or summary and repeats the writer's point of view.

**D** Ss can work alone or with a partner.

> **Answers:** It seems to me that …/I agree that …/I feel that … .
> They occur in the first and last paragraphs.

## LEARN TO use linkers in an opinion essay

**9A** While Ss are completing the table copy it onto the board, so you can add all the phrases to it during this stage and the next one.

**B** You could do this with the whole class, inviting Ss up to the board to write the phrases in the correct column. NB Point out to Ss that all these phrases are followed by a comma.

**Answers:**

| firstly | furthermore | to conclude | in contrast | for example |
|---|---|---|---|---|
| to start with | In addition to this | in conclusion | at the same time as | for instance |
| In the first place | moreover | to sum up | opposed to this | as an example |

**10A** While Ss are making notes, be on hand to help with queries, e.g. about vocabulary.

**B** Group Ss who made notes on the same title together and give them time to exchange ideas and examples.

**C** Ss may not be used to the idea of writing a plan, so you could do an example on the board for the essay in Ex 8, e.g. with notes and ideas for each paragraph. You could direct Ss to the tip before they write their plan.

### speakout TIP

Before you direct Ss to the tip, ask them how the opinion essay they read was organised, i.e. how many paragraphs there were and what the purpose was of each one. Then Ss can compare what they remembered with the information in the tip.

**D** Give Ss plenty of time to write their essay and check it. They could do this as homework if you don't have time in class. Remind Ss about the correction code from the Students' Book, Unit 1 (p10). If there is time in class, Ss could also check their partner's essay.

> **Homework ideas**
> 1 Workbook Ex 1–6, p18–19
> 2 Ss imagine that a year has passed in Jade and Sam's lives and write an email from one of them to a friend, telling them what has happened.
> 3 Ss choose another title from Ex 10A and write the essay.

## FIND YOUR NICHE

### Introduction

Ss practise listening and speaking about niche holidays using future forms and vocabulary for describing locations. They also learn to use uncountable and plural nouns.

#### SUPPLEMENTARY MATERIALS

Resource bank p154 and/or p156

Warm up: bring a selection of holiday brochures.

Ex 3A: prepare enough copies of the sentence halves for each pair to have a set to match.

Ex 3C: prepare question prompts for *weaker classes*.

Ex 3C: if Ss are not from the same country, bring in maps of the UK/the USA/Australia/Canada for a follow up activity.

Ex 8A: Ss need monolingual dictionaries.

### Warm up

If possible, bring in a few holiday brochures from your local travel agent (you only need to use the photos from these to generate ideas for holidays, so they don't need to be in English).

Either: elicit types of holiday and write them on the board, e.g. *camping/skiing/walking/sailing/working holiday; city/beach/flydrive/luxury/spa holiday*. Then put Ss into small groups to categorise the holidays according to criteria such as: *cheap/expensive, boring/interesting, stressful/relaxing*.

Or (if you have more time): put the following prompts on the board: *Location? When? How long? Activities? What to take?* and give Ss a few minutes alone to imagine they have booked a holiday, answering the prompts. Then tell Ss they have a spare ticket for the holiday and they should try to persuade their partner to go with them. Their partner will need to give up their own planned holiday if they decide to go, so they will both need to be very persuasive! After a few minutes, conduct brief feedback to see who was persuaded. NB This activity should allow you to assess Ss' use of future forms. You could make notes of examples of good use of the forms and mistakes to use for discussion and correction after Ex 5.

#### LISTENING

**1A** Direct Ss to the photos and establish what type of holiday is shown in each, i.e. *a trekking holiday, a cooking holiday, a beach holiday*. Give Ss a minute or two to discuss which appeal/don't appeal and why.

**B** You could read this with the Ss, checking *sectors* (parts) and *buzzword* (a fashionable word).

> **Answers:** 'niche' – holidays for people with particular interests; 'flopout' – holidays on the beach where you just 'flop' or relax

**2A** Before you play the recording give Ss a few moments to look through the list and elicit some ideas about what happens on each holiday.

> **Answers:** Thai cooking week 1  Singing on the Nile 5
> Historical cruise 7  Sri Lanka for tea lovers 2
> Bird watching 4  Tour of Chernobyl and Pripyat 6
> Tour of battlefields 3

> **Culture notes**
> Pripyat is a city in northern Ukraine, which was founded in 1970 to house the Chernobyl Nuclear Power Plant workers. It was abandoned in 1986 following the Chernobyl disaster.

**B** Ss should read all the statements before listening to the recording again. Then give them time to compare answers with a partner and correct the false sentences before feedback with the whole class.

> **Answers:** 1 T  2 F – She describes them as similar to/ the same as activity holidays  3 F – He believes in going to a place for a reason and not just because there is a nice view. He thinks people are important.  4 F – You put on a concert  5 T  6 F – The school still has schoolbooks, posters and calendars.  7 T  8 F – She'd prefer a five-star luxury hotel.

**C** Ss could choose one holiday that would appeal to them and one that definitely wouldn't and explain why to their partner. Conduct feedback to see how common the choices were in the class.

### Unit 3 Recording 1

K = Katie Dearham    A = Alison Rice    C = Charlie Connolly

K:  The buzz word de jour is 'niche travel'. Rather than the usual beach flopout, we're turning instead to a growing band of small tour operators offering Thai cooking weeks, trips to Sri Lanka for tea lovers, the ultimate trekking or trekkie experience or poignant visits to obscure battlefields. Well, I'm joined here in the studio by Alison Rice, who's been a travel writer for many years and Charlie Connolly, author and broadcaster, who among other things has travelled the globe in search of the legacy of Elvis Presley. Welcome to you both. Alison, let's start by turning to you first. This definition of niche travel these days, what does it mean to you?

A: I think some people would say we're just talking about activity holidays where, instead of just lying on a beach you follow a particular interest or hobby with like-minded people. Walking holidays, gardening, cookery, painting, yoga, bird-watching – you remember when bird-watching was just for geeks? There's masses of bird-watching holidays. Battlefields, music, theatre festivals – these are all pegs around which we can build a holiday.

C: I do believe in going to a place for a reason and rather than just 'cause there's a nice view or something. I'm a big believer in people. I think people make a place and the atmosphere of a place.

K:  What would your favourite niche holidays that you've come across recently?

A: For me, it's definitely singing. If you google 'singing holidays' you'll find 416,000 entries. Whole choirs go on holiday now, or if you want to just join a choir, you can join a holiday where you learn a piece, rehearse it through the holiday, sailing down the Nile, there is one in Malta next year where you'll be singing the Messiah … and then the holiday ends where you put on a concert for the locals.

C: There is a tour you can do of Chernobyl. It's a one day tour from Kiev and you get to view reactor number four from a hundred metres away and you get to visit the dead town of Pripyat, which is, you know there are schoolbooks still in the school and posters up on the wall and calendars. And they do say it's a hundred percent safe – you're tested for radiation levels when you go and when you come back.

K:  Well, the *Traveller's Tree* messageboard has been littered with postings on this subject. We've heard about Fairtrade holidays in Cuba and southern India, Inca treks. One from a contributor called Portly, who thoroughly enjoyed a historical cruise on the Black Sea. But thank you also to Dilly Gaffe who said, 'Never mind niche. Give me a five-star luxury hotel any time!'

## VOCABULARY locations

**3A** Before the lesson you could prepare copies of the sentence halves and give one set to each pair. Ss can then try various combinations and this should help them to see which halves fit together logically. Encourage Ss to guess meaning from the context of the sentence and to check in their dictionaries only if absolutely necessary. Pronunciation to check: _populated, proximity, summit, remote, unspoilt, barren, peninsula_. NB _As the crow flies = in a straight line._

**Answers:** 2 e 3 a 4 h 5 d 6 b 7 c 8 f

**B** Ss work in pairs to categorise the expressions.

**Answers:** Location/distance: in close proximity to, half-way between, on the edge of, off the coast of, as the crow flies
Names of geographical features: summit, slope, peninsula
Character of a place: densely populated, heavily forested, remote, unspoilt, barren

**C** You could do another example with the class before putting Ss in pairs to ask and answer their questions, e.g. _Who was found to have higher than normal blood pressure?_

### Optional extra activities

I If you feel this will be too challenging for your Ss, you could prepare question prompts to give them:

A _Where / Sir Edmund Hilary and Sherpa Tensing / spend / fifteen minutes?_

_What / they / do / after that?_

_Where / Cape Town?_

_What / most remote / unspoilt / place / UK?_

B _Be / all / Hong Kong / island?_

_Be / Haiti / always / barren?_

_Where / Foula?_

_Where / Lake Baikal?_

2 Ss prepare clues for each other about a country they're both from, e.g.

A: _It's half-way between Rome and Milan._
B: _Florence._

If Ss are from different countries you could give them a map, e.g. of the UK, to help them prepare clues.

## GRAMMAR future forms review

**4A** Tell Ss that all the conversations are about holidays in the future. They should think carefully about how definite the speakers are: do they refer to intentions, arrangements, or just possibilities? Look at the example with the class and establish that _going to learn_ is used because the speaker is referring to an intention. It would be possible to say _He'll learn Arabic one day_, i.e. making a prediction with no intention behind it. Ss can work alone and compare answers in pairs.

**B** Play the recording, stopping after each conversation to check the answers, but don't discuss the rules at this stage.

**Answers:** 2 Are you doing, Yes, we're going 3 The plane lands, we get 4 It's likely to rain, it'll be, I'll check 5 We might go, we could stop off 6 Mike's thinking of going, He's hoping to ask

## Unit 3 Recording 2

I
A: So, are you looking forward to your Nile trip?
B: Yes and Francesco says he's going to learn Arabic … in four weeks!
2
A: Are you doing anything interesting next summer?
B: Yes, we're going to New Zealand in July.
3
A: The plane lands very early on Friday morning.
B: When's the first tour?
A: As soon as we get there, I think.
4
A: It's in Thailand and it says here, 'It's likely to rain every afternoon,
but expect to walk twenty kilometres a day, rain or shine.'
B: I expect it'll be quite hard work.
A: I don't know. I'll check with Tess. She was over there last year.
5
A: We might go to Ukraine this year, we haven't decided yet.
B: Sounds interesting.
A: Yes and then we could stop off in Poland to see Magda on the way home.
6
A: Mike's thinking of going on a trek to Machu Picchu in Peru.
B: It's quite a hard walk, I've heard.
A: Yeah. He's hoping to ask people to sponsor him for charity.

**C** Look at the example with the class and point out that when the present continuous is used for a future arrangement, a future time is usually mentioned (e.g. _next summer_). NB _Are you going to do …?_ Would also be possible but would be a more general intention. _Stronger Ss_ could look through Ex 4A and explain to a partner why each future form is used, before matching the examples to the rules. Although Ss should be familiar with these future forms, they may not have compared them all in this way before, so in a class ensure that you pair Ss carefully to allow _stronger Ss_ to help _weaker_ ones.

**Answers:** 2 – 1B _he's going to learn_, 6A _'s thinking of going, 's hoping to ask_ 3 – 4A _I'll check_ 4 – 4B _it'll be_ 5 – 4A _It's likely to rain_ 6 – 5A _We might go, we could stop off_ 7 – 3A _The plane lands_ 8 – 3A _As soon as we get_

**D** Direct Ss to the phonemic script and explain that it represents how the underlined words sound when they are 'run together' in natural speech. Play the recording once through for Ss to familiarise themselves with the pronunciation, then play it again, stopping after each sentence for Ss to repeat. They could repeat just the underlined words first, then say the whole sentence.

### ⇒ LANGUAGEBANK 3.2 p132–133

There's a lot of information for Ss to take in here, so you may prefer to ask them to read it and do Exs A and B for homework.

**Answers:** A 1 will you come 2 I'm likely to 3 is the bus planning to leave 4 might leave 5 will rain 6 hoping to 7 it's being 12 I'm seeing
B 1 might stay, 'll watch 2 Is Sandra going to be, Will Sandra be, 'll definitely go 3 goes 4 's, is thinking of moving, 'll be 5 is, probably won't finish 6 might see, leaves

## PRACTICE

**5A** You could do an example first, then Ss work alone or in pairs. In feedback, ask Ss which of the rules in 4C each answer exemplifies.

> **Answers:** 1 We're going  2 We'll probably  3 I'm meeting  4 I'm going to use  5 will rain  6 goes  7 I'll stay  8 thinking of  9 I need  10 I'm not likely to

**B** Do an example and change one of the sentences so it is true for you first, e.g. *I'm going to Northern India on holiday this year. I booked a trekking holiday just after Christmas.* Then give students a few minutes to work alone on their sentences.

**C** Model this first by saying another sentence that is true about you and eliciting some examples from the class of follow-up questions they could ask, e.g.

*On Saturday I'm taking my niece to the cinema.*

*What are you going to see?*

*How old is your niece?*

*Are you going in the morning or afternoon?*

Put Ss in pairs and monitor the activity so you can provide feedback to the class afterwards on their use of the future forms.

## SPEAKING

**6A** For *weaker classes* you may want to elicit some examples of questions Ss could ask for each bullet point, e.g. *What kinds of things do you like doing in your free time? Have you got any particular interests? When you go on holiday, do you like staying in a hotel, or do you prefer camping? Do you like self-catering accommodation? Do you like driving holidays, or do you prefer to go by train or bus? Do you like flying? What do you not like doing on holiday? How do you prefer to spend your time on holiday?*

Remind Ss that they need to make notes of their partner's answers.

**B** Ask Ss to think of examples of niche holidays from the lesson so far (they can look back at p35 in the Students' Book if necessary) and any others they've heard of. Put Ss into new pairs, emphasising that they need to design two niche holidays, one for each of their original partners. Circulate and help, encouraging Ss to be creative with their designs.

**C** Before Ss return to their original partners, give them a few minutes to think about how they will present the holiday, including the use of future forms where appropriate, e.g. *Your train leaves at … , You're staying in … , You'll probably need to bring …* Ss should make sure they include at least five different future forms. When Ss have finished, ask one or two to tell the class about the holiday their partner designed and what they think of it.

### Optional extra activities
1 Ss interview you in Ex 6A, then work in pairs to design a niche holiday for you. Pairs then present their holidays and you choose the one you would like to go on.

2 Elicit the names of some famous people that everyone in the class knows and write them on the board. Then write each one on a slip of paper and give each pair of Ss a name. They have to design a niche holiday for that person. When they have finished, they present their holidays to the class, who guess which famous person they were given.

## VOCABULARY *PLUS* uncountable and plural nouns

**7A** Focus Ss on the photo and discuss briefly with the class what they can see, where it might be, etc. Give Ss a minute to read the email then discuss their answer with the class.

> **Answer:** Valerie likes the simplicity. She also mentions the friendly locals, horseback riding and not having access to a TV.

**B** In pairs, Ss could think about the pros and cons of a holiday like this, then compare ideas as a class.

**8A** Look at the examples with the class. If Ss have monolingual dictionaries, show them how the entries for *stairs* and *luggage* show that they are plural [plural] and uncountable [U] respectively. Ss can work with a partner to find the rest of the nouns.

> **Answers:** Uncountable nouns: luggage, soap, cloth, wood, concrete, electricity
> Plural nouns: clothes, glasses, toiletries, outskirts, news, cards

**B** Ss work alone or in pairs to correct the mistakes. They can use their dictionaries to check which nouns are uncountable or plural if they are not sure.

> **Answers:** 1 accommodation  2 facilities  3 advice  4 How much  5 equipment  6 contents  7 means  8 scenery  9 remains  10 whereabouts

**C** You could put Ss into new pairs for this, or they could stand up and walk round the class, asking two or three different people the questions. Conduct feedback to find out how similar or different people's answers were.

> **VOCABULARYBANK** p150 Collective nouns
>
> Ex 3A and B equip Ss with more vocabulary for talking about groups of things. Let them work independently to complete the activity, using a dictionary to check anything they are not sure of. Feed back as a class and discuss question 3B.
>
> **Answers:** 3A 1 bunch  2 gang  3 series  4 flock  5 batch  6 swarm  7 crowd  8 herd  9 pack  10 set
> 3B bunch (e.g. *a bunch of idiots*) gang (e.g. *a whole gang of them*), swarm, pack (e.g. *a swarm/pack of journalists*), herd (e.g. *herds of tourists*)

### Homework ideas
1 Workbook Ex 1–5, p20–21

2 Ss imagine they are on their niche holiday and write an email to a friend about it.

# HOW DOES IT WORK?

## Introduction

Ss practise listening and speaking about games and sports, using phrases for describing procedures and vocabulary related to common actions. They also learn to use mirror questions.

### SUPPLEMENTARY MATERIALS

Resource bank p157

Ex 2–4: If you are able to download/record extracts from some game shows to play in class, you could use these to prompt discussion in Ex 2 and/or for Ss to describe a game in Ex 4.

Ex 5C: prepare definitions for extra practice of mirror questions.

Ex 6A: Ss may need dictionaries.

Ex 7C: be prepared to describe one of the situations in Ex 7A as a model for the class.

## Warm up

Lead into the topic by playing 'Ten Questions'. Think of a game that the Ss will know and tell them to ask you questions about it to find out what it is. The rules are that you can only answer with *yes* or *no* and if Ss haven't guessed the answer after ten questions, you win. If you have time, Ss can then play the game in small groups.

### SPEAKING

**1** Write on the board the name of a game show that most Ss will have heard of and establish what a 'game show' is. Elicit a few more examples and put Ss in pairs (or small groups) to discuss the questions. Ss from the same country can compare which shows they like/dislike and Ss from different countries can describe shows to each other.

### FUNCTION describing procedures

**2A** Focus Ss on the photos and tell them the names of the game shows: *The Weakest Link* (with the host standing in the middle) *Total wipeout* (the person on the plinth) and *Hole in the Wall* (the people in silver suits). Elicit ideas from the class and write these on the board so that Ss can compare them to what they hear in the next stage. Vocabulary to check: *contestant, host, eliminate.*

**B** Tell Ss to listen and compare their ideas to the way the games are described. They should note down some 'key' words to help them.

**C** Ss could draw a table in their notebooks like the one above, to complete while they listen. Give Ss a few minutes to compare their answers with a partner before feedback to the class.

| Answers: | Hole in the Wall | The Weakest Link |
|---|---|---|
| number of contestants | 4 | 9 |
| description of set | studio with swimming pool; twenty metres away there's a wall covered by another 'wall.' | dark studio with blue or red spotlights and each person standing behind a type of desk (podium). The host is in the centre. |

|  | Hole in the Wall | The Weakest Link |
|---|---|---|
| aim of game | Not to get knocked into the pools (by making themselves into the correct shape to get through the hole). | to win money |
| winner | the team who get through the most shapes | the person out of the last two who gets the most questions right |
| best thing about it | the short time (five seconds) they have to get themselves into the correct shape | the host – she's aggressive and can be rude but it's actually funny |

**Unit 3 Recording 4**

1

A: Oh, you must have seen it …

B: … No, I've never even heard of it. How does it work?

A: Well it sounds really stupid, but I'll try to describe it. The way it works is that there are two teams, with two celebs on each team.

B: Two what?

A: Celebs. Celebrities.

B: Oh, right.

A: So anyway, there's a studio with a swimming pool and, at the end, about twenty metres from the pool, there's a wall, actually a giant wall covered by another 'wall', or maybe a sort of curtain …

B: I don't get it. A wall covered by a wall?

A: Yeah, but it's really like a single wall.

B: OK.

A: And the two people from the first team stand at the edge of the pool facing the wall. Then what happens is that the host says 'Bring on the wall!'

B: He does what? [again querying and not confrontational]

A: He says 'Bring on the wall!' Like that, very dramatically. Then the wall starts moving quite fast towards the two people.

B: Who are in front of the pool.

A: Yeah and after a few seconds, the curtain lifts off the wall and there's a funny-shaped hole and they have to get through it.

B: They have to get through where?

A: Get through the hole. They have about five seconds to get themselves into the same position as the shape in the hole so that it goes past them and they don't get knocked into the pool.

A: Uh-huh.

B: Yeah and that's the best part because nobody knows what shape the hole will be until the last moment. It could be anything person-shaped and …

B: What do you mean, person-shaped?

A: Well, maybe bent over or maybe with one foot in front of the other and one arm up at an angle, like this.

B: So what's the point?

A: Well, basically the point is NOT to get knocked into the pool. If they don't stand exactly in the shape of the hole, the wall will knock them into the pool. The teams take it in turns to have a go and the winning team is the one who gets through the most shapes.

B: It sounds pretty stupid to me.

A: You sort of have to see it to get it. It's incredibly popular.

2

A: I like it because it's basically a mix between a general knowledge quiz and kind of psychological game.

B: So how does it work?

**A:** Well, there are nine people standing in a semi-circle in a very dark studio with spotlights of one colour – maybe blue or red – so it looks very dramatic. Each one is standing behind a kind of metal podium.

**B:** Standing behind a *what*?

**A:** A kind of desk, made of metal. Anyway, the host stands in the centre.

**B:** Who stands in the centre?

**A:** The host, the woman in charge. Anyway, the first thing they do is answer general knowledge questions. She fires questions at them one by one and the object is for the team to win money by answering a chain of questions correctly.

**B:** Sounds like any old quiz.

**A:** Yeah but if someone gives a wrong answer they lose all the team's money. The key thing is to bank the money as you go along.

**B:** Bank the money?

**A:** Yeah, before a contestant answers their question, they can say 'Bank' and then the total money so far is safely stored and a new chain is started from zero.

**B:** Whoah! It sounds complicated.

**A:** It isn't, when you get the hang of it. So then after they've finished each round, they have to vote on who should get eliminated, you know, who should leave the game, the person who is 'the weakest link' in the team.

**B:** So that's the person who got most answers wrong?

**A:** Yeah, but what usually happens is that people start voting strategically, sometimes they vote off a strong player so that they can win.

**B:** So the winner's the last one left?

**A:** When there are two left, it's the person who gets the most questions right and then that person wins all the money in the bank.

**B:** I still don't understand why it's so popular.

**A:** Well, the main reason everyone watches it is because of the host. She's very aggressive – like a sergeant in the army – and she can be really rude to the contestants but instead of being offensive it's actually very funny. I can't really explain. You *need* to see it.

**B:** What's it called again?

**3A** Match the first pair as an example, then Ss work alone or in pairs on the rest. Vocabulary to check: *key* (important), *object* (aim). Ss could check their answers in the audio script. In feedback you could elicit alternative ways to complete the sentences so Ss see that most of the phrases are more or less 'fixed', e.g.

*Basically, the point/aim is to get as many goals as possible in the time.*

*What happens is that the amount of money goes up.*

*The first/next thing they do is toss a coin.*

*After they've chosen a subject, they have to answer questions.*

> **Answers:** 1f  2g  3a  4d  5c  6b  7e

**B** Ss can work on this in pairs and decide together which phrases are used for the functions in the list.

> **Answers:** 1 to state an overall goal or aim: 2, 6
> 2 to describe details of the procedure: 1, 3, 4, 7
> 3 to highlight something particularly important: 5, 6

**C** Ss could look at the phrases first and think about which words are likely to be stressed, then listen to the recording to confirm/change their predictions.

> **Answers:** 1 The way it <u>works</u> is that  2 <u>Basically</u>, the point is <u>not</u>  3 What <u>happens</u> is  4 The <u>first</u> thing they <u>do</u>  5 The <u>key</u> thing is to  6 The <u>object</u> is for  7 <u>After</u> they've finished

**▶ LANGUAGEBANK** 3.3 p132–133

Point out to the class that the phrases are summarised in the **Language bank**, with further useful examples for describing games and sports. If Ss are having trouble with the word order and/or remembering all the elements of each phrase, they could do Ex A in class.

> **Answers:** 1 The way it works is that  2 The first thing they do is  3 The object is  4 Basically, the point is  5 What happens is that  6 The key thing is to

**4A** Tell Ss to read the description through quickly before they try to complete the gaps, so they have a general idea of the procedure described and can name the game.

> **Answers:** 2 is  3 first  4 do  5 What  6 is  7 they've  8 point/object  9 key  10 football

**B** While Ss write their notes, circulate and provide the vocabulary they need. If any Ss aren't confident about describing a game, pair them with Ss who are to help them make notes. You can move them to different groups for the next stage.

**C** Put Ss into groups of three or four and tell them that each person must finish describing their game/sport before the others guess what it is. Also encourage Ss to refer to their notes but look up and speak, rather than reading aloud. Monitor and make notes of good use of the phrases for describing procedures, as well as any problem areas, for feedback. When the groups have finished, you could ask which were the most difficult games/sports to guess and why.

**LEARN TO** use mirror questions

**5A** Tell Ss they are going to read some extracts from the conversations they listened to about game shows. Ask them to look at B's questions and think about why and how they are used. Then direct them to the rules and give them a minute or two to discuss the correct alternatives with a partner.

> **Answers:** 1 clarify understanding  2 use *do/do what*  3 a suitable question word  4 'do what'  5 statement  6 Stress

**speakout** TIP

Before directing Ss to the tip, discuss briefly why these 'mirror' questions could be useful for them, i.e. they can use them if they don't understand a word or phrase in a conversation, or if they didn't hear exactly what was said, e.g. on the phone. After Ss have read the tip, ask them if they have something similar in their own language(s), which helps the speaker to see what they need to repeat or explain.

**B** Point out to Ss that in three of the questions they only need one word to replace the phrase in italics. They could complete the gaps alone or together as a class.

> **Answers:** 1 You have to do what?  2 The first player writes what?  3 You go where?  4 The aim is to beat who?

**C** Ss should be able to predict where the stress goes. When Ss are repeating the questions, discourage them from making their intonation rise too abruptly on the question word as this will sound rude/aggressive. Instead, show them how to ask the question in a tentative way, with a fall-rise on the question word which will sound friendlier.

**Answers:** 1 A: You have to sauté the potatoes.
You have to <u>do what</u>?
2 A: The first player writes an anagram of the word.
The first player writes <u>what</u>?
3 A: You go to the webinair site.
B: You go <u>where</u>?
4 A: Basically, the aim is to beat the rival team.
B: The aim is to beat <u>who</u>?

### Optional extra activity
Give these definitions of the phrases in italics from Ex 5B to student A, so they can practise the exchanges again and answer B's questions:

*sauté = cook quickly in a little hot oil*

*an anagram = a word that is made by changing the order of the letters of another word*

*webinar = web-based seminar*

*rival team = the team you are competing against*

Then give student B the following phrases and definitions so that student A has a turn asking mirror questions:

*They have to press their **buzzer** if they know the answer. = a small electric machine that buzzes when you press it*

*Make sure the mixture doesn't **curdle**. = become thick, like sour milk*

*The **umpire** has to decide. = the person who makes sure the players obey the rules, e.g. in tennis*

*Put them under a **cloche**. = a glass or clear plastic cover to protect young plants*

## VOCABULARY   common actions

**6A** Check that Ss understand the instructions and the example, then put them in pairs. Suggest that they try to guess whether the instructions refer to a game, machine, or cooking, for as many of the sentences as they can before checking in their dictionaries.

**Answers:** 2 C  3 M  4 M  5 G  6 M  7 C  8 G  9 C  10 M

**B** You could do this with the whole class and get Ss to shout out their suggestions, or alternatively put Ss in pairs.

**Suggested answers:** 1 cards  2 a mixture, sauce, soup  3 an icon or something on a computer screen/a computer mouse  4 a printer, photocopier, fax machine  5 a ball  6 any machine that uses electricity and which you have to plug in before you start using it, e.g. hairdryer, printer, heater  7 flour, icing sugar  8 dice  9 sugar, grated cheese, flour  10 a button on a camera

**C** Be prepared to demonstrate one or two of these first and Ss call out, e.g. *You're unplugging a heater, You're stirring some sauce,* etc. Make sure that one student shuts their book while their partner mimes.

### Optional extra activity
Instead of miming in their pairs, Ss could take turns to read out phrases from 6A with mistakes, for their partener to correct, e.g.
A: *Unplug the photocopier when you're using it.*
B: *No, unplug it when you're <u>not</u> using it!*

## SPEAKING

**7A** Give Ss a few minutes to think about the situations and choose one.

**B** While Ss make notes, circulate and provide vocabulary they need.

**C** You could provide a model of the activity for Ss. Describe your procedure, including a few fairly obscure words/phrases, so that Ss have to stop you and ask mirror questions. You could run this as a competition, giving points to each pair or group who asks a good mirror question. While Ss are describing their procedures, monitor and make notes of good use of language and problem areas for praise and correction in feedback.

> ➡ **VOCABULARYBANK** p150 Sports and activities
> Ex 1A, B and C extend the Ss vocabulary for talking about different kinds of sports, so you might ask Ss to do them in preparation for Ex 4C which requires them to describe a sport or game to the class. Before you start, you might want to go through some of more specialised vocabulary, e.g. *tackle* (to try to take the ball from a player in the opposite team), *shoot* (to try to score a goal by hitting, throwing, etc. the ball towards the goal). Ss work on the collocations in Ex 1A and match them with the pictures in Ex B. During feedback, get the Ss to talk about their experiences of playing any of these sports and to tell you which they might like try in the future.
>
> Ex 2A and B are concerned with sporting idioms. Let the Ss do the matching in pairs and feed back as a class. Then ask Ss to try to find some examples of sporting idioms in their own language and translate them into English.
>
> **Answers:** 1A 1 win  2 beat  3 score  4 shoot  5 chess  6 athletics
> 1B A bounce a ball  B do weight-training  C let in a goal  D tackle an opponent  E play snooker  F win a match
> 2A 1e)  2c)  3d)  4f)  5b)  6a)

### Homework ideas
1 Workbook Ex 1–4D, p22

2 Ss write about another procedure from Ex 7A.

3 Ss do some research on the internet about bizarre inventions and choose one to describe. They could download a picture and bring it with their description to the next lesson for other Ss to read.

# GREAT EXPERIENCES

## Introduction

Ss watch an extract from the BBC programme *50 Things To Do Before You Die*, where five people talk about activities they've done. Ss then learn and practise how to recommend something they've tried and write about an experience.

## Warm up

Lead into the topic by brainstorming the title *50 Things to do before you die*. Write the title on the board (Ss' books are closed) and put Ss into small groups to write as many things that could be on the list as they can in three minutes. Conduct feedback, eliciting examples from each group and writing a list on the board for Ss to refer back to later.

### ▶ DVD PREVIEW

**1** Give Ss a few minutes to discuss the questions, then ask individuals to report their partner's answers to the class. NB If any Ss don't feel they have done anything unusual, they could talk about someone they know who has.

**2A** If you did the warm up activity, Ss could quickly scan the article first, to see which of the activities on their list are mentioned and find out who decided the top fifty things for the programme.

> **Answers:** 1 Members of the public, BBC viewers

**B** Students match the activities mentioned in the article with the photos.

> **Answers:** A wing-walking  B observing rare and exotic
> animals in their natural habitat  C bungee jumping
> D travelling a historic route by train, car or jet plane
> E husky dog sledding

### ▶ DVD VIEW

**3A** As well as writing the five activities featured in the DVD clip, Ss could also write down the number that each activity got to in the top fifty.

> **Answers:** 1 husky sledding (no38)  2 wing walking (no35)
> 3 driving on route 66 (no19)  4 bungee jumping (no 17)
> 5 swimming with dolphins (no1)

**B** Give Ss time to work through the statements alone and/ or with a partner. When you play the DVD again, you could stop after each activity to give Ss time to process what they've heard and make a note of any key phrases that help them decide if the statement is true or false. If Ss are unsure of some of their answers, you could play the DVD again before conducting feedback with the class.

> **Answers:** 1 F – People say they love the silence, the sound
> of the snow and the dogs.  2 T – 'Having the dogs work for
> you and feeling in (or out of) control is where it's at.'
> 3 F – ... pilots would strap their girlfriends to the outside of
> their planes ...  4 T – 'I'm feeling excited, a little bit nervous,
> (I) can't wait, (I'm) raring to go.'  5 F – It's really hard to do
> the waving.'  6 F – It goes to Los Angeles.  7 T – It was seen
> as 'the road to opportunity'.  8 T – 'Great fun.'  9 T – 'Their
> legendary curiosity and playfulness have enchanted us for
> generations.'  10 F – 'They're gentle, responsive', 'so huge
> and so powerful, yet so playful.'

**C** Put Ss into new pairs and give them a few minutes to discuss their order. They could each write their own order and compare them, or try to agree on the same order between them. Tell them to be prepared to justify their order to the rest of the class. In feedback, establish which are the most and least popular activities in the class.

### DVD 3 50 Things To Do Before You Die

P = presenter   HC = Helen Child   AT = Andy Thomas
W = Woman    RO = Rebecca Over   KE = Kyle Emert
DF = Dave Ferris   NB = Nick Bryant   NBr = Nick Brans
LR = Lucia Rushton   AW = Alan Woods   KS = Katie Siddals

**P:** At number 38 it's husky sledding. I've come to Saariselkä in Finland for a test drive. Absolutely beautiful here, the snow is just like … it's got little bits of crystal all over it and you can really take it in because the dogs are doing all the hard work.

**HC:** Just the sound of the snow and the dogs panting with all the silence around, I think that would be fantastic.

**AT:** Totally silent apart from the sound of the sled and the dogs' paws. Incredible.

**W:** Are you ready?

**P:** As I'll ever be. This is much, much more exhilarating than just sitting in the sled, actually having the dogs work for you and feeling like you're in (or out of) control is definitely where it's at.

**P:** Meet Rebecca Over, an estate buyer from Surrey, who like hundreds of you crazy people, wanted nothing more than to be strapped to the outside of a plane and take part in your very own wingwalking display. The craze started when World War One pilots would strap their poor girlfriends to the outside of their planes to entertain the crowds at air shows. We sent Rebecca off to Rendcomb in Gloucestershire.

**RO:** I'm feeling excited, a little bit nervous, can't wait, raring to go.

**P:** So buckled and braced our daredevil is ready to go.

**RO:** The wind is really, really strong and it's really hard to do the waving. It's been wonderful, an amazing day.

**P:** Still in America now and time to go west on the legendary Route 66: 2400 miles, eight states, three time zones, one incredible journey.

**KE:** Once upon a time it was, the kind of the thing to do.

**P:** The famous route from Chicago to Los Angeles was used by thousands of Americans attempting to flee the hard times of the Great Depression and for many it's remembered as the road to opportunity.

**DF:** I'd love to experience what they did travelling over two and a half thousand miles and experience that wonderful feeling of getting somewhere which is better.

**P:** Next up something you've let get as high as 17 on this list. You're crazy, it's bungee jumping.

**NB:** The feeling you get when you jump off, fall off, dive off, or whatever, is just awesome.

**NBr:** Just to fly like that and just sort of end up being stretched and bounced back up, great fun.

**P:** Throughout history they've intrigued mankind with tales of their mystical powers and super intelligence; their legendary curiosity and playfulness have enchanted us for generations. Thousands and thousands of you have bombarded us with emails and calls to say the number one thing to do before you die is to go swimming with dolphins.

**LR:** They're absolutely amazing animals. They're so gentle they're so, um, sensitive.

**AW:** Once you swim with them, you don't want to … you don't want to leave them.

**KS:** A one-off, magical experience.

**P:** And it was incredible. It's … it's amazing because, they're so responsive and they have, they feel fantastic. Don't you? You feel wonderful, you feel so lovely. And they're so huge and powerful and yet so playful and, I'm really, really lucky to be here with them.

## speakout a recommendation

**4A** Check that Ss understand the instructions, pointing out that these don't need to be particularly unusual activities, just two that they would recommend, e.g. going camping or backpacking, riding a horse/donkey/camel, visiting a wildlife park, working on a farm, skateboarding, water skiing, scuba diving, windsurfing. You could demonstrate how Ss should answer the three questions, e.g.

*1 Activity: windsurfing.*

*2 How felt before: nervous, not very confident.*

*While: very frustrated but determined to pull the sail up.*

*After: exhausted but pleased that I'd managed to stay up for longer than a few seconds!*

*3 Worth trying because: you really test your strength and balance as you try to stand up and pull the sail up; you get a great feeling of freedom when you're surfing along the water and a feeling of achievement.*

Give Ss time to make notes on their own. Circulate and help with vocabulary, etc.

**B** After you have played the recording, Ss can compare their answers to the questions.

> **Answers:** 1 Jumping off a three-metre platform into water. 2 before: really nervous; during: frightened/scared; after: amazed at how scared he'd felt 3 because it made him understand something about fear and taught him about how well he can (or can't) control his feelings

### UNIT 3 Recording 7

M = Man

M: I'm not the kind of person who likes extreme activities like bungee jumping or sky diving and in fact I'd never do any of those sorts of things. So the activity I'd like to recommend may seem quite boring to some of you and very simple: it's jumping off of a three metre platform into water.

Anyway, I'll try to explain why it was so special. A few years ago I was at a lake with a friend and there was a jumping platform about three meters above the surface of the lake, you know the sort of thing, made of wood and anyway people were jumping off it into the water and having a good time, so we decided to try it. We waited till there was no one around, because neither of us was feeling particularly courageous. I remember walking to the edge of the platform and looking down and thinking to myself. 'The water is a long way down!' I felt really nervous but eventually I gathered my courage and walked back a few steps, then I ran and jumped into the water.

Actually, I didn't exactly jump into the water, I jumped into the air, or that's what it felt like. Air all around me, for ages. It felt like some of the longest few seconds of my life. I was determined to keep my eyes open, but involuntarily they closed out of fear. I braced myself for impact, which came eventually of course and it almost hurt, the way I hit the water and travelled quickly to the muddy bottom. I swam to the edge and climbed up to the level of the platform again. My friend had just done her jump and was also climbing out. I was amazed how scared I'd felt and at the fact that I hadn't been able to keep my eyes open. I told myself that if I did it again, I could surely keep my eyes open and relax and enjoy it. I drew in a deep breath, ran and jumped into the air … and it was exactly the same as the first time.

I'd recommend this experience because it really makes you understand something about fear, in a situation where in fact there's no danger. Maybe for some people it's not a big deal, but for me it was because it taught me a lot about myself and how well I can control my feelings, or not.

**C** Before you play the recording again, give Ss time to read through all the phrases. Vocabulary to check: *challenging* (particularly difficult and testing), *exhilaration* (feeling very excited and happy), *determined* (having a strong desire to do something). For phrases that have several alternatives, tell Ss to tick the alternative they hear.

> **Answers:** I'm not the kind of person who likes extreme activities. The activity I'd like to recommend may seem quite boring. I'd recommend this experience because it makes you understand something about fear.

### Optional extra activity

To give Ss more practice with the key phrases before they prepare to recommend their activity, do a 'disappearing drill'. Write or display the phrases on the board, then rub out or cover some of the alternatives, e.g.

*I'm not the kind of person who likes (extreme experiences/ _____ /spicy food) but …*

*It's one of the (best/most exciting/_____) things I've ever done.*

*I'd recommend this experience because it makes you understand (yourself/something about fear/ _____).*

Ss have to tell you the phrase with the missing alternative. You can then continue to remove words until you just have the 'bare bones' of the key phrases left.

**D** Give Ss time to prepare their recommendation before you put them into groups. Monitor the group work and make notes of good language use and areas for improvement to discuss in feedback.

## writeabout an experience

**5A** Give Ss a minute or two to read the extract, then elicit the activity from the class.

> **Answer:** looking at orang-utans in their natural habitat (photo B on p40 in the Students' Book)

**B** Before Ss write their entry, ask them what other kinds of things Stacey wrote about in her entry, e.g. at the beginning (what made her decide to go and look at orang-utans, which country she went to, who she went with, where she stayed) and after the extract on the page (how she felt when their eyes met, whether she saw any more orang-utans on the trip, what her travelling companions thought of it, etc). Ss can write their entry in class or for homework.

**C** You could either collect in all the entries and pass them round for other Ss to read, or put them on the walls of the classroom. Ask Ss to make a note of the most interesting entries as they read them, then put them in pairs to discuss the experience they'd most like to have, giving at least two reasons for their choice. In feedback you could have a show of hands to find out which was the most popular experience.

### Homework idea

Ss research the top fifty things to do before you die on the internet (there are a number of websites devoted to the topic) and choose three they'd like to do. They write a short paragraph about why they've chosen each one.

# LOOKBACK

## Introduction

The aim of these activities is to provide revision and further practice of the language from the unit. You can also use them to assess Ss' ability to use the language, in which case you need to monitor but avoid helping them. You may feel that you don't need or have time to do all the activities. If so, you could allocate the activities that would be most beneficial for your Ss, or get individual Ss to decide which activities they'd like to do.

### BEHAVIOUR

**1A** You could run this as a team game. Tell Ss to close their books and put them into teams of three to five. Put the sentences on the board one at a time. When a team is ready with the answer they put up their hands and call out the missing vowels (there are penalty points for calling out the complete words first), then the complete phrase. Award points for accuracy and good pronunciation.

> **Answers:** 1 gives in  2 criticises  3 compliments  4 neglects  5 takes care  6 puts off  7 gets on with  8 pays attention

**B** Ss discuss the characteristics in pairs, then compare their ideas as a class.

### USED TO, WOULD, BE/GET USED TO

**2A** You could start by putting the title *How do you improve your speaking?* on the board and asking Ss to predict what the writer will say. Ss work alone or in pairs to complete the gaps. NB To give Ss an extra challenge tell them to cover the box and complete the gaps with their own ideas first.

> **Answers:** 2 writing  3 write  4 getting  5 use  6 I'd  7 would  8 get

**B** Put Ss in pairs to discuss which of the writer's ideas they've tried or would like to try, as well as any other ways of improving their speaking they've used or heard of. Conduct feedback with the class.

### FUTURES REVIEW

NB Ex 3 reviews predictions and Ex 4 reviews plans, intentions and arrangements. You may want to direct Ss to the relevant section of the **Language bank** on p132 so they can review the rules before attempting each exercise.

**3A** Focus Ss on the headlines and check that they understand key vocabulary, e.g. *lifespan* (the length of time that someone will live), *exhausted* (all used), *soars* (increases quickly). Then put Ss into groups and tell them to write one prediction for each headline.

> **Example answers:**
> 1 The average lifespan is likely to increase to 100 years.
> 2 Italian will definitely never become a universal language.
> 3 The internet could be banned worldwide, but it's not likely to be.

**B** Ss work alone to write their predictions, giving a reason for each one.

**4A** You could elicit the first line of the first dialogue as an example, then Ss can work alone or with a partner to write the rest. Ss should write in their notebooks so they can use these prompts for oral practice in the next stage.

> **Answers:** 1
> A: What are you doing on Friday?
> B: I might go to Julia's party or maybe I'll go to the cinema.
> A: I'm going to Julia's party so I'll give you a lift if you want.
> B: Thanks. I'll phone you as soon as I decide.
> 2
> A: How are you planning to use your English in the future?
> B: I'll probably try and/to get a job with/in an international company. How about you?
> A: I'm thinking of applying to go to an American university. Who knows? I might get in!
> B: I'm sure you will.

**B** Once Ss have finished practising the conversations, they could repeat them, making at least one change to each of Student A's and Student B's contributions, e.g.

A: *What are you doing after the lesson?*

B: *I might go straight home or maybe I'll go for a coffee.*

A: *I'll probably go for a coffee so I might see you in the café.*

B: *OK. I'll see how I feel.*

In feedback, invite a few of the pairs to act out their new conversations.

### LOCATIONS

**5A** You could run this as a board race with Ss in two or three teams. Tell Ss to close their books. Give each student in the team a number and write one of the phrases with the jumbled word in brackets on the board. As soon as a team has worked out the word, their number 1 runs to the board and writes it up. The team gets a point if it's correct. For the next phrase, the number 2 in each team runs up and so on.

> **Answers:** 2 peninsula  3 crow  4 slope  5 forested  6 proximity  7 edge  8 remote, unspoilt

**B** Ss need to think of four places, one for each phrase they choose.

### PROCEDURES

**6A** You could start by asking Ss what they think an Oyster card is/does. If anyone has used one in London, they could explain how it works to the class or a partner.

> **Answers:** 2 the  3 it works  4 happens  5 that  6 main thing  7 After

**B** Give Ss about five minutes to write their tips. Then, before Ss compare their tips, remind them of the mirror questions on p39, which they can use to check anything they don't understand. Ss can work in small groups or stand up and walk around the room telling each other their tips. Monitor and make notes of good language use and problem areas for praise and correction in feedback.

## OVERVIEW

## AND THE MORAL IS

### Introduction

Ss practise reading, speaking and writing about stories, using narrative tenses. They also learn some common English sayings and how to use adverbs in a story.

### SUPPLEMENTARY MATERIALS

Resource bank p158 and/or p160

Warm up: be prepared to tell Ss about an important possession of yours and the story behind it. Take the possession into the lesson to show the Ss if possible.

Ex 6A: be prepared to tell a personal story that illustrates one of the sayings in Ex 5A and prepare a list of at least eight key words to help you tell the story

### Warm up

Diagnose Ss' use of narrative tenses via a storytelling activity.

Either: Ss tell a 'chain story' round the class. Start by eliciting some key words that are to be included in the story, e.g. a day, a time, a city, a country, the names of two people, the names of two/three objects and one method of transport and write these on the board. Invite a student on one side of the classroom to start the story and to include one of the key words from the board. Once they've said a couple of sentences, they 'pass' the story on to the next student and so on. The idea is that once the story reaches the last student on the other side of the classroom, all the key words have been used and that student finishes the story.

Or: Tell Ss about an important possession of yours and the story behind how you got it, e.g. who gave it to you, when, why, etc. or where, why and when you bought it. Then put Ss in pairs to tell each other the story behind an important possession of theirs.

### READING

**1A** Draw two columns on the board and write the story titles at the top of each column, then make sure that Ss cover the texts before directing them to the pictures. Elicit one or two ideas from the class about what they can see, then put Ss in pairs to predict what might happen in the stories. Conduct feedback, writing some of the Ss' ideas in the columns on the board for them to compare with the actual stories.

**B** Give Ss about five minutes to read the stories, then they can compare what they've read with the ideas on the board. You could elicit a few ideas for the endings from the whole class, then put Ss in pairs to write them, using about three sentences for each ending. Invite two or three pairs to read out their endings to the class. Vocabulary to check: tide (go out/come in).

**C** Give Ss a minute or two to read the endings and discuss briefly with the class who came closest to either of the endings in their predictions.

**2A** Tell Ss to cover Ex 2B while they do this exercise. You could look at the first bold word with the class, as an example, reminding them to use the part of speech, the context and the 'look' of the words to help them, e.g. strolling: it's a verb, it's similar to walking ('and started walking') and is something you do to relax. Put Ss in pairs to look at the rest of the words and make a note of possible meanings.

**B** Ss work alone and compare answers in pairs, before feedback to the class.

> **Answers:** 1 stranded 2 futile 3 strolling 4 intrigued
> 5 passed away 6 on the road to 7 low 8 owing to

**C** Give Ss time to discuss the stories and think about the moral or 'message' in each one. Elicit their ideas.

> **Possible answers:** Starfish: *Even small actions make a difference/No effort is futile/Every creature, however small, is worth saving*
> Hospital window: *Anyone can see beauty if they have the imagination/You don't need to have eyes to see*

## GRAMMAR narrative tenses

**3A** You could suggest that Ss use different ways of highlighting the three tenses, e.g. a circle for past simple, a wavy line for past continuous, a box for past perfect and a straight line for past perfect continuous (these could also be in different colours). Ss compare their answers in pairs. *Stronger classes* could also discuss why each verb tense is used.

> **Possible answers:** Past simple: *decided, arrived, parked, started, noticed,* etc.
> Past continuous: *was feeling, was going down, was beginning, was strolling,* etc.
> Past perfect simple: *'d driven, 'd never seen, had been washed (passive)*
> Past perfect continuous: *had been working,*

**B** Ss read the rules alone, then underline the verb forms and check their answers with a partner. You could ask Ss what effect using the four different verb forms has on the story, i.e. adding more variety and making it more interesting to read.

> **Answers:** a) past simple  b) past continuous.  c) past perfect simple  d) past perfect continuous: (You can point out that the past prefect continuous tense is also often used, as it is here, to give a reason for a past action or situation, i.e. *she'd been working* explains why she was feeling exhausted.)

**C** Remind Ss that the main verbs (which carry the meaning) are usually stressed and the auxiliary verbs (*be, do*) are not, so they are 'reduced'. You could look at the rest of sentence one with the class, as an example.

**D** Play the recording, stopping after each sentence to check the answers. Play the recording a second time for Ss to repeat.

> **Answers:**
> 1 A woman was feeling tired because she (had) (been) working
>      /ə/   /ɪ/
> 2 … thousands of starfish which (had) (been) washed
>      /ə/   /ɪ/
> 3 Two old men (were) staying in the same hospital room.
>      /ə/
> 4 He (had) (been) put in the bed right next to the window.
>      /ə/   /ɪ/

> **Teaching tip**
> If Ss have difficulty repeating complete sentences, build them up gradually, e.g. start by drilling the main verb, then add the auxiliary, then the rest of the phrase, etc.
> Example: *working – been working – had been working – because she had been working – because she had been working all day.*

> ➡ **LANGUAGEBANK** 4.1, p134–135
> The **Language bank** has an example timeline for each tense, which visually-orientated Ss may find helpful for understanding the differences between them. You could use Ex A and B in class before attempting the more complex story in Practice Ex 4A.
>
> **Answers:** A 1 had forgotten 2 was robbing 3 had just been painted 4 had been using
> B 1 ended 2 was working 3 heard 4 had been playing
> 5 ran 6 saw 7 joined 8 were searching 9 found
> 10 had been 11 had gone/went 12 was going
> 13 had heard 14 opened 15 had been sleeping

## PRACTICE

**4A** First, check that Ss know who Socrates was: a classical Greek philosopher. Then ask them to read the whole text quickly without worrying about the gaps and find out why he welcomed the second man to Athens. Ss then work in pairs to complete the gaps. Vocabulary to check: *stare* (look at someone/something for a long time without moving your eyes), *stab someone in the back* (do something that harms someone who trusts you), *frown* (demonstrate this rather than trying to explain), *approach* (move towards), *consider* (think about).

> **Answers:** 1 was standing 2 noticed 3 had been staring 4 asked 5 had come 6 looked 7 told 8 had been standing 9 approached 10 had just arrived 11 was considering 12 replied

**B** Ss discuss possible titles in pairs. Alternatively, you could give them three or four possibilities to choose from, e.g. *Life is what you make it/Give respect and you will earn it/A positive attitude to moving/Do you deserve to move to Athens?*

## VOCABULARY sayings

**5A** Put the example *Every cloud has a silver lining* on the board and ask Ss what they think it means (good things come out of bad things). Explain that this is a saying, i.e. a short, well-known statement that expresses an idea many people believe is true. Put Ss in pairs to match the rest of the halves and think about their meaning.

> **Possible answers:** 2 f) Your actions, good or bad, will have consequences for you.
> 3 e) There's usually truth in every rumour/if that's how it looks, that's probably how it is.
> 4 c) When something or someone has hurt you, you tend to avoid it subsequently.
> 5 b) Adapt yourself to the customs of the places you visit.
> 6 a) If someone or something is still alive, there is hope for recovery.
> 7 h) If you don't take risks, you won't achieve anything.
> 8 d) Don't worry about something that hasn't happened yet.

**B** Check that Ss understand *talent show* and do the first one with the class. Ss work in pairs on the rest.

> **Answers:** 1 nothing ventured, nothing gained.
> 2 When in Rome do as the Romans do. 3 every cloud has a silver lining. 4 Once bitten, twice shy. 5 what goes around comes around. 6 where there's smoke, there's fire.
> 7 let's cross that bridge when we come to it.
> 8 where there's life there's hope.

**speakout** TIP

Read the tip with the Ss and ask them why people only say the first part of a saying, i.e. they expect the listener to know it because the sayings are so well known. Point out that the second half of the sayings in Ex 5A and B can be left out. Ss could practise this in pairs: Student B closes his/her book and Student A reads a line from a dialogue in Ex 5B, then Student B answers with the first part of the appropriate saying. Students A and B then swap roles.

**C** If your Ss are from different countries, make sure that the pairs (or small groups) are mixed for this, so that Ss can compare across cultures. If Ss are from the same country, they could make a list of the three most popular sayings in the country at the moment.

## SPEAKING

**6A** You could start by telling Ss a personal story that illustrates a saying, as a model. Before the lesson, prepare a list of key words to include in the story, as in Ex 6B. Tell the story, referring to your list occasionally. Ask Ss to guess the saying and show them the list of key words you used.

**B** Ss prepare their stories alone.

**C** Before you put Ss into groups you could remind them about listening 'actively', e.g. by showing interest/sympathy/surprise and commenting on the story as it develops. NB tell Ss not to try to guess the saying until the person has finished telling the story.

## WRITING a story

**7A** Focus Ss on the title and the picture and ask them to speculate on what happens in the story. Then give them a few minutes to read the story and answer the question.

> **Answer:** He changes the saying because his experience was the opposite of what the saying means. He does it to be funny/ironic.

**B** Ss read the story and answer the questions alone, then discuss answers with a partner.

> **Answers:** 1 He puts the same saying (or a version of it) in both the first and last paragraphs.
> 2 The second paragraph – the author uses the past continuous, past perfect continuous, past simple.
> 3 Paragraphs 3 and 4 – the author uses past simple, past continuous, past perfect simple, past perfect continuous. Point out that the past perfect is used more in paragraph 4 because it refers back to actions that happened (*friends got tired of laughing, left the beach*), or started (*falling in the water*) earlier in the story
> 4 The writer expresses his feelings throughout paragraphs 3 and 4 by using adverbs such as *stupidly* and by sometimes simply saying how he felt, e.g. *I felt embarrassed.* He says what he learnt in the last paragraph.

## LEARN TO use adverbs

**8A** Direct Ss to the first adverb (*apparently*) as an example, then tell them to circle the rest as quickly as they can.

**B** Suggest that Ss copy the table into their notebooks so they have more room to write the adverbs. In feedback avoid going into the meaning of the adverbs as this is dealt with in the next stage.

> **Answers:**
>
> | adverbs of manner | attitude markers | time markers |
> | --- | --- | --- |
> | hopefully | apparently | finally |
> | awkwardly | stupidly | eventually |
> | dejectedly | naturally | |
> | | fortunately | |
> | | unsurprisingly | |

**C** Encourage Ss to look back at the adverbs in context to help them guess the meanings. Ss discuss answers in pairs before feedback with the class. Pronunciation to check: *dejectedly, apparently, awkwardly, eventually*.

> **Answers:** 1 naturally, unsurprisingly 2 dejectedly 3 apparently 4 awkwardly 5 finally, eventually

**speakout** TIP

Give Ss a time to read the tip then ask them where most of the adverbs occur in the story – mainly in the third and fourth paragraphs where the writer is describing the action (adverbs of manner) and commenting on what happened (attitude markers). Explain that using too many adverbs (i.e. more than ten) will make the story awkward and unnatural.

**9A/B** Encourage Ss to make notes and do a rough first draft of their story. They could give it to a partner to check before writing the final draft (this could be done at home).

> ▶ **VOCABULARYBANK** p151 Verbs used in stories
>
> Ss complete the exercises in pairs without using a dictionary and using a process of logical deduction to help them guess those words they don't know. Feed back as a class or let the Ss use bilingual and monolingual dictionaries to check anything they are not sure of.
>
> If the Ss speak the same language, it could be an interesting exercise to ask them to compare the metaphorical use of the verbs in Ex B with similar expressions in their own language.
>
> **Answers:** A 1 E 2 C 3 I 4 F 5 G 6 D 7 A 8 H 9 B
> B 1 crawled 2 wade 3 wandering 4 creeps 5 limped 6 tiptoeing 7 slide 8 staggered 9 marches

> **Homework ideas**
>
> 1 Workbook Ex 1–6, p23–24
>
> 2 Ss read a short story in English online, e.g. something like www.classicshorts.com (correct at the time of going to press) and report back in the next lesson.
>
> 3 Ss write the story from the warm up to the lesson (either the chain story, or the story of a favourite possession).
>
> 4 Ss research the life of a famous person and make notes in English to bring to class and use in 4.2, Ex 8.

# A LIFE IN SIX WORDS

## Introduction

Ss practise listening and speaking about regrets, using *I wish, If only* and *should have* and related vocabulary. They also learn to use multi-word verbs in life stories.

### SUPPLEMENTARY MATERIALS

Resource bank p159 and/or p161

Ex 4C–D: bring in pictures of people in strange/awkward situations from magazines, newspapers or the internet to prompt Ss to invent a forum entry.

Ex 6–7: monolingual dictionaries should be available.

Ex 8A: be prepared to tell a life story using some of the multi-word verbs.

## Warm up

Tell Ss to close their books and write on the board: *Ernest Hemingway (American author), ten dollars, baby shoes, six words.* Put Ss in pairs to discuss how these could be linked, e.g. in a story, then ask them to share their ideas with the class. Tell Ss to open their books and read the text *A Life in Six Words* to see if any of their ideas were correct.

### LISTENING

**1A** Focus Ss on questions 1–3 and give them a few minutes to read the text about the radio programme. Put them in pairs to compare their answers and to discuss question four, then conduct feedback with the whole class.

**Possible answers:** 1 It could be about a baby that didn't survive, or a friendship that broke up before the writer had a chance to give the mother the baby shoes.  2 To talk about the six-word stories that people have contributed to his online magazine and the book that has been published. 3 It was a story that someone contributed.

**B** Give Ss time to read the three questions and tell them to make notes about the answers while they listen.

**Answers:** 1 Everyone has a story. Story telling should be democratic.
2 The number of contributions (15,000 in a couple of months) and the fact that so many were sad – he expected more to be funny or playful.
3 regret or disappointment: 'It's tough out there'.

**C** You could start by looking at the example and discussing with the class what happened in the person's life and whether they think it's a story of regret/disappointment or not. Then direct them to the other three stories and play the recording again. NB These stories are in the last part of the recording.

**Answers:** 2 Wasn't born a redhead. Fixed that.  3 Found true love. Married someone else.  4 Never should have bought that ring.

**D** Tell Ss to discuss in their pairs what happens in stories 2–4, then to decide which story is the most interesting/the most positive/the saddest.

### UNIT 4 Recording 2

I = Interviewer   L = Larry Smith

I: In the 1920s, Ernest Hemingway bet ten dollars that he could write a complete story in just six words. He wrote, 'For sale: baby shoes, never worn.' He won the bet. An American online magazine has now used that to inspire its readers to write their life story in six words and they've been overwhelmed by the thousands who took up the challenge. They've published the best in a book which they've given the title of one of the submissions: *Not quite what I was planning.* I asked the editor, Larry Smith, what made him think of the idea.

L: Well, on the site, *Smith Magazine*, we tell stories in all sorts of different ways. Our whole idea behind the site is that story-telling should be egalitarian, you know, democratic. Everyone has a story, we say that over and over. That's our tag line. But in telling different types of stories since we launched a couple of years ago, we found that you had to give people parameters. So playing off the great literary legend, the Hemingway story, we thought, 'Let's ask our readers their six-word life story, a memoir' and see what happened. We really didn't know what would happen.

I: And what did happen?

L: It was incredible. In a couple of months we got fifteen thousand entries and I was just blown away. Funny, poignant – I really believe that everyone has a story and most of us aren't going to write for the *Guardian* but I was just so inspired by how serious and intense folks took the six-word memoir challenge.

I: OK, but before we look at the examples. It's one thing … because the Hemingway is a story but it's not a story of a life. That seems to be a bit of a challenge to fit that in six words.

L: Well, it's interesting because some folks clearly tried to tell a whole story of a life in six words and you can tell and other times they're telling a moment in their life, right at this moment, something that they're feeling right now. Or perhaps something that's been an evergreen, a thread throughout their lives.

I: Give us some examples.

L: 'Wasn't born a redhead. Fixed that.' This woman took life under control. Whether she just always felt that her soul was a redheaded soul or simply at some point in life she was going to make a switch. She could have quit her job. She changed her hair colour.

I: But a lot of them are … they're quite sad or there's a sense of regret or disappointment in a lot of them.

L: I didn't expect that. I thought people would come back with a lot of funny things, some playful things, plays on words … but those are really interesting reality. People really told us, 'It's tough out there.' 'Found true love. Married someone else.' 'Never should have bought that ring.'

### GRAMMAR | *I wish, If only, should have*

**2A** You could do the first one as an example with the class. Vocabulary to check: *era* (period in history), *gender* (sex), *aspirations* (ambitions, goals), *compromised* (devalued, spoiled), *procrastination* (delay, putting off).

**B** Look at the example with the class and establish that this is something the writer wants very much, but is unlikely to be able to change. You could compare this with *I hope I can do it all again*, which suggests that the writer thinks it's possible. Once Ss have matched the sentences, tell them to underline and label the verb forms that come after *I wish, If only* and *should have.*

**Answers:** a) 4  b) 5 (*If only I wasn't* is also possible)  c) 1  d) 6  e) 3  f) 2

**C** You could write the rules on the board and invite Ss out to complete the gaps.

**Answers:** past simple or past continuous
past perfect
have + past participle

**D** Ss could look at the sentences first and predict which words are stressed (point out that there are at least two in each sentence).

**Answers:** NB The main/strongest stress is on the last word in each sentence.
1 I <u>wish</u> I could do it all <u>again</u>.  2 If <u>only</u> I weren't so <u>anxious</u>.
3 I <u>wish</u> I'd been born <u>twenty</u> years <u>later</u>.  4 If <u>only</u> I hadn't given <u>up</u> on my <u>dreams</u>.  5 I should have <u>stayed</u> where I was <u>happy</u>.  6 I shouldn't have <u>become</u> a <u>doctor</u>.

### Teaching tip

When you want Ss to practise saying a sentence with more than one stressed word in it, you can start by asking them to repeat just the stressed words a couple of times, so they get the rhythm of the sentence. Then they repeat the whole sentence, 'squashing' the unstressed words in between the stressed ones.

Example:

*only – anxious* (x2)   *If <u>only</u> I weren't so <u>anxious</u>.* (x2)

#### ▶ LANGUAGEBANK 4.2 p134–135

The **Language bank** has an example of *I wish* + past continuous and it deals with the issue of *I wish I were(n't)* vs *I wish I was(n't)*. Ex A provides a useful check of the verb forms before Ss attempt the more challenging practice in Ex 3. For a *stronger class* the use of *I wish + would(n't)* to talk about other people's habits is also explained and practised in Ex B.

**Answers:** A 1 have lied  2 liked  3 knew  4 were
5 didn't live  6 'd met  7 have left  8 had
B 1 lived  2 wouldn't party/didn't party, shouldn't have come  3 wouldn't always/didn't always, have remembered  4 wouldn't play/hadn't played, had slept
5 were, weren't/wasn't  6 didn't bite/wouldn't bite, had

### PRACTICE

**3A** Direct Ss to the example and point out that they can't change the words given for the beginning of the new sentence. Ss can work alone or in pairs, then check with the whole class.

**Answers:** 2 I wish I'd/I had grown up in a large family OR I wish I hadn't grown up in a small family.  3 I should have learned another language.  4 If only I were/was more sociable OR If only I weren't/wasn't so unsociable.
5 I should have travelled more when I was younger.
6 If only I'd/I had learnt how to touch type.  7 I wish I didn't lose my temper with people.  8 I wish I could cook (well).
9 I shouldn't have given up doing sport.  10 If only I'd/I had spent more time with my grandfather.

**B** You could demonstrate this by telling Ss which sentences you would tick and give an example of how you would change one of the others. Emphasise that Ss should not change the original 'stem' of the sentence. Give Ss a few minutes to work on their sentences alone.

**C** You could demonstrate this by choosing one student to say one of their sentences and eliciting examples of follow-up questions from the rest of the class.

### VOCABULARY regrets

**4A** Direct Ss to the title of the forum and make sure they understand that the person regrets becoming a lawyer. Then give them a few minutes to put the entry in order and check their answers with the class.

**Answers:** b) f) a) c) e) d)

#### Culture notes

Taking a *gap year* (also known as a *year out* or *year off*) refers to taking a year out of studying to do something else. Many people take a gap year before starting college or university.

**B** Put Ss in pairs and direct them to the phrases in bold in the forum entry. In feedback, check the pronunciation of *hindsight* and *gutted*.

**Answers:** 1 a) It's a pity, I kick myself, I'm gutted
b) With hindsight  c) a missed opportunity
2 I kick myself, I'm gutted (this conveys a sense of strong disappointment)
3 a) it's a pity, I'm gutted  b) I've had second thoughts
c) I kick myself

**C** If a Ss cannot think of a regret, tell them they can invent it or write from someone else's point of view. Circulate and help Ss to use the phrases correctly.

**D** Remind Ss that (apart from phrases such as *Why don't you …? You could … Have you thought of …?*) they can use *should(n't) have, If only* and *wish* as ways of giving advice, e.g. *If only you hadn't …, Perhaps you should've …; Do you wish you'd …?* Conduct feedback, asking a few Ss to tell the class their regret and what advice their partner gave them.

#### Optional extra activities

1 Elicit the names of some famous people who've been in the news recently, e.g. because of problems in their relationships, their lifestyle or being in trouble with the police. Write these on the board. Each student then chooses one person and writes the forum entry from their point of view. When they tell their partners about their regret, the partner first has to guess which famous person they are, then give them advice.

2 As above but instead of names of famous people, bring in pictures (from magazines, newspapers or the internet) of people who look as if they're in awkward/strange situations (e.g. someone sitting on top of their car in the middle of a flood) and put these on the board for Ss to choose from.

### SPEAKING

**5A** Tell Ss to discuss each story in turn, first saying what they think happened and whether they describe any aspect of their own lives. Vocabulary to check: *Alas* (unfortunately), *dashed* (ran), *ditched* (threw away).

**B** Write the following topics on the board to help generate ideas: *career, studies, skills, relationships, journeys, family, home, finances, possessions*. Circulate and help Ss with vocabulary that will enable them to 'condense' their ideas.

**C** Write the story *Wasted my whole life getting comfortable* on the board and elicit some examples of questions that Ss could ask the writer about it, e.g. *How did you get comfortable? What do you wish you'd done instead?* Then put Ss into groups of four to six and suggest that they each write their six-word story on a piece of paper so that everyone in the group can see it.

## VOCABULARY *PLUS* multi-word verbs

**6A** You could do the first part with the whole class. Write the four stories on the board and elicit from Ss where the multi-word verbs are (i.e. verbs with dependent 'particles': adverbs or prepositions). NB Ss will probably be familiar with the term *phrasal verb*, which is used in several learners' dictionaries. Give Ss a minute or two to match the meanings and compare answers with a partner.

**Answers:** 1 turned up – c  2 gave up – f, took up – a
3 settled down – e  4 set up – d, ran out – b

**B** Before putting Ss into pairs, use a simple example to check that they know what an object is, e.g. write on the board *Ditched the map, found better route* and ask Ss how many objects there are (*the map, better route*). Ss can look at their own monolingual dictionaries here and see how similar/ different the *Longman Active Study Dictionary* is.

**Answers:** 1 run out  2 set up  3 set up  4 run out

## speakout TIP

Before Ss read the tip, elicit from them the kind of information that a dictionary gives you about multi-word verbs. Then put them in pairs to look at how the features are shown.

1 If the verb has more than one meaning, these are numbered in bold.

2 Any examples of language in use are given in italics.

3 To show that the verb and particle can be separated by an object, the abbreviation *sth* is put between them and there is a 'two-way' arrow.

4 If a verb can be followed by a preposition this is indicated by a + sign and the preposition in bold.

**7A** Tell Ss to cover the text and look at the photos. If any of them recognise David Attenborough, they could tell the class what they know. Otherwise, ask them to imagine what his life is like, what his job is, etc.

**B** Focus Ss on the three questions before they read the text (tell them not to worry about the verbs in bold at the moment). After Ss have read the text, they could discuss with a partner what they think of Attenborough's life.

**Answers:** 1 editor of children's science textbooks
2 The woman who gave him the job thought his teeth were too big.  3 He has a lot of stamina and he recovers from jet lag easily.

**C** Remind Ss to use the context to help them work out the meaning of the verbs. Once they have matched the meanings and checked their answers with a partner, Ss could use monolingual dictionaries to check whether the verbs must

be used with an object/can be used without an object and whether the verb can be separated from the particle.

**Answers:** 1 be taken on (take s.o. on: must have an object, can be separated) 2 get over (must have an object, can't be separated) 3 be brought up (bring s.o. up: must have an object, can be separated) 4 turn down (must have an object, can be separated) 5 grow up (doesn't have an object, can't be separated) 6 take to (must have an object, can't be separated) 7 go by (doesn't have an object, can't be separated) 8 put off (must have an object, can be separated) 9 step down  (can be followed by *from* and an object, can't be separated) 10 go on to (must have an object, can't be separated)

## SPEAKING

**8A** Point out to Ss that they need to know some details of the person's life in order to make the notes and use the multi-word verbs. If Ss researched a famous person for homework, they can use the information here. Ss should write notes rather than full sentences, so they sound natural when they tell the life story. Circulate and help Ss to use the multi-word verbs from Ex 6 and 7 appropriately.

**B** You could demonstrate this first, showing Ss how to stop just before the multi-word verb for their partner to guess.

▶ **VOCABULARYBANK** p151 Multi-word verbs (1)
Ss decide on the answers to Ex A in pairs. Check the answers as a class before completing the pronouns in Ex B.

**Answers:**
A a) between the main verb and the particle or after the particle
b) between the main verb and the particle
B 2 The shop had some great clothes but the loud music put **her** off. 3 Fifty people wanted to be extras in the film and the director took **them** all on. 4 Señor Almeida isn't here at the moment. Can you ring **him** back? 5 I finished the essay last night and gave **it** in this morning. 6 If I don't know new words, I just look **them** up in my electronic dictionary. 7 The sound of the doorbell at 2a.m. woke **us** up. 8 Is that a new coat? Anyway, take **it** off and hang it up here.

### Homework ideas
1 Tell Ss to bring one of their favourite books and another type of reading material that they like to talk about.
2 **Workbook** Ex 1–6, p25–26
3 Ss write their story from Ex 5B in exactly fifty words OR write the life story they told in Ex 8A.
4 Ss write a life story from one of the six-word stories in Ex 6A using multi-word verbs.

# IT'S A GREAT READ!

## Introduction

Ss practise speaking about their tastes in reading using phrases for expressing likes and dislikes. They also practise listening and learn to summarise a plot.

### SUPPLEMENTARY MATERIALS

Resource bank p162

Ex 1C: bring in a couple of examples of things you like to read.

Ex 7A: be prepared to tell Ss about the plot of a book you like and explain why they should read it.

## Warm up

Tell Ss to cover Ex 1 and focus them on the photos. Ask them what types of reading material they can see, which ones they are familiar with, which appeal/don't appeal to them and why.

### VOCABULARY reading

**1A** Do question 1 (a *blog* can only be read on a computer screen) then put Ss in pairs. They should use monolingual dictionaries.

**Answers:** 1 blog, e-book, online encyclopedia, website forum  2 lyrics, poetry  3 biography, autobiography, gossip magazine (often blogs)  4 biography, autobiography, online encyclopaedia, manual  5 manga, manual, gossip magazine (*manga* is the same form for singular and plural)

**B** Encourage Ss to think of things to read at work, school, around the home, on public transport, etc. as well as examples of different types of books.

**Some possible answers:** Types of books: thrillers, detective stories, whodunits, romantic novels, historical novels, classics, short stories, etc.
Reading more generally: shopping websites, social networking sites, adverts, news and current affairs magazines, specialist and hobby magazines, newspapers, journals, academic articles, reports, brochures, leaflets, signs, instructions and information on packets, etc.

**C** Demonstrate this by telling the class about things you like reading and showing them the reading material you've brought in. If Ss have brought their own reading materials, they can show them to their partner here. Note down any phrases Ss use to say why they like the material. Ask Ss to rewrite and improve these examples after Ex 4.

### SPEAKING

**2A** Write these questions on the board and tell Ss to close their books. Give Ss time to discuss the questions, then feedback as a class.

**B** Direct Ss to the questions, then give them a minute or two to read the text. Vocabulary to check: *poll* (verb and noun). Ask Ss what they thought of the article, e.g. were they surprised by the different percentages, or by the types of reading material that impressed people the most?

**Answers:** 1 to impress people: friends or potential partners  2 men: news websites, Shakespeare, song lyrics; women: Nelson Mandela's biography, Shakespeare; teenagers: social networking pages, song lyric

### FUNCTION expressing likes and dislikes

**3A** Ss can discuss what kind of book they are, where/when they're set, when they were published, etc.

**B** Suggest that Ss copy the table into their notebooks.

**C** Emphasise that Ss only need to write notes, e.g. a couple of words or a phrase. Give them time to compare answers with a partner and help each other.

**Answers:**

| The Girl with the Dragon Tattoo<br>Amy –<br>Babara ✓<br>Carl ✗ | Barbara likes detective novels; likes the main character – edgy, brilliant but messed up |
| --- | --- |
| | Carl doesn't like detective novels, modern ones too violent |
| | Amy decides to take this books |
| Life of Pi<br>Amy –<br>Babara ✗<br>Carl ✓ | Barbara doesn't like fantasy / could get into it. |
| | Carl thinks it's brilliant – about courage and survival; |
| | exciting, want to know what happens next |
| Pride and Prejudice<br>Amy –<br>Babara ✓<br>Carl ✓ | Barbara thinks it's the most romantic story ever written; |
| | written in beautiful English |
| | Carl loves it, but maybe not for plane journey |

### Unit 4 Recording 4

A = Amy  B = Barbara  C = Carl

C: So, Amy, when's your flight?

A: Tomorrow at one. It's twelve hours so I need a good book. Any ideas? Barbara?

B: Well, I've just finished *The Girl with the Dragon Tattoo* and

C: Didn't they make a film of that?

B: Yeah, apparently it's really good.

A: I haven't read it. It's a sort of thriller, isn't it?

B: Yeah, it's a kind of mixture between a thriller and a detective story, set in Sweden. I thought it was great. I mean I'm a big fan of detective novels anyway but what I really liked about it was the main character, the girl

C: … with the dragon tattoo?

B: Yeah. She's really edgy, strange, kind of brilliant but really messed up at the same time.

C: I'm not that keen on detective novels and the modern ones are usually too violent for me, so I don't think I'd like it.

A: Well, it's definitely a possibility. What would *you* recommend then?

C: What about *Life of Pi*? Have either of you read it?

A: No.

B: I started it but I just couldn't get into it …

C: It's brilliant. It's about this Indian kid who's stuck on a boat in the middle of the ocean with a dangerous tiger and a zebra and some other animals

A: Sounds very strange.

C: No, it's actually all about courage and survival. It'd be really good for a long plane journey – you won't be able to put it down for the whole twelve hours, it's so exciting, you'll just want to know what's going to happen next.

A: Uh huh.

C: But you didn't finish it?

B: No, actually, to be honest, I couldn't stand it and I gave up after about a quarter of the way through. I suppose I'm not really into fantasy and …

C: It's not really fantasy, it's, er, what do they call it, magic realism.

B: Whatever, I just couldn't get into it. Amy, why not try one of the classics? You know, something like *Pride and Prejudice*? Do you like Jane Austen?

A: I dunno, I mean, I've seen the movie and the TV adaptation and I liked them, but I dunno, she's not exactly an easy read.

B: Oh, you should try it. I've read it about, what, ten times and it has to be the most romantic story ever written … The thing I love about it is the writing, the English that she's used is so beautiful.

A: I know what you mean but it just seems a bit, well, a bit serious for a plane journey.

C: Yeah, I agree. I love it too, but maybe not for a plane journey.

A: Actually, you know what? I might try the first one you said, *The Girl With The Dragon Tattoo*. What's the overall story? You know, without giving too much away?

B: Well, it's about …

**D** Ss discuss their choices then share their ideas as a class and find out which is the most popular choice.

**4A** Ss should write the correct sentences in their notebooks so they can refer to them in the next two stages.

> **Answers:** 1 I'm a big fan of detective novels. 2 What I really liked about it was the main character. 3 I'm not that keen on detective novels. 4 I just couldn't get into it. 5 I couldn't stand it. 6 I'm not really into fantasy. 7 The thing I love about it is the writing.

**B** Give Ss time to analyse the phrases in pairs, then conduct feedback with the whole class.

> **Answers:** 1 I'm not that keen on, I just couldn't get into it, I couldn't stand it, I'm not really into (NB. I couldn't stand it expresses the strongest dislike.)
> 2 It starts with 'What' and the words 'about it was' come before 'the main character', with the result that 'the main character' is emphasised.
> 3 It starts with 'The thing' and the words 'about it is' come before 'the writing', with the result that 'the writing' is emphasised.
> 4 I'm not a big fan of, What I really didn't like about it was, I'm very keen on, I'm really into, The thing I hate about it is …

**C** Point out that several of the sentences have more than one main stress and remind Ss to look for the words that carry the meaning of the sentence. Play the recording, stopping after each sentence for Ss to check and repeat. Encourage Ss to use the stresses to help them sound convincingly positive or negative when they repeat the sentences.

> **Answers:** 1 I'm a big <u>fan</u> of <u>detective</u> novels. 2 What I really <u>liked</u> about it was the <u>main character</u>. 3 I'm not that <u>keen</u> on detective novels. 4 I just couldn't get <u>into</u> it. 5 I couldn't <u>stand</u> it. 6 I'm not really <u>into</u> fantasy. 7 The thing I <u>love</u> about it is the <u>writing</u>.

**5A** Go through the example with the class, showing them that the words in brackets have been used unchanged and that the meaning of the new sentence is the same as the original. Ss work alone on the transformations.

> **Answers:** 2 I can't stand reading e-books on my computer – it hurts my eyes. 3 I'm not a big fan of gossip magazines. 4 I'm really into reading anything by Stephen King. 5 What I like best is that lots of different people contribute to the forum. 6 I can't get into *Manga* or other types of comics. 7 The thing I like is the way his lyrics sound so natural.

**B** If you and the Ss have brought in examples of favourite reading material, display these at the front of the class, to prompt ideas. Give Ss time to write their sentences.

**C** Suggest that Student A reads all three sentences before Student B tries to guess. Choose a few Ss who did well to read out their sentences for the rest of the class to guess.

> ➠ **LANGUAGEBANK** 4.3 p134–135
>
> Show the class that the phrases are summarised in a table.
>
> > **Answers:** 1 I'm not that keen **on** opera. 2 I can't **stand** depressing books like that one. 3 The thing I liked **most** about it was the surprise ending. 4 I'm not really **into** sci-fi books or films. 5 **What** I love about Lee's films is that there's always a message. 6 I'm a big fan **of** historical novels. 7 What I like **about** her acting is that she brings something special to every role. 8 I'm **not** into classical music.

**LEARN TO** summarise a plot

**6A** Ask Ss what they remember about *The Girl with the Dragon Tattoo* from the conversation they listened to. Then tell them to read the summary and try to predict the missing words before they listen to the recording. Vocabulary to check: *clippings, a genius, punk clothes*.

> **Answers:** 1 is hired 2 wants 3 finds 4 is helped 5 wears 6 is 7 uncover 8 put

**B** Tell Ss to look through the summary at all the verbs that were missing and decide what they have in common. Direct them to questions 1–3.

> **Answers:**
> 1 the present simple (sometimes in the passive) NB the present perfect could also be used.
> 2 Using present verb forms makes the plot more immediate, as if the reader/listener is experiencing as they read/listen.

**SPEAKING**

**7A** You could start by telling Ss about a book you like. If Ss have brought in a favourite book, tell them to make notes about it and think about how to use it to illustrate what they're saying, e.g. to show the other Ss the main characters or the setting on the front cover. Give Ss some suggestions for phrases they can use, e.g.

1 *Has anyone read/heard of … by …?*

2 *It's a thriller/romance/historical novel set in … (time/place). It's about … who …*

3 *The thing I really … / What I … / I'm really into …*

4 *I recommend it to anyone who … / You should definitely read it if you're a fan of …*

**B** Put Ss into small groups of three to five and tell them that they aim is to persuade the others to read their book.

> **Homework ideas**
> 1 Workbook Ex 1–3, p27
> 2 Ss write an email to a friend recommending a book.

# TESS OF THE D'URBERVILLES

## Introduction

Ss watch an extract from the BBC's serialisation of *Tess of the d'Urbervilles*, where Angel Clare carries Tess and her companions across a flooded path on the way to church. Ss then learn and practise how to describe and write about a favourite TV/film moment.

## Warm up

Lead into the topic by brainstorming types of film and TV programme. Write them into two columns on the board, then put Ss in pairs to discuss which ones they like/don't like and why. Remind Ss of the phrases for describing likes and dislikes in the previous lesson.

Examples of TV programmes: *comedy series, soap opera, costume drama, documentary, reality show*

Examples of films: *thriller, romance, comedy, costume/historical drama, action, science fiction*

### DVD PREVIEW

**1** Direct Ss to the questions. Check that Ss understand that *set* (usually in the passive) refers to the place where (or time when) the story happens. Give Ss a minute or two to read the programme information and answer the questions.

> **Answers:**
> 1 In Wessex, a semi-fictional area of southern England.
> 2 They're all dairymaids; they're all in love with Angel Clare.
> 3 Ss predict what Angel does, then see if they were right when they watch the extract.

### ▶ DVD VIEW

**3A** You could play the extract with no sound for the first viewing. Ss can tell quite a lot about how the women are feeling from their expressions and reactions (they could add some adjectives of their own, e.g. *jealous, disappointed*, etc.). Vocabulary to check: *eager* (wanting very much to do or have something), *thrilled* (pleased and excited), *awkward* (embarrassed), *expectant* (waiting for something), *agitated* (anxious, not calm), *contented* (happy).

You could also ask Ss to imagine what each person is saying at certain points of the extracts and make a note of their predictions to compare with the dialogue when they watch the extract with sound.

> **Answers:** 1st woman: eager, pleased
> 2nd woman: nervous, awkward
> 3rd woman: expectant, excited
> 4th woman: agitated, contented

**B** Give Ss time to look through the quotes before you play the DVD again. You may need to play the extract a third time for Ss to confirm/change any answers they're unsure of.

> **Answers:** 1 Tess. She means there's no need to be nervous about being carried by Angel.
> 2 Angel. He's commenting on the fact that Retty's much smaller and lighter than Marion.
> 3 Izzy. She wants to kiss Angel and asks Tess if she'd mind (because Tess is his 'favourite').
> 4 Angel. He's carried the other three women just so he can spend a few moments with her.
> 5 Angel. He means that he didn't expect to have this moment with Tess, not that he didn't expect the road to flood (as Tess suggests).

**DVD 4 Tess of the D'Urbervilles**

I = Izzy  R = Retty  T = Tess  MC = Mr Clare  M = Marion

I: We can't get there without walking through it.

M: That's that then, I'm going back to bed.

I: Marion, get back here, now.

MC: Good morning ladies and how lovely you all look. Now I see the problem. Perhaps I can be of assistance. Who's first?

I: First for what, sir?

MC: I'll carry you across the water. And don't go away.

R: I'm supposed to put my arms around his neck and put my face against his and feel his arms around me and put my face against his. I don't think I can.

T: There's nothing in it, Retty.

R: That's what you say. I think I'm going to burst.

M: Thank you, Mr Clare.

MC: Retty, a nice easy one this time.

I: I'm going to kiss him. I don't care what happens I'm going to kiss him. You wouldn't mind would you if I tried? I know that you're his favourite and all.

T: Izzy.

I: But I've got to try, haven't I? I might never get another chance. How do I look? Do I look pretty? Tell me, Tess.

T: Very pretty, Iz.

I: Here I go. Wish me luck.

MC: What are you doing?

T: I think I can climb along the bank after all.

MC: Tess, no!

T: Really I'm quite all right.

MC: Tess!

T: And you must be so tired.

MC: I've undergone three quarters of the labour just for this moment.

T: They are much better women than I, all of them.

MC: Not to me.

T: I'm not too heavy?

MC: Compared to Marion you're like gossamer; you're a billow warmed by the sun.

T: That's very pretty. I seem like that to you.

MC: I didn't expect an event like this today.

T: Nor I. The water came up so quickly.

MC: That's not what I meant, at all. Ladies.

M: Come on, we'll be late.

I: I was sure he was going to kiss me.

**C** Give Ss a few minutes to discuss the questions, then invite them to share their opinions with the class.

> **Possible answers:** Escapism: many people are fascinated by seeing how people lived in an apparently simpler and less stressful world, with wide divisions between gender roles and rich/poor, but without modern conveniences, technical and medical advances, etc. For many, the fascination is the costumes themselves: how attractive they make people look, how difficult they'd be to wear, etc.

## speakout a favourite scene

**4A** If any Ss are familiar with *Fawlty Towers*, you could ask them to explain to the class what kind of programme it is, who the main characters are, etc. Otherwise, direct Ss to the questions and play the recording.

> **Answers:** 1 Mrs Richardson, an old customer who complains a lot and is deaf.  2 Basil pretends to talk to Mrs Richardson but he's miming, so she turns her hearing aid up. This happens twice and when it's at full volume he shouts at her and it's <u>very</u> loud.

## Optional extra activity

For *weaker Ss* who might struggle to understand exactly what happened, write the following on pieces of A4 paper and stick them on the board in the wrong order (or put them on slips of paper and give each pair of Ss a set). Ss listen and decide on the correct order:

– *Mrs Richardson makes Basil Fawlty dislike her by being grumpy and complaining a lot.*

– *Basil goes into her room.*

– *He pretends to speak to her but he's miming.*

– *She thinks her hearing aid is turned down, so she turns it up.*

– *Basil mimes again.*

– *She turns her hearing aid up to full volume.*

– *Basil shouts at her.*

**B** First, go through the key phrases with the class and check the following: *absolute* is used for emphasis. It could also be for a negative opinion, e.g. *an absolute disaster; cool* (in this context, clever, excellent); *send shiver up s.o's spine.* Tell Ss to put a tick above the option they hear in the phrase.

**Answers:** I've seen this (hundreds of) times and it's my absolute favourite. It always makes me laugh. It's like a lesson in comic acting. My favourite scene is the scene with … It's very cleverly done. If you've never seen it, you really should.

## Unit 4 Recording 7

*Fawlty Towers!* I absolutely love *Fawlty Towers!*, I've seen this hundreds of times and it's my absolute favourite. It always makes me laugh – in fact, it makes me cry with laughter sometimes … can't get enough of it. And the main character, Basil Fawlty, played by John Cleese, is absolutely brilliant. It's like a lesson in comic acting; the more bad things that happen to this man the more we laugh.

My favourite scene is the scene with Mrs Richardson and Basil Fawlty. And, it's very, very cleverly done. Mrs Richardson wears a hearing aid and Basil Fawlty hates Mrs Richardson – she's a terrible grumpy old complaining customer who he really doesn't like. So he comes into the room and he mimes at her – so he moves his mouth but he doesn't make any sound – so that Mrs Richardson turns up her hearing aid so that she can hear him.

And then he mimes again and he moves his mouth again not making any sound so she can't understand why she can't hear him, so she turns up her hearing aid again. And then once he's sure that her hearing aid is on full volume he shouts at her, 'Mrs Richardson!' – of course which deafens her and, it's – it's, it's very, very funny and it's amazing because he gets his own back on her 'cos she's been awful to him so, he, you know, he kind of wins in the end but, … Oh it's just brilliant. If you've never seen it you really should see it. There were very few episodes made. I think there were only –only ever one series, maybe eight episodes … something like that … I'm not entirely sure about that, but not very many made and, they're – they're really, really fantastic. Everyone is absolutely priceless.

## Optional extra activity

To give Ss more alternatives for the key phrases and more practice, write the following words on the board and ask Ss to decide which of the key phrases they fit into: *many, creatively, hilarious, imaginatively, loads of, gripping, fantastic, beautifully, lots of, one.*

Do some substitution drills by prompting Ss to change one word in the phrase when they repeat it, e.g.

T: *It's very cleverly done.*

Ss: *It's very cleverly done.*

T: *Creatively*

Ss: *It's very creatively done.*

T: *It's an amazing scene.*

Ss: *It's an amazing scene.*

T: *Hilarious*

Ss: *It's a hilarious scene.*

**C** Ss should only write notes for this so that they sound more natural when they're talking. Also, remind them to use the present tense to describe what happens and the present perfect if they need to explain what happened before that moment. Circulate and help as necessary.

**D** Encourage Ss to listen 'actively' while their partner is speaking, e.g. by saying *Uhuh, Yeah, Really? Oh no!* Ss could also work in groups of four to six to talk about their favourite moments, then decide which they'd most like to see of the other moments they heard about. Monitor the activity and note examples of good language use and problem areas to deal with in feedback.

## writeback a description of a scene

**5A** Give Ss a minute or two to read the extract and write the name of the film in the gap in the first line. Vocabulary to check: *crew, cast.*

**Answer:** A science-fiction film: *Star Trek*

**B** You could start by analysing the structure of the description. Put Ss in pairs and ask them to decide on the purpose of:

– the first sentence (a very brief summary of what the whole film is about)

– the rest of the first paragraph (explains what happens)

– the second paragraph, apart from the last sentence (explains why the writer likes/chose this moment)

– the last sentence (describes what effect the moment has on the writer)

While Ss are writing, circulate and provide vocabulary, etc. but don't correct their work at this stage.

**C** You could either get Ss to swap their descriptions with a partner, or collect them in and stick them on the wall for Ss to walk round and read.

## Homework ideas

1 Ss write a second, final draft of their description, having first checked it for accuracy.

2 Ss could explore the BBC website for *Tess of the D'Urbervilles* (www.bbc.co.uk/tess (correct at the time of going to press)) and report back to the class.

# LOOKBACK

## Intoduction

The aim of these activities is to provide revision and further practice of the language from the unit. You can also use them to assess Ss' ability to use the language, in which case you need to monitor but avoid helping them. You may feel that you don't need or have time to do all the activities. If so, you could allocate the activities that would be most beneficial for your Ss, or get individual Ss to decide which activities they'd like to do in class.

## SAYINGS

**1A** You could run this as a board race. Tell Ss to close their books and put them into two or three teams. Write the pairs of prompts on the board one at a time. One student from each team runs up to the board and tries to write the saying in full. Award a team point to the first student to write the saying accurately.

**Answers:** 1 Let's cross that bridge when we come to it. 2 Nothing ventured, nothing gained. 3 When in Rome do as the Romans do. 4 Once bitten, twice shy. 5 Where there's life there's hope. 6 Where there's smoke there's fire. 7 What goes around comes around. 8 Every cloud has a silver lining.

**B** Ss could either work in pairs for this or stay in their teams if you did a board race in Ex IA. The first pair or team member to run to the board and write all three sayings correctly wins points.

**Answers:** 1 We'll cross that bridge when we come to it. 2 Where there's life there's hope. 3 What goes around comes around.

**C** Ss work alone on paraphrasing three sayings. Circulate and check that they don't use any of the words from the original sayings.

**D** Ss can work in pairs or small groups for this.

## NARRATIVE TENSES

**2A** Start by asking Ss to read the text quickly and answer the question: *Does the man spend more time working on his house or his garden? (his garden).* Vocabulary to check: *a limp* (a way of walking when one leg is hurt), *fall apart* (be in very bad condition), *collapse* (fall down suddenly). Then Ss can work alone or with a partner to complete the gaps. You could also refer them to the **Language bank** on p134 to check the rules for narrative tenses.

**Answers:** 1 was 2 had lived/had been living 3 was falling apart 4 hadn't painted 5 looked 6 walked (or *used to walk*) 7 was always working 8 always said (or *used to say*) 9 came 10 'd never walked 11 looked 12 saw 13 was watching 14 'd been watching 15 came

**B** Give Ss a few minutes in pairs to brainstorm possible endings, then to write the one they like best. You could make this more challenging by giving them a specific number of words to use (e.g. thirty) or by telling them to include three different narrative tenses. Ss can read out their endings and the class votes on the best one.

## EXPRESSING REGRET

**3** Ss work alone or with a partner to correct the phrases.

**Answers:** stomached – gutted  decisions – thoughts  sadness – pity  possibility – opportunity  hitting – kicking  looking back – hindsight

Ss could write a reply to Charlotte from Bea, sympathising/ offering advice/telling her about something job-related that she regrets, etc.

## I WISH, IF ONLY, SHOULD HAVE

**4A** Do the first one as an example, then tell Ss to write the rest of the sentences in their notebooks. Point out that they need to think carefully about which other words to change in the original sentence (e.g. *too little* changes to *more*, not *too much*).

**Answers:** 1 I wish I'd finished university. 2 If only I'd spent more time with my friends in secondary school. 3 I should've travelled more when I was younger. 4 I wish my partner liked the same kinds of music as me. 5 If only I had an interesting job./If only I didn't have a boring desk job. 6 I wish I had enough/more time for sport.

**B** You could tell Ss to write their wish list on a separate piece of paper, so that they can pass it on to another student (see alternative suggestion below). Topics for Ss to use in their 'wish list' could be: studies, childhood, jobs, travel, family, friends, relationships, hobbies, appearance, health, etc.

**C** You could demonstrate this using two *strong Ss* in an open pair. Alternatively, for more written practice, you could collect in Ss' wish lists and redistribute them for another student to complete. Ss then have to guess whose wish list they were given.

## EXPRESSING LIKES AND DISLIKES

**5A** You could run this as a competition. Tell Ss to close their books and put them into teams of three to five. Write the words in the box on the board, then display the sentences one at a time. Teams confer and put their hands up when they have an answer and you award points for correct answers. You could award extra points if Ss can finish the phrase convincingly.

**Answers:** 1 into 2 What 3 that 4 thing 5 get 6 fan 7 stand

**B** If Ss were in teams for 5A, they could continue to win points by putting the phrases into the past.

**Answers:** 1 I was really into … 2 What I loved about it was … 3 I wasn't that keen on … 4 The thing I liked most about it was … 5 I just couldn't get into … 6 I was a big fan of … 7 I couldn't stand …

**C** You could start by giving an example of your own as a model for Ss. Tell them the name of the programme, what type of programme it was, what you liked/disliked, what other people in your family thought of it, etc. Emphasise that Ss should write notes rather than full sentences, so they sound more natural when they're speaking.

**D** Monitor this practice and make notes of good language use and areas for remedial work. In feedback, invite a few Ss to report back about their partner's TV programme, then give Ss some examples of their good use of language and errors for them to discuss and correct.

# 5 IDEAS

## OVERVIEW

**BBC VIDEO PODCAST**
If you could start a business, what would it be?

This video podcasts looks at the topic of the starting your own business. Use the video podcast at the start or the end of Unit 5.

## BRIGHT IDEAS?

### Introduction
Ss practise reading and speaking about inventions and change, using articles and vocabulary related to change. They also learn about compound nouns.

### SUPPLEMENTARY MATERIALS

Resource bank p163 and/or p165

NB: There is a lot of work on vocabulary in this lesson, so it would be particularly helpful for Ss to have access to monolingual dictionaries.

Ex 2C: Ss could use monolingual dictionaries.

Ex 3A: prepare a handout with the complete sentences. (see *Alternative idea*)

Ex 5A: Ss could use monolingual dictionaries.

Ex 7C: Ss could use monolingual dictionaries

### Warm up
Put Ss into small groups of three or four to discuss how the world has changed in the last fifty years/in their lifetimes. Write the following prompts on the board to guide their discussion: *communication, travel, work, leisure, food, health, home.* After a few minutes conduct feedback, asking each group to share their ideas.

### READING

**1** Tell Ss to cover the texts on p56 and focus them on the photos. Elicit some ideas from the class as to why the car is one of the worst inventions and put Ss in pairs to write a reason for each invention. Then discuss the Ss' ideas as a class.

**2A** Ss should read the texts quickly, *skimming* them to get enough information to complete the headings. They will have a chance to read the texts in more detail in the next two stages.

**Answers:** 1 E 2 F 3 B 4 A 5 D 6 G 7 C

**B** Direct Ss to the example and point out that they're not looking for the exact words in sentences 1–7, just the same idea. Give Ss time to read the texts in more detail for this and to compare answers with a partner.

**Answers:** 2 mobile phones 3 nuclear power 4 fast food 5 (reality) TV 6 atomic bomb/nuclear weapons 7 a car

**C** You could do number 1 as an example with the class. Tell Ss to look carefully at the <u>form</u> of the verbs in the definitions/synonyms to help them find the words/phrases in the texts. If Ss have access to monolingual dictionaries they could use them to check their answers.

**Answers:** 1 frowned upon 2 have devastating effects (on) 3 courtesy of 4 booming 5 take over from 6 making its debut 7 numbered (phrase: (X's days are numbered) 8 wake up to

### Optional extra activity

If you want to give Ss some practice of this vocabulary, put the following questions on a handout or write/display them on the board and ask Ss to complete the gaps with the correct form of one of the words/phrases:

*1 Do you think e-books will ever _____ _____ _____ paper books? (take over from)*

*2 What kinds of business _____ _____ in your country at the moment? (be booming)*

*3 Do you know anyone who owns a house _____ _____ their parents? (courtesy of)*

*4 When did MP3 players _____ _____ _____ in your country? (make their debut)*

*5 What kinds of music were _____ _____ when your parents were teenagers? (frown upon)*

*6 What's the best way of making people _____ _____ _____ the dangers of smoking? (wake up to)*

Ss then work in pairs, asking and answering the questions.

**D** If Ss have trouble thinking of inventions, you could prompt with ideas, e.g. drugs, alcohol, money, computers, blogs, violent video games, food additives, plastic surgery.

## GRAMMAR articles

**3A** Tell Ss to cover the text on p56 before they start this exercise. You could do number 1 as an example with the class, then put Ss in pairs to help each other complete the rest. For *stronger classes*, once Ss have checked their answers with the text, tell them to discuss why the answer is *a(n)*, *the* or *( – )* in each case.

**Answers:** 1 The, – , – 2 a, the 3 – , the, the
4 the, the, the, the 5 – , – , the
*the is used here because it's followed by a phrase with *of*. Other examples include: *the end of* (the road), *the top of* (the stairs), *the music of* (Beethoven)

### Alternative idea

For *weaker classes*, or Ss who don't have an article system in their own language, omit Ex 3A. It may be too challenging if the Ss are unsure of the rules of usage. Instead, give Ss the complete sentences on a handout, or write/display them on the board. Ask Ss to underline all the examples of articles in the sentences and, in pairs, discuss why each one is used. Then move on to Ex 3B.

**B** Complete the first rule as an example with the class and ask Ss for examples of the rule from the sentences in Ex 3A. Ss work on the rest of the rules alone or in pairs, finding examples for each one.

**Answers:** 1 – (e.g. *British men and nineteen percent of women*) 2 a(n) (e.g. *a lawsuit*) 3 the (e.g. *The World Health Organisation, the fast food chain*) 4 the (e.g. *the modern automobile, the wealthy*) 5 – (e.g. *America*) 6 the (e.g. *in the late 1880s*)

**C** Demonstrate the two different ways of pronouncing *the*, then put Ss in pairs and tell them to take turns to read the sentences aloud to each other and listen for the pronunciation of *the*. In the meantime, write the sentences on the board so that you can ask Ss to come out and circle/underline *the* in feedback. Play the recording and check the answers with the class. Ss could also repeat after the recording.

**Answers:** 1 <u>The</u> interesting thing is that many of (the) people who hate it are (the) ones who watch it.
2 <u>The</u> automobile has done less well, however, since <u>the</u> economic crisis.
3 Those who voted for (the) car mentioned (the) harm it does to <u>the</u> environment as (the) biggest problem.

**D** Complete the rule with the class and point out that sometimes a word may begin with a vowel, e.g. *ones*, but the <u>sound</u> it begins with is a consonant sound: /w/.

**Answers:** vowel, consonant

---

**⟱ LANGUAGEBANK** 5.1 p136–137

The rules for using articles are presented in tabular form, which provide a concise record and may help visually oriented learners to clarify the differences. NB: If your Ss still feel overwhelmed by the number of rules, tell them to ask themselves: 'Is it something new/something general/something we already know?' You could set Ex A for homework or for extra practice in class if Ss have trouble with Ex 4.

**Answers:** 1 – 2 the 3 the 4 the 5 a 6 a 7 a 8 the
9 – 10 – 11 – 12 the 13 a 14 the 15 the 16 the
17 – 18 – 19 the/a 20 the

---

## PRACTICE

**4** Start by writing the title *Bicycle chosen as best invention* on the board and ask Ss to predict the following: *Which country do you think chose it? Why do you think it's the best? Which invention do you think came second, the internet, the radio, or computers?* Ss read the text quickly (without worrying about the missing articles at this stage) to see if their predictions were correct. Then discuss briefly with the class what they found surprising in the text and whether they think the results would be the same in their countries. Ss then complete the gaps and compare answers in pairs before feedback with the class. Vocabulary to check: *innovation, harness, trail behind.*

**Answers:** 1 The ('The humble' is often used to introduce something that is simple/not advanced, but useful, e.g. 'the humble match') 2 a 3 – 4 an 5 the (*the* is used with superlatives) 6 an 7 the 8 the 9 The 10 – 11 the 12 an

## VOCABULARY change

**5A** You could start by writing all the inventions in 1–8 on the board (Ss should have their books closed) and putting Ss in pairs to discuss how these inventions changed people's lives. Pronunciation to check: <u>micro</u>scope, <u>pest</u>icides, anti<u>bio</u>tics. After a brief feedback session with the class, set up the matching exercise. Ss could use monolingual dictionaries to check unfamiliar words. Pronunciation to check in feedback: trans<u>formed</u>, <u>altered</u>, bene<u>fi</u>cial, detri<u>men</u>tal, en<u>han</u>ced, dis<u>tort</u>ed, revolu<u>tion</u>ised.

**Answers:** 2 b) 3 e) 4 c) 5 d) 6 h) 7 f) 8 a)

**B** Give Ss a few minutes to discuss the phrases in pairs.

**Answers:** Changed: transformed, revolutionised
Positive: had a benefical effect on, enhanced
Negative: damaged, had a detrimental effect on

**C** Tell Ss to find three statements in Ex 5A that they <u>both</u> agree with and be prepared to give reasons for their choices.

**D** Put pairs of Ss together into groups of four or six. Encourage both Ss from each pair to speak to the group.

## SPEAKING

**6A** To generate ideas for this activity you could bring in some pictures (from magazines or the internet) of inventions and put them on the board or round the room. Suggestions: *kettle, calculator, light bulb, watch, sunglasses, pacemaker, radar, umbrella, vacuum cleaner, X-ray.* Ss work alone to write notes about two inventions. You could tell them to try to include at least two of the verbs/phrases from Ex 5.

**B** Once the pairs have agreed on the most important invention, they should spend a few minutes adding any more relevant information to the notes about it and making them as persuasive as possible for the next stage.

**C** Ss are now in groups of four, discussing two inventions. During this stage and the next monitor and make notes of good language use and any problem areas for feedback at the end.

**D** Ideally, put four pairs together so that you have eight Ss discussing four inventions. Emphasise that all eight Ss must agree on the final order of the inventions. To finish off you could invite one student from each group to come up and write their order on the board and have a class vote on the two most important inventions.

## VOCABULARY *PLUS* compound nouns

**7A** Focus Ss on the pictures and give them a minute or two to discuss what each invention is for and which were the most/least successful.

**B** Ss read and complete the entries alone, then compare answers with a partner. Ss should not worry about the exact meaning of the words in bold at this stage.

**Answers:** 1 jet pack  2 wrist radio  3 bottle top  4 ring pull

**C** Ss match the definitions alone or in pairs. They could use monolingual dictionaries to check their answers.

**Answers:** 2 outlook  3 breakdown  4 breakthrough
5 downside/drawback  6 outcome

**8A** Before Ss try to complete the gaps you could direct them back to the compound nouns in bold in Ex 7B and ask them how compound nouns are made. Then give Ss a few minutes to complete the information alone or with a partner.

**Answers:** 1 outlook, breakdown, breakthrough, downside, drawback, outcome  2 trade-off  3 breakdown, breakthrough, trade-off, drawback (but *off* and *back* are also adverbs)  4 outlook, outcome

**B** Emphasise that Ss only need to write the compound noun, not the complete sentence. They may need to listen again to check which part is stressed.

**Unit 5 Recording 2**
1 There's been a <u>break</u>through.
2 It's a <u>trade</u>-off between cost and safety.
3 The long-term <u>out</u>look is very good.
4 The <u>down</u>side is I get paid less.
5 There's only one <u>draw</u>back
6 There's been a <u>break</u>down in communications.
7 What was the <u>out</u>come of the meeting?

**C** Direct Ss to the encyclopaedia entries in Ex 7B and point out that each one is about two sentences long and contains at least two of the compound nouns they've studied. Put Ss in pairs to discuss and write their entries. Circulate and help as required.

**D** The entries could be stuck on the walls and Ss walk around guessing the inventions. In this way they see all the entries that the class has written.

**▶ VOCABULARYBANK** p152 Compound adjectives
Ex 2A and B move the Ss on from looking at compound nouns to compound adjectives. Ss complete the exercises individually then compare the answers in pairs. In feedback, explain that whilst many compound adjectives are hyphenated, some have become single words, e.g. *waterproof, handheld* and that this is something that tends to happen over time. However, in many cases, both the hyphenated and unhyphenated version of a compound adjective can be considered conrrect.

**Answers:** 2A 1 c)  2 i)  3 j)  4 a)  5 d)  6 e)  7 g)  8 f)
9 h)  10 b)
B A energy-efficient lightbulb  B handheld GPS system
C waterproof watch  D pocket-sized camcorder
E eco-friendly detergent  F solar-powered torch

**Homework ideas**
1 Workbook Ex 1–5, p32–33

2 Ss find a short, fairly simple text (e.g. on the internet) describing an important invention and blank out ten or more articles. They bring the gapped text to the next lesson for their partner to complete.

3 Ss write a paragraph each about what they consider to be the best and the worst invention of all time. They should aim to include at least two of the vocabulary items related to change, two compound nouns and two of the words/ phrases from Ex 2C.

4 Ss do Ex 1A on p152 (**Vocabulary bank**) in preparation for the next lesson, which is about advertising.

# CONSUMER CRAZY

## Introduction

Ss practise listening and speaking about advertising using conditionals and related vocabulary. They also learn to make written comparisons and write a report.

### SUPPLEMENTARY MATERIALS

Resource bank p164 and/or p166

Warm up: Bring in a variety of advertisements from glossy magazines.

Ex 1A: prepare A4-sized copies of the six questions in the questionnaire.

Ex 2A: Ss should use monolingual dictionaries.

Ex 2B: be prepared to give an example from your experience.

Ex 6B: provide paper and coloured pens, etc. if Ss are making posters (see *Optional extra activity*)

## Warm up

Bring in a variety of magazine adverts.

<u>Either</u>: put Ss in pairs or small groups and give each pair/group an advert to discuss: they should decide whether it's effective and why/why not, then share their ideas with the rest of the class in feedback.

<u>Or</u>: display the adverts on the walls and ask Ss, working with a partner, to walk round discussing which advert they like best/ least and why. Conduct feedback and see if there is a clear winner/loser.

### LISTENING

**1A** Write the title of the questionnaire on the board and check that Ss understand *IQ* (intelligence quotient, or level). Tell Ss to cover Ex 2 before they start looking at the questions.

#### Alternative idea

To encourage more discussion during this activity copy the questions (and question numbers) onto pieces of A4 paper or card. Tell Ss to write the numbers 1–6 in their notebooks so they can keep a record of their answers.

Either: put Ss into small groups and give them one question each to discuss and make notes on, then on a signal from you they pass their question to the right. This continues until they've answered all six questions.

Or: display the questions on the board and Ss discuss them in pairs, making notes on their answers.

**B** Ss listen and confirm or change the notes they made in Ex 1A. Vocabulary to check: *saturated* (describing a market = 'overcrowded with products'), *intuitively* (based on feelings rather than evidence), *lacquer* (a liquid painted onto wood or metal to make it shiny).

**Answers:** 1 200  2 above  3 oil or lacquer, cigarette smoke  4 ten past ten; because it's a positive image: it looks like either a smile or a tick  5 a) red; b) green; c) blue; d) purple; e) yellow and orange  6 Because it suppresses the appetite

**2A** Give Ss a few minutes to decide on the alternatives and look up any words that they can't guess from the context, then play the recording again. Ss can confirm/change their answers in pairs before feedback with the class.

**Answers:** 1 saturated  2 Choice  3 cheaper  4 costs  5 stylist, oil  6 sad  7 precision  8 children

**B** Ask Ss to think of examples from their personal experience, which support or contradict the statements. You could start by giving an example of your own, e.g. of a time when you bought something even though it cost more than a similar product. Alternatively, you could ask Ss to discuss which of the expert's theories they found the most interesting.

### Unit 5 Recording 3

I = Interviewer  E = Expert

I:  We often hear that competition is beneficial but how exactly does it work?

E:  OK. Let's imagine a Coke machine somewhere, anywhere, selling a hundred cans a day. Now, Pepsi comes along and puts up a machine next to it, how many cans would each machine sell?

I:  Fifty?

E:  That's what most people think. In fact, each machine would probably sell two hundred cans a day, unless the market was saturated.

I:  That's hard to believe … What's the explanation?

E:  Well, what happens is that the question in the consumer's mind is no longer 'Should I get a Coke or not?' but 'Which soft drink should I get?' Choice makes people want things.

I:  Ah, that's interesting. What about pricing?

E:  Well, there are several schools of thought on this. People are expected to think 'If I see two similar products at different prices, I'll buy the cheaper one' but, in fact, that's often not how consumers behave. For example, if I were to introduce a new lipstick and I wanted to compete with a product priced at 4.99, should I price mine above or below the competition?

I:  OK – I have a feeling you're going to tell me above, but it seems natural to undercut your competitor.

E:  We've found that with certain types of products, if you price your product just above the competition's price – so let's say 5.49 – you'll actually end up with a bigger share of the market.

I:  Why's that?

E:  We intuitively feel that if something costs more, it's better. People will pay more provided the difference is small. They'll think, 'Well, why not? I deserve the best.'

I:  OK. Turning to the appearance of advertisements, what tricks are used to make products more appealing?

E:  Take this advertisement for a hamburger chain. Big picture of a juicy hamburger with fresh tomatoes and lettuce …

I:  Makes me hungry just looking at it.

E:  Yes, it's fine to look at ….as long as you don't eat it. It probably has a hundred percent beef in it, real tomatoes and lettuce … but to make it so shiny, a food stylist has painted the meat with oil or maybe lacquer; and what appears to be steam rising off the meat is probably cigarette smoke blown onto the hamburger just before the picture was taken.

I:  I've just lost my appetite.

E:  And look at these advertisements for watches. What time is it on this watch?

I:  Ten past ten.

E:  And on these?

I:  Ten past ten – in all of them. Why's that?

E:  There are two theories. One is that with the hands in this position, the face of the watch conveys a smile. The other theory is that it's a bit like a tick symbol. In either case the consensus is that the message is positive.

I:  And if a watch showed 8.20 it wouldn't sell as well?

E:  Presumably not. 8.20 is a very sad-looking time.

I:  What about colour in advertising?

E:  It's crucial. We have built-in associations for every colour, for instance red is associated with risk and with energy, so you see it in adverts for energy drinks, cars and sports equipment. Green on the other hand denotes safety, so it's often used for medical products. Yellow and orange supposedly stimulate the appetite, so they're used for food ads; blue on the other hand suppresses the appetite … it's linked more to intellect and precision, so you see it in adverts for high-tech products. And purple is an interesting one: surveys show that around seventy-five percent of young children prefer purple to all other colours. So you'll see bright purple in advertising for toys for example.

I:  Well, thank you. I'll never shop the same again. And neither will our listeners.

### Extra idea

For *stronger classes* do some work with the following verb+noun collocations from the listening. Put Ss into small groups and write the first part of each collocation on the board. The groups race to complete all the collocations and are awarded points for each correct one. Further points can be awarded for good example sentences using the collocations.

*introduce a new product (to the market)*

*price (a product)*

*undercut (a competitor)*

*saturate (the market)*

*stimulate (the appetite)*

*suppress (the appetite)*

## GRAMMAR conditionals

**3A**  This should be mainly revision for Ss at this level, although the use of the more formal *If I were to …* may be unfamiliar. Some Ss may also not be used to seeing *should* for advice as one of the alternatives in the main clause. *Stronger classes* could cover a–d and work in pairs to name the types of conditional and highlight the form in sentences 1–4, before doing the matching task. In feedback point out that the order of the two clauses can be reversed and that when the *if* clause is second there is no comma in front of it.

**Answers:** 1 b)  2 a)  3 d)  4 c)

**B**  Tell Ss they need to write *zero, first* or *second* in gaps 1a)–c). You may also want to check *hypothetical* (not real) and *likely* (will probably). Ss work in pairs then check answers with the class.

**Answers:** 1a) second  1b) first  1c) zero  2 were to

**C**  You could do this with the whole class or give Ss a minute or two to find the conjunctions alone first. Elicit/point out that *as long as* is less formal than *providing/provided*.

**Answers:** if and only if as long as, providing/provided if not unless

**4A**  You may need to play the recording twice for Ss to write down the complete sentences. Give them a minute or two to check what they've written with a partner.

### Unit 5 Recording 3

1   I'll <u>buy</u> it if you bring the <u>price</u> down.
2   I'd <u>buy</u> it if it weren't so <u>expensive</u>.
3   If I were to get a <u>luxury</u> car, it'd be a <u>Ferrari</u>.
4   I'll <u>come</u> as long as you let me <u>pay</u>.
5   You <u>can't</u> come in unless you're a <u>member</u>.

**B**  Put Ss in pairs to underline the stressed word in each clause, reminding them that the stress falls on the word which carries the meaning. You may only need to play the recording one more time, stopping after each sentence for Ss to repeat and confirm their answers.

**⟫ LANGUAGEBANK** 5.2 p136–137

Ss can read the grammar summary at home or in class. Point out the use of *suppose/supposing* and *imagine* instead of *if* (under 'spoken grammar'), especially if you intend to give Ss Ex B and C for practice. For a mixed ability class, you could give Ex A to *weaker Ss* and Exs B and C to *stronger Ss*. Then give out answer keys for Ss to check their own work.

**Answers:** A 1 'll ask  2 sent, were to send  3 to have  4 would/might give  5 don't call  6 rains  7 isn't  8 to agree
B 1 provided  2 unless  3 Supposing  4 Providing  5 unless  6 Imagine
C 1 you promise to keep it a secret.  2 they don't pay our expenses.  3 to lose your job tomorrow.  4 we don't have enough time.  5 you don't stop being aggressive with me.  6 to meet them in the street.

## PRACTICE

**5A**  To familiarise Ss with the text before they choose the correct alternatives, tell them to read it through quickly and answer these questions: *What is a viral advert?* (a video that spreads via email) *Do they always work?* (No, only if they are funny/entertaining/clever enough). Vocabulary to check: *launch* (start), *susceptible* (easily influenced), *novel* (new and unusual), *smart* (clever), *edgy* (innovative). Ss can work on the alternatives alone or in pairs, then check answers with the class.

**Answers:** 1 would  2 providing  3 will  4 As long as  5 grows  6 provided  7 will spread  8 were to send  9 Unless  10 won't

**B**  You could give an example of your own first, either describing a viral advert or a TV/internet advert.

## SPEAKING

**6A**  Give Ss a few minutes in pairs to read the guidelines and discuss how effective they think the advert would be.

**Answers:** mosquito repellent

**B**  Put Ss in pairs and tell them to follow the pattern: situation – problem – solution and give them up to ten minutes to work out a sequence of events and make notes to use as prompts in the next stage.

**C**  Join pairs into groups of four or six to tell each other about their adverts. The other students decide if it would be entertaining enough to catch on and, if necessary, make suggestions for improvements. Encourage the listeners to use conditionals when giving feedback on the ideas, e.g. *I think this would be really effective because …; If you (changed)…, people (might/would)…; I think it would work better if you …*, etc.

## Optional extra activity

1 For Ss who enjoy acting:

Put Ss into small groups to work out the advert, then give them time to practise acting it out. One student can be chosen to provide a 'voiceover', commenting on and explaining what's happening in the advert. Ss then act out their advert for the class.

2 For Ss who enjoy being creative:

Ss create a poster for their advert, describing what happens and illustrating it with pictures. They then present their poster to the class. You will need to provide large sheets of paper, coloured pens, etc. for this option.

For both options, there can be a vote at the end to decide on the best advert.

## VOCABULARY advertising

**7A** Start by discussing with the class what different things advertisers can do to make sure consumers notice their product (e.g. invent a short phrase that people will remember, or an image that will remind people of the product, get someone famous to say they use it, etc.) Then direct Ss to the words in the box and complete the first question with the class, as an example. Ss can work alone or with a partner. They may need to consult monolingual dictionaries. In feedback, check the difference between: *make* and *brand (a brand is the 'identity' of a product, which may include the name, symbol, colour combination, e.g. Coca-Cola, whereas the make simply refers to the company that makes the product, e.g. Ford) jingle* and *slogan*. Pronunciation to check: *comme̲rcials, endo̲rse, promo̲te, lo̲gos, campa̲igns, slo̲gans, i̲nfluence, adve̲rtise*. Also point out that *cold call* can be a noun or a verb.

**Answers:** 1 commercials 2 slogans 3 makes 4 brands
5 endorse/promote 6 logos 7 influence 8 jingle
9 campaigns 10 advertise 11 pop-ups 12 cold calls

**B** Put Ss in pairs and tell them to take turns to ask/answer the questions. Conduct feedback, asking a few Ss to comment on their partner's most interesting answers.

> ➡ **VOCABULARY BANK** p152 Advertising and business
> Ex 1A and B consolidate and extend the Ss vocabulary for the topic of advertising and business. Ss should discuss and complete the two exercises in pairs, using a dictionary to check anything they are not sure about. Feedback as a class, eliciting example sentences containing the collocations where possible.
>
> **Answers:** 1A 2 a meeting 3 a price 4 a business
> 5 a market
> B 1 demonstrate, promote 2 postpone, cancel
> 3 increase, reduce 4 manage, expand 5 re-enter, see a gap in

## WRITING a report

**8A** Tell Ss to cover the right hand column of the page. Elicit some examples of gadgets, e.g. digital camera, MP3 player, mobile phone, watch, cordless headphones, video game console, then give Ss a few minutes to write their list of factors.

**B** Put Ss in pairs to compare their lists and to explain their order to each other.

**9A** Check that Ss understand the term *smartphone*: a mobile phone that can also send and receive email, browse the internet, etc. Direct them to the list of factors on the left hand side of the chart to compare with the list they made in the previous stage. Then give them a minute or two to answer the question.

**Answers:** 1 men: most: useful/practical features least: price
2 women: most: fashionable least: size
3 teens: most: my friends have the same least: brand loyalty

**B** Once Ss have read the report they could work with a partner on the questions, then check their answers with the class.

**Answers:** 1 All the factors are mentioned except 'fashionable'.
2 The student wrote that price is more important for men than for women, but the opposite is true.
3 first: introduction, second: highlighting similarities for men and women, third: highlighting differences for men and women

## LEARN TO make written comparisons

**10** Point out to Ss that a variety of phrases for comparing the different groups are used in the report, to avoid it becoming repetitive. Ss work alone finding the phrases, then compare answers in pairs.

**Answers:** 1 affect both groups more or less equally/there is no difference in/show only a slight variation
2 There are significant differences in/is/are far more important for men than for women/place greater importance on/showed an interesting contrast to
3 First of all/For example/However/On the other hand

**11A** Direct Ss to the chart and elicit the most obvious difference, i.e. the importance that teenagers place on friends having the same phone. Point out that Ss could use the phrase *far more important* for this point of contrast. Put Ss in pairs to note down four more points and choose appropriate phrases to use with them.

**Possible answers:** The fact that their friends have the same is far more important for teenagers than for men and women.
Teenagers place more importance on the price of the phone.
There is very little difference in how much brand loyalty or looking successful affect their choice; the same is true of price and how fashionable the phone is.
Teenagers place less importance on usefulness and practical features than both men and women.
One factor affects all three groups more or less equally: the results for size show only a slight variation.

**B** Ss could work alone or help each other to write the paragraph about teenagers. Circulate and help them to use the phrases accurately.

## Homework ideas
Workbook Ex 1–5, p34–35

# WHAT DO YOU THINK?

## Introduction

Ss read about and practise brainstorming ideas, using phrases for suggesting ideas and related vocabulary. They also practise listening and learn to show reservations.

### SUPPLEMENTARY MATERIALS

Resource bank p167

## Warm up

Ask Ss to close their books and put them in pairs. Tell them to discuss and make a list of as many ideas as they can for making sure they only speak English in class. After three minutes, invite Ss to share their ideas and see which are the three most popular. NB: This topic is also used in the **Workbook**, p36, Ex 1A: Ss could refer to the ideas there and see if there are any they didn't think of.

### READING

**1A** If you used the warm up idea, elicit from Ss that this was an example of 'brainstorming'. Discuss the questions with the whole class, or give Ss a few minutes to discuss them in pairs first.

**Possible answers:** Brainstorming involves generating and writing down as many ideas as you can on a topic, usually with a group of people. It's used by companies, e.g. for problem solving, for developing/naming/marketing a new product, etc.

**B** Ask Ss what 'it' could refer to in the first sentence, then give them a few minutes in pairs to look at the other sentences.

**C** Tell Ss that each of the five sentences in Ex 1B refers to one of the five 'rules' and give them a minute or two to read and compare their ideas.

**Answers:** 1 quantity 2 a predictable or absurd idea 3 criticise an idea 4 the shy people 5 write down the ideas

### VOCABULARY adjectives

**2A** Direct Ss to the adjectives in bold and put them in pairs to discuss the meaning of any they are familiar with, then match the definitions. Pronunciation to check: *weird, obscure, absurd*.

**Answers:** 2 awful – dreadful 3 impractical – unrealistic 4 aiming very high – ambitious 5 obvious – predictable 6 not obvious – obscure 7 senseless – absurd 8 clever, excellent – brilliant

**B** You could suggest that Ss think of real examples for this practice, e.g.

A: *The weather was awful yesterday, wasn't it?*
B: *Yes, it was dreadful;*
A: *I thought (X) was a really clever film.*
B: *Yes, it was brilliant, wasn't it?* etc.

### FUNCTION suggesting ideas

**3A** Introduce the topic, asking Ss why children don't like eating vegetables and what their parents did to try to make them eat vegetables when they were young. Then give them a few minutes in pairs to discuss and write down three ideas (at least).

**B** Ss can tick any ideas that they thought of and add new ones to their list. Briefly discuss with the class which idea(s) they liked best.

**Answers:** 1 purple vegetables 2 giving a prize to kids who eat two veggies a day 3 a school gardening programme 4 what happens if you don't eat your veggies 5 forbidding kids to eat vegetables 6 vegetarian recipes on cereal boxes or websites 7 viral campaign featuring a video with a celebrity (maybe a rapper)

### Unit 5 Recording 5

A: OK, let's try to do this quickly. We've got just a few minutes. Who's taking notes?
B: I'll do that.
A: Good. OK, let's brainstorm.
C: Colour. Purple vegetables.
B: Purple vegetables. Yeah.
A: Or a competition. A prize to kids who eat their two veggies a day.
B: OK …
A: Or a gardening programme in schools.
B: What do you mean?
A: If kids grow vegetables, they'll want to eat them.
B: Right.
C: Have the opposite? What happens if you *don't* eat your veggies.
B: I'm not sure about that.
A: Hey, we're brainstorming.
C: OK. How about this? Forbid them from eating vegetables, at school at least. No veggies allowed. Then they'll want them.
B: I'll write it down … any more?
A: Something with recipes, like put vegetarian recipes on the back of cereal boxes.
B: Or on websites.
A: Viral campaign. Short video with a celebrity. A famous rap star rapping about eating vegetables.
C: OK.
A: Is that it?

**4A** While they listen, Ss cross off any ideas on their list that are rejected and write the reasons next to them. They circle the one that is chosen.

**Answers:** Reasons for rejecting ideas:
• purple vegetables: supposed to be healthy but would need to use chemicals to colour the vegetables
• giving a prize to children who eat two veggies a day: not original, difficult to organize
• a school gardening programme: too complicated to set up
• vegetarian recipes on cereal boxes or websites: wouldn't mean anything to kids and the point is to get children to eat a more balanced diet, not to make them vegetarians.
Idea chosen:
• viral video, but with fantasy characters, not a celebrity

**B** Give Ss a chance to look through the phrases first and try to predict/remember what was said. Ss could also copy the sentences into their notebooks to give themselves more space to complete the gaps. Play the recording again, then put Ss in pairs to compare their answers before group feedback.

**Answers:** 1 do you feel 2 about 3 you consider 4 strike* 5 'd be great 6 Suppose we
(*In phrases like *How does it strike you?* or *It strikes me as strike* means *think*)

**C** You may want to drill the phrases with the whole class before putting Ss into pairs to practise.

> **Teaching tip**
> To help Ss to hear the movement in pitch you will need to exaggerate your model when drilling and encourage Ss to imitate you. You can indicate that the phrase starts on a high pitch and gradually falls by using your hand. Point out to Ss that using a higher pitch is important because it makes the speaker sound interested/polite, whereas a low pitch can sound bored/rude.

**D** Put Ss in pairs to order the phrases. After checking their answers, you could drill the phrases, once again modelling a mid-high pitch range to show politeness (especially important when disagreeing with someone's ideas in a discussion).

**Answers:** 1 It's not original enough  2 I think it's too complicated to set up.  3 It doesn't grab me. ('grab me' means 'capture my attention', 'inspire me')  4 I think we're on the wrong track.  5 I'm torn between that idea and the viral campaign. (or 'I'm torn between the viral campaign and that idea')  6 Let's go with that.

**Unit 5 Recording 6**

A: OK, let's look at the list and cut it down. Here, I'll put these up on the screen.
B: How do you feel about this idea? The purple vegetables? You know kids, they love purple.
C: Actually, that could be a problem. We're trying to sell something healthy and we put a chemical in it to make it look attractive.
A: Good point, yeah. What about having a competition? If the prize is right, children will do anything.
C: Oh, so whoever eats the most vegetables in an hour wins?
A: No, I was thinking of whoever eats two vegetables a day for a week or something …
C: To be honest, it wouldn't be my first choice.
B: It's not original enough. And too difficult to organise.
A: Would you consider the gardening campaign? We set up little vegetable gardens near schools … maybe even have a competition …
B: Yeah, they could send in photos to a website and …
C: Well frankly, I think it's too complicated to set up. We need something that's fairly simple in terms of organisation. Something that we can control and monitor easily.
A: How does the recipe idea strike you?
B: It doesn't grab me. Sorry.
C: I was going to say the same. To put it bluntly, it's all wrong. It wouldn't mean anything to the kids, maybe only to their parents.
A: Fair enough.
C: Uh, with respect, I think we're on the wrong track here.
A: Yeah?
C: I think it'd be great if we could get kids into vegetarianism.
B: What do you mean?
C: Well, you know how all children love animals … we could use that to make them want to stop eating meat, maybe use cute pictures of animals next to meat.
A: Oh no, that's gross! Anyway, the point is not to make children vegetarians, just to get them eating a more balanced diet.
B: I agree. I know this sounds weird but we could go for a 'negative' campaign. It could be done in a funny way. We could use fantasy characters in a cartoon …
A: As a matter of fact I was thinking of that myself. The ones who don't eat their veggies are the weak ones …
C: Yeah …
A: So what do we think?

B: At the moment I'm torn between the cartoon and the viral campaign … a rapper would be perfect …
C: Suppose we try combining the two ideas and have a viral campaign but not with a celebrity, with cartoon characters?
B: I like it.
A: OK, let's go with that.

**⟱ LANGUAGEBANK** 5.3 p136–137

Refer Ss to the tables in the **Language bank** so they can see the phrases for suggesting and reacting summarised. Ex 5A could be done in class as preparation before Ss move on to the flow chart on p63.

> **Answers:**
> A: What do you **think** about naming our language school 'Tongues4U'?
> B: That's an awful idea.
> C: How do you **feel** about Talk2Me?
> A: It doesn't **grab** me.
> B: I think it's not **original** enough.
> C: Would you **consider** English246?
> B: I think we're on the wrong **track** here. All these numbers.
> A: How does *Language Lab* **sound**?
> B: Hmmm … Not bad.
> C: I'm torn **between** *Language Lab* and *Lingo Lab*.
> A: Lingo is a bit **obscure**.
> B: Let's **go** with *Language Lab* then.
> C: That's a **brilliant** idea.

**5A** Ss could brainstorm their own ideas for getting people to walk to work before looking at the list here. Discuss briefly with the class which idea(s) they think is (are) best and why.

**B** Ss should write out the full conversation in their notebooks, so they can use the prompts here for practice in the next stage. Point out that they need to be careful with the verb forms in the phrases and refer them back to the **Language bank** if they need to check.

> **Answers:**
> A: How do you feel about putting articles in popular newspapers?
> B: It doesn't grab me.
> A: How does the idea of using a celebrity strike you?
> B: It's not original (enough). I think we're on the wrong track. It'd be great if we could get (some) doctors to promote the idea.
> A: Would you consider a Walk to Work Week?
> B: I'm torn between that idea and using the doctors.
> A: Suppose we try combining the two ideas?
> B: OK. That seems like/to be the best suggestion.
> A: Right. Let's go with that.

**C** Remind Ss to use the prompts, rather than the full sentences they've written and to pay attention to their intonation. Monitor the practice and be prepared to give Ss feedback on their use of the phrases and their intonation.

### LEARN TO show reservations

**6A** You may want to explain to Ss that a 'reservation' in this context is a feeling of doubt about an idea. Put them in pairs to look at the comments.

**Answer:** 1–5 = negative  6 = neutral,

**B** Ss work alone or with a partner to find the missing words in the audio script.

**Answers:** 1 Actually  2 To be honest  3 Frankly  4 To put it bluntly  5 With respect  6 As a matter of fact

**C** Warn Ss that they should be careful how they use this comment. They will need to be especially careful with their intonation!

**Answer:** To put it bluntly ('bluntly' means in a direct and honest way, which may upset people)

### speakout TIP

Before directing Ss to the tip, you could tell them to read aloud to each other the negative comments in 6A <u>without</u> the missing phrases and ask them what effect they have (i.e. they sound very direct and could offend the person who made the suggestion).

**7A** Tell Ss to write the numbers 1–6 in their notebooks and to write a plus (+) or minus (-) sign next to the number when they hear the phrases.

**Answers:**
1 Actually, I think it's … (+)
2 Actually, I think it's … (-)
3 As a matter of fact, I feel that … (-)
4 As a matter of fact, I feel that … (+)
5 To be honest, it's quite … (-)
6 To be honest, it's quite … (+)

**B** Play the recording again, stopping after each phrase for Ss to repeat.

### SPEAKING

**8A** Put Ss in groups of three to five for this. Tell them to select a topic and brainstorm ideas following the 'rules of brainstorming' they studied at the beginning of the lesson. Tell them to write down all the ideas they generate, but not to comment on them yet.

**B** Remind Ss to try to incorporate some of the phrases for suggesting ideas and expressing reservations during the discussion and evaluation of the list of ideas. Monitor and note down examples of good language use and problem areas for feedback.

**C** Before Ss tell the class about their ideas, refer them back to the adjectives in Ex 2A and suggest they use one or two when explaining why they chose/rejected an idea, e.g. *We decided that it was too ambitious … At first it seemed a bit weird, but then we realised …*

**Optional extra activity**
While each group is presenting their idea, other Ss write down a question they'd like to ask about it. Then, at the end of each presentation, allow a few minutes for questions 'from the floor'.

**Homework ideas**
1 Workbook Ex 1–3, p36

2 Ss write a conversation based on the flow chart in Ex 5B, using one of the topics from Ex 8A.

3 Ss write an email telling a friend about the brainstorming session in Ex 8, explaining which was the best idea and why the others were rejected.

# GENIUS

## Introduction

Ss watch an extract from the BBC programme *Genius*, where people present ideas for new products or services and a celebrity guest decides if they are genius (very clever, brilliant). Ss then learn and practise how to present a business idea and write an advert for their product.

### SUPPLEMENTARY MATERIALS

**Ex 5B**: bring in examples of adverts with the 'problem → solution' structure.

**Ex 5C**: provide paper and coloured pens for Ss to prepare their advertisements.

## Warm up

Tell Ss to close their books and write the word *Genius* on the board. Explain that this is the name of a BBC programme and give Ss a few minutes in pairs to discuss what they think happens in the programme. Invite each pair to share their ideas with the class.

### DVD PREVIEW

**1A** Direct Ss to the statements, then give them a minute or two to read the text and decide in pairs if they're true or false. Vocabulary to check: *wild and wacky* (crazy and silly in an amusing way), *grill* (ask someone a lot of difficult questions), *provoke* (make people react).

> **Answers:** 1 F – Members of the public present their ideas. 2 T  3 F – The celebrity guest decides which ideas are 'genius'.

**B** Put Ss into pairs or small groups and tell them to think of at least one benefit and drawback for each of the ideas, as well as deciding on the most 'genius' idea. Conduct feedback with the whole class, to see if one idea emerges as the most popular.

> **Possible answers:**
> Sell socks in threes:
> Benefits – if a sock gets lost in the wash, you'll still have a pair.
> Drawbacks – you could end up with a lot of extra socks that you don't need.
> 'Democrobus:' Benefits – could cut down bus journeys because the bus won't stop unnecessarily.
> Drawbacks – time could be wasted discussing/arguing about where the bus should go.
> Food via taps: Benefits – saves a lot of time and effort.
> Drawbacks – would have to be a soft or liquid consistency that could go through a tap.

### ▶ DVD VIEW

**2A** Focus Ss on the questions and play the recording. NB You could pause the recording just after the 'piano choir' finishes singing and ask Ss to predict whether the idea will be judged 'genius' or not, then play the rest of the recording for Ss to see the decision. Ss discuss their answers to the questions in pairs, then with the class. They could also discuss what they think of the idea and whether they agree with the judge's decision. Vocabulary to check: *chorister* (a singer in a choir), *key* (the parts of a musical instrument that you press with your fingers to make it work), *keyboard* (row(s) of keys on a musical instrument like a piano).

> **Answers:** 1 People with the most potential (the possibility for development).
> 2 A 'piano choir': a choir which is controlled by the keys of a piano. Each member of the choir is linked to a different key on the piano.
> 3 Each member of the choir holds a candle shaped electric light, which is wired to the appropriate key on the piano: when the light goes on, the chorister sings their note.

**B** Put Ss in pairs and give them a few minutes to discuss the tips.

**C** As you play the recording again, Ss call *Stop!* when they see Dan doing/not doing something on the list of tips.

> **Answers:** Dan isn't over-prepared; he makes eye contact most of the time; he includes humour (he has a deadpan style which makes the audience laugh); he speaks clearly; he doesn't show his back.

### DVD 5 Genius

DG = David Gorman  DH= Dan Haythorn  L = Laurie  S = Stuart  V = Voice

**DG:** And, hello to you also. And hello to you. Hello and welcome to Genius: a show all about you and your ideas. If you think you might be a genius we can give you the chance to prove it: all you have to do is email us with your cleverest notion. We invite the people with the most potential to join us and it's here that we work out once and for all who really is a genius. OK Stuart, let's see what you make of our final idea tonight. It comes from Dan Haythorn from north west London.

**DH:** Dear Genius, imagine hooking a piano keyboard up to a choir, so that each key caused a different chorister to sing that note. Someone playing the keyboard would then be essentially playing a choir. I've never seen this done before and I would really like to.

**DG:** Would this, this choir … a person in the choir, a chorister, is that note. That's what they represent.

**DH:** Yeah, well each, note would, um, be assigned to a different chorister, so someone would be middle C, someone would be C sharp and etcetera the length and breadth of the keyboard. And, you press that key it would prompt them to sing that note.

**DG:** But it's not something an ordinary musician could ever own?

**DH:** No you couldn't have it at home really no, not unless … not unless you happen to have live a choir of some sort.

**DG:** We obviously, we thought about doing it in the studio and Thorin, our prop man, made an artist's impression of how he imagined it would look. He's imagining wires with lights from each key to the choir and we thought it was worthy of investigation so we have had a piano rigged up to lots of little candle lights. So if … if we can bring that in first of all.

Now just in case anyone thinks that this is just like a rehearsed thing and that this machine doesn't work I think we're the perfect people to prove that this is … this is real. OK, you can see we've got the white keys, the black keys that correlate precisely with the white keys and the black keys on this piano. You don't mind if we do this, do you Laurie?

**L:** Ah, no.

**DG:** OK. After all we built it. I think we should. Just hit anything you like at random, a kind of … What has he ever done to you? And, well I think that you should maybe give it a go. Laurie … you're the man who knows.

**L:** Mm, yeah. Any particular style?

**DG:** Um, I think we should go classical.

**L:** Something classical, OK.

**DG:** Now apart from making Dan's dream come true, is this idea Dan Haythorn and his piano choir – genius or not?

**S:** I think it's only begun to realise its potential. It's genius.

**V:** Genius.

## speakout a business idea

**3A** Put Ss in pairs and direct As and Bs to their list of business ideas. Give them a few minutes to read through their three ideas, then tell each other about them and choose one that they both like.

**B** Ss should aim to make their presentation about two to three minutes long. They also need to give their product a 'catchy' name and think about how they could use visuals in the presentation, e.g. a picture of the product, a graph showing sales forecasts, etc. While Ss prepare, circulate and help with vocabulary, etc. Ss could draw a table and make notes about their product in the first column, then complete the second column while they are listening to the presentation in the next stage.

|  | 1 | 2 |
|---|---|---|
| Name of product | | |
| Why is it such a good idea? | | |
| Where will it be sold? | | |

**C** Vocabulary to check: *yummy* (delicious), *pretzel* (a hard salty biscuit baked in the form of a stick), *gimmick* (a trick to make you want to buy the product), *dissolve* (become liquid), *disposable* (intended to be used for a short time and thrown away).

> **Answers:** 1 Yummy Utensils 2 They create no rubbish, because you can eat them, or if you throw them away, they dissolve. So they're environmentally friendly. 3 In the supermarket, with picnic supplies or in the snack section.

**D** Before you play the recording again, go through the key phrases with the class and check: *anticipate* (expect), *envisage* (imagine), *have expertise* (special skills or knowledge) *be a hit* (be popular), *differentiate oneself* (show a difference from) *track record* (the things a person or organisation has done which show how good they are at their job). Once Ss have listened again for the key phrases, you could elicit from the class ways of completing the following:

1 *We would like to introduce you to an idea* that (*will change the way you eat/think about travel/shop/sleep*).

2 *We have particular expertise in the field in that we have* (*studied/worked in/spent a lot of time in*).

3 *We differentiate ourselves from the competition by* (*using local products/giving customers a guarantee/providing excellent customer support*).

4 *Our track record shows that we can* (*meet deadlines, stick to a budget, keep costs down*).

Then give Ss time in pairs to practise saying the phrases to each other.

> **Answers:**
> We would like to introduce to you an idea that …
> What makes our idea special is that it's not just practical …
> We envisage this product being sold in supermarkets.
> We think that Yummy Utensils will be a hit with …

### Unit 5 Recording 9

W = Woman  M = Man

W: We would like to introduce to you an idea that will change the way you eat: Yummy Utensils. As you can guess, we're talking about knives, forks and spoons that you can eat.

M: You'll never have to throw plastic knives, forks and spoons in the rubbish again. At the end of your lunch, after you finish eating, you simply eat your utensils, like this.

W: Yummy Utensils are made of a special vegetable and flour mixture, are strong enough to cut meat and pierce salad, but easy to digest after you chew them.

M: They're tasty too – a bit like pretzels. Here, would you like to try one?

W: What makes our idea special is that it's not just practical and it's not a simple gimmick.

M: No, Yummy Utensils are not just practical and fun, they're also environmentally friendly. Just think of all of the resources that go into making plastic utensils, which are just thrown into the rubbish and become a permanent part of the waste that we litter the planet with. Yummy Utensils are made from natural ingredients, using the same processes as are used to make bread products and of course create no rubbish at all.

M: Even if you don't eat your Yummy Utensils and throw them in the rubbish, they dissolve within days. So there's no damage to the environment.

W: We envisage this product being sold in supermarkets, in the same section where you buy picnic supplies. But don't be surprised if they're sold in the snack section – they taste better than some snack foods. And they're certainly better for you.

M: We think that Yummy Utensils will be a hit with families in particular, since they're the biggest consumers of disposable utensils.

W: And kids love having a fork or spoon they can eat. We've done some market testing and it was amazing how much the children enjoyed them.

M: In the future we are planning to develop a sweetened version which will make Yummy Utensils the perfect dessert.

W: Thank you for your attention and we welcome any questions.

**4A** Direct Ss back to the presentation they prepared in 3B and suggest that they review it, adding some of the key phrases in appropriate places. They should also decide which of them is going to start the presentation and at what point they're going to hand over to their partner, etc. Then put the pairs together to help each other before they 'go public' with their presentations. Give Ss time in their pairs to make any changes to their notes.

**B** Encourage the Ss who are listening to make a few notes on each product and write any questions they have for the presenters. Ss then decide on the product they like best and vote for it.

## writeback a product leaflet

**5A** In pairs Ss look at the advert and discuss what they think of the product. Feedback as a class. Elicit what features it has that are supposed to make you want to buy the product (e.g. the picture, the way that the advert sets up a problem and gives you the answer).

**B** Ss match the features and compare answers with a partner.

> **Answers:** 3, 4, 1, 2

**C** Put Ss in pairs to prepare their advertisement. Provide paper and coloured pens if possible.

**D** Stick the advertisements on the board or round the walls.

> **Homework idea**
> Ss write an advertisement for another product from the lists they looked at in Ex 3A.

# LOOKBACK

## Introduction

The aim of these activities is to provide revision and further practice of the language from the unit. You can also use them to assess Ss' ability to use the language, in which case you need to monitor but avoid helping them. You may feel that you don't need or have time to do all the activities. If so, you could allocate the activities that would be most beneficial for your Ss.

### CHANGE

**1A** Before you start this, ask Ss to close their books and, in pairs, make a list of as many words as they can for talking about change in both a positive and negative way. Then tell Ss to look at the exercise and see if they remembered all the words. Focus them on the example and give them a minute or two to write their sentences.

**Answers:** 2 It's had a beneficial effect on the quality of life of people in the developing world. 3 It's damaged family relationships. 4 It revolutionised the way people think about war.

**B** You could discuss sentence 1 with the class, then put Ss in pairs to discuss the other three.

**Possible answers:** 1 TV, cinema, a violent video or computer game 2 medicine, better crops, provision of water pumps/wells, etc. 3 TV, computers/the internet 4 News broadcasts, 24 hour news, photographs of war, a particular war film

### ARTICLES

**2A** You could start by writing *basketball, windsurfing* and *scrabble* on the board and ask Ss to tell you as much as they can about them. Then put Ss in pairs to complete the questions. You may want to refer Ss to the section on articles in the **Language bank** on p136 while they work on this.

**Answers:** 1 The 2 – 3 a 4 The 5 – 6 the 7 a 8 – 9 a 10 an 11 the 12 the 13 – 14 the 15 the 16 – 17 the 18 –

**B** Give Ss a few minutes to answer the questions. You could ask one student from each pair to come and write their five answers on the board before checking on p160 and see which pair(s) had the most correct answers.

**Answers:** 1a 2b 3b 4c 5a

### CONDITIONALS

**3A** Tell Ss to close their books and write the title *Seducing Shoppers* on the board. Ask the class for ideas about what the text will say, then tell them to read the text quickly and see if they were right. You could also ask them to think of an alternative title for the text (e.g. On the shelf, The science of product placement, The right place, etc.). Then give Ss a few minutes to choose the alternatives and compare answers in pairs. They could refer to the **Language bank** on p136 to check anything they're unsure of.

**Answers:** 1 Supposing 2 would 3 could 4 would 5 are 6 will put 7 provided 8 would put 9 were to 10 wouldn't 11 are 12 unless

**B** Ss can discuss the questions in pairs or small groups, then share their answers with the class.

### ADVERTISING

**4A** You could run this as a competition in teams. Display one group of words at a time. When a team has the answer, they put up their hands and call out the missing vowels only. Then ask members of the team to tell you the complete words and give extra points for good pronunciation.

**Answers:** 1 advertise, promote, endorse 2 slogan 3 make, brand, logo 4 influence 5 advert, commercial, campaign

**B** Ss could continue to win points by explaining what each group of words has in common.

**Answers:** 1 all are verbs that refer to selling a product 2 all are made up of/consist of words 3 all are linked to a company name 4 all are verbs that refer to changing someone's thinking 5 all are nouns that refer to ways of selling a product

### SUGGESTING IDEAS

**5A** You could run this as a race. Put Ss in pairs and give each pair a copy of the conversation. As soon as a pair find and correct all the mistakes, they bring the exercise to you to check. Stop the race after two or three pairs have corrected the mistakes.

**Answers:** A: It's 'd be great if we could have the class party at a four-star hotel.
B. I think it's (much) too ambitious and expensive. How much do you feel about the school cafeteria?
C: That doesn't grabbing me. What How does Pizza Hut strike you?
A: I think we're on the wrong truck track here. That's not enough elegant enough.
B: OK. Supposed we try the Four Seasons or the Hilton?
A: Yeah, I'm tearing torn between the two, but the Four Seasons is closer.
C: OK. Let's go with that.

**B** If you feel it will be too challenging for Ss to memorise the whole conversation, give them a copy of the conversation with key parts blanked out. Tell Ss to practise the conversation using the 'skeleton' to help them, e.g.

A: _____ we could have the class party at a four-star hotel.

B. I think it's too ambitious and expensive. _____ the school cafeteria?

C: That_____ me. How _____ Pizza Hut _____?

A: I think we're _____ That's not elegant enough.

B: OK. _____ the Four Seasons or the Hilton?

A: Yeah, _____the two, but the Four Seasons is closer.

C: OK. _____ that.

**C** Elicit some reasons why the class might decide to have a party, e.g. end of course, new Ss joining the class, Christmas, etc. Get the class to choose one of the reasons and tell them they're going to plan the party. Put Ss in groups and remind them to appoint someone to write their ideas down. Write the five categories they need to brainstorm on the board: *place, food, activities, music, dress.* Give them time to brainstorm all the categories.

Remind Ss to try to use some of the phrases for suggesting ideas. They can write the phrases on a piece of paper, then tick a phrase every time they manage to use it in the discussion.

# 6 AGE

## OVERVIEW

## THE TIME OF MY LIFE

### Introduction

Ss practise reading and speaking about ages and generations using modal verbs and phrases and related vocabulary. They also learn about word formation.

### Warm up

<u>Either</u>: Prepare a handout with sayings about age (collections of sayings can be found on the internet), e.g.

*Age is an issue of mind over matter. If you don't mind, it doesn't matter.* Mark Twain

*Wrinkles should merely indicate where smiles have been.* Mark Twain,

*Do not regret growing older. It is a privilege denied to many.* Author Unknown

*Middle age is when your age starts to show around your middle.* Bob Hope

*Forty is the old age of youth; fifty the youth of old age.* Victor Hugo

*Growing old is mandatory; growing up is optional.* Chili Davis

*Youth is a disease from which we all recover.* Dorothy Fulheim

*Thirty-five is when you finally get your head together and your body starts falling apart.* Caryn Leschen

Put Ss in pairs to discuss what the sayings mean, which they agree with/like best, etc. then conduct feedback with the class.

<u>Or:</u> Put Ss in pairs and write *young, middle-aged* and *old* on the board. Ask them to:

1 decide on an age range for each group;

2 think of three adjectives they associate with each group.

Ss compare their ideas with the rest of the class in feedback. This will work best in a class where there is a range of ages and Ss will have different perceptions of what 'old' is, etc.

### SPEAKING

**1**  Direct Ss to the box and discuss the advantages and disadvantages of being ten years old as a class. Then put Ss in pairs to discuss the rest.

### VOCABULARY

**2A**  Focus Ss on the example and give them a few minutes to match the other phrases. Points to check in feedback: the phrases in 1–3 all need an appropriate possessive adjective; *elderly* is more polite than *old*; *maturity* is the noun from *mature* and is used with the verb *have*.

**Answers:** 1f 2c 3a 4e 5h 6g 7b 8d

**B** Put Ss in pairs to discuss the questions, then conduct feedback to find out where they agree/disagree. Monitor Ss' use of the vocabulary and help them with any pronunciation problems at this stage.

---

▶ **VOCABULARYBANK** p153

Ex 1A and 1B extend the topic of age and ageing into health and common ailments. You might introduce the activity by asking the Ss what sort of illnesses and health problems people commonly suffer from as they get older, so you can naturally review items which will come up in Ex B, such as *arthritis, stroke* and *near/shortsighted*. Allow the Ss plenty of time to match the symptoms to the pictures and to check their ideas in a dictionary before going on to make a diagnosis in Ex B. Feed back as a class.

**Answers:** 1 A 1 E 2 A 3 B 4 C 5 F 6 G 7 H 8 D 9 I
B a) 3 b) 8 c) 4 d) 9 e) 1 f) 7 g) 6 h) 2 i) 5

---

### READING

**3A** Direct Ss to the title of the website forum and give them a few minutes to read and match the ages to the entries. Vocabulary to check: *hang out with* (spend time with), *take someone/something for granted* (not to appreciate or show you are grateful), *outdo someone* (do better/be more successful than someone), *yell at* (shout at*), *outgrow something* (no longer need or want something as you grow older).

**B** Ss work in pairs and compare their answers

**Answers:** A 15 B 65 C 20 D 30 E 10 F 45

**C** Ss work alone then compare answers and underline any phrases that helped them choose the person/people.

**Answers:** 1 F *'... how comfortable I feel in my own skin. I've outgrown the need to seek other people's approval.'*
2 A *'I can stay out late now'*; C *'The best thing ... living away from home.' 'I only go when I feel like it.'*
3 B *'... it's the fear of growing older'*
4 B *'... we're lucky enough to have the money to do it.'* E *'I don't need to worry about money.'*
5 D *'I feel obliged to give everyone the impression that I'm successful. ... so I pretend I have a good job ...'*
6 F *'I don't have a worst thing ...'*

**3D** Put some prompts on the board for Ss to think about while they discuss this, e.g. *work, finances, friends, interests, relationships, health, future.*

---

### GRAMMAR modal verbs and phrases

**4A** You may want to check that Ss have identified the modal verbs correctly before directing them to complete the table (they could copy it into their notebooks so they have room to write these examples and the ones from Ex 4B). While Ss work in pairs to complete the table, draw it on the board. You can then invite Ss to come up and add the verbs during feedback.

**Answers:** 2 can  3 ought to  4 don't have to  5 mustn't
6 have to  7 had to  8 should

| obligation (strong) | *have to*<br>*had to* | prohibition | *mustn't* |
|---|---|---|---|
| obligation (weak) | *ought to*<br>*should* | permission | *can* |
| lack of obligation | *don't have to* | ability | *can* |

**B** Some of these phrases, e.g. *feel obliged to, be supposed to, be allowed to* will probably be less familiar to the Ss. Once they have matched the phrases to the rules, check the meaning and form (e.g. which verbs/phrases are followed by *to*) and ask Ss to add them to the table. Also check the positive forms *be allowed to* and *'ll be able to.*

**Answers:** 1 c)  2 d)  3 a)  4 h)  5 g)  6 e)  7 f)  8 b)

| obligation (strong) | *have to*<br>*had to*<br>*make*<br>*feel obliged to* | prohibition | *mustn't*<br>*not be allowed to* |
|---|---|---|---|
| obligation (weak) | *ought to*<br>*should*<br>*be supposed to* | permission | *can*<br>*let*<br>*be allowed to* |
| lack of obligation | *don't have to*<br>*don't need to* | ability | *can*<br>*won't be able to*<br>*will be able to*<br>*managed to* |

**5A** Tell Ss to write the numbers 1–6 in their notebooks and that they will hear two sentences for each number. Play the recording, stopping after each number to give Ss time to write.

**B** Ss may need to listen again in order to identify the stressed words. Ask them what the difference is between the positive and negative (in the positive, the modal verb is not stressed, it's a *weak form*). To practise this, you could drill only the stressed words in each sentence first, then drill the complete sentence, e.g.

*go   we must go*

*mustn't go   we mustn't go*

You may also want to point out to Ss that that after *must/ mustn't, can't, couldn't, shouldn't* the final *t* is dropped before a vowel, e.g. *You shouldn't listen to me.*

---

**Unit 6 Recording 1**

1   We must <u>go</u>. We <u>mustn't</u> <u>go</u>.
2   I can <u>come</u>. I <u>can't</u> <u>come</u>.
3   You should <u>listen</u> to me. You <u>shouldn't</u> <u>listen</u> to me.
4   We're supposed to <u>go</u>. We're <u>not</u> supposed to <u>go</u>.
5   You ought to <u>ask</u>. You <u>oughtn't</u> to <u>ask</u>.
6   You're allowed to <u>come</u>. You're <u>not</u> allowed to <u>come</u>.

▶ **LANGUAGEBANK** 6.1 p138–139

The **Language bank** has a summary of the present and past forms of all the modal verbs and phrases. There is also a note about the use of *was/were able to* and *managed to* vs *could*. Ss could do Ex A and B for homework, or use Ex B for oral practice as a team game: display the sentences one at a time on the board and the first team to put their hands up and say the correct answer wins a point.

**Answers: A** 1 had to  2 needed to  3 were supposed to  4 managed to  5 couldn't  6 able to  7 let  8 allowed to  9 have to  10 obliged to  11 can  12 should
**B** 1 I managed to fall asleep.  2 We were obliged to stay for dinner.  3 You're allowed to listen to your MP3 player here.  4 He wasn't able to see anything.  5 She ought to leave before dark.  6 We were supposed to pay before going in (but we didn't.)  7 Adults (over 18) aren't allowed to enter this disco.  8 We had to have a passport.

**Optional extra activity**

To give Ss more practice in manipulating the present and past forms of the verbs orally put Ss in pairs and give Student A and Student B a set of sentences each, e.g.

Student A
*1 I'm supposed to finish my work before I leave.*
*2 They're allowed to come with us.*
*3 We had to do lots of exams at school.*
*4 I can't afford a new car.*
*5 She didn't need to wear a uniform.*

Student B
*1 My brother never let me borrow his car.*
*2 Our teacher makes us work hard.*
*3 I feel obliged to invite him to the party.*
*4 We didn't have to get up early.*
*5 He never manages to catch the early bus.*

Ss take turns to read out one of their sentences. Their partner repeats the sentence, changing it into the past or present as appropriate.

## PRACTICE

**6A** Ss work alone to complete the sentences. Make sure they understand that in some cases there is more than one possible answer.

**Answers:** 1 won't be able  2 couldn't/wasn't able to  3 let  4 was supposed to  5 make you  6 manage to  7 'll be able to  8 don't have to/don't need to

**B** You could demonstrate this first by changing one or two of the sentences to give your opinion. Once Ss have compared their answers, ask them to report back on opinions that they had in common with their partner and/or which of their partner's opinions they found the most interesting/surprising/amusing.

## SPEAKING

**7A** Give Ss time alone to think about the three questions and make some notes for their answers. You may want to remind them to try to use the modal verbs and phrases and the vocabulary related to age.

**B** Put Ss in groups of three to five to discuss the questions. Monitor and make notes on language areas for improvement in feedback.

**Teaching tip**

To use feedback time for teaching, rather than simply correction of errors that Ss made in the speaking activity, make a note of things Ss say that are not incorrect, but very simple, or awkward. In feedback write the phrase/sentence on the board and encourage Ss to improve it with more sophisticated English. You could prompt them by writing up an 'improved' version with gaps in it, e.g.

original sentence: *I think I'm a young adult but old people think I'm a child.'*

improvement: *I think of <u>myself</u> <u>as</u> a young adult, but people from older generations <u>see</u> <u>me</u> as a child.*

## VOCABULARY *PLUS*   word formation

**8A** Give Ss a minute or two to complete the sentences and check answers with a partner.

**Answers:** 1 appreciation  2 achievements  3 preference  4 advice

**B** Ss should copy the table into their notebooks. While Ss work in pairs to complete the table, draw it on the board so that they can come up and add the nouns during feedback. Encourage Ss to use dictionaries.

**Answers:**

| -ion | -ment | -ence | -ice |
| --- | --- | --- | --- |
| appreciation | achievement | pretence | advice |
| reaction | involvement | interference | practice |
| obligation | judgement | preference | |
| impression | encouragement | | |

**9A** Put Ss in pairs to say the words to each other and try to identify the stress position. Point out that the stress stays the same in some pairs of nouns and verbs and shifts in others.

**Answer key:** 1 ap<u>pre</u>ciate, appreci<u>a</u>tion  2 o<u>blige</u>, obli<u>ga</u>tion  3 ach<u>ieve</u>, achieve<u>ment</u>  4 en<u>cour</u>age, encourage<u>ment</u>  5 pre<u>fer</u>, <u>pre</u>ference  6 inter<u>fere</u>, inter<u>fer</u>ence  7 ad<u>vise</u>, ad<u>vice</u>  8 <u>prac</u>tise, <u>prac</u>tice

**Teaching tip**

Show Ss a way of recording stress patterns which can help them to 'visualise' the pattern and avoids the distraction of the spelling. Use large circles for stressed syllables and small circles for unstressed syllables, e.g.

appreciate oOoo    appreciation oooOo

**9B** You could stop the recording after each pair of words for Ss to check and repeat.

## Unit 6 Recording 2

1 appreciate — appreciation
2 oblige — obligation
3 achieve — achievement
4 encourage — encouragement
5 prefer — preference
6 interfere — interference
7 advise — advice
8 practise — practice

**9C** Ss can work in pairs to complete the rules.

**Answers:** 1 -ice, -ment  2 –ion  3 -ence

### speakout TIP

Give Ss a minute or two to read the tip and think about how to change the sentence. Point out that they will need to use a verb with the noun they use to replace the original verb.

**Answer:** *We were having a discussion about which film to see but neither of us could make a decision and in the end we just had an argument about it.*

#### Optional extra activity
To provide more practice of the stress patterns Ss work in pairs and look at the box in Ex 8B. Student A says a verb and Student B responds with its matching noun. If Student A thinks the stress is correct, Student B says a verb and Student A responds with the noun and so on.

**10A** Give Ss a few minutes to complete the sentences alone. When they are ready, they can compare their completed sentences in small groups

**Answers:** 1 impress  2 obligations  3 reaction  4 advice 5 judge  6 pretence  7 practise  8 interfere  9 encouragement 10 preference

**B** Ss may also think that some of the sentences are true of both groups. Tell them to be prepared to justify their opinions in feedback.

#### Optional extra activity
Show Ss that many of the nouns they've been working with collocate with common verbs. Tell SS to write the headings *have, make* or *give* in their notebooks. Explain that you're going to read out some nouns and they need to write them under the verb they're often used with. Read out the nouns below in random order:

| have | make | give |
|---|---|---|
| a preference for | an impression on | advice |
| a reaction to | a pretence of | encouragement |
| an obligation | a decision | |
| an appreciation of | | |
| an argument about | | |
| a discussion about | | |

You could also give Ss some sentence heads to complete, e.g. *I hate having arguments about …*

*I've always had a preference for … rather than …*

*(name of film/book) made a great impression on me.*

*(name of person) always gives me good advice.*

*I think young people should be given a lot of encouragement to …*

### VOCABULARYBANK p153 Word formation

Ex 2A and B give the Ss more practice with word formation and build their awareness of the common patterns for the different parts of speech. Give them plenty of time to complete the table, using dictionaries to help, before feeding back as a class.

**Answers:**

| noun | verb | noun | verb |
|---|---|---|---|
| contribution | contribute | argument | argue |
| explosion | explode | development | develop |
| intention | intend | government | govern |
| invasion | invade | treatment | treat |
| completion | complete | investment | invest |
| creation | create | arrangement | arrange |
| noun | verb | noun | verb |
| defence | defend | reversal | reverse |
| offence | offend | removal | remove |
| occurrence | occur | disposal | dispose |
| existence | exist | approval | approve |
| coincidence | coincide | survival | survive |
| reference | refer | proposal | propose |
| noun | verb | noun | verb |
| closure | close | employee | employ |
| signature | sign | payee | pay |
| exposure | expose | addressee | address |
| mixture | mix | trainee | train |
| pleasure | please | interviewee | interview |
| failure | fail | divorcee | divorce |

#### Homework ideas
1 Ss write an entry about themselves for the website forum. They could also interview members of their family and write entries for them.

2 **Workbook** Ex 1–5, p37–38

3 **Vocabulary bank** Ex 2, p153

4 Ss imagine they're taking a course in something new, e.g. dancing, cookery, pottery, another language. They write an email to a friend telling them about the course and what they *have to do/are supposed to do/can't do/ don't need to do/aren't allowed to do* in the lessons, for homework, etc.

# FUTURE ME

## Introduction

Ss practise listening and speaking about the future using the future perfect and future continuous and vocabulary related to optimism/pessimism. They also learn to use linkers of purpose and write a letter.

### SUPPLEMENTARY MATERIALS

Resource bank p169 and/or p171

**Ex 1A:** be prepared to help Ss guess your four predictions for the year ahead.

**Ex 7A:** Ss should use monolingual dictionaries.

**Ex 9A:** be prepared to talk about your hopes and plans for the next five years.

## Warm up

Write this question on the board: *Do you feel optimistic or pessimistic about the future? Why?*

Give Ss a few minutes to think about their answer, then invite them to share their answers in small groups or as a class. To help Ss to focus their ideas you could also write the following prompts on the board: *work, health, transport, food, communication, energy, leisure time.*

### LISTENING

**1A** Tell Ss you are thinking about your life over the next year and write four sentence 'heads' on the board:

*I'll definitely … I'll probably …*

*I'm not likely to … I definitely won't …*

Give Ss clues so they can guess your answers. Give Ss a few minutes to think of their own answers.

**B** Ss either compare answers or do the same as above, i.e. write sentence 'heads' and help each other to complete the predictions by giving clues.

**2** Vocabulary to check: *a glimpse* (when you see something just for a short time or only partly). Once Ss have read the programme information, discuss the question with the class.

**3A** Check that Ss understand the situation by asking: *How old is the woman reading the letter? How old was she when she wrote it? Where was the letter during the time in between?* Tell them to listen and decide if she was optimistic when she wrote the letter. Vocabulary to check: *fancy someone* (to find someone romantically attractive), *have the guts to do something* (be brave enough to do something).

**Answer:** Yes it's optimistic. (she talks about being at university, finding a partner and having children)

**B** Give Ss time to look through the choices. They may already have some ideas for the answers after listening for the first time.

**Answers:** 1 different 2 in the UK 3 with a partner 4 with children 5 happy 6 studying

**C** Ask Ss to predict Laura's answers. Vocabulary to check: *the way her life has turned out* (the way her life is now).

**Answers:** 1 She sees her 16-year-old self as shallow (not very serious, superficial). 2 Yes, she's 'ecstatic' (very happy) with the way her life has turned out.

## UNIT 6 Recording 3

OK … so … I've got the date … Thursday the twentieth of May, 2004. Dear the future me, I hope this letter has found its way to you/me. As I write this I am sixteen in year eleven; and as I read it, I am twenty. I will have changed so much. I can only guess what I will be like at twenty. I envisage myself at Oxford Uni, sitting … oh, this is embarrassing … sitting under a tree by the river in the college grounds. I think I'll be wearing something floaty and a bit indie, but I bet when I get this, it'll be raining.

As I read this, I'll have already remembered that I fancied Tom Squires … there you go, Tom … I'm looking at him now. I wonder if I'll ever have the guts to tell him. I know, I'm a romantic. I hope that hasn't changed. My plans for myself in the following years are to find a man, someone good-looking, romantic and intelligent who shares my interests – or just Tom. Either way, I hope I'll have someone. I don't remember this … and then I think I'll have three children with long brown hair and green eyes.

Well, I'll stop now even though I want to write everything I can down, but I'm running out of time. I hope I'm happy in 2008 and I hope this letter makes me feel good about who I was, or am, as I write this. Keep smiling and while I can't really say bye, but good luck for the future and keep dreaming. Don't change too much, be happy with who you are – I like who I am now more than any other time. Love Laura.

## Unit 6 Recording 4

It all sounds very shallow looking back and reading what I thought I'd be doing or hoped I'd be doing. I think my sixteen-year-old self might have been disappointed with where I am, but because I, as my twenty-year-old self, have sort of grown up and matured. I'm absolutely ecstatic with where I am and it doesn't have to be this perfect sitting-by-a-lake kind of image.

### GRAMMAR future perfect and continuous

**4A** Ss read and match the examples to the meanings. Check that Ss understand *in progress around the time that she opens the letter* by asking: *Will it start raining when she gets the letter or before she gets it?* (before) *Will it stop raining?* (probably not).

**Answers:** 1 a) 2 b)

**B** For *weaker classes* write on the board: *be, past participle, -ing form, have.* Ss can choose from these.

**Answers:** 1 have, past participle 2 be, -ing form

**C** You could discuss this with the whole class. Elicit some other examples of state verbs, e.g. *like, have (possess), seem.*

**Answers:** I'll own – *own* is a state verb and not usually used in the continuous form.

**5** Demonstrate the pronunciation of the weak forms before you play the recording. Write the two sentences on the board and ask Ss to come up and mark the stress and weak forms. Then rub out all the unstressed words.

**Answer key:**
I'll have <u>changed</u> so <u>much</u>.
  /əv/
I <u>bet</u> when I <u>get</u> this, it'll be <u>raining</u>.
         /bɪ/

⟫ **LANGUAGEBANK** 6.2 p138–139

Draw Ss' attention to the use of *by* with the future perfect, the use of the future continuous for something that will happen 'as a matter of course', not as a result of a plan and the use of adverbs and modal verbs with these future forms. If you want to use Ex A and B in class for practice, you could give half the class Ex A and the other half Ex B. Give Ss a key to check their answers when they've finished, then pair up As and Bs. Ss go through the exercise they've done and explain the answers to their partner.

**Answers:** A 1 will/'ll probably be getting off, will/'ll have arrived  2 will/'ll be watching, will have finished  3 will/'ll have eaten, will/'ll be dreaming  4 will/'ll have decided, definitely won't be regretting
B 1 Will you **be** seeing Frank today?  2 Yes, could you tell him I **probably won't** have finished the report until tomorrow.  3 This time tomorrow you'll **have finished** all your exams.  4 And **you'll be** celebrating with your friends.  5 Will you **be using** your computer at lunchtime today?  6 I might **still be using** it when you get back.

## PRACTICE

**6A** Give Ss a few minutes to work on the answers alone. You could do the first one as an example.

**Answers:** 1 'll/will have received  2 will you be watching  3 you'll/ will have fallen  4 you'll/will have drunk  5 will you still be studying  6 you'll/will have passed  7 you'll still like  8 will you be living

**B** Ss can work in pairs or walk round the class and ask each person they talk to two or three questions at random. Before Ss ask each other the questions, direct them to the phrases in the box and check that Ss understand the differences in meaning.

**Possible answers:** 1 I expect so  2 That's quite likely  3 Possibly  4 Perhaps  5 That's pretty unlikely  6 I don't suppose so  7 I doubt it
NB Many of these expressions, such as *possibly* and *perhaps* and *I don't suppose so* and *I doubt it* are very close in meaning. To interpret the exact difference in the degree of probability they express is therefore difficult and somewhat subjective.

## VOCABULARY optimism/pessimism

**7A** Draw a glass on the board then shade in half of it. Ask *Is the glass half full or half empty?* Discuss briefly with the class what the two different ways of looking at the glass mean. Then direct Ss to the quiz and give them time to read it and discuss the vocabulary. Ss should use monolingual dictionaries to check their ideas.

**B** Ss take turns to read out the quiz questions and make a note of each other's answers.

**C** Ss discuss what they think of the analysis.

**8A** Do the first one as an example, then put Ss in pairs.

**Answers:** 1 have mixed feelings about  2 looking forward to  3 has its ups and downs  4 dreading  5 upbeat  6 fills you with optimism  7 filled you with despair  8 cynical

**B** You can either let the Ss work in pairs and take it in turns to ask and answer the questions or alternatively Ss choose the three questions they find the most interesting.

## SPEAKING

**9A** Talk about yourself. Include one or two examples of the future perfect and continuous in your predictions, as well as adverbs such as *probably, definitely* and verbs such as *expect* and *hope*. Give Ss time to make notes.

**B** Ss note down any hopes/plans that they have in common.

## WRITING a letter

**10A** Once Ss have read the letter put them in pairs to discuss Greg's personality. Vocabulary to check: *conform* (to behave according to the usual standards of behaviour which are expected by society), *global downturn* (the slowing down of the economy across the world and the problems that come with it).

**Answers:** a family man (he mentions the family business and the importance of spending time with his kids); a realist (he knows that he tends to give in to family pressure, he realises that he's unlikely to be rich and famous and he mentions the importance of keeping in touch with friends).

**B** Point out that each of the missing sentences introduces what Greg's going to talk about (the topic) in the paragraph that follows. Ss discuss in pairs where the sentences go.

**Answers:** a) 3  b) 5  c) 1  d) 4  e) 2

## LEARN TO use linkers of purpose

**11A** Start by writing the following examples on the board to show Ss that linkers of purpose answer the question *Why?*
*Why is he writing? To see how his future self is doing.*
*Why should he keep in touch with friends? So as to have people around him …*
Direct Ss to the example and put them in pairs to work on the other questions.

**Answers:** 1 a) in order to, so as to  b) because, so that  c) for  2 in order to, so as to  3 in order **not** to, so as **not** to

**B** Direct Ss to the example and point out that they will often need to remove words from the original sentence.

**Answers:** 2 I wish I could get a letter back from you because then I might know what to do next.  3 I hope you took a year off for a round-the-world trip.  4 If you haven't found a partner yet, try to do so soon, so that you don't/won't find yourself alone and lonely in your old age.  5 I imagine you're still doing sport every day so as to impress people.  6 I guess you have to be optimistic to always dream about being rich and famous in the future.  7 Make sure you read this every day in order to remember how you used to be.  8 If you're not happy in your job, try something else in order not to regret wasting years of your life doing something you don't enjoy.

**12** Ss should make notes for each bullet point first, then write a first draft of their letter. Ss swap letters with a partner and check/comment on each other's work. They could write a final draft for homework.

**Homework ideas**
Workbook Ex 1–5, p39–40

# SO WHAT YOU'RE SAYING IS …

## Introduction

Ss read about and practise brainstorming ideas using phrases for suggesting ideas and related vocabulary. They also practise listening and learn to show reservations.

### SUPPLEMENTARY MATERIALS

Resource bank p172

## Warm up

Put Ss in small groups to brainstorm a list of things that they wanted to do/have as teenagers, but that their parents didn't let them do (and why). Ss share their ideas as a class and discuss whether they now agree with their parents' point of view. If your Ss enjoy role-play you could extend this by getting them to act out a situation in pairs: Student A is a teenager who is trying to persuade their parent to let them to stay out late at a party; Student B is the parent who is insisting that they should be home at their normal time.

### VOCABULARY collocations

**1A** Focus Ss on the example and explain or elicit that a collocation is a combination of words that are often used together and sound natural together. Ss can work on the exercise alone or in pairs. Vocabulary to check: *solo, toddler*.

If Ss find this relatively easy, you could direct them back to 3, 7, 9 and 12 and ask them what preposition they'd need to add/change in order to make the other alternative correct.

**Answers:** 2 owning  3 wearing (or *putting on*)  4 staying  5 getting  6 using  7 having (or *signing up for*)  8 riding  9 babysitting (or *taking care of*)  10 travelling  11 staying  12 running (or *being in charge of*)

**B** Direct Ss to the photos and give them a minute or two to discuss them. They could also comment on how old they were when they did any of the things shown for the first time.

**Answers:** owning a mobile phone; riding a scooter; wearing makeup; travelling solo; babysitting for a toddler.

**C** You could give your own opinion about one of the activities as an example. Also remind Ss that they can use modal verbs to talk about this topic, e.g.

*Children shouldn't … until they're at least …*

*I wasn't allowed to … until I was …*

*Parents shouldn't let children under the age of … have/get …*

*It's ok for a teenager to … but their parents need to …, etc.*

**D** Use this feedback to find out which were the most 'controversial' activities.

### FUNCTION persuading

**2A** Make sure that Ss understand and are familiar with the context for the listening activity – a radio phone-in, where members of the general public phone to ask an expert for advice, or to give an opinion on a topic. Direct Ss to the list of activities in Ex 1A and play the recording whilst they tick the activities mentioned.

**Answers:**
owning a mobile phone
using social networking sites
getting your ears pierced

**B** Elicit from the class how many callers they hear (four) and tell the Ss to copy the table into their notebooks so they have more space to make notes about the nature of each caller's problems and the advice that he/she is given.

**Answers: Caller 1:** Problem: 9-year-old daughter runs up mobile phone bill for over £200
DJ's opinion: parents should have set guidelines before giving her the phone
**Caller 2:** Problem: 8-year-old son doesn't want mobile, mother wants him to have one, for security
DJ's opinion: mother is being overprotective, should allow son independence
**Caller 3:** Problem: 12-year-old son spends too much time on the computer
DJ's opinion: Let him, he'll grow out of it, it's normal these days.
**Caller 4:** Problem: 13-year-old son wants to have ears pierced
DJ's opinion: doesn't say, programme ends.

**C** While Ss are comparing their answers, you can monitor their progress and decide whether you need to play (parts of) the recording again.

**D** Ss decide whether they agree with the DJ or what other advice they'd give. Conduct feedback with the whole class.

### Unit 6 Recording 6

DJ = DJ/Presenter  V = Vince  J = Julia  D = Dan  Z = Zara

DJ:  And up next, it's time for 'Just tell me I'm wrong'. Today's topic: how young is too young or, perhaps more accurately, how old is old enough? We've received hundreds of emails and text messages about the right age for a child to have a mobile phone, stay home alone, wear make-up, get their ears pierced, babysit for younger kids … and we've got our first caller, Vince. Go ahead, Vince. You're on.

V:  Hi. My situation is that my nine-year-old kept asking me to get her a mobile, so I bought her one a few months ago. Then last week I got a bill for over two hundred pounds, so I warned her I'd take the phone away from her if it happened again.

DJ:  So I gather your point is whether she's too young to have a mobile?

V:  Yeah, yeah, that's right.

DJ:  Er, surely it's the parents' responsibility to set some sort of guidelines ahead of time.

V:  So what you're saying is I should have given her some rules?

DJ:  Basically, yes. When she first got the phone. OK, thanks Vince. Next caller is Julia. What's your question, Julia?

J:  About the mobile phone thing. I've got an eight-year-old and I worry about him all the time if I can't reach him. You know … anything could happen …

DJ:  So in other words, you want him to have a mobile.

J:  And have it on at all times. But he doesn't want one.

DJ:  Fair enough. Let me ask you a question. When you were eight years old and there were no mobile phones, what did your mother do? I bet you were allowed to go out on your own. Isn't that an important part of growing up and developing a sense of independence and responsibility?

J:  So what you're getting at is that I'm being overprotective?

DJ:  You could say that.

J:  Yeah, but don't you agree that the world used to be a safer place?

DJ:  Surely that's what every generation says. Anyway, thanks for your question, Julia. Let's go to our next caller. Dan, you're on.

D:  Hi, my question's also about technology.

DJ:  OK. Go ahead.

D:  Well, my son, Seth, he's twelve and up till recently he was a normal twelve-year-old, you know, he used to go out with his friends, play football with me, you know … we had a great relationship

DJ: So Dan from what you're saying I'm guessing he doesn't want to spend so much time with you now and you feel …

D: Oh no, it's not that. It's just that he spends all his time on the computer now.

DJ: Isn't that just normal nowadays?

D: It's hard to say. Sometimes at the weekend he spends all day in his bedroom on the computer, on social networking sites or playing games. I don't think it's right. I mean for one thing, he never gets any exercise.

DJ: Don't you think it's just a stage he's going through? I used to spend hours in my bedroom listening to music when I was that age.

D: You mean I should just relax and let him get on with it?

DJ: Yeah, he'll grow out of it. And you can't force him to go and play football if he doesn't want to.

D: I guess not. Thanks.

DJ: OK, our next caller is Zara. You're on.

Z: Um, I was wondering how you would deal with a thirteen-year-old wanting to get pierced ears?

DJ: Thirteen years old? Doesn't she simply want to be like her friends? I imagine a lot of them have pierced ears.

Z: Well … that's it. I'm not talking about a *she*.

DJ: Oh, if I've got it right, you're upset because your thirteen-year-old *son* wants to get his ears pierced.

Z: That's right.

DJ: Ah … so it's because he's a *boy* rather than his age?

Z: I suppose so.

DJ: Well, what's he like socially? Does he have friends who've got …?

**3** Tell Ss they're going to look at some of the language they heard in the phone in. Direct them to the four examples and ask them which two could be used to persuade someone to agree with your opinion (3 and 4). They may also be able to identify that 4 was said by the DJ on the recording. Then give them a minute or two to match the four examples to their meanings. Point out that 4 is a *negative* question, which starts with the auxiliary verb + *not/n't*.

**Answers:** I b) 2 a) 3 d) 4 c)

**4A** You could do the first one as an example, then Ss work on the rest alone or with a partner.

**Answers:** I Surely it's 2 Don't you agree 3 Surely that's 4 Isn't 5 Don't you think 6 Doesn't she simply want

**B** Play the recording again for Ss to check their answers.

**C** Draw Ss' attention to the arrow showing the intonation falling and rising above the final stressed word in each sentence before you play the recording again.

## Unit 6 Recording 7

Surely it's the parents' responsibility.
Don't you agree that the world used to be a safer place?
Surely that's what every generation says.
Isn't that just normal nowadays?
Don't you think it's just a stage he's going through?
Doesn't she simply want to be like her friends?

### Teaching tip

The fall-rise used in these examples is a useful intonation pattern for Ss to learn because it will help them sound polite and interested, rather than too direct/abrupt (often the result of a rising tone) or bored (when there is little or no movement in pitch).

**▶ LANGUAGEBANK** 6.3 p138–139

Point out to Ss the alternatives to *surely* and some common negative questions used for persuading. Ss could do Ex A in class and practise the conversation in pairs before moving on to the more challenging practice in Ex 5.

**Answers:** 2 Clearly they're 3 Isn't it obvious that most 17 year-olds 4 but doesn't it/that depend on the individual? 5 But surely they need (the) time 6 But isn't it a fact that 7 but anyone can see that

**5A** Remind Ss that in a 'gap year' young people often travel overseas and may work while they're away, either for a volunteer organisation or to fund their trip. Give Ss a few minutes to compare their opinions.

**B** Ss should write out the full conversation in their notebooks, so they can use the prompts here to guide them in the next stage, rather than simply reading the conversation out loud.

**Answers:**
A: Don't you think (that) everyone who finishes university should have a gap year?
B: I don't agree. Isn't it better to start working/work as soon as possible so that you (can) get work experience?
A: Yes, but doesn't a gap year give people a different kind of experience?
B: A gap year is just a long holiday. Surely a year working/a year's work is more useful?
A: I disagree. A year off gives people a chance to think about their career.
B: Haven't most twenty-two-year-olds decided by that age?
A: Not always. People often end up in a job they hate. Anyway, surely it's worth trying.
B: I'm still not convinced. I think it's a waste of time.

**C** Remind Ss to pay attention to their intonation on the phrases for persuading. Monitor the practice and be prepared to give Ss feedback on their use of the phrases and their intonation.

### Optional extra activity

Make the practice more challenging for *stronger classes* by removing some of the words in Student A's and Student B's prompts.

### LEARN TO ask for clarification

**6A** Establish that people ask for clarification to make sure they've understood the speaker's message. Give Ss a minute or two to find the phrases before checking with the class.

**Answer:** I So I gather your point is (gather = understand) 2 So what you're saying is …

**B** Ss work alone or with a partner to find the other phrases in the audio script. Then suggest that they copy all five phrases into their notebooks for reference. You may want to play the recording again so that Ss can focus on these phrases and how they're pronounced. Alternatively provide the model yourself and get Ss to repeat the phrases, making sure that they sound friendly and polite.

**Answers:**
I So, in other words … 2 So what you're getting at is (that) (= What you seem to be saying) 3 If I've got it right, …
SS can also include 'you mean …' in this group of phrase.

**speakout** TIP

Give Ss time to read the tip and check that they understand the idea of 'buying' time to think about what to say next. You could elicit other ways they know of doing this, e.g. saying *um, uhuh, I see, right*.

> **Optional extra activity**
> To give Ss practice in asking for clarification in other contexts, put them in pairs and tell them to choose one of the following situations:
>
> 1 Give your partner directions to X.
>
> 2 Explain a recipe to your partner.
>
> 3 Explain to your partner what's involved in a certain job.
>
> Your partner should ask for clarification of anything they don't understand.

**C** Give Ss plenty of time to think about and complete these statements. Circulate and be available to help them put their ideas into words.

**D** Draw Ss' attention to the example and encourage them to continue the exchange beyond the first two lines. During the practice monitor how effectively Ss ask for clarification and give them feedback on this.

### SPEAKING

**7A** Begin by telling both Ss in the pair to write down as many points as they can in support of and against the opinion. They should be able to generate more ideas this way and this also gives you the option of separating them to work with a different partner for the next stage of the activity.

**B** Put Ss into groups of three making sure that they don't work with their partner from the previous stage. Explain that Ss are going to act out three calls to the radio phone-in show and each time they will take a different role: the DJ, the caller with a problem, or the caller who listens and gives their opinion. Direct Ss to their instructions and once they've read them, ask three Ss to start acting out the first situation in front of the class, to make sure that everyone understands what to do. If you want all the groups to move through the three situations at the same pace, use a signal (e.g. clap your hands or ring a bell) to stop them all and tell them to move on to the next one. Monitor and make notes so you can give Ss feedback on their language afterwards.

> **Optional extra activity**
> If you have access to recording facilities, record each group acting out one of the situations, then you can play the recordings for the class and give Ss 'live' feedback on their language.

> **Homework ideas**
> 1 Workbook Ex 1–3B, p41
>
> 2 If Ss have access to English-speaking radio and TV programmes, they listen to a phone-in or chat show and note down the ways of persuading and asking for clarification that the people use.

# HOW TO LIVE TO 101

## Introduction
Ss watch an extract from a BBC documentary about people on the Japanese island of Okinawa and the reasons why they live such long lives. Ss then learn and practise how to have a debate and write a forum comment.

## SUPPLEMENTARY MATERIALS
Ex 4C: Ss may want to use monolingual dictionaries

## Warm up
Put Ss in pairs and ask them to write a list of advantages and disadvantages of living to a very old age. Then invite Ss to share their ideas and see what they had in common.

### DVD PREVIEW

**1** Give Ss a few minutes to discuss the questions in pairs. Then invite them to share their answers to question 2 with the class.

**2A** Focus Ss on the example and give them a minute or two to match the collocations. (Hopefully, some of the items will already have be generated by Ss during the course of the preceding discussion on how to live a long life.)

**Answers:** 2 c 3 a 4 b 5 h 6 d 7 e 8 g

**Optional extra activity**
To help Ss remember the collocations, tell them to cover the left hand column in Exercise 2A, then, working with a partner, try to remember the verb that goes with each of the nouns/adjectives on the right. Then they take turns to 'test' each other: one student closes their book and the other calls out the first part of a collocation for their partner to complete.

**B** Before putting Ss in pairs to discuss the factors, demonstrate that they'll need to use the verbs in the -ing form if they are the subject of the sentence, e.g. *Staying mentally active is very important.*

**3** Focus Ss on the question and give them a minute or two to read the text. Vocabulary to check: *quest* (a long search for something that is difficult to find), *stumble across* (to discover something by chance).

**Answer:** Okinawa, Loma Linda, the mountains of Sardinia People live longer in these places.

### DVD VIEW

**Culture notes**
Okinawa island is part of Japan's southernmost prefecture (also called Okinawa) and is located southwest of mainland Japan. The islands which make up Okinawa Prefecture are also known as the Ryukyu Islands, named after the native culture, which is distinctly different from that of the rest of Japan in terms of language, cuisine, arts, etc.

The climate is subtropical, with temperatures barely falling below fifteen degrees in winter. The seas surrounding Okinawa's islands are considered among the world's most beautiful with coral reefs and abundant marine wildlife.

Towards the end of World War Two Okinawa became the stage of one of the war's bloodiest battles, when American troops invaded the islands. Okinawa remained under US administration until 1972 and several thousands of US military members remain stationed on the controversial US military bases on Okinawa Main Island today.

**4A** Tell Ss just to listen for the two reasons and that they will have a chance to watch the extract again to understand it in more detail.

**Answers:** 1 They eat a lot of different colour vegetables and soya protein. 2 They don't overeat: only until they're eighty percent full.

**B** Give Ss time to read through the statements carefully before you play the DVD again and tell them to make notes to support their answers. Vocabulary to check: *longevity* (living for a long time), *antioxidants* (substances that slow down the rate at which something decays or oxidizes). Also explain that *centenarians* is the term for people who live to hundred years old or more. Put Ss in pairs to compare their answers after they've watched the extract again.

**Answers:** 1 F Okinawa has over four times the percentage of centenarians than in Britain or America. 2 F They don't think about it at all. They 'couldn't care less' what scientists say. 3 T 4 F The antioxidants are from the vegetables, the protein is from the soya. Meat and eggs aren't mentioned. 5 F It means 'Eat until you're about eighty percent full' 6 T In the west, people want to get more for their money.

**C** Ss should read the quotes from the DVD carefully before watching the extract again. You could also suggest that they can choose a certain number (perhaps set a limit of five) of unfamiliar words from the quotes to look up in the dictionary which may help them to predict some of the answers. In feedback you could also ask Ss:
*1 What is Mr Miyagi's way of defying the aging process?* (his exercise routine)
*2 What is 'the most ordinary of places'?* (the fruit and vegetable shop)
*3 What are the crucial properties?* (antioxidants and soya protein)

**Answers:** 1 defying (= *refusing to obey;* fighting would also be possible) 2 phenomenon (*something unusual that is studied because it is not understood*) 3 properties *(powers)* 4 bloated *(very full of food; swollen is related to an injury)*

**D** Give Ss a few minutes to discuss the questions, then invite them to share their answers with the class. Ask *If you could go and live on Okinawa for a year, would you go? Why/Why not?*

### DVD 6 Horizon: How to Live to 101
N = Narrator  C = Craig
N: The remote island of Okinawa is home to one of the longest living communities in the world. In a population of only one million there are nine hundred centenarians, a percentage that's over four times higher than Britain and America. It's a place where age has a different meaning. Where people like Mr Miyagi can expect to live way beyond his 92nd year. Unaware of the latest diet or lifestyle fad, Mr Miyagi has developed his own way of defying the ageing process.
C: They're not thinking about 'Gee, if I do this I'm not gonna live as long if I … I have one extra drink or if I eat this food or …' – they're not thinking about that at all. Most of them couldn't care less what the scientists think – they just go about their business and live. They just happen to live a very long time.
N: The explanation for this extraordinary phenomenon begins in the most ordinary of places. Like every town in Okinawa the fruit and vegetable shop in Agimi lies at the heart of village life. It's here that Bradley and Craig believe the source of the Okinawa miracle can be traced. For the past twenty years Bradley and Craig have been analysing the life-enhancing Okinawan ingredients.

C: Got reds here in the tomatoes, the peppers, you've got green peppers here.

N: They've identified a number of crucial properties that guard the Okinawans from disease, from the antioxidant-rich vegetables that protect against cell damage, to the high quantities of soya proteins. In gimi, one hundred year old Matsu is preparing a traditional Okinawan dish using all the vital ingredients. It's only after the food is served that the most significant Okinawan tradition can be observed.

C: The Okinawans developed also cultural habits over the years that appear to have health protective properties. They have a saying called 'hara hachi bu', eat until you're only eighty per cent full.

N: In a typical day, Matsu only consumes around twelve hundred calories, about twenty per cent less than most people in Britain and America.

C: In the West we're very much focussed on getting more for our money and one of the most popular things is these-all-you-can-eat restaurants. You go and you load up at the, at the, the all-you-can-eat restaurant and you, you walk away with this bloated feeling and you … you may have got your money's worth but you probably didn't get your, your health's worth because what you're doing is just digging yourself into an early grave.

## speakout a debate

**5A** Check that Ss understand the idea of a debate: a formal discussion of a topic, where speakers take turns to give their points in favour of or against the topic and a vote is taken at the end to decide which side wins. You could start by eliciting an example of a point for or against the topic, then put Ss in pairs to write at least one more point for each side.

**B** Ss can make a few notes while they listen, then discuss in their pairs which speaker they agree with. Vocabulary to check: *gender* (male or female), *deteriorate* (to get worse).

**C** First tell Ss to look through the phrases and decide what the purpose of each one is (the first two are for introducing your point, the other four are for referring back to a previous speaker's point). Then play the recording again for Ss to tick the phrases they hear.

> **Answers:** The first point I'd like to make is that … I would like to start off by saying that … I would like to pick up on the point made by …

### Unit 6 Recording 8

W= Woman    M = Man

W: I'm going to speak in favour of the statement: 'Age discrimination should be illegal at work.' The first point I'd like to make is that selecting a person for a job on the basis of their age is unfair. It's as bad as choosing someone because of their gender or race or religion. People should be selected for a job because of their abilities and suitability and not because they are a certain age. For example, if a sixty-year-old person is able, physically and mentally, to do a job they should be judged on the same basis as a thirty-year-old.

M: I want to speak against the statement. I would like to start off by saying that I fully support equal opportunities for people applying for a job. However, I would like to pick up on the point made by Sarah when she said 'if a person is able, physically and mentally, to do a job.' I think we need to be realistic here. As people age, this can affect their energy, their ability to react quickly and their memory. In some jobs it may be vital for people to have high levels of energy, for example in a creative industry such as advertising. Or people need to be able to react quickly, for instance if they are a lorry driver, or be able to concentrate for long periods of time if they are an airline pilot. It is simply a fact of life that, as we age, our mental and physical capabilities deteriorate and that, for certain jobs, younger people are better.

**6A** To decide on the topic you could ask for a show of hands for each one.

**B** Ideally, put Ss in groups of four and make sure there are equal numbers of groups in favour of and against the topic. Ss work together in their group to list the four (or more) points to support their position, then each member of the group takes one point to develop and speak about in the debate. Circulate and provide help with grammar and vocabulary as required. The groups should then spend some time practising making their points so they can make any corrections or improvements necessary before the debate. They also need to be prepared to pick up on points made by other speakers, either from their own group (which they can prepare) or from the opposing group (which they'll have to do 'on their feet').

**C** The debate can be conducted either by putting a 'for' and an 'against' group together, or as a class. The latter would be more appropriate if your Ss need practise in public speaking in English. Ss from opposing sides take turns to stand up and make their points. At the end, Ss can vote for either side's arguments.

> **Teaching tip**
> You may feel that it's appropriate to give Ss individual feedback on their language use for an activity like a debate. Prepare individual feedback sheets (e.g. A5 size), with the name of the student at the top. Divide the sheet into two sections: one for good language use and one for corrections. You can then fill them in as each student is speaking and give them out after the debate.

## writeback a forum comment

**7A** Give Ss a few minutes to read the comment. You could suggest they put a tick next to any points they agree with and a question mark or cross next to those they disagree with or are have mixed feelings about. Invite a few Ss to share their opinions with the class.

**B** Ss number the parts and compare answers with a partner.

> **Answers:** 1 d) 2 c) 3 b) 4 a)

**C** Ss can work on this alone or choose a topic with a partner and write the comment together. Encourage them to use the structure of the forum comment about children taking care of their parents as they get older. You could then collect in the comments and redistribute them for other Ss to read.

> **Homework ideas**
> 1 Ss write a forum comment on a topic from p74–75, e.g. whether a gap year is a good idea or not.
>
> 2 Ss imagine that they are spending a year living on Okinawa and write home to a friend/relative, telling them about the place, the people, the food, the way of life, etc.

# LOOKBACK

## Introduction

The aim of these activities is to provide revision and further practice of the language from the unit. You can also use them to assess Ss' ability to use the language, in which case you need to monitor but avoid helping them. You may feel that you don't need or have time to do all the activities. If so, you could allocate the activities that would be most beneficial for your Ss, or get individual Ss to decide which activities they'd like to do in class.

### AGE

**1A** You could run this as a board race. Tell Ss to close their books and put them in teams. Write/Display the sentences on the board one at a time. A member from each team races to the board to add the missing vowels and win points.

> **Answers:** 1 elderly 2 in their prime 3 coming of age 4 for his or her age, their age 5 Age discrimination 6 Maturity

**B** You could start by telling the class your opinion about sentence 1 and invite them to agree/disagree with you. Then put Ss in pairs to discuss the rest. In feedback ask a few pairs to report back on which sentences they both agreed with and why.

### MODAL VERBS AND PHRASES

**2A** Introduce the topic of amusement parks (Disneyland, etc.) and the people who work in them dressed as animals. Ask Ss whether they think it would be a good job or not and why. Tell Ss to read the text quickly and find three reasons why the writer doesn't like the job (*the costume is very heavy, he can't see properly, the children annoy him*). Give Ss a few minutes to choose the correct alternatives and compare answers in pairs.

> **Answers:** 1 makes 2 'm not able 3 are allowed to 4 aren't supposed to 5 won't be able 6 don't have to 7 don't need to 8 managed to

**B** You could start by telling Ss about the best job you've ever had and explain why, using at least three of the modal verbs and phrases, e.g. *I didn't have to … / I was allowed to … / I could …* Put Ss in pairs to choose a job and make a few notes about the reasons for their choice, using at least three modal verbs and phrases. Ask the pairs to share their ideas and have a class vote on the best job of all.

### FUTURE PERFECT AND CONTINUOUS

**3A** Ss can work alone completing the sentences and compare answers with a partner.

> **Answers:** 1 won't be sitting 2 will definitely have finished, probably won't be speaking 3 'll be 4 will still be communicating 5 will have been replaced

**B** Tell Ss to give reasons for their answers, e.g. *That's not true because I'll be sitting here until 4.30.*

**C** Ss could either write one prediction for each of the topics given or five predictions for one of the topics.

**D** Groups could choose the two most interesting predictions from their discussion to tell the rest of the class.

### OPTIMISM/PESSIMISM

**4A** You could do this as a 'Listen and stop me' activity. Ss should close their books. Tell them you're going to read a story and if they hear you make mistake with the vocabulary they should shout *Stop!* and correct the mistake. Start reading the story and give the class one point each time they stop you in the correct place and another point if they can correct the mistake. Give yourself a point if the Ss miss the mistake or if their correction is wrong.

> **Answers:** 1 had my ups and downs 2 had mixed feelings 3 look on the bright side of things 4 upbeat 5 looking forward to 6 cynical 7 gloomy 8 dreaded 9 taking one step forward and two steps back 10 promising 11 despair 12 filled with optimism

**B** Give Ss a few minutes to discuss what the student brought to class and why it made the teacher optimistic.

### PERSUADING

**5A** You could run this as a race in pairs: the first pair to finish bring their books up to you to check. For *stronger classes* you could also tell Ss to cover the words in the box and work out the missing words themselves.

> **Answers:**
> A: Don't you **agree** that …
> B: But **surely** …
> A: Why? Anyone **can** see that …
> B: But **shouldn't** …
> A: So **what** you're saying is that
> B: But **isn't** it obvious that
> A: Well **clearly** …

**B** Tell Ss to close their books and put the answers from Ex 5A on the board as prompts for them to use while they practise the conversation.

**C** Leave the phrases from Ex 5A on the board for this speaking activity. Ss should spend a few minutes thinking about the topics and making notes before joining a partner to discuss them. If you want to extend the practice you could swap the pairs around so that Ss are working with a new partner. Monitor and make notes of good language use and areas for remedial work. In feedback, invite a few Ss to tell the class whether their partner managed to persuade them to change their opinion about any of the topics, then give Ss some examples of their good use of language and errors for them to discuss and correct.

# 7 MEDIA

## OVERVIEW

**7.1 BEST OF THE BEEB**
GRAMMAR | quantifiers
VOCABULARY | television; multi-word verbs
HOW TO | talk about TV

**COMMON EUROPEAN FRAMEWORK**
Ss can scan quickly through long/complex texts, locating relevant details; can take an active part in informal discussion in familiar contexts, commenting and putting point of view clearly.

**7.2 THE NEWS THAT WASN'T**
GRAMMAR | reported speech
VOCABULARY | reporting verbs
HOW TO | report what someone says

**COMMON EUROPEAN FRAMEWORK**
Ss can understand articles and reports concerned with contemporary problems in which the writers adopt particular stances or viewpoints; can quickly identify the content and relevance of news items, articles and reports; can write an essay that develops an argument systematically with appropriate highlighting of significant points and relevant supporting detail.

**7.3 WHAT'S IN THE NEWS**
FUNCTION | adding emphasis
VOCABULARY | the press
LEARN TO | make guesses

**COMMON EUROPEAN FRAMEWORK**
Ss can summarise extracts from news items, interviews or documentaries containing opinions, argument and discussion.

**7.4 NEWS BLUNDERS** ⊚ B B C DVD
**speakout** | a news story
**writeback** | a newspaper article

**COMMON EUROPEAN FRAMEWORK**
Ss can understand most TV news programmes; can write an article or story marking the relationship between ideas in clear connected text and following established conventions of the genre concerned.

**7.5 LOOKBACK**
Communicative revision activities

📱 **B B C VIDEO PODCAST**
**What kind of new stories interest you?**

This video podcasts encourages students to reflect on the kinds of news stories that they find the most interesting. Use the video podcast at the start or the end of Unit 7.

## BEST OF THE BEEB

### Introduction

Ss practise reading and speaking about television using quantifiers and related vocabulary. They also learn about multi-word verbs.

**SUPPLEMENTARY MATERIALS**

Resource bank p173, p174 and/or p175

Ex 1A, 3C, 10B: Ss need monolingual dictionaries.

Ex 11A: be prepared to give Ss a model of an idea for a thriller, soap opera or TV drama, or news report, incorporating six of the multi-word verbs from Ex 10.

### Warm up

Either: Put Ss in pairs and give them three minutes to brainstorm types of TV programme. Conduct feedback with the whole class and write a list on the board. Then tell Ss to write the headings *regularly/sometimes/never* in their notebooks and, working alone, put the programme types under the headings according to how often they watch them. They then compare answers in pairs or small groups.

Or: Write *Media* on the board and ask Ss what the term includes, i.e. television, radio, newspapers, magazines, the internet. Then put Ss in small groups to discuss which types of media they use most/least and why. Conduct feedback with the whole class.

**VOCABULARY** television

**1A** Discuss the first pair of programmes with the class, as an example. Give Ss about ten mins to discuss/look up the rest of the programme type pairs and make notes for feedback.

**Suggested answers:** 1 Both show real life: a wildlife one features animals, plants, etc; a reality one features people. 2 Both are dramas which involve a continuing story with the same set of characters: a costume drama is usually set in a historical context; a soap opera is set in a contemporary, modern context. 3 Both are comedies/funny: a sketch show has a lot of short comedy pieces; a sitcom is normally a single story and the stories connect in some way from episode to episode although each episode is self-contained. 4 Both are factual programmes: a documentary can be on any factual topic, e.g. scientific, historical, cultural and is made from real footage; a docudrama is often about historical events and includes re-enacted sequences, sequences performed by actors but made to look real. 5 Both involve more than one programme: a series can be factual; in a drama, each episode is usually a different story, but with the same characters; a serial is a single story broken up into different episodes. 6 Both are exciting and often involve danger and facing and solving a problem: thriller can be a combination of genres or types, it can include sci-fi, fantasy, detective, action type content, but it's always made to create excitement (or 'thrills'); a detective series usually focuses only on police work in connection with crime and as a series has the same characters with a different story every episode. 7 Both involve a competition between teams or individuals: a game show can have many formats, including a quiz format; a quiz is limited to question/answer formats. 8 Both are about real events/stories happening at the moment.: a current affairs programme has feature stories about different topics in the news; the news is made up of shorter stories about the most current (immediate) events.

**Alternative idea**

To make this exercise less time consuming, give each pair of Ss one pair of programmes to discuss (or two, depending on the size of your class). Each pair then tells the class about their programmes in feedback, or you could split the pairs and have Ss in two groups telling each other their answers.

**B** You could start by telling the class which programmes you like the most/least and why.

## READING

**2** Tell Ss to cover the text and focus them on the photos. Explain that they need to match them with one of the programme types in Ex 1A. Some of the pictures may correspond with more than one possible programme genre. Avoid checking answers at this stage. Ss can wait to confirm their predictions when they read the article. Instead, conduct feedback with the class about what they imagine the programmes to be about and which ones they would choose to watch.

**Answers:** (programmes in brackets are other possibilities that Ss may guess):
A series (documentary, reality show) B reality show (documentary) C soap opera (sketch show, sitcom) D current affairs programme (the news) E (sci-fi) series (serial, thriller)

**3A** First, ask Ss if they know what *the Beeb* is and direct them to the introduction to the article to find out. Then give them a time limit of three minutes to read the article and match the photos.

### Teaching tip

It's important to give a strict time limit when asking Ss to read a text for the gist, or general idea. Ss don't need to read the texts about the programmes in their entirety or in great detail in order to complete the matching task. This is a useful skill for Ss to have outside the classroom. They may need to read a text quickly so that they can make a decision, e.g. read reviews of several films and decide which one to watch.

**Answers:** *Eastenders* – C *Top Gear* – A
*Strictly Come Dancing* – B *Newsnight* – D *Doctor Who* – E

**B** Look at the first sentence with the class and give Ss a minute or two to find the relevant phrase to show that it's false. When Ss have identified the rest of the phrases/sentences, put them in pairs to compare answers.

**Answers:** 1 aim for greater realism than is found in most soaps 2 has tackled quite a few issues previously unseen on mainstream UK TV, such as racism, unemployment and drug abuse. 3 with its humorous style 4 the four men raced across London 5 with little or no experience of dancing 6 after the viewers' vote 7 Its main presenter 8 Very few politicians enjoy the experience of being 'Paxoed' 9 solving problems, fighting monsters and righting wrongs 10 millions of fans worldwide

**C** Focus Ss on the example and point out that *air* can also refer to programmes broadcast on the radio, e.g. *Radio Two aired a new quiz show last night.* Ss could work with a partner to match the rest of the meanings and check any they are unsure of in a dictionary.

**Answers:** 2 rows (have a row/argument *with* someone *about* something)
3 one-off (adjective and noun: *a one-off performance; the interview was a one-off*)
4 glamorous (often used to describe movie stars, models and other celebrities)
5 renowned (famous because of an achievement or a special skill they have, i.e. dancing)
6 in-depth (also *in-depth study/investigation/interview/analysis*)
7 come under fire (suggests strong criticism)
8 has cross-generational appeal (also *widespread/worldwide appeal*)

**4** Ss could order the programmes from 1–5, starting with the one they'd most like to watch, then compare answers in pairs or small groups. In feedback, ask Ss who has changed their mind about what programmes seem interesting to them since doing Exercise 2 and finding out more information about them.

## GRAMMAR quantifiers

**5A** Establish that quantifiers are words/phrases used with nouns to show quantity. Focus Ss on the first quantifier in the introduction to the text (*a good deal of*) and ask them which category it belongs to (*a lot*), then give them time to find and categorise the rest and compare answers with a partner.

**Answers:** all: *each, every* (*each* means all the people/things considered separately, one at a time; *every* means all the people/things considered together)
a lot: *a good deal of, plenty of, quite a few, lots of*
a moderate or small number/amount: *a few, little, several, few, a little*
zero: *no*

**B** Look at *a good deal of* as an example with the class, then put Ss in pairs to complete the rules.

**Answers:** 1 uncountable 2 singular 3 plural 4 plural or uncountable

**C** Point out that *few* doesn't mean the same as *a few* and *little* doesn't mean the same as *a little*. Give Ss a minute or two to look at the sentences.

**Answers:** 1 some 2 not many 3 not much 4 some

**6A** Tell the students they are going to do a dictation exercise with four sentences. All the sentences will have quantifiers in them. Then play the recording, stopping briefly after each sentence for Ss to finish writing.

**Unit 7 Recording 1**

1   All of us are from Spain.
2   Quite a few of us live nearby.
3   Several of us don't drink coffee.
4   A few of us smoke.

**B** Focus Ss on the example and show them that the sequence of sounds is consonant → vowel and that the *f* sounds like a *v* when it's followed by a vowel sound, so the whole sentence sounds like *Allovusare from Spain*.

**Answers:**
2 Quite a few of us live nearby.
3 Several of us don't drink coffee.
4 A few of us smoke.

**C** Encourage Ss to copy the tempo on the recording so they sound natural as they repeat the sentences.

**Optional extra idea**
Ask Ss where the consonant → vowel links are in *a good deal of* and *lots of* and ask them to write and practise an example sentence for each of these quantifiers.

**⟹ LANGUAGEBANK** 7.1 p140–141

The table in the **Language bank** contains some extra quantifiers which you will need to check with Ss if you want them to do practice Ex A and B.

*most = nearly all* e.g. *most people, most of the people here*

*any = all, it doesn't matter which*, e.g. *I'll watch any reality show – I love them!*

*neither = not one or the other*, e.g. *neither politician could answer the question.*

You could run Ex A as a competition in pairs. Read the text aloud for the class and when you reach a set of alternatives, the first pair to put their hands up with an answer is awarded a point if it's correct.

**Answers: A** 1 a large number  2 each  3 both  4 some
5 either  6 Any  7 Very few  8 no  9 plenty of  10 Neither
**B** 1 very few  2 a little  3 A few  4 quite a few
5 very little  6 either  7 any  8 any

**PRACTICE**

**7A** Ss can work in pairs to correct the sentences. You could do the first one with the class as an example.

**Answers:**
1 I watch very **few** sports programmes.
2 **Every programme has/All (the) programmes have** a commercial break every ten minutes.
3 The weekend schedules usually include **a few/several** talent shows, at least three or four.
4 You can watch **a lot of/lots of/quite a few** popular programmes online.
5 I like **every** programme/**all programmes/any** programme about hospitals or emergencies.
6 I once spent quite **a few** days watching a box set of the series *Lost*.
7 I think a **great deal/a lot/lots** of TV has been dumbed down.
8 We have plenty **of** detective shows; we don't need more.
9 Lots **of** the best shows are US imports, such as *The Wire*.
10 I think a **little/some** news is OK but not 24-hour news non-stop.

**B** You could demonstrate this first by changing one or two of the sentences to make them true for you/your country.

**C** Put Ss in pairs and tell them to make a note of any opinions that they have in common. In feedback, encourage them to tell the class some of these, using *We both (think)…, Neither of us thinks …, etc.*

**Optional extra activity**
Ss write one or two paragraphs about 'must-see' programmes in their countries, incorporating vocabulary from Ex 1A and 2C and quantifiers. Circulate and help Ss to 'proofread' and correct their work, if necessary writing a second draft. The descriptions can then be put on the walls round the classroom for other Ss to read and decide which programmes they'd like to watch. If Ss are from the same country, they write the descriptions without naming the programmes and the other Ss have to guess which programmes are being described.

**SPEAKING**

**8** Ss work in pairs and discuss the questions.

**9A** Put pairs together to make groups of four. Groups discuss the questions.

**B** When they've finished discussing the questions, the groups should spend a few minutes preparing their results to tell the rest of the class, using quantifiers where possible, e.g. *Quite a few of us …, Only a few of us …, None of us …, Most of us …, We all …, etc.* Ss share their ideas with the whole class, or in new groups (see below). Finally, bring Ss together for you to give feedback on their language use.

**Teaching tip**
Regroup the Ss by giving each member of the group a letter (e.g. A–E for a group of five), then putting all the As together, all the Bs together and so on. In their new groups, Ss tell each other the results of their discussions. This will give more Ss a chance to speak than conducting feedback with the whole class.

**VOCABULARY *PLUS*** multi-word verbs

**10A** Tell Ss to read the quotes then work with a partner to find and underline the multi-word verbs and decide which programme they think the quotes come from. You could identify the first multi-word verb in quote 1 as an example with the class. Vocabulary to check: *appealing, (attractive), summit meeting* (an important formal meeting between the governments from two or more countries), *negotiations* (formal discussions to try and reach an agreement) *fooled* (tricked or deceived).

**Answers:** 1 Top Gear (has brought out, break into)
2 Newsnight (have broken down, are pulling out of)
3 Strictly Come Dancing (takes me back)  4 Doctor Who (turns out)  5 Eastenders (came across, put up with)

**B** Focus Ss on the example and remind them to use the context when trying to work out the meaning of the verbs. Ss work alone for a few minutes and compare answers in pairs. At this stage you could also ask Ss to decide whether each verb takes an object or not (transitive or intransitive) and whether the verb and particle can be separated. They could use dictionaries to help with this.

**Answers:** 2 fail or end unsuccessfully – break down (intransitive, inseparable) 3 meet by chance – come across (transitive, inseparable) 4 introduce (a product) or make something available – bring out (transitive, separable) 5 make somebody remember – take back 6 tolerate – put up with (transitive, separable) 7 enter something with difficulty – break into (transitive, inseparable) 8 end somebody's involvement or quit – pull out of (transitive, inseparable)

**Teaching tip**
Show Ss how to check in a monolingual dictionary whether a verb is transitive or intransitive and separable or inseparable. The symbols are usually [T] for transitive and [I] for intransitive and a separable verb is shown with an object and a two-way arrow between the verb and particle: *bring sth ¤ out.*

**C** Focus Ss on the example and ask them how the meaning of *turn out* is different here from how it is used in the sentences in Ex 10A. (In Ex 10 *turn out* means *to happen in the end* and refers to the identity of a person, but here *turn out* means *to come* or *to appear* and refers to people gathering together for an event). Put the Ss into pairs to look at the rest. Ss could use dictionaries to check any they are really unsure of.

**Answers:** 2 S: meetings, negotiations and machines can 'break down' or fail.
3 D: If someone comes across in a particular way they seem to have particular qualities.
4 D: If you bring something out, you make it easier to see
5 D: If someone takes back something they said, they are saying that they didn't mean it
6 D: If you put someone up you let them stay in your house for a short time.
7 S: both mean 'enter with difficulty' although if you 'break into' a building it is usually a criminal act.
8 D: if a train/car/bike/bus etc. pulls out, it moves away from a stopping position to start moving or to join the rest of the traffic.

**11A** You could start by giving Ss a model, i.e. tell them your idea for a story or report: *the main character comes across some old school friends on a social networking site, starts to exchange messages, enjoys it because it takes her back to her school days. Then one of the old friends says he's coming to her town, can she put him up for a couple of nights? She agrees but is slightly disappointed. His behaviour is rather odd and he spends most of the time hidden away in his room. This brings out the detective in our main character, who starts to find out more information about him and it turns out that he's on the run from the police. What should our heroine do?*

Put Ss in pairs and tell them to brainstorm some ideas for a story or report first, then write up the best one. Circulate and help Ss to use the multi-word verbs correctly. NB If Ss are struggling to include six verbs, you could reduce the target to four.

**Optional extra activity**
To provide Ss with some more multi-word verbs to choose from for their stories/reports, direct them to **Vocabulary bank**, Ex 2 on p154. Provide Ss with an answer key for the exercise, so they can choose to do it if they wish and at their own pace.

**B** You could combine pairs into groups of four for this, or Ss could walk around the room and tell two or three other people about their idea.

➠ **VOCABULARYBANK** p154 Multi-word verbs (2)
Ex 2A introduces some new multi-word verbs which can have different meanings. Let the Ss work in pairs to read the pairs of sentences and deduce the two different meanings of the verbs in bold. Encourage them to find a synonym for each (see the answer key below). Allow them to check their ideas in a dictionary to help complete the table in Ex B.

**Answers:** 2A 1a) raise b) mention 2a) delay b) causing me not to like 3a) reject b) lower the heat 4a) base our assessment b) pass 5a) employed b) fought/tackled
2B 1 take on 2 turn down 3 go by 4 put off 5 bring up

**Homework ideas**
1 Workbook Ex 1–5, p46–47
2 Vocabulary bank Ex 2, p154
3 Ss write about their family's or friends' attitude to the radio and newspapers, using quantifiers, e.g.
*Quite a few people in my family listen to the radio in the car.*
*Very few of my friends read a newspaper from cover to cover,* etc.

# THE NEWS THAT WASN'T

## Introduction

Ss practise listening and speaking about the news, using reported speech and reporting verbs. They also learn to use linkers of contrast and write a discursive essay.

### SUPPLEMENTARY MATERIALS

Resource bank p176

Ex 3: download/bring in some descriptions of hoaxes for Ss to read and discuss.

## Warm up

Tell Ss to close their books and write on the board the title *The News that Wasn't* and the question *When is the News not news?* Brainstorm some ideas with the class about what they mean, e.g. a certain topic might not be considered important enough to be 'newsworthy' (as is the case with some stories about celebrities), or a story might be examined so much that it's exhausted and no longer relevant as news. If Ss mention the idea of someone trying to make people believe a story that isn't true, pre-teach *hoax*.

### LISTENING

**1** Check that Ss understand the idea of a *hoax* and a *composite photo*, i.e. when two or more photos are combined. Discuss the photos with the whole class or put Ss in pairs to discuss them.

**2A** Tell Ss just to listen for whether the photo is a hoax or not and play the recording.

**Answers:** Photo A is real. Photos B and C are hoaxes.

**B** Give Ss a minute or two to look at the questions and think about what they already know about the answers, from listening the first time. Play the recording again, then Ss compare their answers in pairs. Vocabulary to check: *sue (to make a legal claim against someone, especially for a sum of money, because you have been harmed in some way).*

**Answers:** 1 People don't like hoaxers and he could be sued by the original photographer for using photos without permission, or by a newspaper for selling them a hoax.
2 To decide if a photo of a famous person (for example a politician) in an embarrassing situation is a hoax or not.
3 A: It's such an extraordinary sight and it would be easy to make a composite.
B: There would be more damage to the tree and the suitcase.
C: It's too well composed, it looks planned.

**3** Ss discuss the questions in pairs for a couple of minutes, then share their examples and opinions as a class.

### Optional extra activity

Bring in some descriptions of famous hoaxes for Ss to read. These can be found on the internet, e.g. at www. museumofhoaxes.com – Top 100 April Fool's Day hoaxes (correct at the time of going to press). Ss discuss which hoax they liked best, which was the most unbelievable, etc.

---

## UNIT 7 Recording 2

P = Presenter  H = Hoaxer

P:  Welcome to Insight, where our topic for the day is hoaxes, specifically photo hoaxes. My producer had to go to great lengths to actually get a hoax photographer to agree to appear on the show, on the condition that we promise to keep his identity secret. So, I'd like to welcome my guest to the show.

H: Thank you.

P:  For starters, can you explain why you want to remain anonymous?

H: Two reasons really. People don't like hoax photographers, because people don't like to be fooled in this way. We make them feel stupid. Also, hoaxers often use photographs taken by someone else and without permission and the original photographer could sue us … or a newspaper can sue you if they discover you've sold them a hoax.

P:  You're playing it safe, then.

H: You could put it that way.

P:  I see. Now I asked you before the show if you'd ever earned money for your hoax work and you said that you often work with the police and detectives. What exactly do you do for them?

H: Well when a politician, for example, appears in a published photograph in any embarrassing situation, say accepting money… sometimes the police ask me to decide if the photograph is a hoax and then they see if they can find out who did it.

P:  Right. OK, well, let's look at some photographs that we found on the Internet – some hoaxes; some not. Talk us through these photographs if you would.

H: OK, this picture of a plane crossing a road looks like a hoax simply because it's such an extraordinary sight. Also, it looks a bit like a composite photo …

P:  What's that?

H: When you combine two or more photos, that's a composite. It's easy to put a picture of a plane over a picture of a road and then put this traffic light here on the right on top, like a sandwich.

P:  So it's a hoax photo.

H: No, it's actually real. I wasn't sure myself, but when I found out it was Beijing Airport, I asked a friend who lives in Beijing and he told me he had seen it with his own eyes a number of years before. There used to be a taxiing runway that actually crossed the road! It's all changed now, of course and these days Beijing has one of the most modern airports in the world.

P:  Sure. Hmm … so … then this one could be real. A suitcase in the top of a tree is such an extraordinary sight, maybe that's why it looks a bit fake.

H: Well, even if you've never seen a suitcase that's fallen from a plane into a tree – and who has? – your common sense tells you that there would be more damage to both the tree and the suitcase.

P:  Then it IS a hoax photo.

H: Yes, a classic composite photo.

P:  Remarkable. Now this one could be real, the man jumping over the canyon. I remember seeing this on the Internet. They said that there was a 900 metre drop underneath. But you're going to tell me it's a composite photo.

H: Not necessarily. This is an interesting example from a number of standpoints. You have to ask yourself how it is that someone was there to take a very well composed photograph of the man jumping. It's too-well composed.

P:  So the whole thing was planned. Still, it's dangerous…

H: Well, in a photograph you never see the whole picture. It looks dangerous, but in fact just below the bottom of the frame here is the ground connecting these two rocks. At most he would have fallen a few metres.

P:  How do you know that?

H: This is a quite well-known place for adventure tourists who visit the Grand Canyon.

P: Have you been there?

H: No, but I've seen photographs.

P: Ah, how do you know those weren't hoaxes …

## GRAMMAR reported speech

**4A** This should be revision for Ss so you could go through these sentences with the whole class.

> **Answers:** 1 c)  2 a)  3 b)  4 a)

**B** Ss could work in pairs on this.

> **Answers:** 1 'Have you ever earned money for your hoax work?'  2 'I often work with the police.'  3 'Could you decide if the photograph is a hoax?'  4 'I saw it with my own eyes a number of years ago.'

**C** You could look at the first question with the whole class then put Ss in pairs.

> **Answers:** 1 The verb forms move one tense back in the past, e.g. present simple becomes past simple, past simple and present perfect become past perfect.
> 2 If what the person says is still relevant or true now, or if it was said very recently, there is no need to change the tense.
> 3 In reported questions we use the normal word order, not the question word order.
> 4 When it is a *yes/no* question (This is the same rule as for indirect questions, e.g. *Could you tell me if Miss Jones lives here?*)
> 5 the (*to*) infinitive
> 6 They are changed so that the point of time reference is clear, e.g. *yesterday* Ð *the day before, today* that day, next week the next/following week

### Optional extra activity

Put some more sentences from the interview on the board or on a handout and ask Ss to change them from direct to reported speech, or vice versa, e.g.

1 Can you explain why you want to remain anonymous?

*He asked me why I wanted to remain anonymous.*

2 Hoaxers often use photographs taken by someone else.

*He said that hoaxers often use photographs taken by someone else.*

3 Talk us through these photographs if you would.

*He asked me to talk through some photographs.*

4 I asked a friend who lives in Beijing if it was Beijing Airport.

*Is it Beijing Airport?*

5 They said that there was a 900 metre drop underneath.

*There's a 900 metre drop underneath.*

6 How do you know those weren't hoaxes?

*He asked me how I knew they weren't hoaxes.*

➡ **LANGUAGEBANK** 7.2 p140–141

If Ss seemed unsure of the rules in Ex 4C, give them time to read through them in class. Otherwise, tell them to read the section for homework. You could give Ss Ex B for extra practice in class. *Stronger classes* could do it as a race in pairs, or as a 'listen and stop me' activity, where you read the story aloud and Ss stop you when they hear a mistake and correct it.

> **Answers:** A 1 where I'd been all day  2 what I'd watched on TV the night before  3 if I'd washed my hands for dinner  4 if I'd got any homework for the next day  5 if I was going to help her with the housework that weekend
> B I was eighteen when I went for my first job interview, at a photo laboratory. The personnel manager asked me **to take a seat** and then asked **what my name was** and I was so nervous that I told him I **didn't** understand the question. Then he wanted to know **if I had** any plant experience; I said that I **had done/'d done** some work in my grandmother's garden. He laughed and said that by 'plant' he had meant 'factory', not 'trees and flowers'. I felt terribly embarrassed and simply told him that I **had/I'd** never worked in a factory. He had my file of photos and he asked **me to talk** about them. I was so nervous that I dropped them all on the floor. Then he asked me if I **had** any referees; I thought he meant the kind of referees they have in a football match, so I told him that I didn't play team sports but that I had been doing long-distance running for years. I was sure that I had messed up the interview, but then he enquired when I **could** start! He wanted me **to start** on the following Monday!

## PRACTICE

**5A** Focus Ss on picture C again and discuss briefly with the class why someone would jump a gap like that and how they might feel afterwards. Introduce the idea of a conversation between the park official and the man and ask Ss what sort of questions the official might ask him. Put Ss in pairs, emphasising that there are no 'set' answers, so they can use their own ideas.

> **Possible Answers:** 1 Q: Are you feeling OK?
> 2 A: Yes, I'm fine, thanks
> 3 Q: Why did you jump?
> 4 A: I wanted to see what if felt like./I wanted to show my family and friends I could do it.
> 5 Q: Did you realise that there was such a big drop?
> 6 A: No, not until I got to the edge.
> 7 B: Have you ever broken any bones doing your stunts?
> 8 A: Well no, but once I twisted my ankle.
> 9 Q: Would you mind coming to the office and helping me complete my report?
> 10 A: First I'll just phone my wife to tell her I'm okay.

**B** Give Ss time to write out the complete conversation in their notebooks, before putting them in pairs to compare answers.

> **Answers:** 1 if he was feeling (OK)  2 he was (fine)  3 why he'd (jumped)  4 he'd (wanted to see what it felt like)  5 if/whether he had/'d realised (that there was such a big drop)  6 he hadn't (until he'd got to the edge)  7 if/whether (he'd ever broken any bones)  8 once he'd twisted his ankle  9 him to come (to the office)  10 first he would/'d phone (his wife to tell her he was okay)

### VOCABULARY reporting verbs

**6A** Nominate different pairs to 'act out' the dialogues and discuss with the class who the people are and the situations.

**B** Direct Ss to the headlines. Check that they understand *champ* (short for champion) and *split* (end of a relationship). Ask them to predict which report goes with which conversation, then read the reports to check their predictions.

**Answers:** 1 C 2 B 3 A

**7A** Complete the first gap in report A as an example. Encourage Ss to use all the verbs they're familiar with first, then check any that they're unsure of in the dictionary.

**Answers:** 1 admitted 2 apologised 3 suggested 4 offered 5 refused 6 insisted 7 agreed 8 promised 9 accused 10 denied 11 threatened 12 persuaded

**B** Ask Ss to find a verb in the reports that is followed by an infinitive with *to*. Put Ss in pairs to find the rest.

**Answers:** 1 infinitive with *to*: offer refuse agree promise threaten
2 *-ing* form: admit (also followed by *that*) suggest deny
3 object + *(to)* infinitive: persuade
4 preposition+ *-ing* form: accuse apologise for insist on

**8** Two *strong Ss* demonstrate this for the class, swapping roles after the first line and continuing with the second line of the dialogue.

**9A** Ask Ss to read through the situations quickly and decide which they would find the most difficult to deal with. Discuss their answers briefly as a class and put them in pairs to complete the questions. Vocabulary to check: *betray* (not to be loyal to), *authenticity* (the quality of being real or genuine), *bonus* (an extra amount of money as reward) *take the credit for something* (to accept praise or approval for something).

**Answers:** 1 b) doing (having done is also possible) c) to pay 2 a) of betraying b) to believe c) on seeing 3 a) to take b) to go c) for breaking 4 a) to do b) asking c) to report

**B** Ss should note down each other's answers and see where they agree. You could also encourage Ss to write an extra answer for any of the situations where they would react differently (e.g. for situation 1: *accuse your colleague of blackmail and threaten to report him to your boss*) and share these with the class in feedback.

### WRITING a discursive essay

**10A** If there are any stories concerning celebrities currently in the news, you could bring in some news headlines and/ or photos and put them on the board for Ss to discuss what they know about the story, what they think of the celebrity involved, etc. Ss could then discuss the statements and think of reasons in pairs.

**B** Put pairs together into groups of four for this.

**11A** Give Ss a minute or two to read the essay quickly and answer the questions. Have a brief discussion with the class about whether they agree with the writer and why/why not.

**Answer:** The essay is about topic 1.

**B** Before Ss answer the questions, you could ask them to decide on the purpose of each paragraph with a partner. Then they can do the exercise to check their ideas.

**Answers:** 1 explains why the topic is of interest 2 gives points for 3 gives points against 4 gives the writer's opinion

### LEARN TO use linkers of contrast

**12A** While Ss circle the linkers, write up the four sentences on the board so you can highlight them in the next stage.

**Answers:** 2 While 3 Although 4 However

**B** Give Ss a few minutes to discuss the questions. You could also ask them which of the linkers can go at the beginning or in the middle of the sentence.

**Answers:** 1 a comma
2 an *-ing* form (e.g. *despite knowing*).
3 The main clauses are:
sentence 1 – Celebrities invite publicity
sentence 2 – others never want or plan for it
sentence 3 – often they are more interested in selling a sensational story
4 the subordinate clause

**C** Ss work on this alone and compare answers in pairs.

**Answers:** 1 Some celebrities are good role models for young people. However, others set a negative example. OR Although some celebrities are excellent role models for young people, others set a negative example
2 Despite the fact that anonymously published internet news is unreliable, many people rely on it as a main source of information OR Despite anonymously published internet news being unreliable, OR Despite the unreliability of anonymously published internet news, … etc.
While anonymously published internet news is unreliable, many people rely on it as a main source of information.
3 While false reports of celebrity deaths are common, some people still believe them. False reports of celebrity deaths are common. However, some people still believe them.
4 Although the scandal damaged his reputation, he still has millions of fans. OR Despite the scandal damaging his reputation he still has millions of fans. OR Despite the fact that the scandal damaged his reputation, OR Despite the damage that the scandal did to his reputation, … etc.

**13A** Ss could decide on a topic in pairs and brainstorm some ideas, then work alone to write notes for each paragraph.

### speakout TIP

Ask Ss what the difference is between a discursive essay and an opinion essay, then give them 1–2 mins to read the tip.

**B** Ss write a first draft in class, then read their partner's work and give them some feedback. Ss write a final draft for homework.

**Homework idea**
1 Workbook Ex 1–5, p48–49

# WHAT'S IN THE NEWS?

## Introduction

Ss practise listening and speaking about the press using phrases for adding emphasis. They also learn to make guesses.

## SUPPLEMENTARY MATERIALS

Resource bank p177

Ex 1A: Examples of tabloid and broadsheet newspapers.

## Warm up

Tell Ss to close their books and put the title *What's in the news?* on the board. Put Ss into groups of three to five to discuss stories that have been in the news for the past few days and make a list of the topics. Write a list on the board.

## VOCABULARY the press

**1A** Ss keep their books closed. Write the headline of the article on the board and check that they understand *tabloids* (newspapers that have a small page size and don't have much 'serious' news). If you have brought in some tabloid and broadsheet newspapers, show Ss the difference. Ask the class for their ideas on the six topics and put them on the board. Give Ss a minute or two to read the article quickly, then check the list of six topics together.

> **Answers:** scandal, money, babies, animals, royalty and winners

**B** Ss read the article in more detail and tick ✓ the types of story they would read, then compare answers with a partner, giving reasons for their choices.

**2A** With *stronger classes* direct Ss to the words in bold and ask them to discuss what they mean in pairs. Then they can do the matching task and check their ideas. Pronunciation to check: *feature* (a special article in a newspaper which deals with a particular subject), *biased* (not neutral), *sensationalism* (when newspapers intentionally present information in a way that is intended to excite or shock people) *tabloid*.

> **Answers:** 2 feature 3 readership 4 columnist
> 5 supplement 6 broadsheet 7 biased 8 sensationalism
> 9 circulation 10 tabloid

**B** Give Ss a few minutes to discuss the questions. Find out which sections of the paper are the most/least popular.

---

> ⇒ **VOCABULARYBANK** p154 Parts of a news website
>
> Ex 1B revises and extends the vocabulary for talking about the press in the context of a news website. Let the Ss work independently to label the diagram of the website and check their answers in pairs. Feedback as a class.
>
> > **Answer key:** As seen in diagram.

---

## FUNCTION adding emphasis

**3A** Give Ss a couple of minutes to discuss the headlines, then ask different pairs to talk about each headline in feedback.

**B** Ss should note down just the letter of each headline in the order that they hear them.

> **Answers:** 1 E 2 A 3 F 4 C

**3C** Tell Ss to listen for one surprising fact in each story. Give them time to compare answers with a partner.

---

> **Answers:** 1 The lottery winners are from the same town but don't know each other. 2 It looks like a picture done by a child but in fact it's bacteria from the moon. 3 Some lions protected a girl from men chasing her. 4 A prince has to pay a fine even though he recommends reducing car use and taking public transport.

## Unit 7 Recording 3

### Conversation 1

A: Can you believe those people who won the lottery?

B: Sorry?

A: Those people who won 43 million euros each.

B: Lucky them! That must be one of the biggest prizes ever.

A: Yeah, but the amazing thing is the two winners are from the same town.

B: So?

A: and they've won separately.

B: What, you mean they didn't do it together?

A: No, they don't know each other.

B: You're kidding. That's absolutely incredible! I mean …

A: Yeah, it's such an amazing coincidence. They're saying that …

### Conversation 2

A: Hi.

B: Hi. Have you seen this picture? Look.

A: No.

B: What do you think it is?

A: It's difficult to say, but I gather it's some sort of painting. It's quite pretty. It looks like one of those done by a child or I guess it could be a computer image.

B: Wrong! It's actually a photo of some bacteria they found on the moon.

A: Really? There's no way I would have guessed that. Let me see again. I suppose it does look like bacteria now I come to think about it.

B: Mind you, I don't believe it. I think it's a tabloid …

### Conversation 3

A: Did you see that story about the kid in Ethiopia?

B: No.

A: It was on the breakfast news this morning. It was about this girl who was being chased by some men. And three lions came out and chased away the men and then stayed and protected her.

B: That is incredible. Why on earth would they do that?

A: What, the lions?

B: Yeah.

A: Maybe they heard her crying. You know and thought she was a cub.

B: Perhaps … but it sounds a bit weird. Why didn't they just eat her?

A: Good question. Er, maybe …

B: That reminds me of a story …

### Conversation 4

A: He looks in a bad mood.

B: Let's look. What happened?

A: He's got to pay a fine. Apparently he left his car in the wrong place.

B: He's got to pay a fine!

A: Yeah.

B: And he's the one who's always talking about reducing car use and taking public transport.

A: Yeah. That's so hypocritical.

B: I thought you liked him.

A: Yeah, well, sometimes he can be such an idiot but he's …

**4A** Focus Ss on the first extract from the recording and point out that the underlined phrase could be left out and the sentence would still make sense. Tell Ss to look at the other sentences in the same way.

**Answers:** 2 absolutely  3 such  4 There's no way  5 does  6 *is* (couldn't be left out but would normally be contracted to 's)  7 on earth  8 the one who's  9 so  10 such

**B** Establish that a word used on its own to add emphasis (e.g. *absolutely*) will always be stressed and in a phrase the stress will be on the 'content' words, e.g. *amazing (thing)* in sentence 1. Encourage Ss to copy the speakers' intonation.

## Unit 7 Recording 4

1  The amazing thing is the two winners are from the same town
2  That's absolutely incredible!
3  Yeah, it's such an amazing coincidence.
4  I suppose it does look like bacteria now I come to look at it more carefully.
5  There's no way I would have guessed that.
6  That is incredible.
7  Why on earth would they do that?
8  He's the one who's always talking about reducing car use.
9  That's so hypocritical.
10 Sometimes he can be such an idiot

### ⏩ LANGUAGEBANK 7.3 p140–141

Ss look at Ex 4A again and try to categorise the different ways of adding emphasis. Direct them to the **Language bank** to check their ideas. Ss could do Ex A for extra practice or instead of Ex 5.

**Answers:** 1 A: What **on earth**'s the matter? You look terrible!
2 B: I've just seen Marco with Claudia. I'm **so** furious, I can hardly speak.
3 A: That's **totally** crazy. I'm sure there's a mistake. Why don't you call him?
4 B: **There's no way I'm going** to phone him.
5 A: But Marco's **such** a great guy and you're **so** good together.
6 B: Well you can be (**really**) sure that Claudia's (**really**) going to regret it.
7 A: I **do** hope you're not going to do anything stupid.
8 B: **You're the one who** told me to fight for him. I'm just following your advice.

**5A** Ss work alone or with a partner to rewrite the sentences.

**Answers:**
1 B: But I **did tell** ~~told~~ you. A few minutes ago.
A: That's **really** helpful! How am I supposed to get ready in time?
B: But you're **the one who** said you never want to go to parties.
2 A: Dave was good-looking but she was **absolutely** crazy about Will.
B: It's sad. **The thing is,** Dave adores her.
A: Yeah and he's really kind, **such** a nice man.
B: What **on earth** shall I say if he asks me about Will?
3 A: I'm quitting my job. It's **such** a bore.
B: I **do** think you'll regret it.
A: You're **the one who** always says I should do what I want.
B: **There's no way I meant** ~~I didn't mean~~ that you should just quit.

**B** Circulate and help Ss to use the phrases for emphasis accurately in their conversations.

**C** You could suggest that Ss write one or two key words in their notebooks from each of A's and B's lines to act as prompts to help them remember the conversation.

### LEARN TO make guesses

**6A** Encourage Ss to complete the sentences with anything that is grammatically correct and makes sense.

**Answers:** 1 must be  2 difficult  3 gather  4 could  5 suppose  6 look  7 Maybe

**B** Put Ss in pairs to look at the words and point out that there's more than one possibility for some of the gaps.

**Answers:** 1 must be – 's surely  2 difficult – hard  3 gather – reckon/imagine/think  4 could – might  5 suppose – reckon/think  6 look – seem  7 Maybe – Perhaps

### speakout TIP

Give Ss time to read the tip and then read out the three sentences and ask them to tell you the categories:
*I'd recommend the wine* = suggestion
*I'd agree that it's …* = opinion
*I'd imagine she's married?* = guessing
NB *I'd say …* is also used for guessing.

**7A** Ss work alone.

**B** Tell Ss not to write out the full conversation.

**Answers:** A: What do you think it is?
B: It's hard to say but I'd imagine it's _____.
A: I think it sounds like _____.
B: I suppose it could be _____.
A: Or it might be _____.
B: Well, I reckon it's _____.

You could encourage *stronger classes* to refer to the past in the conversation, e.g. *What do you think it was?* etc.

**C** Tell Ss to write the numbers 1–5 in their notebooks and after each conversation, to write down the answer they decided on. They can compare their answers with the class.

### SPEAKING

**8A** Pairs can make guesses for all four categories, or concentrate on one. NB Make sure that Ss don't look at the answers yet.

**B** Go through the instructions for the activity, reminding Ss they can use phrases for emphasis when they react to the correct answers (as in the example). Then either put the pairs together into groups of four or six, or split the pairs up into two groups of As and Bs.

**Homework ideas**
1 Workbook Ex 1–4B, p50
2 Ss write dialogues about headlines B and D from Ex 3, using phrases for adding emphasis, as in audio script 7.3.
3 Vocabulary bank Ex 1, p154

# NEWS BLUNDERS

## Introduction

Ss watch an extract from a BBC programme about TV news out-takes. Ss then learn and practise how to retell a news story and write a newspaper article.

## Warm up

Start by eliciting some jobs involved in making the TV news, e.g. producer, researcher, newsreader (also newscaster and anchorman/woman in the US), weatherperson, camera operator. Then put Ss in pairs and ask them to brainstorm the pros and cons of working as a TV newsreader. Conduct feedback with the class.

### ▶ DVD PREVIEW

**1A** You could lead into this by describing one or two favourite out-takes of yours. Then put Ss in pairs to discuss the questions.

**B** To familiarise Ss with the programme information, ask them to read it quickly and find out why mistakes on TV news programmes happen more often nowadays (because the news is non-stop for twenty-four hours). Then put them in pairs to match the words/phrases and definitions.

> **Answers:** 2 strike (commonly used with *disaster* or *tragedy*) 3 technical hiccup (*hiccup* can be used for any kind of small problem or delay) 4 rolling 5 autocue 6 blunder 7 to malfunction

### ▶ DVD VIEW

**2A** Explain to Ss that they will see seven blunders in total and ask them to write the numbers 1–7 in their notebooks so they can make notes about each one. They could use a tick ✓ for blunders they found funny, a cross ✗ for those they didn't find funny and a question mark ? for the ones they didn't understand. They should also write down a few key words to help them remember what happened each time. Ss then compare answers in pairs and help each other with any blunders they didn't understand.

**B** You could play the first blunder and check that Ss understand what happened. Then play the rest of the recording and give Ss time to compare answers.

> **Answers:** Malfunctioning equipment – 1
> People stumbling over their words – 2, 3
> The wrong guest in an interview – 5, 6, 7
> An accident on a live programme – 4

**C** Direct Ss to the extracts and give them a minute or two to predict/remember the missing words.

> **Answers:** 1 wrong 2 thing, is 3 embarrassing (*deeply* means *extremely* and also collocates with *worrying* and *involved*) 4 champion, involving 5 show (*It goes to show* is a common spoken phrase used when an experience proves something to be true)

**D** Give Ss a few minutes to discuss the question, then ask one or two pairs to tell the class their answer and explain why they chose that incident.

### DVD 7 The Funny Side of the News

**1**

**Jeremy Paxman:** Good evening. If the autocue was working I could now read you something, but as it isn't, I can't.

**2**

**Newsreader:** And there'll be live coverage on the BBC of the Democratic convention in New York in just in … under ten minutes, that's in about, ah, ten minutes.

**3**

**Rob:** And that is all the business news for the moment, Riz.

**Riz:** Thank you very much Rob. I'm back with a look at the, headweather … with the headlines after a look at the weather with Rob McElweather.

**Clive Anderson:** News, everybody's got an opinion about it: there's too much of it, it's on at the wrong time, it's too serious, it's too fluffy, it's too short, it's too tall.

**Nicholas Owen:** It's one of the few things on television these days that really is live, so if it starts going wrong, you're gonna see it and probably enjoy it at the same time.

**4**

*Look East* **presenter:** And finally, my thanks to Hugh Smith of Holt and Kay Coulson of Fordham Heath, Colchester for sending me these little and large bottles with, impossible nails and screws through pieces of wood to further tantalise my brain on how they did it … oh … ah.

**Fiona Bruce:** The thing about rolling news is that you have to fill an awful lot of time and things are changing around you and you won't necessarily be that clear about, you know, you know you've got to interview about three or four guests, the order of them might change you're not quite sure who it's gonna be …

**Clive Anderson:** And twenty-four-hour rolling news has created a new category. The right interview with the wrong guest.

**5**

**Interviewer 1:** … higher quality. Managing Director of Internet at NTL, Jerry Rust joins me now, what's gone wrong? What's gone wrong in, ah, in your offer?

**Wrong guest 1:** I'm afraid this is not what I'm talking about, I'm not …

**Interviewer 1:** I'm afraid we obviously the wrong guest here. That's, ah, deeply embarrassing for us.

**6**

**Sophie Raworth:** The Head of the NUT's Education Department is John Bangs. He's in our …

**Wrong guest 2:** Ah you've got the wrong …

**Sophie Raworth:** … Central London Studio … he was in our Central London Studio but he seems to have disappeared so hopefully we shall go back to him later on?

**Clive Anderson:** But the undisputed champion of the Wrong Guest division is the BBC News twenty-four incident involving the charming but inappropriate Guy Goma.

**7**

**Interviewer 2:** So what does this all mean for the industry and the growth of music online? Well Guy Kewney is the Editor of the technology website, ah, News Wireless. Hello, good morning to you.

**Guy Goma:** Good morning.

**Interviewer 2:** Were you surprised by this, verdict today?

Guy Goma: I'm very surprised to see this verdict to ... to come on me, because I wasn't expecting that.

Kevin Bakhurst: It was an item in one of the business slots on News 24 and the Business Producer went downstairs to reception and said, 'Is Guy here for *BBC News*?' and Guy Goma put his hand up ... There were two Guys there, but the wrong Guy put his hand up first and came upstairs and as you know he was here for a, he was here for an interview but it wasn't for an interview for News 24, it was an interview for a job.

GMTV presenter: The Sun headline is 'Big Bluffer', we find the Beeb news ... Beeb news show's accidental 'expert' ...

Clive Anderson: And for a while, Guy Goma found himself living the celebrity lifestyle. But anyway, it goes to show just how much the public love a good news blunder.

## speakout a news story

**3A** Before Ss look at the exercise, use pictures A–C to pre-teach *snow globe, paper clip* and *door knob*. Then ask Ss in pairs to decide how these three objects could be connected in a story and discuss their ideas as a class. Introduce the story and explain that *swap* and *trade* both mean to exchange something with someone so that you each get what you want. Tell Ss to number the items from 2–6 and play the recording. Check answers with the class and ask Ss what they thought of the story.

> **Answers:** 2 a pen  3 a door knob  4 a snow globe  5 a part in a film  6 an empty house

**B** Give Ss a minute or two to look through the key phrases before you play the recording again. At this point you may want to check: *It sounds a bit out there* (unconventional, eccentric), *random* (without any particular reason, aim or pattern).

> **Answers:** Did you hear the story/read the news about ...?
> Apparently what happened was ...
> According to the report ...
> I don't remember all the details, but ...
> As I recall ...
> My impression was that ...

### Unit 7 Recording 7

M = Man  W = Woman

M: Did you hear this story in the news about this guy that swapped a paper clip, for a house?

W: No.

M: It sounds a bit out there but apparently what happened was he started ... he was at his desk looking for a job or phoning up about jobs ...

W: Yeah.

M: ... and, um, he saw a paper clip on his desk and he thought, I wonder what I can do with this paper clip – whether I can swap it for something.

W: Oh.

M: Anyway, so he got onto the internet and he made this website – I think it's called the-red-paper-clip dot com.

W: Right.

M: And he put this, this on the internet, photographs it, puts it on and sees if anyone wants to swap something with him.

W: And did, did anything happen?

M: Yeah, so first of all, I don't remember all the details but as I recall two Vancouver women, um, took up the first challenge and they swapped the paper clip with, I think it was a pen shaped like a fish they had found ...

W: Random.

M: Yeah – they had found on a camping trip, yeah random. But he meets up with all these people he doesn't just send the things. And so then from that, I believe, this guy in Seattle wanted the pen and, swapped it for a door knob. And the door knob, was swapped for something to do with camping.

W: Oh so he kept trading up each time.

M: Yeah he kept trading, trading up so and then that was swapped for a beer keg I think. Apparently what happened was all these people were ... the same sort of thought patterns as him and they wanted to sort of meet up and it was about a social event as well.

W: Ah.

M: Anyway, the next thing he got was a snow globe and, according to the report, it said a film director wanted it and said he'd swap it for a part in his film. And then this town decided, they had this house in this town and that they would swap the house for a part in this film.

W: No! So he went all the way from the red paper clip to getting a house.

M: ... a house. And my impression was that he, he was just crazy at the beginning but he, he ended up having this – I'm not sure how good the house was but, well, yeah.

W: Well, better than a paper clip.

M: I know basically that's what happened.

W: Wow!

**C** Get the Ss to work alone on their story. Be available to help with vocabulary, etc.

**D** Ss work in groups of three to five. Remind those listening to use words/phrases to show they're interested and to take notes. After they've all told their stories, they could discuss which story was the most interesting/the funniest/the weirdest, etc. then tell the rest of the class what they decided.

## writeback a newspaper article

**4A** Give Ss a minute or two to number the items. Vocabulary to check: *breakthrough,* (an important discovery or event which helps improve a situation or a solve a problem), *enterprising* (good at thinking of and doing new things), *mayor* (the person who is leader of the group that governs a town or city).

> **Answers:** 1 a neon sign  2 an afternoon with Alice Cooper

**B** Tell Ss they're going to look at some ways of avoiding repetition in their writing. They can work on the tasks alone or with a partner then go through the answers with the class.

> **Answers:** 1 objects, items, article  2 A Canadian man, Blogger Kyle Macdonald, the 26-year-old, the Canadian, the enterprising trader
> Point out to Ss how to use the examples in 2: *a + nationality + noun (a British teenager); noun + name (actor Trudi Brown); the (age)-year-old; the + nationality; the + adj + noun (the lucky winner).*

**C** Encourage Ss to start by writing notes and making a plan for their article. Circulate and help as required. When ready, Ss write their first draft, then show it to you or to a partner for comments and suggestions.

> **Homework ideas**
> 1 Ss write another newspaper article.
> 2 Ss research redpaperclip.com (correct at the time of going to press) on the internet and report back on their findings in the next lesson.

# LOOKBACK

## Introduction

The aim of these activities is to provide revision and further practice of the language from the unit. You can also use them to assess Ss' ability to use the language, in which case you need to monitor but avoid helping them. You may feel that you don't need or have time to do all the activities. If so, you could allocate the activities that would be most beneficial for your Ss, or get individual Ss to decide which activities they'd like to do in class.

### TELEVISION

**1A** You could set a time limit – for example two minutes – for Ss to find the fourteen different types of TV programme in the wordsnake, working either alone or in pairs, before feeding back as a class.

> **Answers:** sketch show  sitcom  the news  costume drama  quiz  serial  documentary  detective series  game show  current affairs programme  opera  reality show  thriller  wildlife programme

**B** You could set a time limit for this, e.g. three minutes and see which pair has written down the most examples for each category.

> **Answers:**
> laugh – sketch show, sitcom, reality show, game show
> learn something – documentary, current affairs programme, quiz, docudrama
> just relax and watch real people – reality show, game show
> catch up on the news – current affairs programme, the news
> test your knowledge – quiz

### QUANTIFIERS

**2A** You could do the first sentences as an example, then give Ss a few minutes in pairs to do the rest. Remind Ss to look carefully at the verb forms used (singular or plural) and that the sentences are about just two people.

> **Answers:** 1 Both  2 Neither  3 quite a few of  4 a little  5 hardly any  6 Neither  7 every 8 Each  9 several  10 a few

**B** Ask two Ss to demonstrate the first example and point out that if the answer is not the same for both of them, they need to say *One of us (enjoys airports), but the other (doesn't).* Choose a few Ss to tell the class some of their answers in feedback. You could extend this by asking Ss to choose a famous celebrity couple, or a movie/cartoon couple and tell them to change the sentences as if they are answering for that couple. The idea is to produce some amusing answers!

### REPORTED SPEECH

**3A** You could do the first sentence as an example with the class. Ss work alone and compare answers with a partner.

> **Answers:** 1 Last week, an interviewer asked me what my biggest weakness was.
> 2 The other day, a complete stranger walked up to me and asked what I'd/had been doing lately.
> 3 Once, I was trying on trousers and the shop assistant asked if I would like/wanted to try a bigger size.
> 4 Every day, my flatmate asks me to do the dishes and then says he'll do them next time.
> 5 At the end of a first date, the girl asked me when I wanted to get married.
> 6 At 3a.m., my phone rang and the person asked if I was sleeping.

**B** You could start by telling Ss which question would make you feel most uncomfortable and why. Then put Ss in to small groups to explain their choices. You could extend this by asking Ss to imagine that someone did actually ask them the questions and tell their group how they replied, e.g. (for no1) *I told him I didn't have any weaknesses!*

### REPORTING VERBS

**4A** Focus Ss on the example and put them in pairs to help each other with the rest of the exercise.

> **Answers:** 2 making  3 to lend  4 going  5 to pay  6 for being  7 to quit  8 on paying  9 of being  10 to do

**B** Encourage Ss to read out the questions to each other, focusing on appropriate stress and intonation. For *weaker classes* you may want to drill the questions first. To extend this, ask Ss to choose two (different) questions each to ask other people in the class, then to stand up and walk round asking the questions and making a note of the answers they get. Ss then go back to their original pairs and report the answers to their partner, e.g. *Everyone said they'd always apologise for being late. One person said he'd refused to pay a bill: it was in a restaurant – his pizza was burnt!*

### ADDING EMPHASIS

**5A** You could run this as a race in pairs: as soon as a pair has finished the exercise they bring their books up to you to check.

> **Answers:** 1 so  2 so  3 very  4 the  5 the  6 she

**B** You could demonstrate this first by taking the role of Student A yourself and asking a *strong student* to take the role of Student B, e.g.

**You:** *There's no way that I'd ever borrow money from a friend.*

**Student B:** *What makes you say that?*

**You:** *Well, it's embarrassing if they don't pay you back.*

**Student B**: *How do you mean?*

**You:** *You know, you don't want to ask them for the money in case they've forgotten, or …*

After Ss have practised in pairs for a few minutes they could report some of the conversations back to the class, e.g. *My partner told me her hometown's a boring place because there's nowhere to go out at night. When I asked her what she meant by that, she said there were some cafés and pubs, but no clubs.*

# 8 BEHAVIOUR

## OVERVIEW

## IT'S A TOUGH CALL

### Introduction
Ss practise reading and speaking about difficult decisions using conditionals and related collocations.

### SUPPLEMENTARY MATERIALS
Resource bank p178 and/or p180

Ex 1B, 7A: Ss should use monolingual dictionaries for the *Optional extra activity* and when preparing to talk about a difficult decision.

### Warm up
Ask the class for an example of an important decision that a person may have to make in their life, then put Ss pairs to make a list of examples. Write the examples on the board in feedback and discuss with the class which they think are the most difficult decisions to make.

Examples of decisions: *whether to go to university or not and which one to go to/what subject to study; what career path to take; whether to change jobs; what car/house to buy; what town/country to live in; whether to get married/have children/get divorced; what to do about problems in a friendship/relationship.*

### READING

**1A** Direct Ss to the photos and write the headlines on the board to avoid Ss getting distracted by the texts.

**Answers:**
Hiker risks life – B
Mother turns son in to police – A
Couple ordered to return cash – C

**B** Ss could discuss what happened in pairs and agree on two sentences to give the details of the situation and describe what happened for each headline.

**Optional extra activity**
In order to check some key items of vocabulary from the texts and to encourage further prediction, write the following words on the board and ask Ss to decide which article they're from:

*cash in, footage, shelter, hypothermia, heartbroken, luxuries, temptation, stranded, toughest*

Encourage Ss to use monolingual dictionaries to check the meaning of unfamiliar words.

**C** Give Ss about five minutes to read the texts and discuss how accurate their predictions were with their partners.

**2** First, establish with the class what different people are mentioned in the articles, i.e. *Sakamoto, his fellow hikers, a park spokesman, Sandra Matthews, Simon Matthews, Carl Ruiz, a family friend, Dorothy Millet, Alan and Megan Beecham, a spokesman for the lottery company.* Then look at the first statement as an example with the class and put Ss in pairs to discuss the rest.

**Answers:** 1 Sandra Matthews, the mother who turned her son in. 2 Alan or Megan Beecham, who found the lottery ticket. 3 One of the two climbers who was trapped in the snowstorm. 4 Carl Ruiz, shop manager who was robbed. 5 Dorothy Millet, who lost the lottery ticket. 6 Spokesman for the lottery company. 7 Akira Sakamoto, who saved the two hikers. 8 Simon, whose mother turned him in.

### Optional extra activities

1 To give Ss practice in guessing meaning from context, ask them to find the following words in the text and guess what they mean:

(Hiker risks life) *makeshift, poncho, evacuated;* (Mother turns son in to police) *stuffing, option;* (Couple ordered to return cash) *prove, recovered.*

Ss write a simple definition for each word, then check with a monolingual dictionary.

2 For extra speaking practice, Ss role-play one or more of the following conversations:

a Sakamoto and the two hikers when he finds them on the mountain.

b Sakamoto and the two hikers after they've been discharged from hospital.

c Sandra Matthews and the police officer she sees at the police station.

d Sandra Matthews and Carl Ruiz.

e Alan and Megan Beecham after they find the ticket.

f The lottery representative and Alan and Megan Beecham.

**3** Ss can discuss the situations in pairs or small groups, then share their ideas with the class. In the feedback session find out which decision the majority of the class thinks was the most difficult one to make overall.

### GRAMMAR conditionals

**4A** Ss at this level should be familiar with the concept of 'unreal' present and past conditionals, but may not be confident in using modal verbs with these forms, or in referring to the past and present in the same sentence. Start by asking Ss which newspaper stories each of the four sentences refers to. Then, while Ss underline the verbs, write/display the sentences on the board so you can highlight the verbs and later label them with the answers to Ex 4B.

**Answers:** I If I <u>were</u> in the same situation, <u>I'd find</u> it difficult to <u>turn</u> my son <u>in</u>.
2 If she <u>hadn't saved</u> the receipt, we <u>might</u> never <u>have recovered</u> her money
3 If <u>I'd been paying attention</u>, I <u>wouldn't have dropped</u> the ticket.
4 If he <u>had left</u> them there, they <u>wouldn't be</u> alive now.

**B** Look at the first sentence with the class and establish that it refers to an imaginary situation. Put Ss in pairs to do the rest of the exercise.

**Answers:** I All four sentences refer to imaginary situations.
2 I present, 2 past, 3 past, 4 both (*had left = past, wouldn't be = present*)

**C** Tell Ss to look back at the example sentences in Ex 4A to help them with this. For *stronger classes* suggest that Ss cover the words in the box and try to complete the rules from their own knowledge first. When you've checked their answers, ask Ss to look again at the sentences in Ex 4A and reverse the order of the clauses. Elicit/Point out that when the main clause is at the beginning of the sentence like this, a comma in the middle is not necessary. You could also drill the four sentences at this stage, showing Ss that when they pause briefly on the comma, their pitch shouldn't drop.

**Answers:** I past simple, past perfect, past perfect continuous.
2 modal + infinitive, modal + have + past participle

**5** Direct Ss to the phonemic script and see if they can predict the matches first. Play the recording and ask Ss what happens to the h in *have* (it disappears). Then play the recording again for Ss to repeat the sentences. Point out that it's quite common to leave out the *if* clause like this when it's understood from the context.

**Answers:** Id) 2a) 3c) 4b)

⫸ **LANGUAGEBANK** 8.1 p142–143

Ss could read the notes and do Exs A and B for homework. You may want to direct Ss to the example of the mixed conditional *If* + past simple, modal + *have* + past participle and point out that the past simple usually refers to a state or habit/repeated action, e.g. *If we lived nearer to the airport, we could've given him a lift. If you spoke a bit more quietly, she might not have heard what you said about her.* Also direct Ss to the note about using *was* in spoken English, rather than *were*.

**Answers:** A I a) 2 b) 3 b) 4 a) 5 a)
B 2 If you had/'d invited me to the party, I would have come. OR: I would have come to the party if you had/'d invited me.
3 If Ludmila hadn't lost all her money on the stock market, she'd be rich now/she would have been rich now. OR Ludmila would be rich now/would have been rich now if she hadn't lost all her money on the stock market.
4 If Greg had been travelling fast, he might have hit the motorcyclist. OR Greg might have hit the motorcyclist if he had/'d been travelling fast.
5 If they hadn't stopped the fire, it could have destroyed most of the building. OR The fire could have destroyed most of the building if they hadn't stopped it.
6 The plant wouldn't have died if you had/'d watered it. OR If you had/'d watered the plant, it wouldn't have died.
9 Mei-li couldn't have afforded the car if she hadn't just won some money. OR If Mei-li hadn't just won some money, she couldn't have afforded the car.
10 If we hadn't been working together in Tokyo, we wouldn't be/wouldn't have been married now. OR We wouldn't be/wouldn't have been married now if we hadn't been working together in Tokyo.

### PRACTICE

**6A** Start by asking Ss to read the email quickly and answer the following questions:

*Who stole the laptops?* (Shaun)

*Who got sacked?* (Nick)

*Who lied?* (Nick)

Ss complete the gaps alone and check answers in pairs.

**Answers:** 1 hadn't been working  2 wouldn't have seen  3 might have spoken  4 hadn't asked  5 would have told  6 weren't/hadn't been  7 were/was  8 might not have lost  9 'd/had known  10 would you have told

**B** You could give Ss the following sentence heads to complete:

*I would've … because …*

*I wouldn't have … because …*

*I might've … because …*

*I couldn't have … because …*

**Optional extra activity**
Ss either write Shaun's email in reply to Nick, or role-play the conversation when he finally answers Nick's call.

### VOCABULARY  collocations

**7A** You could start by writing the following on the board (Ss should have their books closed) and asking Ss to think of a suitable verb for each gap:

1 _____ a decision

2 _____ one's principles (strong ideas about what's right or wrong)

3 _____ the pros and cons (good points and bad points)

4 _____ a situation

Add any acceptable suggestions that Ss give you to the board, then direct them to the first word web and give them a minute or two to think about the verb that doesn't collocate. Then put them in pairs to work on the rest. They should use monolingual dictionaries to check any verbs they're unsure of.

**Answers:**
a decision – do (*make* is correct)
one's principles – make
the pros and cons – decide
a situation – argue

**B** Look at the first definition with the class and establish that the two missing verbs have the same meaning. Also point out that this is the case for the rest of the definitions, although there may be some difference between them in the level of formality, e.g. *postpone* vs *put off*, *betray* vs *go against*, *stick to* vs *follow*, *weigh up* vs *compare* or *assess*. Pronunciation to check: *postpone, betray, compare, analyse, examine, assess.*

**Answers:** 1 come to, arrive at  2 postpone, put off  3 stick to, follow  4 go against, betray  5 compare, analyse, weigh up, examine  6 analyse, examine  7 assess, weigh up

**Optional extra activity**
For personalised practice, write the following sentence heads on the board for Ss to complete with their own ideas:

1 I often find it easier to _____ a decision than to …

2 I would only _____ my principles if …

3 If I spend too long _____ the pros and cons, …

4 It's easier to _____ a difficult situation if …

Ss the compare and discuss their answers in pairs or small groups.

**8A** Give Ss a minute or two to read through the situations and decide which one is more difficult and why. Discuss this briefly with the class, then give SS a few minutes to complete the texts.

**Answers:** 1 weighed up/assessed  2 go against/betray  3 came to/arrived at  4 examined, compared, analysed, weighed up  5 stick to, follow  6 put off, postponed

**B** Give Ss a few minutes to discuss the situations and compare their decisions.

### SPEAKING

**9A** Ss should make some notes about their own difficult situations so they can answer the questions in Ex 9B.

**Optional extra activities**
If Ss have trouble thinking of a situation:

Either: give Ss the situations below to choose from:

1 You were offered a room in a flat share and you really wanted to move out of home, but your family didn't want you to and you didn't want to upset them.

2 You were offered a free holiday with a friend's family, but you had exams coming up and you needed to study.

3 You saw something expensive in a shop that you'd been looking for for ages, but you were supposed to be saving money for a ….

Ss imagine they were in the situation and decide what they did.

OR: Ss think of a famous person, e.g. a politician, an actor, a footballer who's been in the news because of a difficult situation they've been in. In 9B, Ss can 'be' the famous person, answering as if the situation happened to them.

**B** You could start by talking about a difficult situation that you were in. Invite different Ss to ask you questions 1–6 and answer them incorporating some conditionals and some collocations in your answers.

**C** At this stage the support of the questions from Ex 9B is removed and Ss describe the whole situation and their reaction to the group. Monitor the groups and note down any good language use and problems for feedback and discussion later.

**Homework ideas**
1 Workbook Ex 1–5, p51–52
2 Ss write up a few situations from Ex 9C for the forum.
3 Ss prepare word webs for verbs such as: *make, do, take, have,* or for nouns such as *money, an email, an exam, a business* (refer to Unit 6, p74 in the Students' Book for other possibilities) and bring them to the next lesson to compare.

# BODY CLOCK

## Introduction

Ss practise listening and speaking about attitudes to time using -ing forms and infinitives and vocabulary related to feelings. They also learn to use an informal style and write an informal article.

### SUPPLEMENTARY MATERIALS

Resource bank p179 and/or p181

Warm up: prepare a handout of quotations about time (an alternative to writing them up the board).

Ex 9A: Ss need to refer to monolingual dictionaries.

## Warm up

Either: Write/Display the following quotations about time on the board (or put them on a handout) and put Ss into small groups to discuss what they mean, which ones they agree with, which one they like best and why. Conduct feedback, inviting the groups to share their opinions.

1 *Time is the most valuable thing a man can spend.* (Theophrastus, Philosopher)

2 *Nothing is a waste of time if you use the experience wisely.* (Rodin)

3 *Calendars are for careful people, not passionate ones.* (Chuck Sigars)

4 *It's a strange thing, but when you are dreading something and would give anything to slow down time, it has a disobliging habit of speeding up.* (J.K. Rowling)

5 *Time is a dressmaker specializing in alterations.* (Faith Baldwin)

6 *Time is what we want most, but what we use worst.* (William Penn)

Or: Write the title *Body clock* on the board (SS should have their books closed). Put Ss in pairs or small groups to discuss the following questions:

1 What is your body clock?

2 How are people's body clocks different?

3 How does your body clock affect your life?

Conduct feedback with the class.

### VOCABULARY feelings

**1A** You could start by asking Ss to guess which type you are, then telling them the answer and some of the reasons for it. If Ss know each other fairly well, they could guess their partner's 'type' in the same way.

**B** Direct Ss to the quiz and invite the class to comment briefly on what the pictures show. Then ask Ss to find another answer for number 1, before giving them time to work through the rest of the exercise, alone or in pairs. They may want to check some of the vocabulary in a dictionary: in order to encourage them to rely on their own guessing skills, you could suggest that they limit the number of words they look up to three or four. Pronunciation to check: <u>groggy</u>, <u>cringe</u>, <u>alert</u>.

**Answers:** 1 alert, at your sharpest, on the ball  2 wide awake  3 groggy, at your lowest ebb  4 have a sense of dread  5 bright and breezy, have a spring or a bounce in your step  6 despise (it) with a passion  7 not (be) that fussed  8 cringe

**C** Student A closes his/her book while Student B reads out the questions and choices and vice versa. Ss then read the key and see if it coincides with what they said in 1A. Finish with a quick show of hands to see how many of the different types are in the class.

**2A** Start with an example of your own, e.g. for *a lark: I feel groggy if I wake up later than 8 a.m.* Circulate and help Ss as they write their sentences.

**B** Focus Ss on the example and put them in pairs.

> ▶ **VOCABULARYBANK** p155 Feelings
>
> Ex 1 revises vocabulary for talking about feelings and introduces some new items. For Ex A, Ss can check the words in their dictionaries if they have difficulty in matching them with the correct group.
>
> In feedback, elicit the differences in degree between the adjectives in each group and also about shades of meaning – e.g. that within the group *delighted, glad, cheerful, delighted* is the strongest adjective, *glad* is usually used in relation to a specific event or thing, e.g. *glad about the good news* and *cheerful* can be used to describe someone's general mood, e.g. *I'm feeling cheerful this evening.* Completing Ex B will help Ss to get a good grasp of these differences in shade and degree of meaning.
>
> **Answers:** 1A Happy – glad, cheerful, delighted
> Unhappy – miserable, depressed, upset
> Angry – cross, livid, furious
> Frightened – petrified, apprehensive, terrified
> Confused – disorientated, puzzled, mystified
> B 1 cheerful  2 cross  3 apprehensive  4 upset
> 5 disorientated

### LISTENING

**3** Ss should think about the good and bad points about being a lark or an owl. In feedback, compile a list of their ideas on the board.

**4A** Tell Ss they're going to hear eight different speakers talking about being a lark or an owl. They should copy the list of good/bad points that the class has compiled on the board into their notebooks, so they can tick off the ones that are mentioned.

**B** Put Ss in pairs to discuss and label the statements, then play the recording again for them to confirm/change their answers.

**Answers:** 1 L  2 O  3 O  4 O (an owl is quoting her parents, who are larks)  5 L  6 O  7 L  8 O

**C** Give Ss a few minutes to discuss their answers.

### GRAMMAR -ing form and infinitive

**5A** Focus Ss on the example and suggest that they circle the correct answer so it stands out. Ss can work in pairs and help each other with this. Suggest that if they're not sure of an answer, they could read the sentence aloud, trying out the different forms, to see which one 'sounds' right. Vocabulary to check: *would rather (would prefer to)*, *tend (often do a particular thing)*.

**Answers:** 2 wake  3 dancing  4 getting up  5 eat  6 to be  7 to be  8 Being  9 to sleep  10 understand

**B** Check that Ss understand the terms *infinitive, infinitive with to* and *-ing form* by writing *go, to go* and *going* on the board and asking them which is which. You may want to check the following verbs from the table: *consider* (to think about), *end up* (to do something you didn't plan to do), *had better* (to make a suggestion or give advice).

**Answers:**

|  | -ing form or infinitive or infinitive with to | example sentence |
|---|---|---|
| after a preposition | -ing | 3 |
| to express purpose | infinitive with to | 6 |
| after let and make | infinitive | 2, 10 |
| as part of a semi-fixed phrase, e.g. it's good/better/best and it's the best time | infinitive with to | 7 |
| as a subject or object (or part of one of these) | -ing | 8 |
| after modal verbs | infinitive | 5 |
| after certain verbs such as enjoy, not mind, despise, avoid, keep, consider, imagine, end up | -ing | 4 |
| after certain verbs such as want, would like, tend, prepare | infinitive with to | 9 |
| after had better and would rather | infinitive | 1 |

**C** This exercise shows Ss that because the form of the modal verbs *must* and *can* doesn't change, they need to use an appropriate form of *have to* and *be able to* for expressing obligation and ability. Direct Ss to the example and remind them about the rules in Ex 5B. After Ss have had a minute or two to discuss their answers, play the recording.

**Answers:** 2 having to  3 to be able to  4 being able to

**6** Play the recording, stopping after each sentence for Ss to mark the stressed words and weak forms (unstressed vowel sounds). Then play it again for Ss to repeat.

**Answers:** 2 I <u>hate</u> having to <u>get</u> up in the winter.
/tə/
3 I <u>don't</u> seem to be able to <u>start</u> the computer.
/tə/    /tə/
4 I I <u>enjoy</u> being able to <u>watch</u> the sunrise.
/tə/

---

### ➡ LANGUAGEBANK 8.2 p142–143

Direct Ss to the **Language bank** in class if you think they'll benefit from seeing more examples of the uses of *–ing* and the infinitive. You could do Ex A as a team competition: write/display the sentences one at a time on the board for teams to discuss: to liven this up, when they're ready with the answer, the team members could make a sound like a 'buzzer' that people press, e.g. in a televised competition.

**Answers:** A 2 There's no point **in going** to bed now – we have to get up in an hour.
3 Do you expect **me to know** all the answers?
4 **Listening** to your MP3 player during class is rude.
5 My parents never **let me stay** out past 8 o'clock.
6 We all look forward **to seeing** you in person.
7 You'd better **get ready** – the taxi's arriving in ten minutes.
8 The trip was a good opportunity **to practise** speaking English.
9 They're used **to speaking** English with each other even though they're both Japanese.
10 I phoned the station **to ask** about departure times.
B 1 Have you considered becoming a doctor?
2 I've managed to pass my driving test – after three tries.
3 My mother taught me to type without looking.
4 We avoided talking to each other all through the party.
5 Jorge expects to finish the painting by the end of the week.
6 My computer keeps freezing whenever I hit the delete button.
7 Could you remind me to lock the door, Jan?

### PRACTICE

**7A** You could start by putting the three questions on the board and asking the Ss to complete them. Then ask Ss to discuss possible answers to the questions in pairs. Conduct feedback briefly and give Ss time to complete the answers, still in their pairs.

**Answers:** 1 to do  2 undertaking  3 exercising  4 eating  5 feel  6 digesting  7 to dip  8 putting  9 do  10 being able to remember  11 studying  12 to take  13 getting  14 to study

**B** Give Ss a minute or two in pairs to discuss what surprised them most about the answers.

### SPEAKING

**8A** Ask Ss if they know what their attitude to time is and put the following questions on the board for them to discuss with a partner:

*How do you feel about …*

*keeping to deadlines?*

*public transport arriving late?*

*people arriving late, e.g. at a meeting place, or for a dinner party at you house?*

*working late?*

Tell Ss they're going to hear about different attitudes to time and that they should simply tick the speaker(s) they agree with.

**B** Put Ss into groups of three to five and give them time to discuss their attitudes. Monitor the discussion and note down examples of good language use and problems for feedback and discussion/correction later.

**Unit 8 Recording 4**

S1 = Speaker 1    S2 = Speaker 2    S3 = Speaker 3    S4 = Speaker 4
S5 = Speaker 5    S6 = Speaker 6

S1:  I do prefer to keep to deadlines and if I don't I tend to get a bit stressed out, I don't like to disappoint people and I like to feel as though I'm quite organised. I don't mind working late sometimes if it's to get something finished and I feel much more satisfied getting something completed at the end of the day and I'm more likely to go home and relax. But, otherwise, I'll end up going home and just thinking about everything that I've got to do the next day, so that stresses me out more.

S2:  I think it's really important for transport, public transport to be punctual when you're working and that, that's – that's just normal but I think when I'm on holiday I'm a bit more relaxed about whether trains or buses are a little bit late, obviously you don't want to waste a whole day waiting for your transport when you want to get from A to B and you want to make the most of your holiday but, yeah, I think I'm definitely more relaxed when I'm abroad than when I'm in my own country …

S3:  Yeah I was, taught from an early age that time keeping's really important. Because of that I find it quite annoying when other people don't have that same sort of line of thought. An example I can give is my friends at university, they were always late. It makes me feel incredibly frustrated because, obviously, you're there on time waiting and it can be quite lonely at times.

S4:  I generally don't have a problem at all with people turning up late because it gives me time 'cos I'm generally running late anyway so, it gives me plenty more time to get myself ready. If we're preparing for a dinner party and people turn up late it really doesn't worry me at all. It gives me plenty more time to get ready …

S5:  If I'm holding a dinner party and people come late then usually I'm quite annoyed because I'm quite organised and so the food will probably be ready and so I'll be a little bit cross that perhaps the dinner will be ruined.

S6:  Deadlines are important but I try not to let them stress me out too much, I just try to forget about the pressure and get the work done. As for working late, I don't mind working late, we all have to do it from time to time.

### VOCABULARY *PLUS* idioms

**9A**  If Ss have access to the *Longman Active Study Dictionary* they could find the two references. Put them in pairs to discuss what information the dictionary gives the about idioms.

> **Answers:** A definition, an example sentence, common collocations, the fact that the phrase is informal.

### speakout TIP

Read the tip with the Ss and point out that the key word is very often a noun or verb. If they have different dictionaries to the *Longman Active Study Dictionary* give them a minute or two to find and compare the entries for the two idioms.

**B**  Look at number one with the class as an example, then put Ss in pairs to do the rest. Encourage Ss to try to guess the meaning of the idioms while they're doing this.

**C**  Tell Ss to copy the eight idioms/phrases into their notebooks first, so they can annotate them.

> **Answers:** 1 pressed  2 cut  3 bide  4 nick  5 once  6 time
> 7 make  8 drag

**D**  Ask a pair of *stronger Ss* to do an example from the class first, e.g.

*B: Does 'pressed for time' mean you don't have enough time?*
*A: That's right! You can also say 'pressed for money'.*
*It's informal.*

**10**  Focus Ss on the example and point out that they need to think carefully about the form of the verb in the idiom.

> **Possible answers:** (the part in bold must be correct)
> 2 You've got to **stop dragging your feet** about which job to take.  3 I was trying to **make up for lost time**.  4 I've told you **time after time** to check your spelling  5 Sorry, **I'm pressed for time**, can we talk later?  6 I fall ill **once in a blue moon**.  7 I got here **in the nick of time**.  8 **I'm biding my time**, something better might come along.

---

> ⇒ **VOCABULARYBANK** p155 Idioms
>
> Ex 2A and B introduce the Ss to some more common English idioms. Give the Ss a few minutes in pairs to match the idioms to the images and with the correct meaning, before feeding back as a class. If Ss are enjoying the topic of idioms, you could ask them to try to find idiomatic expressions in their own language which express the same ideas.
>
> > **Answers:** 2A 1 A 2 B 3 C 4 D 5 E 6 F 7 G 8 H
> > B 1 A f)  2 B b)  3 C d)  4 D e)  5 E c)  6 F h)  7 G a)
> > 8 H g)

### WRITING an informal article

**11A**  Tell Ss to cover the article and look at the three titles. Elicit some ideas about the possible content of an article with each of the titles. Then Ss read the article and choose the title.

> **Answer:** b) Pressed for time?

**B**  Suggest that Ss write the number 1, 2 or 3 next to the line in the article that contains an example to support each answer.

> **Answers:** 1 a student magazine: the tone is light hearted (para 3), *that's what email's for!*
> 2 give advice: (para 1), *here are some ideas that work for me.*
> 3 beginning: (para 2), *make a to-do list and prioritise ruthlessly.* The rest of the paragraph expands on this sentence, explaining it and giving examples.

### LEARN TO use an informal style in articles

**12A**  Look at the first guideline with the class, establishing that there is a personal example in each of the three main paragraphs. Put Ss in pairs to work through the rest.

> **Answers:** 1 T – *I look at my list, One of the shocking discoveries I made, I just realised recently*
> 2 T – three examples of *you* in the first paragraph; four examples of *I* in the second paragraph
> 3 F – *don't, you'd* (para 1)
> 4 T – *well, a couple of, that will just take, a bit like, 'me-time'*
> 5 T – *First of all, Then, Second, Finally, So*
> 6 T – *Have you ever felt …? Or that …?*
> 7 F – *catch up with, get on with, get up,*
> 8 F – There are no examples of the passive in the article.

**B**  Ss can choose one title to brainstorm ideas for, or work on all three.

**C**  Monitor Ss' writing and note down any common problems and some good examples for a feedback session. Ss may then want to redraft the article.

> **Homework ideas**
> 1 Workbook Ex 1–6, p53–54
> 2 Ss write another article from the list in Ex 12B.

# HAVE YOU GOT A MINUTE?

## Introduction

Ss practise listening and speaking about awkward situations using phrases for handling awkward situations and vocabulary related to manner. They also learn to soften a message.

### SUPPLEMENTARY MATERIALS

Resource bank p182

Ex 1A: Ss need to refer to a dictionary.

speakout TIP: give Ss some dialogues to add fillers to.

## Warm up

You could start by telling Ss about an awkward situation (real or invented) that you found yourself in, e.g. a friend borrowed something (a book, an item of clothing) and returned it damaged. Elicit some more examples of awkward situations form the class and ask Ss how it's best to behave when dealing with a situation like this. Ss may say you need to be tactful/honest/direct, etc.

### VOCABULARY manner

**1A** You could do the first one as an example with the class. Pronunciation to check: sup_por_tive, un_help_ful, dip_lo_matic, _tac_tful, _sen_sitive, _sen_sible, con_fron_tational, col_la_borative, ag_gres_sive, as_sert_ive, di_rect, _fo_cused. Ss could check the stress on the words in their dictionaries.

**Answers:** I D – supportive and unhelpful are near opposites
2 S – both mean you try to avoid hurting feelings or making people upset when you communicate with them.
3 D – sensitive means you are easy to hurt, OR that you understand what other people feel and care about their feelings. Sensible means you make good, rational decisions.
4 D – confrontational and collaborative are near opposites. If you are confrontational you like a fight, if you are collaborative you like to work with others.
5 D – aggressive is negative and means you push too much in any situation. Assertive is more positive and means you have the confidence to give your point of view, for instance.
6 S – These are similar. If someone is direct, they say what they mean clearly. If someone is focused, they are clear about what they want to say and are able to say it clearly.

**B** Focus Ss on the example and put them in groups to discuss the situations.

**Possible answers:** breaking bad news: sensitive, tactful, focused
a friend is down: supportive, sensitive
making a complaint: diplomatic, assertive, direct
working on a project: supportive, diplomatic, collaborative, focused
driving or cycling: sensible, focused

**C** Give Ss a few minutes in pairs to try making opposites and saying them aloud to see if they 'sound' correct.

**Answers:** I unhelpful – helpful 2 diplomatic – undiplomatic, tactful – tactless 3 senstive –insensitive, sensible – senseless 4 confrontational – unconfrontational, collaborative, uncollaborative (These opposites exist but are not common.) 5 aggressive – non-aggressive, assertive, unassertive 6 direct – indirect, focused – unfocused

### SPEAKING

**2A** Direct Ss to the photos and ask them what the awkward situation might be in each case. Then look at the three situations together and match the photos. Put Ss in pairs to discuss how to handle the situations.

**B** Give Ss a few minutes to read and discuss the tips. All the tips are valid, so they may agree with them all. You could ask them which they feel are the most/least important.

### FUNCTION handling an awkward situation

**3A** Refer Ss back to the tips in Ex 2B and play the recording.

**Answers:** He follows all the tips. He stays focused when she says she doesn't have the money on her. He's specific, reminding her that she said she'd pay it back later once before and telling her that he feels annoyed; he doesn't say what anyone else thinks. He gives her space by asking 'Do you know what I mean?' He suggests a solution.

**B** Give Ss 1–2 mins to read the statements then play the recording again.

**Answers:** I F (She borrows small amounts each time but they add up to quite a lot.) 2 F (Next week, after she's been paid.) 3 T (He says that she's said she'll pay him back before.) 4 F (He suggests she pays back however much she can afford each week.)

#### Unit 8 Recording 5

J = Jim    L = Liz

J:  Here's your coffee.

L:  Thanks, Jim. Oh, I needed that.

J:  No problem. Hey, Liz, there's something I've been meaning to talk to you about .

L:  Oh yeah?

J:  It's just that ... well ... you know you borrowed some money from me last week?

L:  Oh, right. It was ten euros, wasn't it? ... I don't actually have that on me at the moment.

J:  It's not that, it's ... well ... I hope you don't take this the wrong way, but, um ...

L:  Right.

J:  It's just that this isn't the first time I've lent you money and, er, well you haven't paid it back. I mean, I know it's not a lot, just small amounts each time but it kind of adds up quite quickly ... I dunno. Do you know what I mean?

L:  Yeah . Sorry. I didn't realise. I know I'm terrible with money. I just forget. Look, I promise I'll give it back, but could you wait a week? Until I get paid.

J:  Well, actually, you've said that once before. I don't want you to get the wrong idea, but ... it, you know, never happened. And it makes things slightly awkward. It makes me feel just a bit annoyed. Do you see where I'm coming from?

L:  Oh. Yeah. I suppose so.

J:  Look, I've got a suggestion. I'd feel better if we could work out how much is owed and then you could pay me back a little each week, you know, however much you can afford. How does that sound?

L:  Yeah, yeah. That sounds reasonable.

J:  Okay, great so ...

**4A** Once Ss have completed the phrases with their own ideas, either direct them to the audio script or play the recording again, for them to check.

**Answers:** I meaning (= intending, thinking about) 2 just 3 take (It's just that ... 'softens' the message) 4 what 5 sound

**B** Give Ss a minute or two to read the sentences aloud and think about the stress and intonation, then play the recording.

### Unit 8 Recording 6

There's <u>something</u> I've been <u>meaning</u> to <u>talk</u> to you about.
I <u>hope</u> you don't take this the <u>wrong</u> <u>way</u>, but …
I don't <u>want</u> you to get the <u>wrong</u> <u>idea,</u> but …
The first phrase goes down as it is a completed statement.
The other two phrases go up because they are unfinished.

**C** Ss could practise saying the phrases to each other and comment on whether they sound tactful or confrontational.

> ⯈ **LANGUAGEBANK** 8.3 p142–143
>
> Direct Ss to the summaries of the different types of phrase on page142. Under *suggesting a solution,* establish that a past form is needed after *It would put my mind at ease if (you could …)* and *I'd feel better if you (told me).* Ss could do Ex A before moving on to the more challenging practice in Ex 5 on p99. Once Ss have completed the conversation, they could practise acting it out, making sure they sound appropriately diplomatic/focused, etc.
>
> **Answers:** 1 c) 2 f) 3 b) 4 e) 5 a

**5A** Tell Ss to read through the prompts quickly and match the situation with the appropriate photo (*the girl talking on the phone with the woman looking exasperated in the background*). Give Ss a few minutes to write out the conversation in their notebooks.

> **Answers:** A: Alex, there's something I've been meaning to talk to you about.
> B: Yeah. What's up?
> A: Well, look I don't want you to get the wrong idea but …
> B: But what?
> A: It's just that I've a lot of work and when you're always on the phone I can't concentrate.
> B: Oh, right.
> A: It's quite annoying. Do you know what I mean?
> B: I'm sorry, I wasn't thinking.
> A: I've got a suggestion. Why don't you ask your friends to call your mobile instead of our land line?
> B: You mean I should/could use the phone in a different room?
> A: That's right. How does that sound?
> B: That seems reasonable. I'm really very sorry.
> A: No problem. Forget it.

**B** Ss should only look at the flow chart, not read aloud from their notebooks. Monitor the practice and note down any problems for correction in feedback.

> **Optional extra activity**
> Ss in pairs think about what to say for situation 2 in Ex 2A, the waitress with blue hair and practise the conversation.
> For *weaker classes,* encourage them to write some prompts like those in Ex 5A to help them before they practise. Monitor the practice and ask one or two pairs who did well to act out their conversations for the class. You could have a vote on who dealt with the situation in the most tactful/ effective way.

### LEARN TO soften a message

**6** Tell Ss they're going to hear some extracts from the conversation between Jim and Liz again and give them a

minute to read through the sentences. Explain that the extra words or sounds they'll hear make the sentences sound more realistic for someone who's trying to be tactful and not confrontational. Show Ss how to write *um* and *er* and play the recording.

### Unit 8 Recording 7

1 It's not that, it's … well … I hope you don't take this the wrong way, but um it's just that this isn't the first time I've lent you money and, er, well you haven't paid it back. I mean, I know it's not a lot, just small amounts each time but it kind of adds up quite quickly … I dunno. Do you know what I mean?

2 Well, actually, you've said that once before. I don't want you to get the wrong idea, but … it, you know, never happened. And it makes things slightly awkward. It makes me feel just a bit annoyed. Do you see where I'm coming from?

### speakout TIP

Before Ss look at the tip, ask them to look back at Ex 6 and decide which words are used like a pause and which are used in front of an adjective to soften the message.

> **Optional extra activity**
> For more practice in adding fillers to a conversation, give Ss some four to six line dialogues (on a handout or written on the board) and ask them to add fillers.
> The following situations should naturally generate the need for pauses/getting thinking time and softening the message:
> an invitation to dinner/a party/an event (the person inviting is nervous), e.g.
> A: I was (kind of) wondering if you're (I mean) free on Saturday?
> B: I think so, yes.
> A: (Well, um) There's a jazz (kind of) festival in town in the afternoon. Would you like to (um) go?
> B: That sounds great, I'd love to.
> giving directions (the person giving directions is unsure of the exact route)
> making an excuse for being late (the listener is quite annoyed with the late arrival)

### SPEAKING

**7A** Give Ss time to think how they'd start each conversation. They could also think of a solution that one of the people in each situation could offer.

**B** Ss should take a minute or two to think about which phrases they can use in the conversation and when/how they might need to 'soften' their message. Monitor and note down examples of the phrases and fillers Ss use, for feedback later.

**C** Put Ss in new pairs and give them a minute to prepare as in Ex 7B. Monitor as above. If you have access to recording facilities, you could record some of the role-plays, then play back the recordings for Ss to analyse, e.g. if Ss didn't use many fillers, ask them to identify places where they could have used them.

> **Homework ideas**
> 1 Workbook Ex 1–3, p55
> 2 Ss write conversations for the situations in Ex 7A that they didn't practise in class.

# THE HUMAN ANIMAL

## Introduction

Ss watch an extract from a BBC programme about human behaviour. Ss then learn and practise how to talk about a ritual and write about a family ritual.

## Warm up

Tell Ss to close their books. Put them in pairs or small groups and ask them to think of as many ways as they can of greeting someone, both verbal and non-verbal. These could be from their own country, or from other countries they've visited or heard about. Circulate and provide vocabulary as required. In feedback, take the opportunity to review this and pre-teach other vocabulary that will help Ss with the DVD viewing tasks and the discussion of gestures in their countries, such as: *shake hands, kiss (on the cheek/hand), hold/clasp (someone's hand/arm) hold your palms/hands out/up, hug, bow, rub (noses), slap (on the back)*.

### ▣ DVD PREVIEW

**1A** Give Ss a few minutes to discuss the photos in pairs and answer the questions. Then get feedback from the class.

**Answers:** A – The ritual is a traditional dance. The couples dancing together are dressed in Greek national dress and don't necessarily know each other very well.
B – The ritual is exchanging business cards. The Asian businessmen in the photo are probably new business acquaintances who have just met.
C – The ritual is grinding or preparation of some kind of grain or cereal. The people in the picture look as though they might be from the same family. There is a young boy and an older man and woman who might be his parents.

**B** Ss should read the information quickly and decide which photo(s) are relevant to the programme.

**Answers:** Photo B, also the photo at the bottom of the page of the men touching noses with each other.

### ▶ DVD VIEW

**2A** Ss discuss the questions in pairs, then demonstrate the gestures in feedback.

**B** Establish that Ss only need to count the different handshakes and ways of saying *You're crazy*. They don't need to explain them.

**Answers:** 1 five handshakes 2 six different ways to express *You're crazy*.

**C** Give Ss time to read through the questions before playing the DVD again. You may need to play the recording a third time for Ss to catch all the answers. You could tell them to shout *Stop!* at any points where they need time to write. NB For question five, Ss will need to remember the gestures rather than trying to write a description of each one.

**Answers:** 1 Because he looks at people like a bird watcher looks at birds.
2 many years
3 They shake hands when they start bargaining and can't stop until a deal is struck.
4 It makes both people equal because they are performing identical actions.
5 In Rome: hand taps against forehead, fingers pointing downwards.
In England: 'the temple screw' (one finger against the side of the head) meaning 'He's got a screw loose' OR rotate the finger clockwise at the side of the head, meaning 'His brain is going round and round' OR tap the front of the head several times, meaning 'What does he think he's got inside his skull?' In some countries you do this action with two hands.
In Japan the 'His brain is going round and round' gesture has to be done in an anti-clockwise direction – if you do it in a clockwise direction it means 'He's intelligent'.

**D** Ask Ss why it's important for visitors to Japan to know that you express *You're crazy* by turning your finger anti-clockwise: i.e. because they could be offended if they didn't know that turning your finger clockwise actually means *You're intelligent*. Ask Ss to think of more examples of gestures which could give offence if used wrongly or misunderstood. To prompt them, you could write the following on the board and ask them to think about the gestures used: *OK, goodbye, good, come here, good luck, I'll call you*. You could also demonstrate the phrases: *You do this with your (hands/fingers/head), You make a sign/sound like this*, to help Ss to explain the gestures.

### DVD 8 The Human Animal

DM = Desmond Morris

DM: Back in the late 1960s I was sittng in this very restaurant on the island of Malta talking to my publisher. I drew his attention to the fact that over the other side of the road there were two men who were gesticulating in a particular way. The way they were holding their palms to one side was fascinating me and he said, 'You know, you look at people the way that a bird watcher looks at birds' and I said, 'Yeah, I suppose you could call me a 'man watcher'.

As soon as I said it, it was as if I'd fired a starting gun on a major new project, one that was to engross me for many years to come and take me to over sixty different countries. I was going to do for actions what dictionary makers had done for words. I began making huge charts naming every facial expression, every gesticulation, every movement, every posture. I kept at it for month after month.

One of the first problems I encountered was that even the simplest human action, such as the handshake, has countless variations. Sometimes it's reduced to a mere palm touch, as with these Masai elders in East Africa. But in other countries it becomes more elaborate. In Mali in West Africa the hand shaker briefly touches his own forearm as the palms clasp.

In Morocco the hand shakers kiss one another's hands at the same time as clasping them. And in Turkey, these Kurdish farmers have taken this simple action and converted it into what amounts to a minor ritual. It's the local rule that they can't start bargaining until they're shaking hands and they have to keep on doing so until the deal is struck.

The essential feature of hand shaking is that it's an egalitarian act. Regardless of their social standing, the two people involved are momentarily performing identical actions.

Despite their variations, all these greetings have one thing in common: they're all fine-tuned to the precise context in which they occur.

Because a single message is given in a different way in different countries. The crazy sign: how do you say to somebody, 'You're crazy'? Well, here in Rome you do this, but, in England I would probably do this – the temple screw saying 'he's got a screw loose' – or I might say 'his brain is going round and round', or I might, tap my head saying, 'what does he think he's got inside his skull?' In some countries you do it with two hands; it varies from place to place and, if you go to Japan you have to be careful because if you do it this way it means 'he's intelligent', you have to do it in an anti clockwise direction in Japan if you want to say that somebody is crazy. So, all over the world the same message is given in a slightly different way.

## SPEAKOUT a ritual

**3A** You could tell Ss about a personal ritual of your own to provide them with a model. Examples of personal rituals could be: the order you do things in when getting up in the morning or before going to bed at night, having breakfast at a café and reading the papers every Sunday, etc.

**B** Again, you could give Ss an example here, e.g. eating a big family lunch together on a Sunday, throwing out old possessions on New Year's Eve, etc. NB The word *custom* suggests something done in a particular society because it's traditional, whereas a *ritual* can be something personal.

**C** Tell Ss to make notes on the two questions as they listen.

**Answers:** What is it? It's a ritual for their children's birthdays in the family. They put a paper cloth on a table and write the child's name in coloured sweets, then lay their presents out on the table. Also, the child who doesn't have a birthday that day gets an 'un-birthday' present.
How did it start? They invented it for the first child and it just carried on.

**D** Give Ss time to read through the phrases. Point out that after *This involves* an -ing form is used. Tell Ss to tick the option they hear as well as the phrase. In feedback you could drill some of the different options within the phrases, or put Ss in pairs to practise saying the phrases to each other.

**Answers:** This involves coming down for breakfast …
All the presents are laid out.
It was just something that we invented for the children.

### Unit 8 Recording 8

W = Woman  M = Man

W: So what about you, do you have any family rituals or traditions?
M: We have a, we have a family ritual for the children's birthdays and, that – this involves coming down for breakfast, um, before the children come down, we lay a paper, table cloth and we write in little coloured sweets we write their name and it says if it was Will for instance it would say 'Will is twelve'.
W: Ah lovely.
M: And then the, all the extra little coloured sweets they get put into a bowl so that they're allowed this treat of having sweets for breakfast which is very unusual. And then all their presents are laid out on the table in front of them and then and they come downstairs and you say right it's ready for you to come downstairs now and as they come in we sing Happy Birthday to them and there are all their presents and it says 'Will is Twelve' and then the other child, there's four years' difference between them, always has to have an un-birthday present, just 'cos otherwise they get upset that one of them's getting more –
W: Ah – more presents than all the other ones. And, we take a photograph of that and I've now got a collection of all these photographs, which go 'Will is One', 'Will is Two', 'Will is Three', 'Will is Four' so there's this sort of continuity that goes all the way through –

W: That's lovely.
M: And he's twenty-five now, so we're starting to wonder at what point do we stop doing this.
W: Do they do the same for you and your wife?
M: No not really no it's, – we don't because we're a bit too old for it.
W: For the coloured sweets.
M: Yes and it was just something that we invented for the children, it's not a family tradition it hasn't come down from either of us we just invented it for the first child when they were one and it's just carried on like that, but we, of course we can't stop it now, you know he's aged twenty-six – when he's thirty we'll go 'Will is Thirty'.

**4A** Give Ss time to make notes and circulate and provide help as necessary. Remind Ss to incorporate some of the key phrases where appropriate. Ss could practise their talks in pairs before moving into groups in the next stage.

**B** Put Ss into groups of four to six to present their talks. Remind the listeners to write questions (suggest at least two) to ask at the end of each talk. Monitor and make notes of good language use and problems for discussion and correction in feedback.

## writeback a family ritual

**5A** Tell Ss to read the entry and tell each other if they have memories of similar 'get-togethers' with other families. Vocabulary to check: *vast* (extremely large), *harsh* (difficult, without comforts), *rowdy* (noisy), *set* (go down – when referring to the sun or moon), *dough* (mixture of flour and water for making bread).

**Optional extra activities**
Focus Ss on the following features of the example text so they can incorporate them when writing their own entry:
1 Remind them about the use of *would* + infinitive to talk about past habits by asking them to find all the examples in the entry (there are seven).
2 Show them how the text is structured:
• Background to Stephen's childhood (*I'm from … I spent my childhood …* )
• Introduction to the ritual: where, when, who was involved
• General description of the activities (*kids running … while the adults …* )
• More detailed description of a specific activity (*Then at about 5 o'clock …* )
• The 'highlight' of the ritual (*the best part was …* )

**B** Encourage Ss to make notes first, then write a first draft to show their partner, before writing the final draft. The entries could then be displayed on the board or around the classroom for other Ss to read.

**Homework ideas**
1 Ss write some tips for people visiting their country, telling them about important gestures and their meaning.
2 Ss write a description of another ritual or custom from their family or their culture.

# LOOKBACK

## Introduction

The aim of these activities is to provide revision and further practice of the language from the unit. You can also use them to assess Ss' ability to use the language, in which case you need to monitor but avoid helping them. You may feel that you don't need or have time to do all the activities. If so, you could allocate the activities that would be most beneficial for your Ss, or get individual Ss to decide which activities they'd like to do in class.

## CONDITIONALS

**1A** You could start by writing just the beginnings of the three sentences on the board and asking Ss to complete them so that they are true for them. Then direct them to the exercise, so they can compare the endings given there.

> **Answers:** 1 a) might have studied b) wouldn't have gone c) wouldn't be 2 a) wouldn't take b) would choose c) would find 3 a) would be b) spend c) have ended up

**B** Ss choose one answer each from a), b) or c).

**C** Ss should explain to each other why they chose the answer in each case.

> **Optional extra activity**
> Ask Ss to think of ideas to substitute the following in each of the three sentences:
>
> 1 studying English (e.g. *going to the gym, working for (name of company), wearing glasses, (cookery) lessons*)
>
> 2 live in a different country (e.g. *start my own business, travel for six months, take a year off, meet someone famous*)
>
> 3 computers (e.g. *cars, mobile phones, fridges*)
>
> They then write their own endings and compare ideas in groups.

## COLLOCATIONS

**2** Ss can work on this in pairs.

> **Answers:** 1 analyse, postponed 2 weigh up, come to 3 examine, putting off 4 stick to, go against

## FEELINGS

**3A** You could run this as a competition between two teams. Write/Display the sentences on the board one at a time and give teams time to confer. They put up their hands when they're ready, then call out just the missing letters in the correct order (you could give a point for every correct letter and take away a point for any incorrect letter).

> **Answers:** 1 groggy, alert 2 wide awake 3 cringe 4 sharpest, lowest ebb 5 despise, passion

**B** If Ss are in teams, they could ask these questions in open pairs. A student from one team chooses a student form the opposing team and asks them the question. Points can be given for good pronunciation, interesting answers, etc.

> **Optional extra activity**
> Put the following sentence stems on the board or on a handout for Ss to complete with their own ideas. They then compare their answers in pairs or small groups.
>
> *1 It's important to be wide awake when you're …*
>
> *2 People who are always bright and breezy make me feel …*
>
> *3 If you want to work as a … you need to be on the ball.*
>
> *4 The best thing to do if you feel groggy is to …*
>
> *5 … fill me with a sense of dread.*
>
> *6 I always cringe if I see …*

## -ING FORM AND INFINITIVE

**4A** You may want to let Ss refer to the **Language bank** on p142 while they're doing this exercise. You could make this a race: as soon as a pair has finished the exercise they bring their books up to you to check.

> **Answers:** 1 travelling 2 to learn, hearing 3 to be 4 to do 5 Riding 6 making 7 being able to watch 8 Having to wear

**B** You could start by giving one or two examples about yourself, as a model for Ss. Give Ss a few minutes to work on this alone.

**C** Demonstrate this by saying one of the sentences that is true for you and inviting Ss to ask you at least three different follow-up questions, e.g.

T: *Cooking is one of my favourite ways of relaxing.*

S1: *Really? Why's that?*

T: *Because I like being creative.*

S2: *What kinds of dishes do you like cooking?*

T: *I love cooking desserts and cakes.*

S3: *Do you know how to make cheesecake?*

T: *Yes – would you like a recipe? etc.*

Ss could stand up and walk round the class reading and responding to their statements.

## AWKWARD SITUATIONS

**5A** You could start by putting Ss in pairs, directing them to the three situations in Ex 5B and asking them to rank them in order from most to least awkward. In feedback discuss their reasons for ranking them as they did and ask them what solutions they'd suggest. Ss could then correct the sentences in pairs, or in teams, as a competition. Write the corrected sentences on the board for Ss to refer to in Ex 5B.

> **Answers:** 2 There's ~~nothing~~ something I've **been** meaning to talk to you about. 3 Look, I **don't** want you to get the ~~right~~ **wrong** idea, but … 4 It's just that I've ~~noted~~ **noticed** that … 5 I'd feel ~~brighter~~ **better** if … 6 How would you ~~fill~~ **feel** about that?

**B** After Ss have practised one situation, choose two or three pairs to act out their conversations for the class and give them some positive and constructive feedback. Then ask Ss to change partners for the next situation and choose different pairs to act out for the class afterwards.

## OVERVIEW

**9.1 WITNESS**

GRAMMAR | -ing form and infinitive

VOCABULARY | crime

HOW TO | talk about being a witness

**COMMON EUROPEAN FRAMEWORK**

Ss can understand articles concerned with contemporary problems in which the writers adopt a particular stance or viewpoint; can develop a clear description or narrative, expanding and supporting their main points with relevant supporting detail and examples.

**9.2 SCAM**

GRAMMAR | past modals of deduction

VOCABULARY | synonyms/prepositions

HOW TO | speculate about the past

**COMMON EUROPEAN FRAMEWORK**

Ss can describe events both real and imagined; can convey degrees of emotion and highlight the personal significance of events and experiences; can evaluate different ideas or solutions to a problem.

**9.3 IT'S AN EMERGENCY!**

FUNCTION | reporting an incident

VOCABULARY | verb phrases for incidents

LEARN TO | rephrase

**COMMON EUROPEAN FRAMEWORK**

Ss can pass on detailed information reliably, including details of unpredictable occurrences, e.g. an accident and provide the concrete information required.

**9.4 MAYDAY! ⊙ BBC DVD**

**speakout** | items for a life raft

**writeback** | a lucky escape

**COMMON EUROPEAN FRAMEWORK**

Ss can understand most current affairs/real-life drama programmes; can evaluate different ideas or solutions to a problem, giving the advantages and disadvantages of various options.

**9.5 LOOKBACK**

Communicative revision activities

**BBC VIDEO PODCAST**

**Do you have any phobias?**

This video podcast extends the unit topic to deals with the issue of phobias and the irrational fear people have of certain situations, activities, things, animals, or people. Use this video podcast at the start or end of Unit 9.

## WITNESS

### Introduction

Ss practise reading and speaking about memory and being a witness using the -ing form and infinitive and vocabulary related to crime.

**SUPPLEMENTARY MATERIALS**

Resource bank p183 and/or p185

Ex 1: be prepared to tell Ss about any memory techniques you have.

Ex 3: if you've ever been a witness, be prepared to tell Ss about the experience.

Ex 8A: Ss need to refer to monolingual dictionaries.

### Warm up

Put Ss in pairs and direct them to the three photos on p104–105. Tell them they have a minute to look at the photos and try to remember as many details as possible. After a minute tell all the Student Bs to close their books and explain that Student A should 'test' Student B on the photos by asking questions, e.g. *How many men were in the ID parade?* Student A can then report back to the class about how good their partner's memory was.

**READING**

**1** If you did the warm up, you could ask Ss to be a little more specific about how good their memories are in question 1 by asking *Do you have a good memory for names/faces/dates/facts/conversations?* etc. You could also do an example for question 2 by telling Ss about a technique you have for remembering passwords, PIN numbers, etc, if you have one.

**2A** Give Ss two or three minutes to read through the article quickly and find the information.

**Answers:**

1 Seeing a video of the bus exploding in the 2005 terrorist attacks in London.

2 Seeing a white van or truck leaving several of the crime scenes during sniper attacks in the Washington DC area in 2002.

3 Seeing video footage of the moment Princess Diana's car crashed.

**Culture notes**

**Princess Diana** was the wife of Prince Charles, heir to the throne of the United Kingdom. She died on August 31, 1997 as a result of her injuries from a car crash in Paris. Although the media at first blamed the paparazzi, the crash was found to have been caused by the chauffeur, who lost control of the car at high speed while under the influence of alcohol.

**The Washington sniper** attacks took place during three weeks in October 2002 in Washington, D.C., Maryland and Virginia. Ten people teare killed and three others critically injured in series of shootings. At first thought to be the work of a single sniper, it was later found that two men were responsible.

The London bombings (also known as 7/7) were a series of coordinated suicide attacks on London's public transport system during the morning rush hour of July 7 2005. At 08.50 a.m. three bombs exploded within fifty seconds of each other on three London Underground trains, a fourth exploding an hour later at 09.47 on a double-decker bus in Tavistock Square. The explosive devices were packed into rucksacks and detonated by the bombers themselves, all four of whom died. Fifty-two other people were killed and around 700 were injured.

**B** You could do the first one as an example and establish that *witness testimony still plays an important part in court cases* is the key phrase to underline. Give Ss time to go through the article carefully and mark the statements true or false.
Ss compare answers in pairs before feedback with the class.
Vocabulary to check: *DNA tests* (test that can prove the identity of a person by studying some of their DNA, which is unique for each individual), *forensic* (related to scientific methods for solving crimes), *testimony* (what a witness says in court), *Death Row* (the part of a prison where criminals who are going to executed for their crimes are kept), *traumatic* (emotionally shocking and disturbing), *flee* (to run away)

**Answers:** I F – *Even in these days of DNA tests and other forensic techniques, witness testimony still plays an important part in court cases.*
2 F – *forty percent of people claimed to have seen this nonexistent footage* BUT *some even went on to describe what happened in vivid detail* (i.e. some of the forty percent)
3 T – *But what Ost's study clearly demonstrates is just how easily influenced our memories are.*
4 T – *In many cases, an unreliable memory is not a problem. It just means we forget to send a birthday card …*
5 T – *In 1998, an American study calculated that in ninety-five percent of felony cases – the more serious crimes – witness evidence (in other words, people's memories) was the only evidence heard in court.*
6 F – *witnesses reported seeing a white van or truck fleeing several of the crime scenes.*
7 T – *In twenty percent of cases they pointed to a volunteer.*
8 F – *our memories may be poor and are usually fragmented. A good example is how in car crashes …*

### Optional extra activity
To give Ss practice in guessing meaning from context, ask them to find the following words in the text and guess what they mean:
*recollection, ripped off, vivid, alter, fragmented*

**C** Focus Ss on the example and establish that *it* refers back to the noun *recollection*. When Ss have finished the exercise, explain that this use of pronouns can help them to understand a text when they're reading and also for them to use in their writing to structure the text and avoid repeating the nouns.

**Answers:**
2 It could well be a mental image of a red double-decker bus in Tavistock Square with its roof ripped off by the force of the explosion.
3 Do you remember seeing a video of the bus exploding?
4 But what about CCTV footage? What can you see in that video?
5 Well, the truth is, you shouldn't be able to see anything in your mind's eye because such CCTV footage simply doesn't exist.
6 Many of us think we have a good memory. After all, it's got us through the occasional exam.
7 In many cases, an unreliable memory is not a problem. It just means we forget
8 When they were caught, the sniper suspects were actually driving a blue car.

**3** If you've ever been a witness, you could start by telling Ss about your experience. If Ss think they'd be a good witness, ask them to explain why.

GRAMMAR *-ing* form and infinitive

**4A** You could write the sentences on the board and go through them with the whole class, or put Ss in pairs to discuss them first. The sentences are all in the left hand column of the article.

**Answers:** I seeing 2 to describe 3 to send

**B** If you have a *mixed ability* class try to ensure that *stronger* Ss are paired with *weaker* ones for this activity. Monitor the pairwork closely so you can help any pairs who are struggling. You may want to go straight on to Ex 4C if Ss have coped well with identifying the differences in pairs.

**Answers:** Ia I remembered, then I set the alarm. It was my responsibility to set the alarm.
b I remember now that I thought then that the building seemed very quiet.
2a I didn't phone for the tickets because I forgot, although it was my responsibility.
b I'll always remember the experience of being at the concert.
3a Henri stopped first because he wanted to drink some coffee. He stopped and then he drank.
b He didn't continue driving.
4a Billy finished the training and after that he became a famous dancer.
b Billy didn't stop practising five hours a day.
5a He made an effort to recall her name.
b Then he went through the alphabet, as an experiment.

**C** You could do the first one with the class as an example, then put Ss in pairs to match the rest.

**Answers:** I c 2 a 3 d 4 b 5 e 6 g 7 f 8 h 9 i 10 j
NB: *I'll never* is very commonly used before *forget + -ing*

**5A** Ss need to practise saying the example at natural speed in order to hear the final /d/ sound of *remembered* disappearing. Give them a minute or two to say the other sentences to their partner and listen for the disappearing sounds.

**B** Once you've played the recording for Ss to check and repeat, ask them what the missing letters have in common. (When /d/ or /t/ follow each other the first sound disappears. This is also true when /t/ follows /t/ (as in 2a and 3a) and we when /d/ follows /d/ e.g. *I remembered doing it*),

## Unit 9 Recording I

2a)  I forgot to phone for tickets for the Coldplay concert.

3a)  Henri stopped to drink some coffee to keep himself awake.

b)  Then he stopped driving because he still felt tired.

---

**▶ LANGUAGEBANK** 9.1 p144–145

Direct Ss to the **Language bank** for further examples of the verbs which have a different meaning when followed by –*ing* or an infinitive, as well as a list of verbs which can be followed by –*ing* or an infinitive with no difference in meaning. You could do Ex A in class: put Ss in pairs and tell Student A to cover the right hand column and Student B to cover the left hand column. Student A reads a sentence beginning at random and Student B listens and chooses the correct ending. Then both Ss cover the right hand column and try to remember the ending of each sentence.

**Answers:** A I b)  2 a)  3 c)  4 d)  5 e)  6 f)  7 h)  8 g)
B I to get (*getting* is also possible but the -*ing* form is not used so much in the negative)  2 to investigate  3 seeing  4 to intervene  5 doing  6 to take  7 to tell  8 to identify  9 doing  10 helping/to help

---

## PRACTICE

**6A** Focus Ss on the example and give them a few minutes to work on the questions alone or with a partner. Vocabulary to check: *significant* (important).

**Answers:** 2 to buy  3 to help  4 witnessing  5 thinking  6 to take  7 to become  8 writing  9 studying  10 hiding

**B** Help Ss to sound natural by focusing on the linking at the beginning of some of the questions and drilling them, e.g. *Have you ever …, Do you ever/always …, Has anyone …, How long do you …*

You could then demonstrate the idea of follow-up questions by inviting Ss to ask you one of the questions and answering it, then eliciting two or three examples of follow-up questions that they could ask.

## VOCABULARY crime

**7** You could start by brainstorming different types of crime with the class (Ss close their books). To prompt Ss give them categories, such as crimes which involve:

I damaging something

2 taking something which isn't yours

3 harming a person

4 getting money from someone

Then put Ss in pairs to complete the sentences. Pronunciation

---

to check: <u>pick</u>pocketing, <u>kid</u>napping, <u>tax</u> evasion, <u>van</u>dalism, <u>id</u>entity th<u>ef</u>t, <u>coun</u>terfeiting, <u>ar</u>son, <u>shop</u>lifting, <u>bri</u>bery.

**Answers:** I arson  2 kidnapping  3 vandalism  4 stalking  5 bribery  6 hacking  7 mugging  8 counterfeiting  9 identity theft  10 pickpocketing  11 shoplifting  12 tax evasion

**8A** First suggest that Ss draw a table with twelve rows and three columns, to write their answers in. Put Ss in pairs, emphasising that they should try to help each other work out the answers and only use the dictionary for those they're really unsure of.

**Answers:**

| Crime | Person | Verb |
|---|---|---|
| arson | arsonist | to commit arson |
| kidnapping | kidnapper | to kidnap |
| bribery | – | to bribe |
| identity theft | thief | to steal s/one's identity |
| stalking | stalker | to stalk |
| tax evasion | tax evader | to evade/avoid tax |
| vandalism | vandal | to vandalise |
| mugging | mugger | to mug |
| counterfeiting | counterfeiter | to counterfeit |
| shoplifting | shoplifter | to shoplift |
| hacking | hacker | to hack into sth |
| pickpocketing | pickpocket | to pickpocket |

**B** Ss could try to agree on the most and least serious of the crimes and be prepared to justify their answers to the rest of the class in feedback.

## SPEAKING

**9A** Give Ss a few minutes to read think about the situations and think of what they would do and why. Make sure they understand that they should consider questions a)–c) for each situation and make notes of the answers to use in the discussion activity.

**B** Put Ss in groups of three to five to discuss the situations, nominating one person to keep a record of the questions they agreed/disagreed on. In feedback, encourage Ss to summarise some of their group's answers, e.g. *We'd all …, None of us would …, Most of us said we'd ….*

You could also have a brief discussion about which group's answers were surprising/predictable, etc.

**Homework ideas**

I Workbook Ex I–4C, p60–61

2 Ss look through a newspaper or the news on the internet and write a summary of the types of crime that were reported, e.g. *There were two stories about vandalism in my local paper- in one story the vandals …, in the other they vandalised ….*

# SCAM

## Introduction

Ss practise listening and speaking about scams using past modals of deduction, synonyms and dependent prepositions. They also learn to avoid repetition in writing and write a 'how to' leaflet.

> ### SUPPLEMENTARY MATERIALS
>
> Resource bank p184 and/or p186
>
> Warm up: prepare sets of slip with vocabulary to review/preview
>
> Ex 8C: Ss need to refer to monolingual dictionaries

## Warm up

Write the following on separate slips of paper: *mug, fake, counterfeit, bribe, rob, a scam, shoplifting, identity theft, hacker, pickpocket, a con, tax evasion*. Put Ss in groups of four to six and give each group a set of slips. Demonstrate that Ss should put the slips face down in a pile in front of them and take turns to turn over a slip and define the word for the rest of the group. Whoever guesses the word keeps the slip. If a student doesn't or can't define the word or nobody can guess it, the slip is put to the bottom of the pile. The winner is the person with the most slips. Any words left in the pile can then be looked at and discussed by the group.

### VOCABULARY synonyms

**1A** If Ss have trouble thinking of an example, tell them about *phishing*: you get an official looking email from your bank telling you the information on your account is outdated and providing a link to a page where you can update your information. The link will take you to a webpage that looks identical to the reputable site, but which has been set up by a scammer to collect your personal information.

**B** Direct Ss to the title of the TV programme and tell them that *hustle* is another word for *scam*, mainly used in American English. You could also introduce *con artist* and *victim*. Put Ss in pairs to read the information and discuss the questions. Encourage Ss to try to guess the meanings of the words in bold. NB For a *weaker class*, you may want to revise *fool* (to trick or deceive) and pre-teach *snatch* (to take or take hold of something in a sudden or violent way), *be taken in* (to believe something that isn't true/to be tricked). After a few minutes invite Ss to share their answers with the class and find out which Ss are the most *gullible* (easy to fool).

**C** Focus Ss on the example and give them a few minutes to match the rest, working alone or in pairs.

> **Answers:** 1 pose as  2 fool, deceive  3 distract, divert someone's attention (from sth)
> 4 snatch, grab  5 be taken in (by), fall for  6 swap (sth for something else), switch (sth with something)
> NB: Although these verbs and phrases are used as synonyms in this context, it's worth pointing out to Ss other contexts where some of them can be used:
> pretend to be = behave as if something is true: *pretend to be asleep, pretend you didn't hear*
> grab = to take hold of something suddenly: *She grabbed my arm when she heard the scream.*
> swap = exchange: *Let's swap phone numbers.*
> switch = change form one thing to another: *He's switched jobs; She can switch from Italian to English easily.*

## speakout TIP

Before Ss read the tip, ask them why it's important to learn synonyms. Give them a minute or two to read the suggestions and to rewrite the sentence.

> **Possible answer:** Yesterday was very pleasant. I had a good meal at an excellent restaurant with some lovely people.

You could discuss with the class which way(s) of learning synonyms they've tried and suggest that they try one new one when they next read or write something.

### LISTENING

**2A** Direct Ss back to the TV programme information and tell them to listen for which two of the five scams the people talk about.

> **Answers:** the Bag and PIN Snatch, the Jewellery Shop Scam

**B** Give Ss time to read through the questions before playing the recording again. Ss discuss answers in pairs, then as a class.

> **Answers:** 1 It was taken while she was taking a photo of a couple in a café.
> 2 She talked to someone who she thought was a woman from her bank.
> 3 She gave the woman her name address, account number and PIN.
> 4 She was accused of paying for jewellery with counterfeit money.
> 5 He took the cash and the necklace. He also took the woman away, apparently to the police station.
> 6 Because his boss took £600 from his salary to pay for the stolen necklace.

## UNIT 9 Recording 2

### Conversation 1

L = Lise  J = Jeff

L: So what happened was, I was sitting in a café and this young couple – they looked like tourists – asked me to take a photo of them. And I took their photo and they thanked me and left and then I looked at my seat and realised my handbag had gone, with my mobile, wallet, credit card, keys, everything.

J: No! What did you do?

L: Well, there was a guy on the next table and he saw I was really upset and I explained about the bag and he asked me which bank I was with and he said he worked for that bank and gave me a phone number and let me use his mobile to phone them and stop my credit card.

J: And you believed him?

L: Yeah, I mean I was in a real panic. I was really grateful for his help. Anyway, I phoned the number and talked to a woman from 'the bank' and gave her my name and address and my account number.

J: She sounded genuine?

L: Yeah, completely. I could hear the sounds of the call centre behind her. And she asked me to key in my PIN on the phone and she said they'd stop my card.

J: Wow. So it was a double scam. They got your bag and your bank account details?

L: Yeah, unfortunately. Of course, the guy could get my PIN from his phone.

J: So who actually took your bag?

L: Well, it must have been stolen when I wasn't looking.

J: Right.

L: So it can't have been the young couple because I was looking at them all the time I was taking the photo. Their job was just to distract me.

J: Was it the guy at the next table, then?

L: I think so. He must have taken my bag when I wasn't looking. Then he could have hidden it in his case or he might have given it to another member of the gang.

J: And then he gave you a fake number.

L: Yeah and they must have used a recording of a call centre so that it sounded like the real bank.

**Conversation 2**

D = Dan    I = Ingrid

D: I was badly tricked a few years ago when I was working in a jewellery shop.

I: You never told me about that. What happened?

D: Well, this woman came in and was looking at necklaces. She was young, attractive, well-dressed and then a guy came in shortly afterwards and he was just looking around. But then the woman went to pay for a very expensive necklace that she'd picked out and when she was counting out the money onto the counter, the guy grabbed her, flashed his police ID and said he was arresting her for paying with counterfeit money.

I: No! Wow!

D: So he took the cash and the necklace as evidence, wrote down his contact details and promised me he'd bring the necklace back by the end of the day. I didn't suspect anything. Then he took the woman away, presumably to book her at the police station.

I: And he didn't come back?

D: No and stupid me, I didn't even begin to suspect anything until it was closing time, so then I phoned the police and they had no idea what I was talking about. That was it, end of story.

I: How much was the necklace worth?

D: £600. And my boss took it out of my salary. That's why I quit.

I: So the police ID must have been a fake.

D: That's right. I just didn't check it.

I: And wait a second, was the woman a real customer?

D: No, the woman must have been working with the guy. She couldn't have been a real customer, or she wouldn't have gone with him.

I: But she might have had fake money.

D: I really don't think so.

I: Talk about an ingenious scam …

**3** Ss can work in pairs or small groups. Give them a few minutes to discuss the questions, then get feedback from the whole class.

> **Suggested answers:** She shouldn't have left her bag on the chair.
> She should have picked up her bag or paid attention to her bag while she was taking the photo.
> She should have found the correct number of her bank and not used the man's number.
> She shouldn't have keyed in her pin number.
> He should have checked the policeman's ID.
> He should have phoned the police station to check the ID.
> He shouldn't have allowed the man to take the necklace.

## GRAMMAR past modals of deduction

**4A** For *stronger classes*, first tell Ss to cover meanings a)–c) and discuss in pairs the different in meanings of sentences 1–6.

> **Answers:** 1 a 2 c 3 b 4 a 5 a 6 c

Check that Ss understand the idea of speculating or making a deduction, ie if you're less than 100 percent sure (e.g. *He took my bag.* =I know this, it's a fact.)

**B** While Ss complete the rules, write them on the board so that Ss can come out and complete the gaps in feedback.

> **Answers:** 1 *must/could/might/can't/couldn't* + *have* + past participle
> 2 modal + *have* + *been* + *-ing*
> 3 modal + *have* + *been* + past participle

**5A** You could focus Ss on the phonemic script and see if they can predict how the past modals are pronounced, before you play the recording.

**B** Give Ss a minute or two to look at the sentences in Ex 4A and practise saying them to themselves first. You may then want to tell Ss to look up from their books while they're repeating, so they don't get distracted by the written forms.

---

**⇒ LANGUAGEBANK** 9.2 p144–145

Direct Ss to the **Language bank** for examples of the past modals of deduction in different contexts. You could use Ex A and B in class for some controlled practice before going on to Ex 6. Put Ss in pairs and either allocate an Ex to each pair or ask them to choose one (Ex B is more challenging, so direct Stronger Ss to this one). When Ss have finished, provide them with an answer key to check their answers, then put them together with a pair who did the other exercise and tell them to swap answers.

> **Answers:** A 2 He can't/couldn't have heard you.
> 3 The thieves could/might have got in through the window.  4 I realised I can't/couldn't have saved the document.  5 It must have hurt a lot.  6 Her plane might/could have been delayed.  7 I must have made a mistake.  8 She can't/couldn't have been trying hard enough.
> B 1 must have cost  2 might/could have switched off  3 must have been working late  4 could/might have been thinking  5 can't/couldn't have looked  6 might have been told

---

## PRACTICE

**6** You could start by telling Ss to read through the two accounts quickly and decide which scam is the most ingenious. Then give them a minute or two to complete the gaps and compare answers in pairs.

> **Answers:** 1 might/could have dropped  2 might/could have fallen  3 must have pulled  4 can't have been  5 must have been  6 must have been working

## SPEAKING

**7A** Explain to Ss that they're going to read about a scam and that they should add a few details to it and practise telling it so that sounds as if the scam happened to them. They should also try and work out how the scam worked by thinking about the questions under the story. Put Ss into two groups, As and Bs and give them time to practise and discuss their story.

**B** Pair Ss up so you have one from group A and one from group B in each pair. Ss tell each other their story without looking at the text, then they speculate together about how the scam was done. Remind Ss to use past modals here. Monitor and note down some examples of good use of the past modals and any problems for feedback later. Finally, direct the class to the answers on p162.

### VOCABULARY *PLUS* dependent prepositions

**8A** Encourage Ss to read the headlines out to each other and see which prepositions 'sound' correct.

> **Answers:** I with stealing  2 of taking  3 for selling

**B** Focus Ss on the example and establish that the present perfect is commonly used to introduce news stories, before details of time, place, etc are added using past forms. Elicit the full forms of the other two headlines from the class and write them on the board.

> **Answers:** 2 A woman has accused a con artist of taking her bag and PIN. Active
> 3 A gang has been arrested for selling one car nine times. Passive

**C** Encourage Ss to work together and help each other before checking in a dictionary.

> **Answers:** I of accessing  2 for cheating  3 for causing
> 4 of becoming  5 for employing  6 from travelling
> 7 for saving  8 from being eaten  9 of murdering
> 10 from drowning

**9A** You could start by giving Ss an example as a model, e.g. *A fourteen-year old student is facing a four-mile walk to school every day after being banned from travelling by train for a year. Judi Leigh, who goes to Maryfield High School, was caught on CCTV camera spraying graffiti on the wall of her local station for the third time in a month. The teenager claims that it is a case of mistaken identity.*

**B** Combine pairs into groups of four and ask Ss to take turns reading out their articles and choosing the correct headline.

> ⇒ **VOCABULARYBANK** p156 Dependent prepositions
>
> Ex 3 gives Ss more practice in using dependent prepositions in the context of newspaper headlines. You could write the prepositions *about, in, for* and *from* up on the board to give them some extra help. Let them work independently to try to complete the headlines, then check their answers in pairs.
>
> > **Answers:** I for  2 from  3 for  4 about, of  5 from
> > 6 for  7 about  8 in  9 from  10 for

### WRITING a 'how to' leaflet

**10A** Ask the class for some examples of problems people can have when they visit an unfamiliar city, e.g. with transport – catching the right bus, getting a reliable taxi driver; with shops – being charged more than the real price, being given the wrong change, etc. Elicit some advice for dealing with the problems.

**B** Establish that a *leaflet* is a small piece of printed paper containing information, advertising, advice, etc. As they read, Ss could put a tick ✓ in the margin next to ideas they discussed and a cross ✗ next to the ones they didn't think of. You could invite them to comment on how useful they think the advice is.

**C** Put Ss in pairs and give them a minute or two to look at how the information is organised and made to 'stand out' in the leaflet before they complete the guidelines.

> **Answers:** I title  2 sections, subheading
> 3 fonts, underlining  4 bullet-points  5 contracted

### LEARN TO avoid repetition

**11A** First check with Ss how many verbs in bold there are in the leaflet (eleven). Ss work alone and compare answers in pairs.

> **Answers:** I Never take a taxi  Always ask
> 2 Make sure you carry  Be sure to keep  Be careful to cover
> Try to check  Take time to look
> 3 Phone  Keep  Use  Book

**B** Direct Ss back to the phrases with verbs in bold to help them complete the rules.

> **Answers:** I never  2 a) sure  b) sure  c) careful  d) to
> e) time to

> **Optional extra activity**
> Ss look through the leaflet again for more useful language. Ask Ss to find examples with:
> I *Be careful* and *Take care* and highlight the pattern *Be careful/Take care when* verb + *-ing*.
> 2 *May* – e.g. *you may find yourself …, you may find that …, (x) may happen, (y) may have been done*
> These patterns are often used to describe the possible problems before explaining how to avoid them.

**12** Ss could work in pairs and brainstorm ideas for one of the topics, then write a first draft individually. They then swap their first drafts and, using the checklists in Ex 10C and Ex 11B, give each other feedback. Ss can then write a final draft in class or for homework. The finished leaflets can be displayed round the room or passed round for others to read.

> **Homework ideas**
> I Workbook Ex 1–6, p62–63
> 2 Ss write another 'how to' leaflet from Ex 12.
> 3 Ss find an article that interests them online or in a newspaper and a) underline any dependent prepositions b) circle any synonyms. They bring the article to the next lesson and show their findings to a partner.

## IT'S AN EMERGENCY!

### Introduction

Ss practise listening and speaking about reporting an incident, using appropriate phrases and vocabulary for describing incidents. They also learn to rephrase when their listener doesn't understand.

### SUPPLEMENTARY MATERIALS

Resource bank p187

**Ex 4B**: prepare role cards (see *Alternative idea*).

**Ex 5C**: be prepared to tell Ss about an incident that happened to you.

### Warm up

Tell Ss to close their books and write the title *It's an emergency!* on the board. Put Ss in pairs and give them one minute to brainstorm reasons for calling the emergency services, e.g. you've seen a car accident, someone in your family is very ill, you've been robbed, some friends went out in a boat and haven't returned, a building nearby is on fire, etc. Conduct feedback with the class.

### READING

**1A** Direct Ss to the photos and ask which of the emergency services they would ring, if any.

#### Optional extra activity

Put Ss in pairs and ask them to role-play the call they would make about one of the situations. Give them a minute or two to prepare what to say:

Student A (the caller) thinks about what they've seen when and where it happened, if anyone is injured, etc.

Student B (from emergency services) thinks about what questions to ask the caller about the incident and what advice to give them.

Ss practise their phone calls, then a few pairs act out their call for the class.

Monitor the role-plays closely and make a note of some of the Ss' questions and answers. You could write/display these on the board after Ex 3A for Ss to compare with what they've heard on the recording.

**B** Focus Ss on the questions and give them a minute or two to read about the calls. Conduct feedback with the class and find out which reason Ss consider the silliest via a show of hands. Suggestions for what the person should have done in each case might include:

*They should've called the doctor the/pizza company/the phone company/a friend.*

### FUNCTION reporting an incident

**2A** Tell Ss to make a few brief notes about what happened and that they'll be able to listen for more detail the next time.

> **Answer:** He was robbed by a man posing as a jogger in the park.

**B** Give Ss a minute or two to look through the report and check *incident* (an event, often unusual vs. *accident*, something that is not planned), *serial number* (a number put on an item by the manufacturer), *ethnicity* (ethnic group), *distinguishing marks or features* (something that makes you look different/stand out, e.g. a scar). Pay the recording, pausing after each of

the longer sections to ensure that Ss have time to write their notes.

> **Answers:** Name: Alain Girard
> Date and time of incident: *2.50, 7th June*
> Location of incident: *Park Avenue, near the entrance to the park, 50 metres inside*
> Description of incident (what exactly happened?): *Robbery. Victim was walking out of the park when a man ran into him and stole his wallet.*
> Description of stolen or damaged property or vehicle (serial number, bank card type, value of property, colour, make, model of car, etc.): *wallet, brown leather with credit card, 250 euros and photo of girlfriend*
> Description of suspect or offender (age, sex, ethnicity, build, clothing, distinguishing marks or features, etc.): *tall white male, about twenty, wearing tracksuit bottoms and a grey hoodie. Looked like Vin Diesel*
> Witnesses: *none*
> Contact details: x

### Unit 9 Recording 5

P = Police officer  A = Alain

P: Hello, police. Can I help you?

A: Yes, I'd like to report a crime. I've been robbed.

P: I'm very sorry to hear that, sir. OK, I'll need to take a statement.

A: A statement?

P: To write down some details, if that's all right.

A: Yes, sure.

P: Could you give me your name please, sir?

A: Alain Girard.

P: Right. That's Girard with a J?

A: No, G and it's Alain spelled A-l-a-i-n.

P: Right, Mr Girard. Could you tell me exactly when the incident happened?

A: Just now. About an hour ago.

P: Could you be more precise?

A: Excuse me?

P: Could you give me the exact time?

A: I think at 2.50 or 2.55.

P: That's about 2.50 on the seventh of June. And where did it happen?

A: Park Avenue.

P: Can you pinpoint the exact location?

A: Pinpoint?

P: Tell me exactly where.

A: Oh. It was near the entrance to the park. Just about fifty metres inside.

P: OK. Could you tell me what happened?

A: I was walking out of the park and a man was running towards me and he hit into me hard..

P: He collided with you?

A: Yes and he said 'sorry' and something else, then before I realised what had happened, he had run on. It was only about thirty seconds later that I realised my wallet had gone and that he must have taken it when he hit me, collided with me.

P: But did it cross your mind that it wasn't just an accident?

A: No, it never occurred to me that he'd done it on purpose.

P: Did you run after him?

A: No, my mind just went blank and I stood there not knowing what to do.

P: But you were OK? Not hurt?

A: No, just very shocked.

P: OK. Could you tell me exactly what your wallet looked like and what was in it?

A: It's brown, leather and it has my credit card and about 250 euros and …

P: Hold on a minute, credit card … about 250 euros, yes?

A: And a photo of my girlfriend.

P: OK. So you saw the man. Can you give me a description?

A: Erm, about twenty, white, quite tall. And he was wearing a sweater, grey colour with a … you know … erm, something you put over your head …

P: A hood? He was wearing a hoodie?

A: Yes, that's the word. So I didn't see his face, not clearly. But he looked as if he was just out jogging, you know, he was wearing some sort of dark trousers, for running or for the gym.

P: Tracksuit bottoms?

A: Yeah. I can't remember anything else, it all happened so quickly.

P: So that's a tall white male, about twenty, wearing a grey hoodie and dark tracksuit bottoms?

A: That's right.

P: And did he have any other distinguishing marks or features?

A: Sorry?

P: Anything special or different from normal? For example, a scar on his face or anything like that?

A: No, he just seemed like a normal guy, out running. Nothing special. Except …

P: Yes?

A: He reminded me a bit of that actor, Vin Diesel. But younger. Do you know who I mean?

P: Vin Diesel, yeah. I'll put it down. And you said he said something to you.

A: Yeah but I didn't catch what he said. It was too quick.

P: Right, one last question and then I'll take your contact details. Were there any other people in the vicinity?

A: Vicinity?

P: In the surrounding area – nearby. Any witnesses who saw what had happened?

A: No, there was no one nearby, in the … vicinity.

P: Right, now I just need to take your contact details, Mr Girard and I can also give you a phone number to ring if …

**3A**  Ss could complete the phrases in pencil so they can make any necessary changes when they listen to the recording. They could also refer to the audio script for a final check of their answers. Check that Ss understand *Did it cross your mind …?* (Did you think …?), *It never occurred to me* (I never thought), *My mind went blank* (I couldn't think of anything), *I didn't catch* (I didn't hear/understand).

**Answers:** 1 Before, had  2 only, later that  3 mind
4 occurred  5 blank  6 as  7 happened
8 seemed  9 reminded, of  10 catch

**B**  Look at the first sentence with the class, as an example, then put Ss in pairs.

**Answers:** Describe impressions of a person: 6, 8, 9
Refer to time: 1, 2, 7
Refer to something else: 3, 4, 5, 10 (These phrases all describe the victim's reaction.)

**C**  Ss could practise saying the phrases to each other at natural speed and listening for the 'content' words, i.e. those that carry the important information.

**Teaching tip**

When you play the recording again for Ss to repeat, you could divide the class into smaller groups of about six and nominate groups at random to repeat each sentence. This will add more variety, rather than having the whole class chorus all ten sentences.

**Unit 9 Recording 6**

1  Before I realised what had happened, he had run on.
2  It was only about thirty seconds later that I realised my wallet had gone.
3  But did it cross your mind that it wasn't just an accident?
4  It never occurred to me that he'd done it on purpose.
5  My mind went blank.
6  He looked as if he was just out jogging.
7  It all happened so quickly.
8  He just seemed like a normal guy.
9  He reminded me a bit of that actor, Vin Diesel.
10 I didn't catch what he said. It was too quick.

**▶ LANGUAGEBANK** 9.3 p144–145

Direct Ss to the summaries of the different types of phrase on p144. You could drill some of the alternatives for each phrase that were not on the recording, e.g. *it was only much later that I remembered …, He seemed very strong, He looked like a student, I didn't catch the car number plate.* Ss could do Ex A before moving on to the more challenging practice in Ex 4 on p111 in the Students' Book. Once Ss have completed the conversation, they could practise acting it out.

**Answers:** 1 It never **crossed** my mind until I saw the picture on *Crimebeat* on TV.
2 It **occurred** to me then that I should contact you.
3 Yes. I saw him near the factory. He looked **as if** he was taking photos of the building.
4 When he saw me he went away very quickly and he **looked** guilty.
5 It was only later that I **realised** that there was something strange about how he left.
6 I don't know. It just seemed quite **strange** but then I didn't think any more about it till I saw the programme.

**4A**  Tell Ss to read through the prompts quickly and answer these questions: *What was stolen? Where? Who might have stolen it?* Give Ss a few minutes to write out the conversation in their notebooks, leaving the prompts 'clean' for them to use later for spoken practice.

**Answers:** PO: When was your bag stolen?
C: I was shopping/in a shop and I left it in the changing room.
PO: Did you tell the shop manager?
C: As soon as I realised what had happened, I told the sales assistant.
PO: Didn't it occur to you that it wasn't a good idea to leave your bag there?
C: It crossed my mind but I wanted to ask a friend about the clothes.
PO: Did you see anyone?
C: There was one other woman in the changing room.
PO: What did she look like?
C: She seemed normal. She looked as if she was trying on clothes.
PO: Did you notice anything else about her?
C: She reminded me of my boyfriend's ex-girlfriend.
PO: Could it have been her?
C: It was only later that I realised (that) it could have been.

**B**  Ss should only look at the flow chart, not read aloud from their notebooks. Monitor the practice and note down any problems for correction in feedback.

**Alternative idea:**

To allow Ss to be a little more creative, use role cards instead of the flow chart:

Student A

You're the police officer. Someone calls to report a stolen item. Find out:

1 What was stolen, when and where.

2 Whether the victim knows who stole the item or suspects anyone.

Student B

1 You're the caller. Your bag was stolen from the changing room in a shop.

2 You were trying on clothes. You left the bag to go out and show your friend the clothes.

3 You saw another woman in the changing room. She looked a bit like your boyfriend's ex-girlfriend.

Ss act out the conversations, then they could refer to the flow chart and compare the sequence of questions and answers to their ideas.

Alternatively, half the class use role cards and half use the flow chart. They act out their conversations and compare them.

## VOCABULARY incidents

**5A** For *stronger classes,* tell Ss to cover the box and try to think of an appropriate verb to put in the gap.

**Answers:** 1 got stuck  2 is on fire  3 knocked (it) over
4 broken down  5 fallen off  6 locked (myself) out
7 got knocked out  8 run over

**B** Focus Ss on the example and put them in pairs to discuss the other sentences.

**Possible answers:** 2 fire department  3 police
4 car breakdown and recovery service  5 ambulance
6 police, locksmith, housemate  7 ambulance  8 vet, friend

**C** If one of these situations has happened to you, you could tell Ss about it as a model. Then put Ss in small groups to talk about their experiences. The groups could choose one experience to tell the rest of the class about.

⟱ **VOCABULARYBANK** p156 Cars and accidents

These two activities in the **Vocabulary bank** expand Ss vocabulary for describing car accidents and incidents with motor vehicles. Ss can work in pairs to label the diagram of the car for Ex 1, using a dictionary if necessary to help them with anything they are not sure of. In feedback, check pronunciation and word stress of any new items.

Before attempting Ex 2, check the meaning of to *skid* (to slip), *pull out* (to start moving onto a road or a different part of a road), *swerve* (to change direction suddenly) and *collide* (to hit something violently). Ss work in pairs to match the correct verb phrases with the images.

**Answers:** 1  1 E  2 C  3 A  4 B  5 D  6 H  7 K  8 F  9 L
10 E  11 G  12 I
2  2 swerved  3 overtook  4 exceeded the speed limit
5 scratched  6 collided with  7 pulled out  8 drove in the wrong lane

## LEARN TO rephrase

**6A** Check that Ss understand *rephrase* (saying the same thing using more familiar words, so it's clearer) and give them a minute or two to find the examples. You could also ask Ss what the caller does when he doesn't understand (he says *Excuse me?* or repeats the word that was unfamiliar: *pinpoint?*)

**Answers:** 1 Could you give me the exact time?
(= rephrasing of *Could you be more precise?*)
2 Tell me exactly where. (= rephrasing of *Can you pinpoint the exact location?*)

**B** In feedback, point out that sometimes the police officer rephrases what the caller said and gives him the correct word for what he was trying to say.

**Answers:** 1 d)  2 e)  3 c)  4 b)  5 a)

**C** When Ss have checked their answers you could ask them what new words the caller learnt from this conversation (*collided, hoodie, tracksuit bottoms*) and direct them to the *speakout tip.*

## speakout TIP

Read the tip with the Ss and point out that the use of rephrasing helped the conversation to 'flow' more smoothly for both the caller and the police officer.

**Optional extra activity**

For more practice in rephrasing, write the following questions on the board:

Do you remember what you were doing *prior to the incident?* (7)

Was *there any damage to the vehicle?* (4)

Are any of *the occupants* trapped inside? (2)

Is it *causing an obstruction?* (3)

Does he *appear to be in a stable condition?* (5)

Put Ss in pairs and tell them to match the questions to five of the situations in Ex 5A (numbers given in brackets), then rephrase the parts in italics using more familiar vocabulary (they can use dictionaries to check). The pairs then act out the phone calls and the person answering the call rephrases the questions to help the caller understand.

## SPEAKING

**7A** Direct Ss to their pictures and make sure they keep them hidden from each other. Student A should spend a few minutes thinking how to explain the route that the burglar took to get into and out of the house. If there are words they don't know, they need to paraphrase them. Student B studies the picture and the names for different parts of the house.

**B** Tell Ss that Student B needs to draw the burglar's route with Student A's help. Student A can ask B for help with vocabulary. At the end they can show each other their pictures. Monitor and write down examples of good use of rephrasing for feedback.

**Homework ideas**

1 Workbook Ex 1–3B, p64

2 Ss write an email to a friend about an incident that happened to them, who they reported it to, what happened in the end, etc.

# MAYDAY!

## Introduction
Ss watch an extract from a BBC programme about people being rescued from a sinking cruise liner. Ss then learn and practise how to negotiate choices for a difficult or dangerous situation and write about a lucky escape.

## Warm up
Direct Ss to the photo and discuss what they can see. Ask questions to elicit key vocabulary for the lesson, e.g.

*Why's the helicopter there?* (To rescue people from the sea/a ship.)

*What's the person wearing?* (a safety harness)

*What's happening to him/her?* (He's/She's being airlifted.)

*What's the weather like?* (There's a gale/there are gale force winds.)

*How would you feel if you were on board a ship in this weather?* (Worried/scared that it might sink.)

### Culture notes
1 *Mayday* is an emergency code word used internationally as a distress signal in voice radio communications. It derives from the French *venez m'aider*, meaning 'come and help me'. The call is always given three times in a row (*Mayday, Mayday, Mayday*) to prevent mistaking it for some similar-sounding phrase under noisy conditions.

2 The BBC programme is called *999* because this is the number for the emergency services in the UK.

### DVD PREVIEW

**1A** Put Ss in pairs and give them a few minutes to agree on the three worst things, then share their answers with the class. Vocabulary to check: *hull* ( the main part of a ship), *the crew jump ship* (the crew leave the ship when they're not supposed to), *lifeboat* (a small boat carried by ships for people to use if the ship sinks).

**B** Direct Ss to the questions and give them a minute or two to find the answers in the text. Vocabulary to check: *cruise liner* (a large ship for sailing slowly for pleasure), *evacuation* (the process of sending people to a safe place from a dangerous place), *vessel* (a ship or large boat).

**Answer:** Moss Hills, his wife and other members of the entertainment team organised the rescue. Ss can speculate about why they had to do this – guessing from the list of situations in Ex 1A that the crew weren't in charge for some reason.

### DVD VIEW

**2A** Put Ss in pairs and give them a minute or two to order the events, then compare answers with the rest of the class.

**B** Play the DVD for Ss to check. In feedback compare the Ss' order from Ex 2A and discuss briefly why the captain and crew got off the ship when the storm hit and what Ss think of their behaviour.

**Answers:** 2 e  3 d  4 f  5 b  6 c
NB If Ss are unsure about the order of d) and e): 'Suddenly the power went off. Unbelievably, the senior crew <u>had already jumped</u> ship'.

### Optional extra activity
Refer Ss back to the list of things in Ex 1A and ask which of them did <u>not</u> happen.

**Answers:** someone falls into the water, an airlift harness breaks (although a state of panic is avoided initially, we can probably assume that one develops when passengers realise there are no lifeboats left).

**C** Give Ss time to read through the extracts carefully and predict the missing words before playing the DVD again.

**Answers:** 1 atmosphere, party  2 packing, panic
3 charge of  4 pour, avoid  5 winds, assist  6 board

### DVD 9 *999*

MB = Michael Buerk     MH = Moss Hills     PW = Paul Whiley
MB: Tonight on 999 holiday hell on a sinking cruise liner: one man's incredible story. The sea can be a dangerous place but when you go on a big ship, a ferry or a cruise liner, you'd hardly expect it simply to sink underneath your feet. But that's exactly what happened to the 581 passengers and crew on the cruise ship Oceanos that went down off South Africa in 1991. Husband and wife singers Moss and Tracy Hills felt at home on board the Oceanos. So as the entertainment staff got things ready for the opening night's party, no one worried about the storm that was battering South Africa's east coast.

MH: There was a great atmosphere when we set sail. It's kind of typical … there's always … people are partying … it's the whole sail away party. It's one of the highlights of a cruise. I went upstairs to go and check on our musical equipment and on my way up there I saw three security guards running down the passageway, so I followed them and saw crew members packing their bags and everyone was in a real state of panic. I knew something was wrong, I then went up to the lounge, then suddenly the power went off.

MB: Unbelievably the senior crew had already jumped ship.

MH: And next thing we just sort of started running everything. It was myself and Julian and the Cruise Director, my wife Tracy and we were getting people and just loading them into lifeboats.

MB: By 4a.m. three hundred and fifty people, including the crew, had got off, leaving the entertainers in charge of the frightened passengers.

MH: There were just over two hundred people still left on board and nowhere to get off: we had no more lifeboats.

MB: Water continued to pour through the hull but the gravity of the situation was kept from the passengers to avoid panic.

MH: I'm an entertainer. We're used to leading with people, everyone just looked to us to … to see the whole thing through. So I went on and I filled my pockets with sweets and then I'd, like, give people … adults and everyone … I'd give them sweets.

MB: Eight hours had passed since the lights went out and still there was no sign of help. Each wave tore deeper into the ship's damaged hull: but the Captain's early Mayday had been heard and as the ship wallowed in the boiling ocean, the largest air-sea rescue in history was about to begin … Swinging uncontrollably in gale force winds, two Navy divers were dropped on board the ship to assist with the rescue.

PW: Once I was on deck I went up with the first passenger just to show everybody once and from then on everyone was on their own – we sent two people in the harnesses at a time.

MB: Paul organised the airlift of passengers from one end of the ship with Moss at the other.

MH: As soon as I had two in the harness and ready to go I'd signal the chopper guys and they'd get … the harness would go up … and then you'd send the next two out. We had 12 passengers left: myself, Tracy and we had, um, Robin was on the bridge, so there's 15 people left on board and they disappeared to go and drop those passengers off. We're waiting and we wait and we wait and then they didn't come back.

MB: After 40 minutes there was still no sign of a helicopter.

MH: Turns out they'd run out of fuel and … and there was no fuel available there.

PW: Yes, time was passing and there was less and less space on the boat, um and everyone was just, ah, waiting, waiting for … for choppers.

MB: Having refuelled, the helicopters returned just as Moss was giving up any hope of being rescued.

PW: As we got into the harness and I looked down on the vessel I was sad to the point where, you know, I was … I was emotional. I had a bump in my throat – I was really … you look at the vessel and you think that, ah, so much has happened in such a short time, yeah and there's nothing more we could do – there's just no way of saving it, there's no way.

**D** Put Ss in pairs to discuss the questions for a few minutes, then continue the discussion as a class.

---

**Optional extra activity**

Ss work in pairs and role-play an interview with one of the people (the captain, a passenger, Moss Hills) from the Oceanos. Give interviewers a few minutes to prepare some questions first. When Ss have practised their interviews, ask a few pairs to act theirs out for the class. Ss can write up one of the interviews in the form of a newspaper article for homework.

---

### speakout items for a life raft

**3A** Tell Ss to look through the list and check they understand what all the items are. While they listen, Ss should make brief notes about why an item is rejected/kept.

---

**Answers:** lighter – rejected: can't start a fire on a raft, not a priority to cook a hot meal, just survive.
blanket – kept: keep warm, use as a towel, protect you from the sun.
hand mirror – mentioned but no decision made

---

**B** Ss look through the key phrases before listening again. Ss should tick the phrases they hear and underline the option in each phrase. Vocabulary to check: *priority/ prioritise* (the most important thing/put in order of importance), *essential/ vital/crucial* (very important), *dehydrate* (lose water from your body). When Ss have checked their answers, highlight the use of the *-ing* form in *I can't see the point of* … and *to prevent you from* ….

---

**Answers:**
it depends on what (the life raft is made out of)
It's not exactly top priority to be able to (cook a hot meal)
I'd say that (a blanket is) essential.
to keep you warm (obviously)
That hadn't occurred to me.

---

**C** Circulate and help while Ss make notes on their six items. Encourage Ss to incorporate some of the key phrases and to practise talking about their items on their own before joining a group in the next stage.

**D** Put Ss into groups of four or five and explain that the goal is to agree on six items. A spokesperson for each group could then read out the list to the class and see what they all have in common. Monitor and note down good examples of language use, particularly the key phrases and any problems, for discussion and correction later.

---

**Unit 9 Recording 8**

W1 = Woman 1    M = Man    W2 = Woman 2

W1: So we really need to decide then, what it is we get rid of and what is absolutely essential to keep on the life raft, I think that's probably the most important thing isn't it?

M: I'm sure it's easy to get rid of a few things, isn't it?

W2: Like what?

M: Well, I'm not sure about the lighter. I mean, we can't really start a fire on a raft, can we?

W2: No.

W1: I suppose it depends on what the life raft is made out of, doesn't it?

M: Yeah, but it's not exactly top priority to be able to cook a hot meal, you know, when you really just need to survive.

W1: So no lighter?

M and W2: OK.

W1: OK. So what do you think is important?

W2: I'd say that a blanket is essential.

W1: Interesting choice. What for?

W2: Well, you can use it for a lot of different things. To keep you warm obviously, but you can use a blanket as a towel if you get wet.

W1: If you fall in the water.

W2: … for example. And a blanket can protect you from the sun.

M: That hadn't occurred to me. Okay, I'm convinced. So what else?

W1: Well I can't see the point of taking the hand mirror can you?

M: Actually, I can. Because if …

---

### writeback a lucky escape

**4A** You could start by writing the title *A lucky escape* on the board and recap with the class why the passengers on the Oceanos had a lucky escape. Then put Ss in pairs to brainstorm other ideas for a lucky escape. Direct Ss to the first word string in Ex 4A (they should cover the story below) and either put them in pairs to invent a story, or elicit a story round the class, inviting one student at a time to add more to the story, using the next word in the chain.

**B** Ss read the story and discuss the answers to the questions in pairs.

**C** Ss could choose a word string in pairs and brainstorm ideas for the story before writing a first draft, then exchange stories and make any suggestions for improvements.

**D** Ss' stories can be put round the walls of the classroom for others to read and comment on.

---

**Homework ideas**

1 Ss write another 'lucky escape' story using the word string they did not use in class.

2 Ss write a newspaper article about the rescue on the Oceanos.

3 Ss research on the internet what happened to the captain of the Oceanos.

---

# LOOKBACK

## Introduction

The aim of these activities is to provide revision and further practice of the language from the unit. You can also use them to assess Ss' ability to use the language, in which case you need to monitor but avoid helping them. You may feel that you don't need or have time to do all the activities. If so, you could allocate the activities that would be most beneficial for your Ss, or get individual Ss to decide which activities they'd like to do in class.

### -ING FORM AND INFINITIVE (2)

**1A** You could start by either asking Ss to read through the article quickly and think of a suitable title for it, or putting Ss in pairs to brainstorm advice they'd give to someone who'd been mugged, then read the article to see if their ideas are mentioned.

**Answers:** 1 doing 2 to check 3 being 4 falling 5 to find 6 shaking 7 drinking 8 to phone 9 seeing 10 to do

**B** Ss discuss their opinions of the article in pairs and/or as a class. They could then go on to write a similar article (using -ing forms and infinitives) for someone whose house has been broken into.

### CRIME

**2A** You could divide the class into teams for this and set a time limit. The team who has the most crimes on their list when time is up wins points.

**Answers:** (from page 106 – Ss may think of others)
1 stalking 2 kidnapping 3 hacking 4 arson 5 tax evasion
6 vandalism 7 bribery 8 mugging 9 counterfeiting
10 identity theft 11 shoplifting 12 pickpocketing

**B** Ss can stay in their teams for this and do it as a board race. Read out the descriptions one at a time (Ss should have their books closed so they can't look ahead) and as soon as a team thinks of the answer, one member runs up and writes the crime(s) on the board. Points can be awarded for correct answers, but deducted for incorrect spelling.

**Answers:** 1 arson, vandalism 2 stalking, kidnapping, mugging, pickpocketing
3 hacking, counterfeiting, identity theft 4 tax evasion, bribery 5 shoplifting

**C** Put Ss in pairs or small groups to discuss this and the reasons why those crimes are more often in the news.

### SYNONYMS

**3A** Give Ss a few minutes to rewrite the questions. They could also practise saying the questions at natural speed in preparation for the pair work in part B.

**Answers:** 1 distract you 2 grab 3 pose as someone 4 deceiving 5 fallen for

**B** Encourage Ss to ask follow-up questions after their partners have answered. You could demonstrate this by inviting Ss to ask you one or two of the questions first.

### MODALS OF DEDUCTION

**4A** You could start by reading out the situations to the class (with their books closed) and encourage them to make guesses about what happened using modals of deduction. Then direct Ss to the options and give them a minute or two to rewrite them.

**Answers:** 1 b) His friends might/could have sent mail to the old address. c) The postman can't/couldn't have delivered the letters. 2a) She might have been practising in an empty concert hall. 2b) She must have been deaf, so no-one clapped. 2c) The audience can't have/couldn't have liked the music.

**B** Encourage the class to think of two more explanations for each situation before they read the solutions on p161, e.g. *someone else must have taken the letters; the lock on his post box might have been broken, so they fell out and blew away; the pianist must have asked the audience not to clap for some reason; it might have been in a country where the custom is not to clap,* etc.

### DESCRIBING AN INCIDENT

**5A** For *stronger classes,* you could tell Ss to cover the box and try to remember the appropriate words for the gaps first, then check with the words in the box.

**Answers:** 2 reminded 3 realised 4 went 5 happened 6 didn't catch 7 happened 8 crossed 9 if 10 like

**B** You could start by looking at one of the incidents with the whole class as an example and elicit some ideas about how to use the sentences. Then put Ss in pairs to work on a different incident and circulate to help with language as required.

**C** You may want to refer Ss back to the flow chart on p111 before they start the role-play. Monitor and make notes of good language use and problems for feedback and correction.

## OVERVIEW

## MOVING EXPERIENCES

### Introduction

Ss practise listening and speaking about films using relative clauses and adjectives for describing films. They also learn to write descriptively and write a film review.

### SUPPLEMENTARY MATERIALS

Resource bank p188 and/or p190

**Ex 1B:** Ss need to use monolingual dictionaries

**Language bank:** p147, 10.1, **Ex A–C:** prepare answer keys to hand out to Ss.

### Warm up

Brainstorm types of film. Put Ss in pairs and give them two minutes to make a list of as many types of film as they can. Ask Ss to discuss their favourite and least favourite types of film, giving reasons for their preferences.

### VOCABULARY adjectives

**1A** Direct Ss to the photos and give them a minute or two to decide which film genre is shown in each photo (*action film, romance or romantic film, science fiction film*) and discuss which types of the film they like/don't like and why.

**B** You could do another example with the class then put Ss in pairs, encouraging them to guess the words they don't know before checking in a monolingual dictionary. Point out that there are three adjectives for each box. Pronunciation to check: *predictable, awesome, horrific, unforgettable, brilliant, electrifying, poignant.*

#### Answers:
full of action/suspense – gripping, fast-paced, electrifying
frightening – creepy, chilling, horrific
emotional/often sad – moving, touching, poignant
not good – predictable, weak, dull
very good – awesome, brilliant, unforgettable

**C** Do one example with the class, demonstrating that Ss should try putting *very* (used only with gradable adjectives) or *absolutely* (used only with extreme adjectives) in front of each adjective and see which sounds better. When Ss have indentified all five ungradable/extreme adjectives, you could elicit other adverbs that can be used with them (*utterly, totally, completely, absolutely* and *really,* which can also be used with gradable adjectives).

#### Answers: The five ungradable/extreme adjectives are:
gripping, awesome, horrific, unforgettable, electrifying

**2A** Put Ss in groups of three to five and give them a minute or two to write down five films they all know.

**B** Focus Ss on the example and check how many of the adjectives from Ex 1A are used by Student A in the description. Then emphasise that each of the other Ss should ask a *Yes/No* question before anyone can guess the film.

## LISTENING

**3** Ss read the information and discuss their answers with a partner or the whole class.

> **Possible answer:** People listen to the programme because it is varied and interactive and gives people useful information.

**4A** Before you play the recording, you could find out if anyone has seen or heard of the film *Let the right one in* and ask them to tell the class what it's about. Give Ss a moment to read through the options in questions 1–3, then play the recording.

> **Answers:** 1 loved  2 slow-paced  3 the director

**B** Give Ss time to read through the extracts and try to predict some of the missing words before you play the recording again. Ss can discuss their answers in pairs.

> **Answers:** 1 Creepy creepy*  2 brilliant brilliant*  3 carefully paced  4 chilling  5 horrific  6 unforgettable  7 poignant  8 awesome
> * Point out that the speaker repeats himself for emphasis; he also does the same with *very* (no. 2) and *really* (no. 4).

**C** Put Ss in pairs or small groups to discuss the questions.

### Unit 10 Recording 1

E = Edith Bowman    J = James King

E: Right, another two couple of films to look at. Now I heard about this and I really want to see it. Are you starting off with *Let the Right One In*?

J: I certainly am. Creepy, creepy horror film this one. It's the story of a twelve-year-old boy, real loner boy, real kind of geek at school, bullied at school, who befriends his new neighbour, who's a twelve-year-old girl. She happens to be a vampire. And this is set in very snowy and very bleak Sweden. It's a brilliant, brilliant film, it really is very, very good, because I think it's so bleak, because it's a very – although it is a horror film, it's a very quiet horror film, you know it's very sort of slow and really carefully paced, really not showy at all. And because of that, I think really, really chilling and actually sometimes you're laughing and the most horrific things are happening on screen because this boy, you know he's in love with this girl, he wants to help her. You know and even though really horrible things are happening on screen, you actually giggle a bit and I love that … when you really don't know how to feel, you just feel uncomfortable.

E: Almost the film is running your emotions for you.

J: Absolutely. And I think a really unforgettable film. They are going to do an American version of this, which could be quite good. I think it's the guy who made *Cloverfield*, Matt Reeves has said that he wants to make an American version of this. But go and see this original version because it really, it really does show you that, you know, in horror films, restraint can be a very powerful thing and it doesn't just have to be really loud and just loads of blood and guts. You can have something that's really poignant and …

E: … and beautiful.

J: … and beautiful at the same time as being really chilling. And the two kids in this are well, just awesome. I haven't stopped thinking about it since I've seen it, it's a really special film, *Let the Right One In*.

E: How many stars?

J: One, two, three, four, five stars!

E: Yay! Oh, wow …

## GRAMMAR  relative clauses

**5A** For *weaker classes*, you may want to start by eliciting what each pronoun is used for, i.e. *who* – people, *which* – things, *whose* – belonging to, *where* – place, *when* – time.

> **Answers:** 1 which  2 which  3 which  4 who  5 who  6 which  7 which  8 when  9 which  10 who  11 whose  12 where

**B** For *weaker classes*, you may want to look at question 1 with the whole class and establish which relative clauses are defining/non defining. Establish that the relative clause starts with the relative pronoun *who, which,* etc. To help Ss see the difference between the two types of clause you could read out some of the sentences without the relative clauses and elicit which ones still sound 'complete' and which ones don't.

> **Answers:**
> D: 1, 2, 3, 5, 8
> ND: 4, 6, 7, 9, 10, 11, 12
> 2 ND (It may help Ss to think of the commas and/or full stop as parentheses around the clause as showing that it is extra, non essential information)
> 3 *Which* refers to the whole preceding clause or phrase, i.e. (the fact that) 'Eli is a vampire and she needs blood' and 'the insecurities and horrors of growing up'
> 4 1, 2, 3, 5, 8 (the defining relative clauses)
> 5 3, 5, 8 (in these examples, the relative pronoun is the object of the relative clause)
> 6 The preposition is at the end of sentence in 5 and 7; in 9, it's before the relative pronoun, *which*.

**6** While Ss underline the relative clauses, you could write the extract on the board without the clauses, so you can focus Ss on the intonation in the next stage.

> **Answers:** who is bullied by other kids
> which gives Oscar a real possibility of striking back against the bullies.

**7A** Play the recording a couple of times for Ss to hear the lower pitch on the non-defining clauses. You can then add the clauses to the extract on the board, but write them on a slightly lower line, to show Ss visually how the pitch drops. Tell students that the drop in pitch is a way of indicating the parentheses round the extra information.

**B** Encourage Ss to start repeating the extract as soon as it starts.

> **Possible answers:**
> C 1 The man who is marrying Suzanne is very lucky.
> 2 The house where I used to live burnt down yesterday./The house I used to live in burnt down yesterday.
> 3 Pablo Picasso, whose father was also an artist, spent his early childhood in Malaga.
> 4 The moment I realised I wanted to be an actor was the most important moment of my life.
> 5 The holiday I enjoyed most was in Canada./The holiday I most enjoyed was in Canada.
> 6 Usain Bolt, who won three gold medals at the Beijing Olympics, is a famous Jamaican runner.
> 7 I lived with a guy whose name was Jon while I was a student./While I as a student I lived with a guy who name was Jon.
> 8 This is the sort of occasion when you should make a speech.

➠ **LANGUAGEBANK** 10.1 p146–147

Give Ss time to read through the rules and example carefully, particularly if they've found Ex 5 challenging. To give Ss controlled practice, they could do Ex A,B and/or C in class. In a *mixed ability* class, give Ex A–B to *weaker Ss* and Ex C to *stronger Ss*: provide a key for Ss to check their work, then pair up Ss who've done different exercises to exchange answers.

**Answers:**
A 1 which 2 who 3 whose 4 who 5 who
6 where 7 who/which 8 when 9 which 10 which
11 which 12 which
B replaced by *that*: 1, 2, 7, 9, 10, 11, 12
omitted: 7, 10, 11

## PRACTICE

**8A** Focus Ss on the example and give them time to work through the exercise on their own. Ss compare answers in pairs before checking with the whole class. Remind them to use a lower pitch for non-defining relative clauses.

**Answers:** 2 Megastar Zac Efron, who shot to fame in *High School Musical*, gives an emotional and mature performance in his latest film.
3 *Invictus* is a story about leadership and forgiveness at a critical period when Nelson Mandela had just become president of South Africa.
4 The film *Star Trek* was based on a popular TV series which has been watched all around the world.
5 The film, which is directed by Marc Forster, is Daniel Craig's second outing as James Bond.
6 Adrian Brody plays a Jewish refugee who is a famous Polish piano player in *The Pianist*.
7 *Lost in Translation* is a film about two Americans in a Tokyo hotel who meet and form an unusual bond.
8 *The Hurt Locker*, which was made in Jordan, is a gripping story about the insanity and foolishness of war.

**B** Ss write a sentence about each film using the sentences in Ex 8A as models.

**C** Put Ss in groups of four. To make this more fun, tell Ss to say *Beep!* instead of *this film/these films*.

## SPEAKING

**9A** Complete some of the sentences so that they are true for you. Ss complete the sentences, working alone.

**B** First, elicit some examples of appropriate follow-up questions, e.g.

A: *My favourite actress is Toni Colette, who was in* Japanese story *and* Muriel's wedding.

B: *Really? What's so special about her?*

A: *Well, she always plays different characters, she's not type cast.*

Ss report back to the class about their partner's answers.

## WRITING a review

**10A** Start by directing Ss to the pictures and asking if anyone has seen the film and what they thought of it, or what they know about it. Put Ss in pairs to discuss the questions.

**Answers:**
2 to help people decide if they want to see a film
3 plot summary, actors' names, recommendation, setting of the film, reviewer's opinion of different elements
(You don't usually find the ticket prices because they vary from cinema to cinema, nor the a description of the film's ending because people don't want to know that before they see the film.)

**B** Ask Ss to read the review and decide how many stars (out of a possible five) the reviewer would give it and ask any Ss who've seen the film if they agree with the reviewer. Tell Ss to choose a topic from the box in Ex 10A question 3 to write next to each paragraph.

**Answers:** 1 setting of the film 2 plot summary
3 reviewer's opinion of different elements
4 recommendation

## LEARN TO write descriptively

**11A** Direct Ss to the third paragraph and give them time to find two adverbs followed by past participles.

**Answers:** skilfully directed, poignantly acted

**B** Put Ss in pairs to complete the phrases. Suggest that they try saying the combinations to see if they sound correct.

**Answers:** 1 skilfully/sensitively/poignantly 2 poignantly/convincingly/skilfully/sensitively 3 widely/overwhelmingly/highly 4 harshly/widely/heavily/overwhelmingly

**12A** Ss can work alone or with a partner who's seen the same film.

**B** While Ss write their first draft make a note of any common problems, so that you can give some feedback on these before Ss write their final draft in Ex 11D.

**C** Before exchanging reviews, Ss could write (on a separate piece of paper) a star rating for the film. The person reading their review should then guess how many stars they gave it and check with them when they hand it back.

**D** Ss can write their final draft in class or for homework.

**Homework ideas**
1 Workbook Ex 1–5, p65–66
2 Ss write a review of a play, concert or CD.

# POPULAR CULTURE

## Introduction

Ss practise reading and speaking about popular culture using participle clauses, vocabulary related to the arts and two-part phrases.

### SUPPLEMENTARY MATERIALS

Resource bank p189 and/or p191

**Ex 1B**: put all the questions from 'Popular Culture Q & A' on a handout (see *Alternative idea*).

**Ex 4B**: Ss need to use monolingual dictionaries.

**Ex 4B**: prepare a copy of vocabulary definitions (see *Optional extra activity*).

**Ex 5A**: be prepared to answer one of the questions, using some words/phrases from the unit so far.

## Warm up

Lead into the topic by putting the title *Popular culture* on the board and discussing with Ss what it means to them.

### READING

**1A** Ss could discuss the photos (of the actors at the bottom of the page and pop star at the top) in pairs or as a class and decide what the most difficult aspects of these two different types of performing could be. Ask them to consider which they think is most difficult/challenging – performing as an actor or as a singer.

**B** Direct Ss A and B to their five questions. Emphasise that Ss should only look at their own text. You could put all Student As and Student Bs together in two groups. They can take turns to read out the question for the group to discuss, then read the answer to check their ideas.

### Alternative idea

1 Extract all ten questions from A's and B's texts and either write/display them on the board or give them to Ss on a handout. Ss predict the answers in pairs and make a note of their ideas.

2 To pre-teach unfamiliar vocabulary, write the following pairs of items on the board and ask Ss in pairs to predict which answer each pair is from, using a dictionary to help them if necessary:

*manipulate, purism;*
*a commodity, money launderers;*
*a disposable camera, a knack for timing;*
*amplification, vibrations;*
*glycerine, a prop;*
*a backing track, stationary;*
*a stand-up comedian, freebies;*
*crossing boundaries, a definitive answer;*
*unheard of, a portfolio of work;*
*humiliating, insulting.*

Ss can check how many they predicted correctly when they read the texts.

**C** Emphasise that Ss should summarise the answers, rather than simply reading them aloud to their partners. You may want to give them a few minutes to think about how to summarise the main point of each answer before putting them in pairs, e.g. they could note down one or two key words to refer to. When Ss have heard all the answers, they could discuss which ones they found most interesting/surprising/predictable, etc. and share their ideas with the class.

### GRAMMAR participle clauses

**2A** Tell Ss to read the article quickly and find the answer to the question.

**Answer:** So that people don't ruin their day by taking photos or asking for autographs.

**B** You could start by asking Ss how each clause would be written with a full verb, rather than a participle, i.e.
1 *stars who are registered*
2 *paparazzi who are trying*
3 *public who are seeking*
4 *Names which involve*
5 *who were married*
6 *and used*
7 *and knew.*

You could look at rule 1 with the class to check that Ss understand what present and past participles are.

**Answers:** 1 present participle, past participle
2 *1, 2, 3, 4, 5* 3 present participle, past participle

**C** Direct Ss to the pairs of sentences and point out that the meaning of both sentences in the pair is the same. You could also elicit that using a participle clause is more economical. Go through the rules with the class.

**Answers:** 1 a present participle 2 the same

### speakout TIP

Before Ss read the tip, direct them back to the text in Ex 2A and ask them why they think it's a good idea to use participle clauses (they help you avoid repetition and make your writing more economical and 'polished'). Read the tip with the class and elicit how to improve the sentence *I stayed at home and I read the paper and I watched TV.* (*I stayed at home reading the paper and watching the sport on TV.*)

Also point out that in the complex sentence *The people stopped at the border were all Americans*, 'stopped' means 'who were stopped' – we know this because a past participle is used for a passive clause.

### Optional extra activity

Ss look for more examples of participle clauses in the Question and Answer reading texts on p119 and p163.

… the range of works and styles of painting <u>regarded as art</u> …

… the average person <u>sitting at his or her home computer</u> …

… as much as someone <u>working with a computer</u> …

A big star <u>auditioning for a part</u> …

The closest such actors get to anything <u>resembling an audition</u> …

Heavy metal <u>played softly</u> sounds stupid …

… for dealing with members of the audience <u>interrupting their performance</u> …

Some comedians, <u>known for their</u> …

**LANGUAGEBANK** 10.2 p146–147

Give Ss time to read through the rules and examples and to notice the three main reasons for using participle clauses. You could use Ex A in class for a short controlled practice activity.

Ss could do Ex B for homework.

**Answers:**
A 1 walking, waiting  2 chatting, noticing
3 Hidden  4 waiting  5 injured  6 Disgusted, watching
B 1 The taxi almost drove over a man lying in the street.
2 I don't know those people living next door to me.
3 Some factories forced to close during the recession still haven't reopened.  4 The army led by Napoleon advanced towards the hill.  5 Those apartments overlooking Central Park are the most expensive.
8 Hundreds of young people camping along the river illegally were chased away by the police.  9 She closed her eyes, listening to the sound of the building site, wishing she wasn't there  10 The wedding taking place tomorrow is the Mayor's son's (wedding).

### PRACTICE

**3A** Do the first sentence as an example. Ss work alone or with a partner on the rest of the sentences.

**Answers:**
1 People taking photos should ask their subjects' permission first.  2 Films based on books are usually disappointing.
3 It's great to see rock stars in their sixties still playing concerts.  4 Architecture designed in the 1960s is generally quite ugly and ought to be pulled down.
5 Photos of people posing for the camera don't work as well as spontaneous pictures.  6 Film and TV stars appearing in the theatre attract huge audiences.  7 Jokes involving racial stereotypes are not funny.  8 Photos altered to make celebrities look thinner should be banned.

**B** You could give your opinion on the first sentence as an example and invite Ss to agree/disagree. Then put Ss in pairs to discuss the sentences, or ask Ss to walk around the room choosing sentences at random to discuss with different people. Conduct feedback with the whole class and find out if there are any sentences that everyone agrees with.

### VOCABULARY the arts

**4A** Tell Ss they're going to read three forum comments about the same singer. Give them a couple of minutes to read and underline the adjectives which reveal the writer's attitude. They should then decide whether the overall tone of each comment is positive, negative or mixed and mark it ✓ ✗ or – accordingly.

**Answers:** 1 ✓ 2 ✗ 3 –

**B** Look at *creating a stir* with the class as an example. Establish that, from the context, the meaning is positive and ask Ss what other meanings of *stir* they know, i.e. to mix something up or cause strong feelings. Put Ss in pairs to discuss the rest and check in their dictionaries.

**Answers:**
**to create a stir:** to cause a feeling of excitement (or sometimes annoyance)
**ground-breaking:** using new ideas, innovative
**(to get/have) rave reviews:** noun – strong praise for a new performer, music, film, play etc.
**a sell-out:** a performance, sports event etc for which all the tickets have been sold
**must-see:** (informal) something that is so good, exciting or interesting that you think people should see it.
**hype:** noun [U] (informal) publicity – when something is talked about a lot on TV, in the newspapers, online etc. to make it seem good or important.
**a letdown:** (informal) something that disappoints you because it is not as good as you expected.
**a flop:** a film, show, plan, or product that is not successful
**mainstream:** the most usual ideas or ways of doing something which are accepted by most people.
**alternative:** different from what is usual or accepted.

**Optional extra activity**
Put Ss in pairs and give a copy of the answers above to Student A who 'tests' Student B by reading out a definition and asking them for the correct word. They then swap roles, e.g.

A: *Something that disappoints you because it's not as good as you expected.*

B: *A letdown?*

A: *Correct!*

**C** Ask Ss to write their forum entry on a separate piece of paper so they can be passed round the class for other Ss to look at.

**D** Ss pass their entry to the person on their right, who reads it and passes it on, etc. If a student is interested in a performance, they could write any questions they have about it on the piece of paper underneath the forum entry for the writer to answer when they get the entry back. Or, if a student has seen the same performance, they could write a further comment, saying whether they agree (as in the examples in Ex 4A).
Make sure everyone gets their original entry back and give Ss the opportunity to answer questions/reply to comments written on their entries.

**VOCABULARYBANK** p157 Music

Ex 1 and 2 revise and extend the Ss vocabulary for talking about musical instruments and musical performance. For Ex, let Ss work individually or in pairs to label the musical instruments before feeding back as a class. During feedback, extend the discussion into Ex 2 and find out which Ss in the class play instruments or which they would like to learn.

**Answers:**
1 1 E 2 J 3 I 4 L 5 C 6 H 7 F 8 K 9 D 10 B 11 G 12 A
2 1 c) 2 d) 3 e) 4 a) 5 g) 6 h) 7 f) 8 b)

## SPEAKING

**5A** You could start by answering one of the questions yourself, as a model. Then give Ss time to look through the unit for language they could use in their answers and write down some key phrases to prompt them in the next stage.

**B** Put Ss in pairs and encourage them to listen 'actively' to each other while they're talking about their experiences, e.g. by asking questions, commenting on what their partner says, showing interest/surprise, etc.

**C** Group Ss so they're not with their partners from the previous stage. Tell the listeners in each group to make a note of any questions they want to ask while each person is making their recommendation and remind them to ask their questions when everyone has spoken. Monitor the group work and note down examples of good language use and problems for discussion and correction later. Conduct feedback, asking Ss to tell the rest of the class which thing/person they would most like to go to see/hear and why.

## VOCABULARY PLUS two-part phrases

**6A** Focus Ss on the example sentences and give them a minute or two to discuss what the two-part phrases mean.

**B** Refer Ss to the dictionary entry, pointing out that a good dictionary will always have an example sentence to help them understand the meaning, as well as a definition. You could also ask Ss if they've come across any other two-part phrases like this and whether they have similar phrases in their own language.

**7A** To help Ss match the pairs, point out that they often contain two opposite ideas, or repeat the same word/idea. Ss could work on this in pairs, saying the combinations to each other to see if they sound plausible.

**Answers:**
peace and quiet   leaps and bounds   pros and cons
on and on   rough and ready   now and then   sick and tired
ups and downs   through and through   give and take

**B** When Ss have checked their answers, play the recording again and tell them to listen to the way *and* is 'squashed' between the two words so that it seems to become part of the first word in the pair.

**8A** Ss could start by reading the sentences together and predicting where some of the more 'literal' word pairs might go. Then they read their definitions and examples and complete only the five sentences for their five word pairs.

**Answers:**
1 peace and quiet  2 now and then  3 through and through
4 sick and tired  5 leaps and bounds  6 ups and downs
7 on and on  8 give and take  9 pros and cons
10 rough and ready

**B** Monitor closely and help Ss sort out any confusion, e.g. if they've both put their word pair in the same sentence, refer them back to their dictionary definitions and examples to work out which one doesn't fit.

**C** Give Ss a few minutes to discuss the ideas, then invite them to share some of their opinions with the class.

---

**➡ VOCABULARYBANK** p157 Two-part phrases

Ex 3A and B introduce the Ss to more two-part phrases which are commonly used in spoken English. Let the Ss work in pairs to try to complete both exercises, avoiding the use of dictionaries in possible. Feed back as a class. If Ss are enjoying the topic, ask them if they can find equivalent expressions in their own language.

**Answers:**
3A 1 later  2 leave  3 swim  4 take  5 nothing  6 death
7 miss  8 another
B a) 2  b) 5  c) 4  d) 7  e) 1  f) 8  g) 3  h) 6

### Optional extra activity

Tell Ss you're going to ask them for some pieces of information, which they should write *in random order* on a clean sheet of paper in their notebooks. Tell them to write down:

*a place you'd go to get some peace and quiet*

*somewhere you used to go a lot but now you only go to every now and then*

*a book or film that you'll never get sick and tired of*

*a book or film that goes on and on for too long*

*someone who's an animal lover through and through*

*someone whose English has improved in leaps and bounds*

*a band whose songs are a bit rough and ready*

*a band whose music you listen to on and off*

Ss then show each other what they've written and guess what each piece of information means, e.g.

*'War and peace'– Is that a book that you'll never get sick and tired of?*

*That's right!*

### Homework ideas
1 Workbook Ex 1–5, p67–68
2 Vocabulary bank p157, Ex 3

# ON YOUR LEFT …

## Introduction
Ss practise listening to and giving a tour, using appropriate phrases. They also learn vocabulary for giving dimensions and how to express estimates.

### SUPPLEMENTARY MATERIALS
Resource bank p192

Ex 3B: Prepare sets of cards for a matching activity (see *Optional extra activity*).

## Warm up
Ss should have their books closed. Tell them to write down the names of two cities they've visited and three places of interest to see in each city. Ss then either work in groups or stand up and walk round the classroom, telling each other about the cities and places they've chosen, with reasons for their choices. Conduct feedback, asking Ss which cities sounded most appealing to them.

### SPEAKING
**1** Direct Ss to the photos and give them a few minutes to discuss the questions. NB Avoid telling Ss the answers to question 2a) as this will become apparent when they listen to the recording. If some pairs don't have many ideas for question 2b) you could bring the class together to pool any information they have about the two places and write it on the board for them to copy: they can then tick the information that is mentioned when they listen to the tour.

### FUNCTION giving a tour
**2A** Tell Ss to write the letters from the photos (A–F) in order as they listen.

**Answers:** 1 B 2 F 3 D 4 A 5 C 6 E

**B** You could suggest that Ss copy the list of places into their notebooks, so they have more space to write notes about them. Give Ss time to compare answers in pairs, adding anything they missed to their own information. You may want to play the recording again, for Ss to 'fill out' their notes.

**Answers:**

| | |
|---|---|
| 1 The Blue Note Jazz Club | It's one of the best jazz clubs in the neighbourhood. |
| 2 The Café Reggio | The first owner brought cappuccino to the US, the original cappuccino machine is there. |
| 3 Greenwich Village in general | It's a centre of artistic life and attracts writers, dancers, poets; it was a big part of 60s folk music scene. |
| 4 Washington Square Park | People play chess there every day. The arch was modelled on the Arc de Triomphe in Paris and was built in 1889 to celebrate 100th anniversary of inauguration of George Washington. |
| 5 The Bodleian | Named after founder Thomas Bodley, the Bodleian is a (circular) library, which has a copy of every book published in the UK; any student can use it. |
| 6 The Oxford colleges | There are 38 Oxford colleges. |
| 7 The Bridge of Sighs | It connects the two sides of Hertford College; is modelled on bridge in Venice. |
| 8 New College | The college was founded in 1370. |
| 9 The 'Schools' | Students take their exams there; biggest room can seat 500 students. |
| 10 Christ Church College | It's the biggest and most famous college at Oxford; Harry Potter feasts were filmed in the Great Hall. |

### Unit 10 Recording 4
W = Woman   M = Man
**Conversation 1**
W: So here we are in Greenwich Village.
M: It looks very different from the rest of New York.
W: Yeah, the streets are quite narrow and the buildings aren't as high.
M: It does look quite village-like.
W: Yeah, but it's quite big. It extends out west that way to the Hudson River, north above Washington Square. We'll go up there in a bit.
M: And you lived here?
W: When I first came to New York, yeah. In an apartment just around the corner, on West Third Street. Actually, you can see the building over there.
M: Near The Blue Note Jazz Club?
W: Yeah.
M: I've heard of The Blue Note.
W: It's pretty famous. There are some great jazz clubs around the neighbourhood and that's one of the best. We can see a show there one night if you want.
M: That'd be great.
W: Now up here on the left is the Café Reggio. It's where I used to hang out and read when I wasn't working.
M: Looks good.
W: Their cappuccino is great. The story goes that the original owner brought cappuccino to America. You can see the original cappuccino machine inside.
W: Cool. We could stop and have a coffee.
M: Maybe a bit later? Let's head over to Washington Square Park and then circle back.
M: OK – lead the way!

W: A lot of these clubs we're walking by have a real history. As I'm sure you know, Greenwich Village has always been a centre of artistic life – very bohemian. It's always attracted famous writers, dancers and poets. And in the sixties, it was a big part of the folk music scene: Simon and Garfunkel, Joni Mitchell, Bob Dylan, you know.
M: Before my time! Now what's this?
W: This is Washington Square Park. We'll walk into the park on this side. Can you play chess?
M: A bit, yeah.
W: Any of these guys here would be happy to challenge you to a game of chess. They're here all day, every day.
M: Maybe next time – I'm not that good! What's the arch over there? It looks like the Arc de Triomphe in Paris.
W: Well it should, that's the Washington Square arch. It was modelled on the Arc de Triomphe and built in 1889 to celebrate the hundredth anniversary of the inauguration of George Washington as president.
M: Could we sit down a second? I need a break.
W: Why don't we retrace our steps and go back to the Café Reggio?
M: Sounds good. I could really do with a coffee.

## Conversation 2

W = Woman    M1 = Man1    M2 = Man2

M1: So, this is Radcliffe Square.

W: Wow! Is this right in the centre then?

M1: Pretty much.

M2: What's that?

M1: Hold on. Let's just get off our bikes … Right, so that building in front of us is the Bodleian, named after the founder – Thomas Bodley. Believe it or not, despite the fact that it's circular, it's actually a library.

W: Cool!

M1: Yeah, it gets a copy of every book published in the UK.

M2: Who can use it?

M1: Any student at the university. Of course, each college also has its own library – you know the university's divided into colleges, right?

M2: Right. How many colleges are there?

M1: Just under forty. Well, thirty-eight to be exact.

W: So that means thirty-eight libraries?!

M1: Mm but they're not all as big as the Bodleian. Anyway, we'll need to get back on our bikes for the next bit …

---

M1: Can you hear me if I talk as we cycle along?

M2: Yeah.

W: OK, but don't go too fast. I'm not very steady on this thing!

M1: So, here's the famous Bridge of Sighs, connecting two sides of Hertford College.

M2: I've seen the original.

M1: What, of the bridge? In Italy, you mean?

M2: Yeah, it's in Venice. Beautiful.

M1: OK. We'll go past New College and then onto the High Street.

M2: Is that New College there?

M1: Yep.

W: How 'new' is new?

M1: Roughly 1370.

W: You're kidding!

M1: No, really! Interestingly, the oldest college was actually only founded a hundred or so years earlier! Uh-oh, watch out on this corner …

M1: That's the 'Schools'. It's where the students take their exams. Apparently, the biggest room can seat somewhere in the region of 500 students although I haven't seen it myself. Anyway, we're turning right here. The street's cobbled, so be careful.

M2: How many students are there at the university in total?

M1: To be honest, it depends. In term time, you'd probably get upwards of twenty thousand.

M2: Many international students?

M1: Some, but most are from the UK. We'll finish by cycling down this way to Christ Church. We can actually go inside if we're quick. It's well worth a visit.

M2: Christ Church is another college?

M1: Yeah, the biggest and probably the most famous. Have you seen any of the Harry Potter films?

M2: No …

W: I have!

M1: Oh, well you'll recognise the Great Hall. It's where they have the feasts in Hogwarts School. You know that bit when Harry …

**3A** Put Ss in pairs to work on the answers. Check that Ss understand *head over to* (go in that direction), *retrace our/your steps* (go back the way we/you came).

> **Answers:** 1 head  2 circle  3 retrace  4 modelled
> 5 celebrate  6 named  7 founder  8 As (I'm sure you) know
> 9 Interestingly  10 Apparently  11 worth

**B** Give Ss a time limit for checking their answers, so they don't get too distracted by the long recording script.

> **Optional extra activity**
> To give Ss controlled practice of some of the key phrases from the recording, prepare sets of sixteen cards (one set for each pair of Ss) with the following 'half 'phrases:
>
> 1 head | over to
> 2 circle | back*
> 3 retrace | our steps
> 4 modelled | on
> 5 built | to celebrate
> 6 named | after
> 7 well worth | a visit
> 8 as I'm sure | you know
>
> Ss first match the phrases, then take turns to turn over one card from each pair and 'test' each other.
>
> * *head back* is also possible

**C** Play the recording and encourage Ss to copy the intonation pattern. You could model the same words with falling intonation, to show Ss that this sounds off-putting, whereas the fall-rise is used by the speaker to keep the listener engaged, as well as sounding enthusiastic.

> ⮕ **LANGUAGEBANK** 10.3 p146–147
>
> Direct Ss to the summaries of the different types of phrase on p146. Draw Ss' attention to the phrases which are not in Ex 3, i.e. *Supposedly, Strangely, Believe it or not* (under 'commenting on facts') and *to commemorate, in honour of, burnt down / destroyed / rebuilt / restored in* (under 'giving facts') and drill them briefly to make sure Ss can pronounce them. Ss could do Ex A for controlled practice: once they've corrected the conversation, they could act it out, paying attention to their intonation.
>
> **Answers:**
> A: So here we are at Margit Island, named **after** a nun whose father was once king.
> A: Yeah, **interestingly** at one time it was three islands and only used by people who had land here.
> A: **Supposedly** these caves run for miles.
> A: The story **goes** that when there was an invasion, the local people hid in these tunnels
> A: That's the Vajdahunyad Castle. It was modelled **on/ after** a castle in Transylvania.
> A: It was built for the city's millennium exhibition in 1896, to **commemorate** the one thousand-year anniversary of the founding of the state.
> A: Let's retrace our **steps** to Castle Hill.
> A: Exactly and the museum is well **worth** a visit.

**4A** Before Ss look at the prompts, ask them which three places they'd go to if they were visiting Paris. Then tell them to read through the prompts quickly and find out if any of those places are mentioned. Give Ss a few minutes to write out the conversation in their notebooks, leaving the prompts 'clean' for them to use later for spoken practice.

**Answers:**
1 Let's head over to the cathedral, Notre Dame.  2 It's well worth a visit/visiting but we won't/don't have time to look inside today.  3 Yes, it was modelled on a famous Roman arch.  4 To celebrate one of Napoleon's great victories.  5 So here we are at the Eiffel Tower, named after its designer, Gustave Eiffel.  6 Yeah, apparently it can sway six to seven centimetres in the wind!

**B** Ss should only look at the flow chart, not read aloud from their notebooks. Monitor the practice and note down any problems for correction in feedback.

### VOCABULARY dimensions

**5** You could start by eliciting ways of asking about dimensions that Ss already know, using adjectives (*How high/long/wide/ deep is …?*) and *get* + comparative (*get longer/narrower/wider/ deeper/shorter*), then focus on the first question and elicit *height*. Ss should then use monolingual dictionaries to help them find the rest of the nouns and verbs.

**Answers:** 1 height  2 length  3 widen  4 thickness  5 narrows  6 breadth, depth  7 enlarge  8 shorten

**Optional extra activity**
Draw the table below on the board (without some or all of the words in italics, depending on how well you think your Ss will cope with it) for Ss to copy and ask them to complete it:

| adjective | noun | verb |
| --- | --- | --- |
| high | *height* | *raise* |
| long | *length* | *lengthen* |
| wide | *width* | *widen* |
| broad | *breadth* | *broaden* |
| deep | *depth* | *deepen* |
| narrow | *narrowness* | *narrow* |
| short | *shortness* | *shorten* |
| large | *size* | *enlarge* |

### LEARN TO express estimates

**6A** Give Ss a minute or two to find the examples, working alone or with a partner.

**Answers:** 1 just under  2 roughly  3 or so  4 somewhere in the region of  5 upwards of

**B** Tell the students to think about whether the phrases express the idea of 'more than' or 'less than' a given number to help them decide with which expressions they might be replaced.

**Answers:** 1 fewer than – just under  2 more than – upwards of  3 approximately – roughly, or so, somewhere in the region of

**C** Before you play the recording, tell Ss to work in pairs and read aloud the two alternatives for each answer, so they familiarise themselves with the numbers. Explain that they will have to decide which of the two options corresponds to the information that they will hear in the audio.

**Answers:** 1 b)  2 b)  3 a)  4 a)  5 a)  6 b)

### Unit 10 recording 6

1 It's roughly 1,500 metres in length.
2 There are upwards of 35 corridors.
3 It's just under 1,200 metres above sea level.
4 It's somewhere in the region of 715 km.
5 It's two metres or so at its thickest point and then it narrows.
6 You get approximately 370 to the euro.

**D** Give Ss time to think about and note down their estimates alone first, then put them in pairs to read out their estimates in turn and agree/disagree, e.g.

A: *I'd say there are roughly 450 students in our school.*

B: *I reckon it's upwards of 500.*

Conduct feedback, inviting the class to compare their estimates.

### SPEAKING

**7A** Give Ss time to make notes about what the tour of their town or city would include and to think about how to incorporate some of the language from Ex 3–6. If Ss are from different countries, they can work alone on their tours. If Ss are studying away from home, they may want to design a tour of the city where they're staying. Circulate and provide help as required.

**B** Put Ss in pairs and monitor the 'tours', noting down examples of good language use and problems for discussion and correction later.

**Alternative idea**
You may want to ask Ss to finish preparing their tours at home, so they can research some facts about the places they've included and find some photos/maps, etc. that they can use to bring the tour to life. Ss then bring what they've found to the next lesson and give their tours.

**Homework ideas**
1 Workbook Ex 1–3, p69

2 Ss imagine they're visiting a city and write an email to a friend telling them about some of the important sights.

# BANKSY

## Introduction

Ss watch an extract from a BBC programme about a graffiti artist called 'Banksy'. Ss then learn and practise how to discuss the pros and cons of ideas for a town project and write about a work of art.

## Warm up

Ss should have their books closed. Ask the class to think about the following question: *If you could buy any work of art to put in your house, what would you buy?* Put Ss in pairs to describe and discuss their choices, then invite the class to share their ideas.

### ▶ DVD PREVIEW

**1A** Direct Ss to the photos and background image on the page. Make sure they know what graffiti is and are aware of some of the controversy surrounding it. Check the following vocabulary: *deface* (spoil the appearance of sth), *striking* (unusual or interesting enough to be noticed), *provocative* (intended to cause a reaction), *hideous* (very ugly), *messy* (dirty, untidy).

### Culture notes

*Graffiti* is the name for images or lettering scratched, scrawled, painted or marked in any manner on property. Graffiti has existed since ancient times, with examples dating back to Ancient Greece and the Roman Empire. In most countries, defacing property with graffiti without the property owner's consent is considered vandalism, which is punishable by law. Sometimes graffiti is employed to communicate social and political messages. To some, it is an art form worthy of display in galleries and exhibitions. To others it is merely vandalism.

**B** Focus Ss on the three questions and give them a minute or two to find the answers in the text. Vocabulary to check: *pioneering* (introducing new ideas), *fetch* (be sold for).

**Answers:** I Banksy is a graffiti artist, possibly from Bristol, whose work is considered art and is sold for a lot of money. 2 (Possible answers) Because his graffiti work is illegal and he risks being arrested; because he might benefit from being anonymous; because (perhaps) he's more than one person. 3 Because Banksy might be from Bristol.

### ▶ DVD VIEW

**2A** Direct Ss to the list of people, warning them that some of the people appear very briefly and two of the men (Man 1 and Man 3) speak twice. Ss could note down any key words that help them decide on the speaker's opinion.

### Answers:

I Spud Murphy: V ('spoils people's lives)
2 Woman I: A ('I think it's art.')
3 Man I: V ('makes a mess', 'untidy', 'so wrong')
4 Man 2: A ('I definitely think it's art.)
5 Woman 2: A ('quite exciting')
6 Woman 3: V (feels 'horrified')
7 Man 3: A (says 'messy' initially, but then 'very, very artistic', etc.)
8 Man 4: A ('I don't find that particularly offensive.')

**B** Give Ss time to read through the sentences carefully and try to predict the missing words. You may want to play the recording again.

**Answers:** I queuing 2 addressing 3 laws 4 accepted 5 pleasing, good/positive

---

### DVD 10 The One Show

AC = Adrian Chiles  CB = Christine Bleakley  CB = Cerrie Burnell
KB = Kate Brindley  SM = Councillor Spud Murphy ...
M = Man 1/2/3/4  W = Woman 1/2/3

**AC:** Depending on who you ask, graffiti is either vandalism pure and simple or, ah, as valid an art form as any other.

**CB:** As Cerrie Burnell's discovered, nowhere does the debate rage harder than in Bristol, where the work of the most famous graffiti artist of them all has gone on show.

**CB:** One of the pioneers of modern graffiti art is the mysterious artist known only as Banksy. His work started on street corners and sell for hundreds of thousands of pounds. And with a brand new Banksy exhibition just opened here in his native Bristol, has graffiti art officially gone mainstream?

**KB:** Oh it's been really popular. We've been astounded by the numbers of people coming through the door and queuing down the street. Five and a half thousand, six thousand a day and it's attracting everyone. Lots of different people from lots of different communities, but also from all over the country – people that don't necessarily come to museums are coming to see the show.

**CB:** Do you ever worry that you might be encouraging vandalism by having this kind of show at your gallery?

**KB:** I don't see us as encouraging vandalism – the spray-painting work is onto canvas and so it's actually addressing his work in a different way.

**CB:** But what about all those defaced trains and bus stops? Bristol is also home to a very busy anti-graffiti task force.

**SM:** Graffiti is vandalism; art is art. Well it, it spoils lots of people's lives. I mean people that try to look after their property and paint their houses and walls and things like that ... somebody that comes along in the middle of the night and paints on there all kinds of rubbish – and you can't have the laws for one and not for the other; you can't say that Banksy's OK to do it because he paints a nice picture, but a kiddy that does a stupid thing on the side of a thing, he can't do it because it's stupid. That wall that they're just doing now will be clean when they leave, but I bet you by the end of the week somebody will have painted something on it. People coming in from all over the world see this and think, 'What a dump!' And it's a beautiful place, Bristol.

**CB:** So has graffiti really become a credible and accepted art form, or is it seen by most as just vandalism? Let's find out what the people of Bristol really think.

**W1:** I think art.

**M1:** It just makes a mess of everywhere.

**M2:** I definitely think it's art.

**W2:** I think it's quite exciting sometimes.

**CB:** And how do you feel when you see it on the streets?

**W3:** Horrified.

**M3:** Sometimes it can be a bit messy.

**M4:** If it's a ... a nice picture ... some kind of mural on the side of a tube train that could be considered to be art, I don't find that particularly offensive.

**M1:** I think it's untidy ... and defacing public buildings, I just think it's so wrong.

**M3:** Very, very artistic, very pleasing to the eye and sometimes it has a good message too: a very positive message maybe about peace or love or about the environment or whatever the case may be.

---

**3** Ss could work in pairs or small groups to discuss the statements.

## speakout a town project

**4A** Give Ss a minute or two to look through the list and check they understand what all the projects are: *theatre workshop* (a space where people can practise any skills related to the theatre, such as acting, dancing, stage lighting, etc.) *state-of-the-art* (using the most modern designs, materials, etc.) *multiplex* (a cinema with several screens) *a botanical garden* (a large public garden where different types of plants are grown for scientific study). While Ss listen, they should also make brief notes about why each person likes the particular project they have chosen to support.

> **Answers:**
> Tim: state-of-the-art multiplex – most beneficial, would bring jobs, provide entertainment for young people.
> Sarah: botanical garden – good for different age groups, also blind people and those with disabilities; education centre good for young people.
> Nigel: theatre workshop space – to stop young people getting bored & hanging around: will motivate them, parents will come to performances. Could be multi purpose, e.g. has sprung floor for dance classes, etc.

**B** Ss look through the key phrases before listening again. Ss should tick the phrases they hear and underline the option in each phrase. Once Ss have listened again and checked their answers, they could look at the audio script and underline three or four more phrases that they think would be useful.

> **Answers:**
> I'm really in favour of (the state-of-the-art multiplex cinema)
> I think that it would be (most useful and beneficial for the community)
> We have to consider (the maintenance)
> Can you see the (older) generation (wanting it, liking it)?

**5A** Give Ss time to choose and discuss two projects and make notes to show how their projects fulfil the three criteria given. They should also think about how to incorporate the key phrases when presenting their ideas in the next stage. NB If Ss are from different towns/cities and are studying away from home, they could choose a project for the town or city where they're studying. Circulate and provide help and advice with language as required.

**B** Put Ss into groups of four to six to discuss and agree on one project. Monitor and note down good examples of language use, particularly the key phrases and any problems, for discussion and correction later.

**C** You could ask one student from each group to act as spokesperson, or ask each student from each group to present one aspect of their chosen project.

### Unit 10 Recording 8

S = Sarah   T = Tim   N = Nigel

S:  Right well we have our shortlist for the new feature that we're going to put into the town centre, which one gets your vote Tim?

T:  I'm really in favour of the – the state-of-the-art multiplex cinema I think that it would be most useful and beneficial for the community. I think it will be used a great deal, I think it would bring jobs to the area and I think it would provide entertainment and activities for young people.

N:  The only thing that would concern me though is that that's going to be very, very expensive.

T:  Um hm.

S:  I mean, I personally would prefer the botanical garden.

T:  Oh.

S:  Because I think that that will satisfy the needs of many different age groups. I think it would be very good for wheelchairs, for … for blind people, for people with disabilities, there would be areas that would be excellent for young people and lots of learning opportunities in the education centre. And we know from past experience that the older age group certainly enjoy gardens.

T:  The only thing that would concern me on that is that you mention youth, but I don't think that you're going to get as many young people involved in a botanical garden. I think if it was interactive then it would be … but just as a thing that was showing I'm, I'm not so sure.

N:  Well I don't want to harp on about costs again but we have to consider the maintenance of this botanical garden. There are very high maintenance costs involved.

S:  Oh so, Nigel what, what would you prefer?

N:  Well – My vote would go to the theatre workshop space for young people. And I know we said we don't want to discriminate against any … we don't want to leave out certain members of our society, but I think we've got a problem in this town about kids getting bored, hanging around on street corners, they need something to do and a theatre workshop space is going to get them … it's going to give them a routine, it's going to give them a motivation and then when they do their shows, they're bringing along their grandparents, their parents, I feel it's very inclusive.

T:  Can you see the older generation, wanting it, liking it?

N:  I think the older generation want to be sure that kids aren't hanging about the streets with nothing to do.

S:  And could that, theatre workshop space be used for other things as well?

N:  Absolutely.

S:  Could it be used for meetings, for other sections of society?

N:  … Aerobics … there's going to be a sprung wooden floor so there'll be dance classes, yoga, pilates, multi purpose …

## writeback a work of art

**6A** Give Ss time to read about the competition, then elicit some more ideas for works of art, buildings, rooms, etc. that Ss could write about. Ss make notes about what they would choose and why, then compare their ideas in pairs.

**B** When Ss have ticked the things in the box that the writer mentions, they could also look at the purpose of each paragraph: 1 What/Where it is and why the writer likes it?; 2 Who made it, the materials and colours?; 3 a summarising comment.

> **Answers:** setting (nearby river)  when it was made (twentieth century)  material (titanium)  colour (silver/gold)  who made it (Canadian architect Frank O Gehry)  why he/she likes it (an 'awe-inspiring structure'/reminds him/her of different things)

**C** Ss write a first draft for their entry, then swap with a partner and comment on the accuracy of the language, how persuasive the entry is, etc. Ss could write their final draft for homework.

> **Homework idea**
> Ss write another competition entry.

# LOOKBACK

## Introduction

The aim of these activities is to provide revision and further practice of the language from the unit. You can also use them to assess Ss' ability to use the language, in which case you need to monitor but avoid helping them. You may feel that you don't need or have time to do all the activities. If so, you could allocate the activities that would be most beneficial for your Ss, or get individual Ss to decide which activities they'd like to do in class.

## ADJECTIVES

**1A** You could run this as a game of 'Backs to the board'. Put Ss in two teams and ask one volunteer from each team to come and sit with their back to the board. Write an adjective from p116 on the board: the rest of the team has to give their volunteer clues to help them guess the word and the first one to do this wins their team a point. A new volunteer form each team comes up and the game continues.

**B** Ss complete the comments alone or with a partner.

> **Answers:**
> 1 moving (*poignant* and *touching* are also possible)
> 2 predictable 3 gripping (*brilliant, electrifying* and *unforgettable* are also possible) 4 dull

**C** Ss could write their comments with a gap for the adjective, then pass them to the next pair to complete.

## RELATIVE CLAUSES

**2A** Ss can work on this alone or with a partner.

> **Answers:** 1 whose 2 where 3 that 4 where 5 whom 6 which

**B** Elicit some examples of how to change the first sentence, e.g.

*A person whose main interests include reading detective novels/ playing computer games/photography/cooking.*

Also point out that in sentence 3, the sentence could read *someone who knows how to speak English/play the guitar really well/cook, etc.*

Ss work alone to change the sentences.

**C** Direct Ss to the example and put them in groups of three or four, or ask them to stand up and walk round the class, talking to at least three other Ss. Conduct feedback with the class about the most useful/interesting information they found out.

## PARTICIPLE CLAUSES

**3A** You could run this as a competition with Ss in teams of four to six. Ask each team to choose a sound which they can use as a 'buzzer' when they're ready to answer a question. Display the questions one at a time on the board. Ss 'buzz' to answer and are given one point for a correct participle and a further point for a correct answer to the question (you could also deduct points for Ss shouting out answers rather than 'buzzing').

> **Answers:**
> 1 standing, made 2 started, known 3 played, involving, taking 4 crowned, defeated 5 awarded
> 6 living, using, called 7 consisting, rolled 8 written, featuring

**B** Ss can work either in pairs or individually to answers the questions in the quiz.

**C** Feed back on the answers as a class or let Ss check their answers on their own on p161.

> **Answers:**
> 1 Sydney Opera House 2 Apple Inc. 3 squash 4 Napoleon Bonaparte 5 Oscar 6 the Inuit 7 sushi (makizushi)
> 8 *Hamlet*

> **Optional extra activity**
> Ss work in pairs and write their own trivia quiz of four or five questions. Each question should contain at least two participle clauses. When Ss have written their quizzes, they can either put them round the walls or leave them on a piece of paper on their desks for other pairs to walk round and try to answer. In feedback, Ss could comment on the best/most challenging questions.

## THE ARTS

**4** Ss could work on this in pairs. You could run it as a race, asking the first pair to finish to bring their answers up to you to check.

> **Answers:**
> 1 flop 2 rave 3 sell out 4 let-down 5 hype 6 must-see

> **Optional extra activity**
> Ss write four descriptions of performers, shows, CDs, exhibitions, celebrities, etc. using at least one of the words related to the arts in each sentence, e.g. *There was a lot of hype surrounding this film about, but when it came out, most people thought it was a real let-down.* Ss read out their sentences to a partner, who has to guess what they're describing.

## GIVING A TOUR

**5A** For *stronger classes,* you could tell Ss to cover the box and try to remember the appropriate words for the gaps first, then check with the words in the box.

> **Answers:** 1 It **was** built in the 17th century by the ruler Shah Jahan in **honour** of his dead wife. As **you** may know, it's made of white marble and it is well **worth** a visit. (The Taj Mahal)
> 2 It was **named** after its designer and was built in 1889. The **story** goes that many Parisians hated it because it was too modern. (The Eiffel Tower)
> 3 Parts of it were **rebuilt** many times. Believe **it** or not, more than 2 million Chinese may have died in its construction. (The Great Wall of China)

**B** Ss can work in pairs to write their sentences, using at least two of the phrases from p122–123 in each sentence.

**C** You could do this with the whole class, or put Ss in groups of six to eight. One pair reads out their sentences and the others make guesses. The pair who guesses first wins a point, but every wrong guess gives the pair who wrote the sentences a point.

| PAGE | UNIT | PHOTOCOPIABLE | LANGUAGE POINT | TIME |
|---|---|---|---|---|
| 143 | 1 | Happy flatmates | **Vocabulary: describing personality**<br>review vocabulary for describing personality<br>practise speaking skills by describing people | 20 mins |
| 144 | 1 | How do I feel? | **Vocabulary: describing feelings**<br>review vocabulary for describing feelings<br>practise adjective/noun word formation | 25 mins |
| 145 | 1 | Good cop, bad cop | **Grammar: indirect questions**<br>practise forming indirect questions<br>practise speaking skills in interviews | 40 mins |
| 146 | 1 | Talk about … | **Grammar: present perfect and past simple**<br>review the present perfect and the past simple<br>personalised fluent speaking practice | 45 mins |
| 147 | 1 | How can I help you? | **Functional language: managing enquiries**<br>practise functional language for making and managing enquiries | 25 mins |
| 148 | 2 | Scrambled issues | **Vocabulary: social issues**<br>review vocabulary for social issues<br>free speaking practice on social issues | 45 mins |
| 149 | 2 | You're on camera | **Vocabulary: surveillance**<br>review vocabulary for surveillance<br>practise speaking skills by discussing surveillance | 25 mins |
| 150 | 2 | A brief history of energy drinks | **Grammar: the passive**<br>practise forming questions in the passive<br>review different passive tense forms | 25 mins |
| 151 | 2 | It's a perfect world | **Grammar: present perfect simple and continuous**<br>practise using the present perfect simple or continuous according to context | 25 mins |
| 152 | 2 | Big issues | **Functional language: supporting your view point**<br>practise giving opinions and supporting them with reasons and examples | 40 mins |
| 153 | 3 | Carlo's car | **Vocabulary: describing behaviour**<br>review vocabulary for describing behaviour<br>practise speaking skills by telling a story | 20 mins |
| 154 | 3 | Treasure hunt | **Vocabulary: describing locations**<br>review vocabulary for describing locations<br>practise describing and explaining | 20 mins |
| 155 | 3 | Am I getting used to it? | **Grammar: *used to, would* and *be/get used to***<br>review and practise the structures *used to, be/get used to* and *would* | 35 mins |
| 156 | 3 | Questions of the future | **Grammar: future forms review**<br>practise a range of future forms by answering questions | 40 mins |
| 157 | 3 | The new football | **Functional language: describing procedure**<br>practise describing procedures<br>practise mirror questions | 45 mins |
| 158 | 4 | What's my saying? | **Vocabulary: idioms**<br>review idioms from 4.1<br>practise speaking skills by telling an anecdote | 35 mins |
| 159 | 4 | Change it! | **Vocabulary: phrasal verbs**<br>review the phrasal verbs from 4.2 | 25 mins |
| 160 | 4 | Past consequences | **Grammar: narrative tenses**<br>practise using narrative tenses<br>guided sentence writing | 35 mins |
| 161 | 4 | Spiralling regret | **Grammar: *I wish, if only, should have***<br>practise with *I wish, if only* and *should have*<br>free speaking practice talking about regrets | 35 mins |
| 162 | 4 | Literary critics | **Functional language: expressing likes and dislikes**<br>practise expressing likes and dislikes<br>review language for describing books and reading | 35 mins |
| 163 | 5 | Compound snap | **Vocabulary: compound nouns**<br>review compound nouns in the context of invention and innovation | 25 mins |
| 164 | 5 | Talking advertising | **Vocabulary: advertising**<br>review vocabulary for advertising<br>practise speaking skills by defining words | 25 mins |
| 165 | 5 | Ahead of its time | **Grammar: articles**<br>review the use of articles | 25 mins |
| 166 | 5 | Conditional dominoes | **Grammar: conditional structures**<br>review conditional structures<br>practise speaking skills by discussing and evaluating conditional statements | 30 mins |

## Student A

**Housemate names**
- Sam
- Josh
- Gemma
- Lucy
- Sara

**Personality**
- a people-person
- a good laugh
- a geek
- be out until the early hours
- be particular about
- be into
- pull one's weight
- tight-fisted
- be down-to-earth
- keep to oneself

| 1 Housemate name | 2 Housemate name | 3 Housemate name | 4 Housemate name | 5 Housemate name |
|---|---|---|---|---|
| | | | | |
| Personality | Personality | Personality | Personality | Personality |
| 1. | 1. | 1. | 1. | 1. |
| 2. | 2. | 2. | 2. | 2. |

- **(Start)** Josh thinks Sam's glasses make him look like **a geek**, and he really is one!
- Lucy is always realistic about things.
- The two male housemates are next to each other.
- The housemate who gets home late is next to the housemate who **keeps to himself**.
- The housemate who's fun to be with is standing up.
- Josh is **a people person** and is next to Gemma.
- The **tight-fisted** housemate is next to the housemate who feels it's very important to never leave washing-up in the sink.
- The housemate who **is really into** theatre is between a male and female housemate.

## Student B

**Housemate names**
- Sam
- Josh
- Gemma
- Lucy
- Sara

**Personality**
- a people-person
- a good laugh
- a geek
- be out until the early hours
- be particular about
- be into
- pull one's weight
- tight-fisted
- be down-to-earth
- keep to oneself

| 1 Housemate name | 2 Housemate name | 3 Housemate name | 4 Housemate name | 5 Housemate name |
|---|---|---|---|---|
| | | | | |
| Personality | Personality | Personality | Personality | Personality |
| 1. | 1. | 1. | 1. | 1. |
| 2. | 2. | 2. | 2. | 2. |

- The housemate who doesn't **pull her weight** with cleaning the house is not sitting on the sofa.
- All the housemates think the person lying on the floor is mean with money.
- The boring housemate who's obsessed with computers is next to the housemate who's **a good laugh**.
- The **down-to-earth** housemate hates Sara and is as far away from her as possible.
- The housemate who really likes theatre is next to the housemate who doesn't do their share of the housework.
- The housemate who is **out until the early hours** is in the middle.
- The housemate who**'s particular about** the washing-up is next to the sociable person.
- The introverted housemate is next to Lucy.

| | | | |
|---|---|---|---|
| I've been saving money to do this for three years and tomorrow I'm finally going to set off on my trip round the world.<br><br>*How do I feel?*<br>**excited** | I've just won $5m on the lottery. I can give up my job and do anything I want!<br><br>*What's the feeling?*<br>**excitement** | I am a visitor at the home of a couple who argue all the time. They keep asking me to take sides.<br><br>*How do I feel?*<br>**awkward** | I'm meeting my partner's parents for the first time and making conversation is difficult.<br><br>*What's the feeling?*<br>**awkwardness** |
| I've not slept for thirty-six hours and I can hardly keep my eyes open.<br><br>*How do I feel?*<br>**exhausted** | I've been baby-sitting five very active four-year-old children all day.<br><br>*What's the feeling?*<br>**exhaustion** | The workmen arrived on time and finished the job when they said they would.<br><br>*How do I feel?*<br>**satisfied** | I am very happy with my life as it is, there's not much I want to change about it.<br><br>*What's the feeling?*<br>**satisfaction** |
| My teenage son didn't come home last night and he always calls if he's going to be late.<br><br>*How do I feel?*<br>**anxious** | I need to catch a connecting flight and my flight is delayed.<br><br>*What's the feeling?*<br>**anxiety** | My team lost the final.<br><br>*How do I feel?*<br>**disappointed** | The world champion fell over and missed winning an ice-skating medal at the Olympics.<br><br>*What's the feeling?*<br>**disappointment** |
| I still can't find a parking space. I've been looking for over half an hour.<br><br>*How do I feel?*<br>**frustrated** | I've got lots of urgent emails waiting for me, but my internet connection is down.<br><br>*What's the feeling?*<br>**frustration** | I'm about to give a presentation to fifty people I've never met. They are all experts in the field and probably know more than me.<br><br>*How do I feel?*<br>**nervous** | I am going to ask my partner if they want to marry me. I don't know what they are going to say.<br><br>*What's the feeling?*<br>**nervousness** |
| I slapped my friend on the back and told him to hurry up, but when he turned round I saw it was a stranger.<br><br>*How do I feel?*<br>**embarrassed** | I am going to introduce my colleague to the new boss, but I just can't remember her name.<br><br>*What's the feeling?*<br>**embarrassment** | I lost my wallet and spent one hour looking for it. I've just found it in my coat pocket.<br><br>*How do I feel?*<br>**relieved** | Your friends were on a plane that crashed. You've just found out nobody was injured.<br><br>*What's the feeling?*<br>**relief** |

## Good cop

You are a detective investigating the theft of five priceless works of art from the Metropolitan National Gallery of Art. There was no sign of the thief/thieves breaking into the building and you suspect the Director of the gallery may be involved. The Director is a highly respected and famous art expert and has been Director for over twenty years. There are rumours about her/him illegally selling valuable paintings to rich private collectors, but they may not be true and he/she may be completely innocent. You are going to interview her/him and you need to:

- find out what he/she was doing on the night the paintings were stolen
- search their house(s)
- access their bank accounts
- close the gallery for at least four days
- check their personal emails
- look at CCTV footage from the gallery
- ask about the rumours.

Remember:

The Director is a very important person and you are worried about wrongly accusing someone so respected and well-known. Therefore be as polite and as diplomatic as possible and only ask them indirect questions. Your partner is not going to be so polite and you need to make any direct questions your partner asks into indirect ones.

## Bad cop

You are a detective investigating the theft of five priceless works of art from the Metropolitan National Gallery of Art. There was no sign of the thief/thieves breaking into the building and you suspect the Director of the gallery may be involved. The Director is a highly respected and famous art expert and has been Director for over twenty years. There are rumours about her/him illegally selling valuable paintings to rich private collectors, but they may not be true and he/she may be completely innocent. You are going to interview her/him and you need to:

- find out what he/she was doing on the night the paintings were stolen
- search their house(s)
- access their bank accounts
- close the gallery for at least four days
- check their personal emails
- look at CCTV footage from the gallery
- ask about the rumours.

Remember:

The Director is a very important person but you don't care. You think he/she is highly suspicious and believe he/she is using their good reputation to hide criminal activity. You don't care about seeming rude and you are going to only ask the Director direct questions.

## Gallery director

You are the Director of the Metropolitan National Gallery of Art. You have been Director for over twenty years and you are a famous and respected art expert. You are friends with many rich and powerful people. However, you are deeply dishonest and greedy. You arranged for five priceless paintings from your gallery to be stolen and sold to wealthy private collectors. They paid you $200m for the paintings. This money was paid into your Swiss bank account. You supplied the thieves with the keys and alarm codes. The paintings have already left the country. The police are going to interview you. You are a very private person and dislike the police, but of course you need to be helpful and convince them that you are not involved in the thefts.

# TALK ABOUT ...

## Grammar: present perfect and past simple

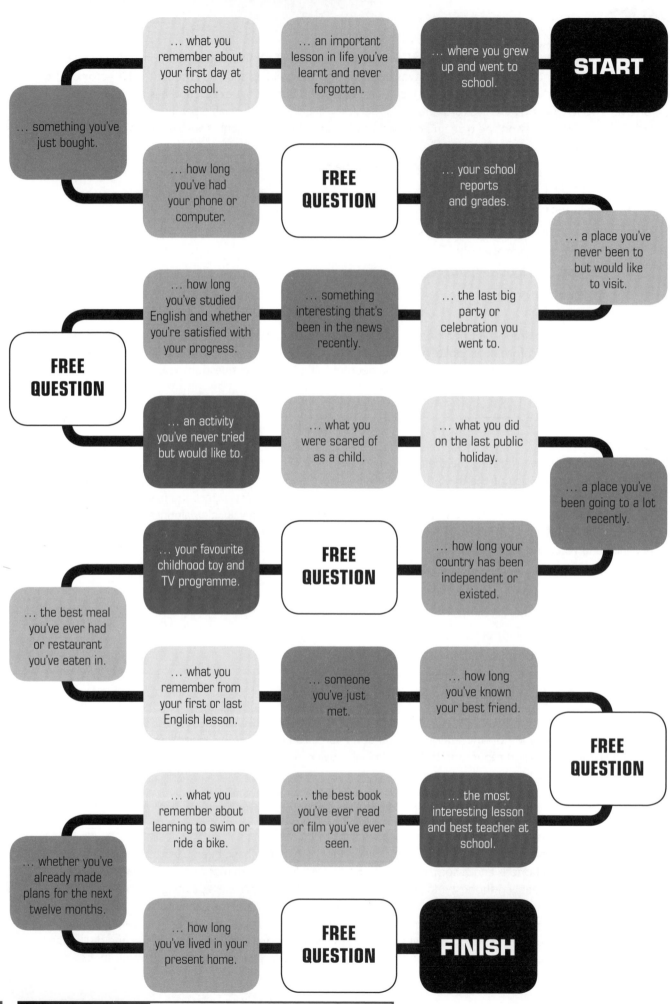

... what you remember about your first day at school.

... an important lesson in life you've learnt and never forgotten.

... where you grew up and went to school.

**START**

... something you've just bought.

... how long you've had your phone or computer.

**FREE QUESTION**

... your school reports and grades.

... a place you've never been to but would like to visit.

... how long you've studied English and whether you're satisfied with your progress.

... something interesting that's been in the news recently.

... the last big party or celebration you went to.

**FREE QUESTION**

... an activity you've never tried but would like to.

... what you were scared of as a child.

... what you did on the last public holiday.

... a place you've been going to a lot recently.

... your favourite childhood toy and TV programme.

**FREE QUESTION**

... how long your country has been independent or existed.

... the best meal you've ever had or restaurant you've eaten in.

... what you remember from your first or last English lesson.

... someone you've just met.

... how long you've known your best friend.

**FREE QUESTION**

... what you remember about learning to swim or ride a bike.

... the best book you've ever read or film you've ever seen.

... the most interesting lesson and best teacher at school.

... whether you've already made plans for the next twelve months.

... how long you've lived in your present home.

**FREE QUESTION**

**FINISH**

## Student A – Making enquiries

**There is a power cut on your street and you have had no electricity for twelve hours. You phoned the power company just after it happened and were told to phone back later in the day after they had investigated the problem. You are now phoning for a second time.**

- Find out when the power will be switched on again.
- Find out what the problem was and if it will happen again.
- Find out why there are not any engineers working on the problem now (there were some this morning).
- Find out what compensation you can expect to receive.
- Explain how inconvenient it has been and how unhappy you are with the situation.

**Phone Customer Service now!**

## Student A – Managing enquiries

**You work in the customer service department of a national bank, CTB. You deal with customer complaints and problems. A customer is going to phone you regarding a cloned cash card. Their money was stolen but the bank has not refunded it yet.**

- Ask for personal and bank account details as well as security passwords.
- Apologise that the computer system is really slow today.
- Explain that the customer has not received a refund because the bank has not received a police crime reference number yet.
- Explain refunds take a minimum of ten working days.
- Explain customers should not normally have to pay overdraft charges in these circumstances. You can ask your supervisor to refund the charges immediately.

**Start the conversation with:** *Hello this is CTB. This is* (name) *speaking. How can I help you?*

## Student B – Managing enquiries

**You work in the customer service department of a national power company, EGON Power. A customer experiencing a power cut is going to phone you for the second time about the problem.**

- Ask for their personal details and account number.
- Apologise for the fact that the computer system is really slow today.
- Explain that the problem is complex and will take up to three days to repair as special equipment is needed.
- Explain that engineers only work for eight hours and then another team arrive.
- Compensation is paid after thirty-six hours with no power.

**Start the conversation with:** *Hello this EGON Power, I'm* (name). *How can I help you?*

## Student B – Making enquiries

**Your cash card was cloned and over $1500 was taken from your account. The bank accepted it was not your fault and promised to refund the money. Three weeks later they have not done this and you are now paying overdraft charges.**

- Explain the situation to the customer service representative.
- Find out why the money has not been refunded and when you will receive it.
- Explain that you have already given the bank the police crime reference number.
- Explain that you need money desperately as you have to pay your rent this week.
- Find out why you are paying overdraft charges. It is not you fault that your account is overdrawn.

**Phone Customer Service now!**

| Scrambled Issue | Unscrambled Issue | Idea one | Idea two | Idea three |
|---|---|---|---|---|
| tbed | debt | *Educate children at school about how to manage their money.* | *Banks should only lend money to people who can definitely pay it back.* | *Governments should provide loans with low interest rates to help poor people.* |
| oghtudr | | | | |
| croiedv | | | | |
| sssenmeholes | | | | |
| loopultin | | | | |
| citemods cenvileo | | | | |
| sensenkrund dan grud ubesa | | | | |
| toprevy | | | | |
| klac fo kingrind rewat | | | | |
| manfie | | | | |
| stobyie | | | | |

## Councillor A

You are a local councillor and your town has a number of problems:

1 Motorists drive too fast through the narrow streets.

2 Vandalism and drunkenness are a problem in the town centre. Families and elderly people keep away.

3 Attacks by dangerous dogs are becoming more common.

4 Gangs are selling illegal fake goods in the town centre.

You believe ways to deal with the issues are:

- to install cameras to act as a deterrent but also help the police keep track of trouble-makers and catch wanted criminals.

- to microchip all dogs so the owners of dangerous ones are registered. They can be easily identified and their details handed over to the police.

- to install CCTV in the town centre so the gangs selling fake goods will move out of the town. You believe their presence encourages others to break the law.

## Councillor B

You are a local councillor and your town has a number of problems:

1 Motorists drive too fast through the narrow streets.

2 Vandalism and drunkenness are a problem in the town centre. Families and elderly people keep away.

3 Attacks by dangerous dogs are becoming more common.

4 Gangs are selling illegal fake goods in the town centre.

You believe ways to deal with the issues are:

- not to install CCTV. You believe our surveillance society is not only an invasion of privacy but very expensive. The money could be spent on more police and other towns with CCTV still have these problems.

- not to microchip dogs, as only responsible owners would do this and not the owners of the dangerous dogs.

- not to worry about the people selling fake goods. You don't see the harm in people selling a few fake handbags and sunglasses.

## Councillor C

You are a local councillor and your town has a number of problems:

1 Motorists drive too fast through the narrow streets.

2 Vandalism and drunkenness are a problem in the town centre. Families and elderly people keep away.

3 Attacks by dangerous dogs are becoming more common.

4 Gangs are selling illegal fake goods in the town centre.

You believe ways to deal with the issues are:

- to install surveillance cameras. You believe that if you are a law-abiding citizen and you have done nothing wrong then it doesn't matter that your every move is monitored and logged.

- to use number plate recognition technology to discourage known criminals, some of whom are selling the fake goods, from entering the town.

- to install speed cameras. The evidence that they reduce accidents and make streets safer and nicer places to be is overwhelming.

## Councillor D

You are a local councillor and your town has a number of problems:

1 Motorists drive too fast through the narrow streets.

2 Vandalism and drunkenness are a problem in the town centre. Families and elderly people keep away.

3 Attacks by dangerous dogs are becoming more common.

4 Gangs are selling illegal fake goods in the town centre.

You believe ways to deal with the issues are:

- not to install speed cameras. You believe they cause accidents by people slowing down quickly before them and speeding up after them. The money they make is not spent on improving roads.

- not to install CCTV. It is rare for police to actually look at it for minor crimes like drunkenness and vandalism.

- to encourage citizens to be more responsible and use their camera phones if they see someone committing a crime. You believe this would make individuals more accountable for their actions.

## Student A

Although Irn-Bru from Scotland has never been marketed as ¹ _____, it can claim to be the first. Called Iron Brew at the time, it was first sold in 1901. In Japan, energy drinks have been produced for over fifty years starting with the release of Lipovitan in the 1960s. A lot of Japanese energy drinks do not look like soft drinks at all and are sold in ² _____ _____. These energy drinks are known as 'genki drinks' and are aimed at ³ _____.

Lucozade Energy, first sold in 1929, was originally introduced as a hospital drink for 'aiding the recovery'. However, by the early 1980s it had become an energy drink and was promoted as a ⁴ '_____'.

The first drink designed to improve the performance of sports stars was Gatorade. It was invented in the 1960s for the University of Florida football team, the Gators, hence its name. It was designed to aid ⁵ _____. Gatorade is considered to be safer than many energy drinks and is known more as a sports drink.

⁶ _____, was launched by Pepsi Co in 1985 and was the first energy drink introduced by a major US beverage company. It was discontinued in 1999.

Undoubtedly the most popular energy drink today is Red Bull and it is adapted from a Thai energy drink, Krating Daeng, which means Red Bull. The company was founded by ⁷ _____ in 1987 along with its famous slogan 'Red Bull gives you wings'. The product is marketed aggressively through advertising, tournament sponsorship and sports team ownership.

## Student B

Although Irn-Bru from Scotland has never been marketed as an energy drink, it can claim to be the first. Called Iron Brew at the time, it was first sold in 1901. In Japan, energy drinks have been produced for ¹ _____ years starting with the release of Lipovitan in the 1960s. A lot of Japanese energy drinks do not look like soft drinks at all and are sold in small brown glass medicine bottles. These energy drinks are known as ² '_____' and are aimed at the salaryman market.

Lucozade Energy, first sold in 1929, was originally introduced as ³ _____ for 'aiding the recovery'. However, by the early 1980s it had become an energy drink and was promoted as a 'drink for replenishing lost energy'.

The first drink designed to improve the performance of sports stars was Gatorade. It was invented in the 1960s for ⁴ _____, the Gators, hence its name. It was designed to aid hydration and improve performance levels. Gatorade is considered to be ⁵ _____ and is known more as a sports drink.

Josta, was launched by Pepsi Co in 1985 and was the first energy drink introduced by a major US beverage company. It was discontinued in 1999.

Undoubtedly the most popular energy drink today is Red Bull and it is adapted from ⁶ _____, Krating Daeng, which means Red Bull. The company was founded by a Thai and an Austrian national in 1987 along with its famous slogan 'Red Bull gives you wings'. The product is marketed aggressively through ⁷ _____.

| Student A | Student B | Student C |
|---|---|---|
| 1 I feel emotional and I'm crying.<br>2 I love the cinema.<br><br>**I've just seen a sad film.** | 1 I'm crying but I don't feel emotional.<br>2 I'm cooking.<br><br>**I've been chopping onions.** | 1 I don't have any money left.<br>2 Now I can drive anywhere I want to go.<br><br>**I've bought a new car.** |
| 1 We're at the theatre.<br>2 My partner looks angry and we can't go in.<br><br>**I've forgotten the tickets.** | 1 I feel sick.<br>2 There are five chocolate bar wrappers on the floor.<br><br>**I've eaten five bars of chocolate.** | 1 I'm at the doctor's.<br>2 I always wake up in the night. I feel exhausted.<br><br>**I haven't been sleeping well.** |
| 1 I'm completely wet.<br>2 I didn't take an umbrella with me.<br><br>**I've been walking in the rain.** | 1 I'm celebrating with my partner.<br>2 I met him/her fifty years ago.<br><br>**I've been married for fifty years.** | 1 I'm in pain and my body is red all over.<br>2 I was at the beach.<br><br>**I've been sunbathing.** |
| 1 My boss is angry with me.<br>2 I find it difficult to get up in in the morning.<br><br>**I've been arriving late for work.** | 1 I'm playing football.<br>2 All my team mates are running towards me.<br><br>**I've just scored a goal.** | 1 I'm really anxious.<br>2 It had my credit cards and cash in it.<br><br>**I've lost my wallet.** |
| 1 I'm really happy I passed.<br>2 I'm in a bar with all my friends.<br><br>**I've been celebrating.** | 1 I used to have a beautiful garden.<br>2 All the plants are dead.<br><br>**I haven't been watering my plants.** | 1 Jean is my best friend.<br>2 We became friends when we were children.<br><br>**I've known Jean since we were children.** |
| 1 I really, really like tennis.<br>2 I first played tennis when I was thirteen.<br><br>**I've loved tennis since I was thirteen.** | 1 I'm tired and really hot.<br>2 I was at the gym.<br><br>**I've been working out.** | 1 I'm heavier than I was.<br>2 I can't stop going to the kitchen.<br><br>**I've been eating too much.** |

Start

| | | | | |
|---|---|---|---|---|
| Life was better fifty years ago. | English is destroying other languages. | Football is more important than life or death. | There is nothing wrong with having cosmetic surgery. | Having as many children as you want is not a basic human right. |
| Teachers should be able to use physical punishment. | It's better to be good-looking than intelligent. | Money can buy you happiness. | Terminally ill people have the right to end their life. | We are not alone in the universe. |
| Democracy is the best form of government. | Black is the most elegant colour. | Social networking sites are a waste of time. | Mankind will eventually destroy the planet. | The death penalty is justifiable for some crimes. |
| Citizens carrying guns makes society safer. | Some drugs should be legalised. | Women are more complex than men. | Immigration is generally a positive thing. | You can't be young and wise. |
| Climate change is a myth. | War and terrorism are never justifiable. | The best music has already been written. | Shoplifting is a victimless crime. | A country gets the government it deserves. |

Start

Start

Start

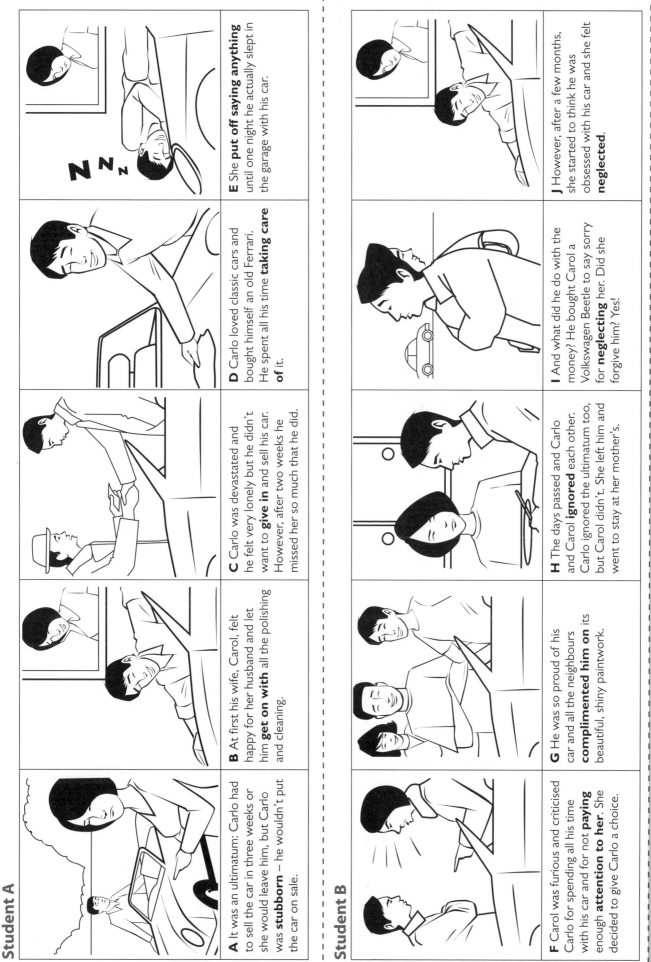

**Student A**

**A** It was an ultimatum: Carlo had to sell the car in three weeks or she would leave him, but Carlo was **stubborn** – he wouldn't put the car on sale.

**B** At first his wife, Carol, felt happy for her husband and let him **get on with** all the polishing and cleaning.

**C** Carlo was devastated and he felt very lonely but he didn't want to **give in** and sell his car. However, after two weeks he missed her so much that he did.

**D** Carlo loved classic cars and bought himself an old Ferrari. He spent all his time **taking care of** it.

**E** She **put off saying anything** until one night he actually slept in the garage with his car.

**Student B**

**F** Carol was furious and criticised Carlo for spending all his time with his car and for not **paying enough attention to her**. She decided to give Carlo a choice.

**G** He was so proud of his car and all the neighbours **complimented him on** its beautiful, shiny paintwork.

**H** The days passed and Carlo and Carol **ignored** each other. Carlo ignored the ultimatum too, but Carol didn't. She left him and went to stay at her mother's.

**I** And what did he do with the money? He bought Carol a Volkswagen Beetle to say sorry for **neglecting** her. Did she forgive him? Yes!

**J** However, after a few months, she started to think he was obsessed with his car and she felt **neglected**.

| Student A | Student B | Student C | Student D |
|---|---|---|---|
| **1** Sail to the remote islands but watch out for extremely strong ocean currents. | **1** On the southern slope of this mountain is a small village. Find an old blind man called Adam. | **1** From this point, you'll be able to see some small islands just off the coast but you'll need transport. | **1** The treasure is buried on the northern island, to the east of the palm tree. Happy digging! |
| **2** **Start**: Your plane will land near the big town on the densely populated side of the island. | **2** You'll find a boat in close proximity to the arch in the cliff. | **2** Don't stop to enjoy the amazing scenery, it's about 100 kilometres west as the crow flies. | **2** He will give you a key. Next, head north through the densely forested region. |
| **3** After about thirty kilometres, the trees will be replaced by barren desert. Don't go across it. | **3** Eventually, you'll reach the beginning of a peninsula. Continue along it to the most westerly point of the island. | **3** From Porto Nico, go west towards the mountains. Look for the one with snow on the summit. | **3** Instead, follow the beautiful unspoilt coastline west. |

**Treasure map**

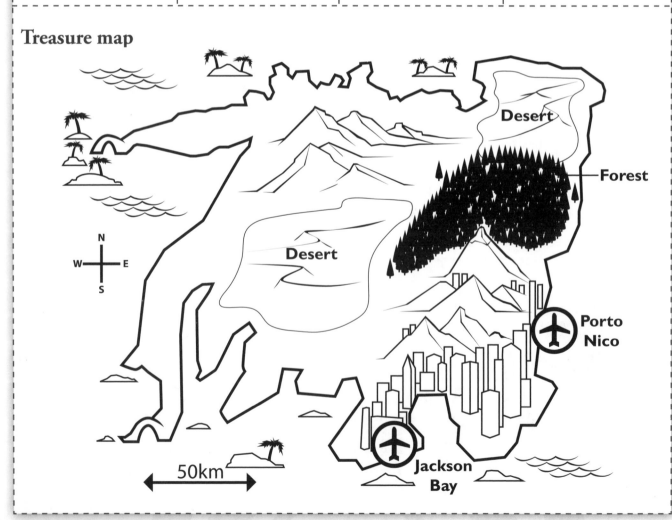

50km

| **Student A** | | **Answers** |
|---|---|---|
| 1 You're now very old but were a model when you were young. | I _____ appear in fashion magazines.<br>I _____ have grey hair and wrinkles.<br>I've _____ not getting compliments any more. | used to/would<br>didn't use to<br>got used to |
| 2 You moved from Spain to the UK a long time ago. | I _____ eat dinner very late, about 11p.m.<br>I _____ drive on the left.<br>I'm _____ not seeing the sun very often. | used to/would<br>didn't use to<br>used to |
| 3 You went completely bald when you were young. | I _____ like going to hairdresser's.<br>I _____ spend a long time doing my hair.<br>I'm _____ wearing a hat. | used to<br>used to/would<br>used to |
| 4 You've recently become a mother/father for the first time. | I _____ be quite selfish.<br>I _____ buy nappies.<br>I'm _____ sleepless nights. | used to<br>didn't use to<br>getting used to |

| **Student B** | | **Answers** |
|---|---|---|
| 1 You gave up coffee some time ago. | I _____ drink about six cups a day.<br>I _____ sleep well.<br>I'm _____ drinking tea instead. | used to/would<br>didn't use to<br>getting used to |
| 2 You were a soldier when you were younger. | I _____ wear a uniform all the time.<br>I _____ be very brave.<br>I _____ the danger and the travel. | used to/would<br>used to<br>was/got used to |
| 3 You've just been banned from driving. | I _____ drive really fast.<br>I _____ have to ask people for lifts.<br>I'm not _____ catching the bus. | used to/would<br>didn't use to<br>used to |
| 4 You've recently got promotion and are now the boss. | I _____ take orders from people.<br>I _____ have my own office and secretary.<br>I'm _____ working even harder. | used to/would<br>didn't use to<br>getting used to |

| **Student C** | | **Answers** |
|---|---|---|
| 1 You're a famous actress. | I _____ go to lots and lots of auditions.<br>People _____ recognise me.<br>I'm _____ all the attention I get these days. | used to/would<br>didn't use to<br>used to |
| 2 You've recently got your first job. | I _____ be so lazy and stay in bed until midday.<br>I _____ ask my Mum for money all the time.<br>I'm _____ being more independent. | used to<br>used to/would<br>getting used to |
| 3 You sold your car and bought a bike. | I _____ drive everyday.<br>I _____ spend ages stuck in traffic.<br>I've _____ to having a shower at when I get to work. | used to/would<br>used to/would<br>got used to |
| 4 You've recently moved out of the city to a village. | I _____ be woken up by traffic.<br>I _____ hear the birds singing.<br>I'm _____ breathing fresh air. | used to/would<br>didn't use to<br>getting used to |

| | | | | |
|---|---|---|---|---|
| **1** START | **2** Your friend needs a lift to the airport. You're not busy and have a car. What do you say to her? | **3** Are you going to go home as soon as the class finishes? | **4** Is your country likely to get a new leader in the next twelve months? | **5** After you get home, what will you do? |
| **10** How many children/grandchildren do you think you'll have? | **9** GO BACK 5 | **8** What's the next book you're going to read/film you're going to see? | **7** Are you doing anything interesting this weekend? | **6** What do you think the weather will be like next week? |
| **11** How long are you going to continue to study English? | **12** How long is it until the break or the end of the lesson? | **13** Are you likely to forget something important soon? | **14** Might you live in another county one day? | **15** GO BACK 4 |
| **20** When is the next public holiday? | **19** Where's your next holiday going to be? | **18** GO FORWARD 3 | **17** When and where are the next Olympic Games? | **16** We're all waiting for your friend. We want you to speak to him and find out where he is. What do you say? |
| **21** GO BACK 2 | **22** Are people likely to visit Mars in your lifetime? | **23** Your Grandma tells you she has lost her glasses. You want to help. What do you say? | **24** Are you going to buy anything expensive soon? | **25** Do you think you might learn another language? |
| **30** The door bell rings. You offer to answer it. What do you say? | **29** What are you planning to do this/next summer? | **28** Do you think you'll ever be rich or famous? | **27** GO BACK 3 | **26** When do you finish your course? |
| **31** Do you think you could become a politician one day? | **32** Do you think you'll live for a long time? | **33** Are you likely to move home in the next six months? | **34** Are you staying in tonight? | **35** FINISH |

You are a group of television executives and you have to invent a new sport or game which will be played on a programme at 7.00 every Saturday evening. With your group, choose at least four of the items below to be used in the new sport or game. Think about the aim of the game, the way it works and the different stages. What are the key things players need to remember and what's the game called?

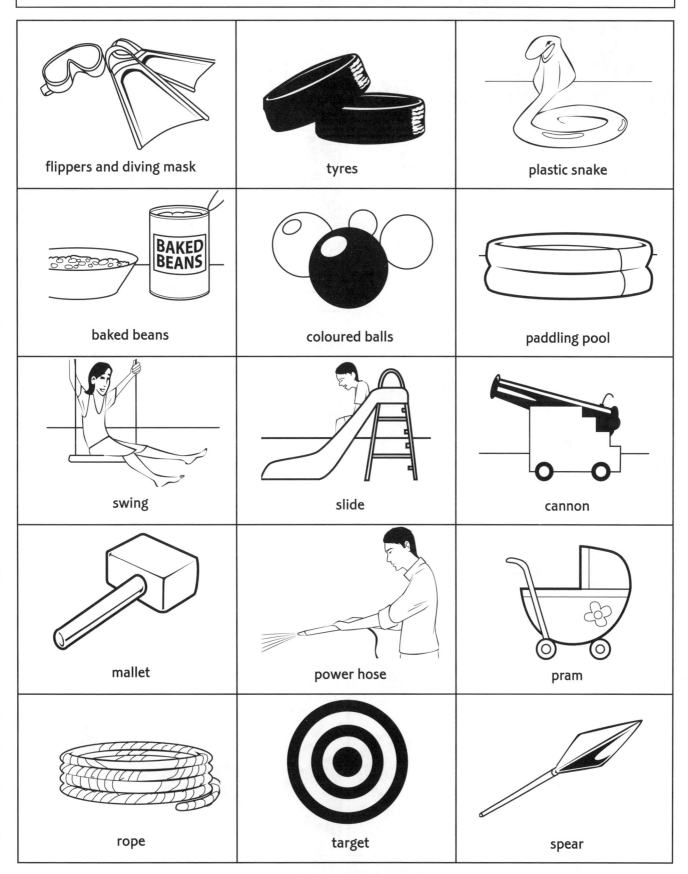

flippers and diving mask

tyres

plastic snake

baked beans

coloured balls

paddling pool

swing

slide

cannon

mallet

power hose

pram

rope

target

spear

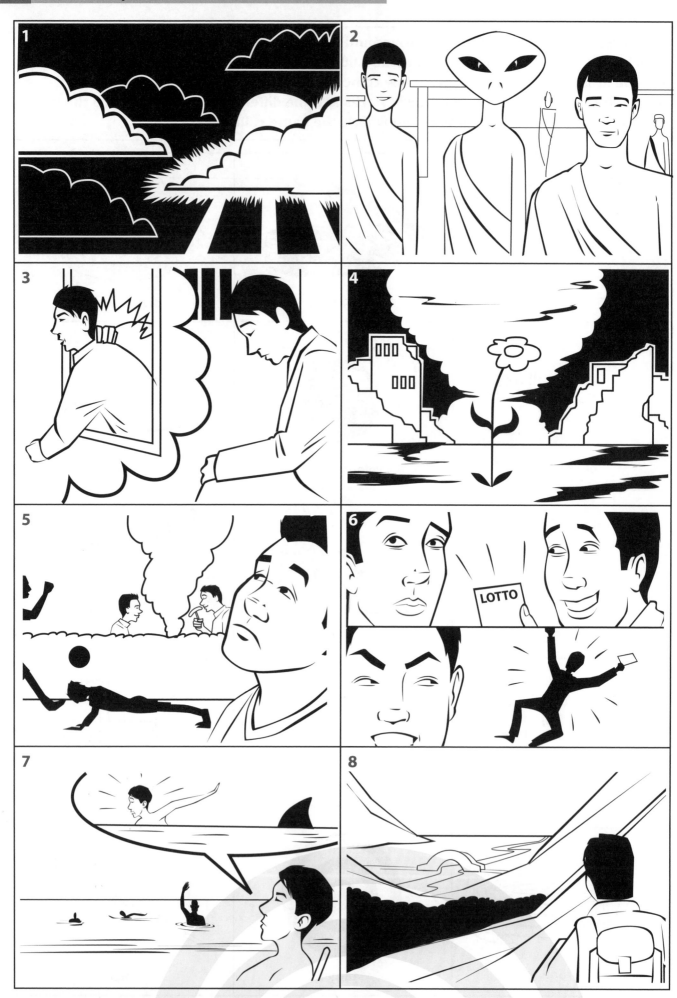

| take up | **1** They arrived two hours late. | **2** After he left the band, he wrote film soundtracks. | **3** I don't think he'll ever get married and have kids. | **4** Many years passed before he forgave his brother. |
|---|---|---|---|---|
| settle down | | | | |
| set up | **5** He went travelling but used up all his money and had to come home early. | **6** I've recently started doing yoga. | **7** I could never stop eating chocolate, I love it so much. | **8** She started the company with her brother in 2001. |
| turn up | | | | |
| run out of | | | | |
| bring up | **9** Finding a dead insect in the lettuce meant I didn't finish my salad. | **10** I liked John from the moment I met him. | **11** Where did you spend your childhood? | **12** He proposed to her but she said no. |
| grow up | | | | |
| take on | | | | |
| take to | **13** The company want to employ 150 new staff. | **14** In the story, Tarzan was raised by apes. | **15** After the scandal, the President resigned. | **16** I'll never recover from the death of my parrot. |
| step down | | | | |
| turn down | | | | |
| put off | | | | |
| get over | | | | |
| go on | | | | |
| go by | | | | |
| give up | | | | |

**Answers**

| **1** They turned up two hours late. | **2** After he left the band, he went on to write film soundtracks. | **3** I don't think he'll ever settle down. | **4** Many years went by before he forgave his brother. |
|---|---|---|---|
| **5** He went travelling but ran out of money and had to come home early. | **6** I've recently taken up (doing) yoga. | **7** I could never give up eating chocolate, I love it so much. | **8** She set up the company with her brother in 2001. |
| **9** Finding a dead insect in the lettuce put me off my salad. | **10** I took to John from the moment I met him. | **11** Where did you grow up? | **12** He proposed to her but she turned him down. |
| **13** The company want to take on 150 new staff. | **14** In the story, Tarzan was brought up by apes. | **15** After the scandal, the President stepped down. | **16** I'll never get over the death of my parrot |

## A day to forget, a night to remember

| | |
|---|---|
| 1 It was a cold, dark night. It was _____ and _____ . | What's the weather like? |
| 2 Jack was tired, he had been _____ all night and now he was driving home. | What had he been doing? |
| 3 It had been the worst twenty-four hours of his life. He had _____ and _____ . | What two things Jack had done? |
| 4 As he drove, he _____ . The roads were empty and he felt alone. | What did he do as he drove? |
| 5 He stopped the car at an all-night diner. He had to _____ and _____ . | What two things did he have to do? |
| 6 It was twenty-four hours since he had _____ and he was starting to go crazy. | What hadn't he done for twenty-four hours? |
| 7 As he entered the diner, the waitress _____ and _____ . | What two things did she do? |
| 8 He didn't even notice her but then he suddenly realised _____ _____ . | What did he suddenly realised? |
| 9 In seconds, they were _____ _____ . | What were they doing? |
| 10 'Could this be real?' he thought. 'Why had she _____ _____ ? | What had she done? |
| 11 And why had he been _____ _____ ?' | What had he been doing? |
| 12 But that didn't matter now. All that was important was _____ _____ . | What was important now? |
| 13 She told him that she _____ _____ . | What did she tell him? |
| 14 All he could say was '_____ !'<br><br>**The End** | What did he say? |

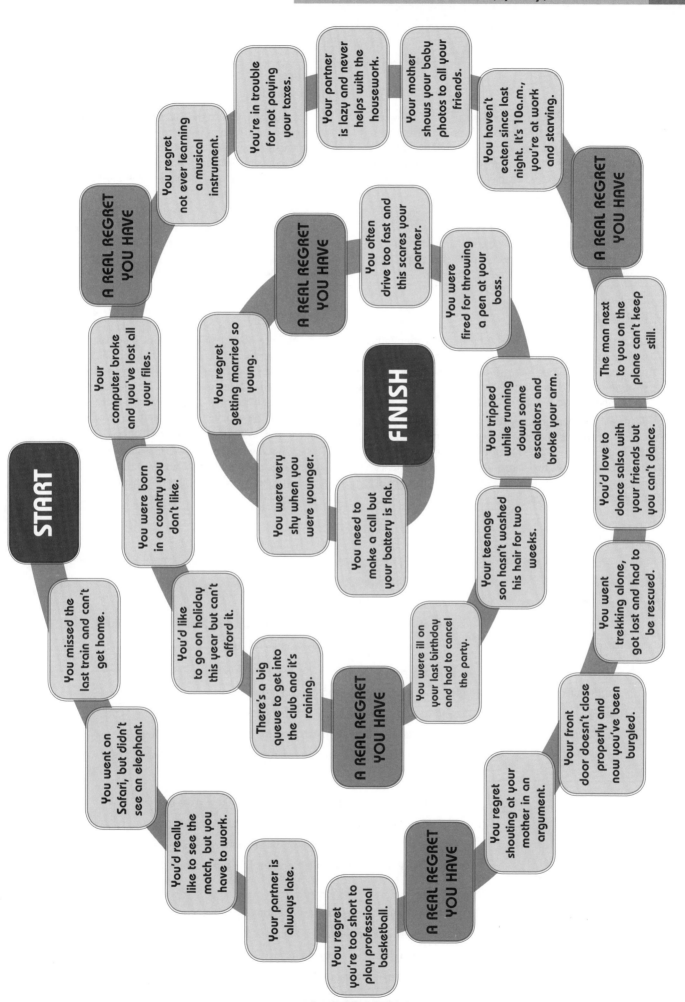

START

FINISH

A REAL REGRET YOU HAVE

You regret not ever learning a musical instrument.

You're in trouble for not paying your taxes.

Your partner is lazy and never helps with the housework.

Your mother shows your baby photos to all your friends.

You haven't eaten since last night. It's 10a.m., you're at work and starving.

A REAL REGRET YOU HAVE

You often drive too fast and this scares your partner.

You were fired for throwing a pen at your boss.

The man next to you on the plane can't keep still.

Your computer broke and you've lost all your files.

You regret getting married so young.

You were very shy when you were younger.

You need to make a call but your battery is flat.

You tripped while running down some escalators and broke your arm.

You'd love to dance salsa with your friends but you can't dance.

You were born in a country you don't like.

You'd like to go on holiday this year but can't afford it.

There's a big queue to get into the club and it's raining.

You were ill on your last birthday and had to cancel the party.

Your teenage son hasn't washed his hair for two weeks.

You went trekking alone, got lost and had to be rescued.

You missed the last train and can't get home.

You went on Safari, but didn't see an elephant.

You'd really like to see the match, but you have to work.

Your partner is always late.

You regret you're too short to play professional basketball.

A REAL REGRET YOU HAVE

You regret shouting at your mother in an argument.

Your front door doesn't close properly and now you've been burgled.

## Blurbs

### Last Rendition
By Jackson Baines

Adi is a singer in a band, but through a case of mistaken identity finds himself suspected of terrorism. Transported around the world, questioned and tortured by different intelligence services, to save himself Adi agrees to work undercover for the CIA. Unable to ever go back to his previous life, his world changes forever.

Baines is the master of the conspiracy theory and he explores important questions of our time, the way governments deal with the problem of terrorism and the question of human rights. A thrilling, action-packed adventure with an incredible twist at the end.

### Lovosice
By Elzbieta Jabrinska

Set in Eastern Europe in the mid 18th century, this is the story of an orphan's battle to survive the horrific experiences of war. Having witness the murder of his parents by enemy soldiers, Pavel and his sister escape but his sister later dies. Starving and alone Pavel decides to look for his aunt's family in the city.

*Lovosice* describes Pavel's long journey across a war-torn country. Beautifully written with incredible descriptions of the bitter eastern winter and how the cruelty of war is interpreted through the eyes of a child. Moving, heartbreaking but unforgettable.

### The Daughters of Altin's
By Roma Bazna

Set in 1960s Albania, widower Altin is the devoted father of four daughters. Following the death of his wife, Altin is unprepared for raising four girls alone. Despite the financial struggle and the arguments, the strong family bond and his unconditional love for his family shine through.

Bazna paints a humorous picture of a rich family life with complex relationships between a grieving father and his children. Share Altin's highs and lows as he watches his daughters grow, find love and eventually experience motherhood. A heart-warming read that is guaranteed to bring a tear to your eye.

### Poison Girl
By Katie G. Elliot

Elana Maurice doesn't fit in at school. Her classmates tease her, her busy parents ignore her and she constructs an incredible fantasy world filled with magical creatures and where she has special powers. As she retreats into this world, she loses her sense of what's real and what's imagined. In the end, her visions seem to be of a dark future, a future which ends in terrible catastrophe.

This is fantasy writing at its best: imaginative, nightmarish, and at times truly terrifying. Elana may be a child but don't be mistaken, Elliot writes for adults not children.

## Role cards

**A**

| | |
|---|---|
| *Last Rendition* | Really liked characters and the twist at the end. |
| *Lovosice* | Couldn't stand it – far too depressing. |
| *The Daughters of Altin's* | Big fan of Bazna. Liked youngest daughter and the chapter on her wedding. |
| *Poison Girl* | Not fond of this – too far-fetched and a bit childish. |

**B**

| | |
|---|---|
| *Last Rendition* | Not really into thrillers – too long and too violent. |
| *Lovosice* | Loved it – the intelligence of main character and gentle style of the writer. |
| *The Daughters of Altin's* | Too predictable and sentimental. Altin is a bit of an idiot (but funny). |
| *Poison Girl* | Really scary but great. Loved the creatures and the black ending. |

**C**

| | |
|---|---|
| *Last Rendition* | Really into this – clever story, lots of action, make a great film? |
| *Lovosice* | Not into it. Pavel was more like an adult than a child. Bad ending. |
| *The Daughters of Altin's* | Not a fan of this kind of book. Slow, boring and clichéd. |
| *Poison Girl* | Wow! Couldn't put it down. Descriptions of Elana's parent's death best bit. |

**D**

| | |
|---|---|
| *Last Rendition* | Not fond of author or conspiracy theories – plot too complex, too many names. |
| *Lovosice* | Really into historical novels. Child's perspective is original, beautifully written. |
| *The Daughters of Altin's* | Full of humour and can really identify with all the family problems. |
| *Poison Girl* | Put off by the main character being a child. Not a fan of fantasy. Unrealistic. |

| | | | |
|---|---|---|---|
| **breakthrough** | Scientists don't often make _____s that are this important. | **breakthrough** | The _____ was made when he was working late in the laboratory one night. |
| **trade-off** | There is a _____ between making the battery bigger and increasing the weight of the product. | **trade-off** | There is a _____ between the performance of the engine and the need for it to be economical. |
| **breakdown** | The engine used in the early model had many _____s. | **breakdown** | Over 100,000 kilometres, this vehicle had no _____s. |
| **outcome** | The _____ of the experiment was not possible to guess. | **outcome** | The _____ of the modifications was an increase in the product's efficiency. |
| **downside** | The _____ of this material is the cost. | **downside** | The biggest _____ of the product was its reliability. |
| **drawback** | The fact it doesn't work underwater is a major _____ . | **drawback** | Even though it had a number of _____s, the first design was chosen. |

## Answers

| | | | |
|---|---|---|---|
| Scientists don't often make **breakthroughs** that are this important. | The **breakthrough** was made when he was working late in the laboratory one night. | The **outcome** of the experiment was not possible to guess. | The **outcome** of the modifications was an increase in the product's efficiency. |
| There is a **trade off** between the performance of the engine and the need for it to be economical. | There is a **trade off** between making the battery bigger and increasing the weight of the product. | The **downside/drawback** of this material is the cost. | The biggest **drawback/downside** of the product was its reliability. |
| The engine used in the early model had many **breakdowns.** | Over 100,000 kilometres, this vehicle had no **breakdowns**. | The fact it doesn't work underwater is a major **drawback.** | Even though it had a number of **drawbacks**, the first design was chosen. |

**Student A**

**Student B**

# The Sinclair C5

| | |  |
|---|---|---|
| 1 | Launched in United Kingdom in 1985, the Sinclair C5 was a battery-assisted tricycle | |
| 2 | created by British inventor, Sir Clive Sinclair. The C5 was steered by the handlebar | |
| 3 | beneath a driver's knees and powered by a small electric motor making it unnecessary | |
| 4 | for the driver to pedal. C5's top speed of twenty-four km/h was the fastest allowed | |
| 5 | in the UK without driving licence. The retail price was £399, plus £29 for delivery, | |
| 6 | which was expensive for the time. Both media and the public ridiculed the C5 during | |
| 7 | 1980s and it was a commercial disaster, selling only around 12,000 units. In fact, the | |
| 8 | design was an impractical one: from the beginning, there were the serious concerns | |
| 9 | about the C5's safety in traffic because it was so low to ground. In addition to this, the | |
| 10 | driver was exposed to the wind and the rain and the cold weather tended to shorten | |
| 11 | battery life. The lack of gears and seat-to-pedal adjustment and the fact that a motor | |
| 12 | overheated on the long hills, were also serious problems. The motor turned out to be | |
| 13 | essentially useless for climbing hills, with even the gentle slopes requiring the driver to | |
| 14 | pedal. Sinclair spent the millions of pounds on developing the C5 and its failure | |
| 15 | bankrupted a company and cost him his reputation. It will long be remembered in the | |
| 16 | UK as the spectacular and comic failure, but was Sir Clive's idea just ahead of its time? | |

| | |
|---|---|
| I just don't remember it. | If products are endorsed by celebrities, |
| people are more likely to buy them. | I won't buy sunglasses, |
| unless they are a well known brand. | If I'm watching something on TV and there is a commercial break, |
| I change channels. | Provided you take the time to shop around, |
| you can get good deals these days. | If I see a new product in the shops, |
| I often try it. | If I go shopping at the weekend, |
| I might buy something new to wear. | If I buy a new mobile in the next twelve months, |
| it'll be the same brand of phone as I've got now. | I won't buy another computer for at least a year, |
| as long as my present one doesn't break. | If I need to a buy a ticket next week, |
| I'll do it on the internet. | If luxury goods were cheaper, |
| people wouldn't want to buy them. | I'd buy a fake watch |
| If it was a good copy. | If I were to start a business, |
| I might open a restaurant or sell fast food. | If companies didn't advertise, |
| we wouldn't buy their products. | If I found out a well-known company used child labour, |
| I'd stop buying their products. | If there wasn't sponsorship, |
| a lot of sports couldn't survive. | If an advert isn't funny, |

You are a team of advertising executives in the marketing department of a soft drinks company, Swapps. The company is going to expand its portfolio of high-profile brands by launching its first energy drink. The energy drinks sector is very competitive and there is a lot of money at stake, so it is essential that the marketing campaign to launch this new product is dynamic and effective.

Hold a meeting with your colleagues to put together your complete marketing campaign. Discuss the categories below and decide on a strategy for each. Prepare to present your campaign to the board of directors.

1 **Decide on the market.**
   Describe the typical drinker. What are they like? (Think about age, gender, interests, what is important to them.) What do they do for a job and in their free time? Why do they need an energy drink?

2 **Decide on the name.**
   Suggestions for the name include: Tiger Teeth, Sharp, Kick, Hyper, Shark Bite, Black Wolf, Blue Monkey and Craze, but maybe you have better ideas?

3 **Decide on the slogan.**
   It needs to be something short and catchy.

4 **Decide on the packaging.**
   What should the can look like? What are the colours and what's the logo?

5 **Decide on how to spend the budget.**
   You have a budget of €30m. Decide how you're going to spend the money.

6 **Decide on the adverts.**
   What happens in the TV and cinema ads? What are the printed ads going to show?

| Type of advert | Cost | |
| --- | --- | --- |
| Prime-time TV ads on six major channels (two weeks) | $20m | Which channels? |
| Whole page ads in ten magazines (three months) | $5m | What kind of magazines? |
| Ads in all national cinemas (two months) | $10m | |
| Whole page ads in five national newspapers (one month) | $5m | Which newspapers? |
| Viral advertising (three months) | $2.5m | Which sites? |
| Sponsor six major sporting events | $5m | Which events? |
| Sponsor six other major events | $5m | Which events? |
| Billboards in the ten largest cities (three months and across the whole city) | $2.5m | |
| Free Samples to public in the ten largest cities (50,000 cans over three months) | $2.5m | Which places – in the street, bars, clubs etc.? |
| Celebrity endorsement (two year contract) | $5m | Who is it? |

## Tell the group about …

1  the last time you bought someone a gift to show your app_____ .

2  your greatest ach_____ so far in life.

3  the last time you pre_____ to be ill.

4  the best adv_____ you've ever been given.

5  how you rea_____ in an emergency.

6  someone bad you became inv_____ with.

7  someone whose jud_____ you respect.

8  an obl_____ you don't like.

9  the last time you made a good or bad imp_____ .

10  the last time someone int_____ in your life.

11  a skill you need more pra_____ at.

12  your pre_____ in holidays.

13  an activity you no longer enj_____ doing?

14  the thing that gives you the most sat_____ .

15  a teacher who gave you lots of enc_____ .

### Student A

You work in a large office and you have found out that your boss, Student B, is leaving for another job abroad. You've also heard that your colleague, Marco, has been promoted and is going to replace Student B. You are really unhappy as nobody likes Marco and every loved working for Student B. You meet Student B at the coffee machine and have a chat.

**Start:** Hi. Congratulations on the new job. You must be really excited about it.

**a** Well, it's hard to **look on the bright side** when your new boss is going to be Marco. Anyway, you never liked him.

**b** No, it's **one step forward and two steps back**. Anyway, I guess we'll just have to do the best we can.

**c** Disappointed!? He told me he was **filled with despair**. The company only made Marco boss to save money. They know nobody likes him and loads of people will quit.

**d** Wow, that sounds **promising!** When can I start?

**e** Yes, we've all had our **ups and downs.** What were the company thinking when they appointed him? I'm really not looking forward to working for him.

**f** Yes, I'd be **filled with optimism** if I were you. You know it's going to be absolutely terrible here without you.

### Student B

You are the boss of a large office but you are leaving this job to work for a bigger company in Spain. You have also heard that your colleague, Marco, has been promoted and is going to replace you. Everyone is really unhappy as nobody likes him and everyone loved working for you. You meet your colleague, Student A, at the coffee machine and have a chat.

**g** Come on, don't be so **gloomy**. Try to look at the positives of having a new boss.

**Finish:** Anyway, must dash. I've got a desk to tidy out! See you later.

**h** You're not alone. I think all your colleagues are **dreading** it too. Jack said he was disappointed about the decision.

**i** Yes, I'm really **looking forward to** working in Spain and some new challenges. I'm really positive about the future.

**j** That's better, you're sounding a bit more **upbeat** now. If you're interested, I may be able to get you a job with me.

**k** I wouldn't say that, I have **mixed feelings** about him but he's good at his job. Sure, we've had a few problems over the years.

**l** I'm not sure that's true, but it's difficult not to be **cynical**. Anyway, whatever the reasons are, a decision like this is not progress or good for the company.

## Gyrkyzstan

Beautiful, isolated Himalayan republic. Very difficult to reach but vast unspoilt mountain landscape.

Last year there was a lot of snow. Not possible for planes to take off or leave for one month!

Wealthy Russian holiday-makers have started going there. Visit it before it changes to just another ski resort!

### Things to do

Summer: trekking, mountaineering, rafting, bungee-jumping and hunting

Winter: some winter sports like skiing – facilities not great

### Things to know

No food or drink allowed into the country.

Alcohol is banned in most places.

No visa needed but $50 exit tax.

Very important to get travel insurance and special insurance for winter sports.

Good idea to take/hire camping equipment.

### Travel

Flights are expensive. No direct flights. Change in Moscow or Tashkent.

Public transport poor.

Hire a minibus and driver (quite cheap).

## Djamenia

Small newly-independent state in sub-Saharan Africa. It has both desert and rainforest.

Was dangerous and politically unstable but now much better. Government killed thousands of rebels.

Oil has been discovered there so it's about to change and possibly suffer environmental damage. Visit it now!

### Things to do

Desert: camel riding, camel trip across the desert, visit ruined cities

Jungle: gorillas, amazing waterfalls and great wildlife

### Things to know

Good idea to take gifts from home to give to people, e.g. pens.

No visa needed. No airport tax.

Get all vaccinations!

Get used to people looking at you and following you – especially kids.

### Travel

Fly to Nigeria or Algeria and then get a flight from there.

Local buses OK but be patient! Very slow!

Your guides and drivers will be armed (heavily)!

In the past not safe to travel – still a bit dangerous.

## The McKenzie Islands

The smallest nation on earth – a group of about twenty coral islands 1,500km west of Hawaii.

Rising sea-levels threaten the islands' existence. Last year inhabitants of the fourth largest island were forced to abandon it. Visit this island paradise before it disappears under the waves!

### Things to do

Beaches: sunbathing, swimming, relaxing in paradise

Sea: diving, snorkelling, sailing, fishing and incredible surfing

### Things to Know

Need a tourist visa. Apply through Australian embassy.

Get your diving licence somewhere else. Very expensive!

Learn some of the local language – the locals will love you for it!

Possibly the friendliest people in the world.

Most accommodation is basic beach huts.

### Travel

Costs a fortune to get there. Flights from Hawaii, Jakarta and Auckland (not scheduled).

Boats between islands are cheap.

Possible to walk everywhere – taxi if you're feeling lazy!

## Kirlian Island

A 1,500 sq km rock in the Southern Ocean. The windiest place on the planet but with a spectacular volcano.

Once only inhabited by a few scientists and fisherman and hundreds of thousands of penguins.

The island has started servicing cruise ships and is starting to lose its character. Get there before it does!

### Things to do

Volcano: crater and lava fields, trekking, spectacular cliffs, rock climbing, bathe in hot springs

Wildlife: penguin and seal colonies

### Things to know

Better in summer – long, cold and dark winters.

Bring own food (though can buy some things – very expensive).

Little accommodation and basic. Book in advance.

Electricity only a few hours a day.

Take camping equipment and outdoor gear.

### Travel

Ships from Australia take seven days and cheap.

Some flights from Australia and Seychelles (not scheduled and very expensive).

Trips to Antarctica are available by boat and plane.

**Grammar: future perfect and future continuous**

| | Futurologist predictions and questions: | Your answer/opinion |
|---|---|---|
| 1 | All the world's governments will have passed laws to limit the global population by 2025. | |
| 2 | You'll be driving an electric car or one that uses an alternative source of fuel by 2020. | |
| 3 | There will be tigers and pandas in zoos but they will have become extinct in the wild. | |
| 4 | 'Space tourists' will be taking trips on special planes out of the earth's atmosphere in the next ten years. | |
| 5 | China will have become the world's number one superpower within the next twenty years. | |
| 6 | We'll be just as obsessed with money but we'll be living in a completely 'cashless' society within ten years. | |
| 7 | The world's fastest athlete will have run 100 metres in under nine seconds by 2020. | |
| 8 | In fifty years, the older generation will be playing more computer games than the younger generation. | |
| 9 | Space exploration will continue but when will life on other planets have been conclusively proven? | |
| 10 | We'll all be watching holographic TV and cinema and reading electronic books before the end of the decade. | |
| 11 | Europe will have become completely unified by 2025. | |
| 12 | We'll be designing and personalising our own products on our home computers within the next ten years. | |
| 13 | Completely different varieties of English will have developed by 2050. | |
| 14 | People will commonly be living to 120 by the end of the 2020s. | |
| 15 | The sale of unhealthy fast food will have been banned in most countries by the mid 2020s. | |
| 16 | More people will be speaking Spanish than English in the USA in thirty years time. | |
| 17 | Climate change will continue but when will the polar ices caps have completed melted? | |
| 18 | We'll be choosing the sex and physical characteristics of our babies before they are born by 2080. | |
| 19 | Your Prediction 1: | |
| 20 | Your Prediction 2: | |

**Tick two topics you would like to discuss from the list below.**

*This class believes that …*

- a family with two parents is the best environment to bring up children.

- there is a lack of positive role-models for young people these days.

- governments need to censor the internet to protect their citizens.

- protecting culture and traditions from globalisation is not important.

- it's not the government's responsibility to look after sick and poor people.

- celebrity culture is harmless fun.

- money should be spent on protecting people rather than endangered species.

- your school days are the best days of your life.

- cosmetic surgery is only justifiable in extreme cases.

- marriage can't be forever in a modern society.

- art is an expensive waste of money.

- modern technology doesn't make our lives better.

- _____ (your suggestion)

## Arguments for

## Arguments against

| wildlife programme | reality show | costume drama | soap opera |
|---|---|---|---|
| • animals<br>• nature<br>• environment | • ordinary people<br>• famous<br>• competition | • past<br>• clothes<br>• story | • continue<br>• story<br>• week |
| **sketch show** | **sitcom** | **documentary** | **docudrama** |
| • laugh<br>• funny<br>• comedy | • comedy<br>• laugh<br>• Friends | • serious<br>• real life<br>• investigate | • real life<br>• people<br>• work |
| **series** | **serial** | **thriller** | **detective series** |
| • every<br>• episode<br>• programme | • episode<br>• story<br>• character | • exciting<br>• action<br>• adventure | • police<br>• crime<br>• investigate |
| **game show** | **quiz** | **current affairs** | **news** |
| • prize<br>• money<br>• win | • questions<br>• prize<br>• guests | • events<br>• reports<br>• investigate | • reporter<br>• events<br>• reports |

| Student A | | Student B | |
|---|---|---|---|
| turn out | take back | turn out | take back |
| break down | put up with | break down | put up with |
| come across | pull out | come across | pull out |
| bring out | break into | bring out | break into |

## Student A

**I can't stand living in this city any longer.**

You can't **put up with** living in this city any longer.

―――――――

**I crashed into the car as it was emerging from a side road.**

You crashed into the car as it was **pulling out** of a side road.

―――――――

**I am not a bad tempered person but she makes me show the worst side of my personality.**

You're not a bad-tempered person but she **brings out** the worst in you.

―――――――

**When you meet her, you get the impression that she is a shy person.**

When you meet her she **comes across** as shy.

―――――――

**It's difficult for our company to enter such a competitive market.**

It's difficult for your company to **break into** such a competitive market.

―――――――

**I was really worried but in the end what happened was OK.**

I was really worried but in the end, it/everything **turned out** OK.

―――――――

**The negotiations between the management and the union have failed.**

The negotiations between the management and the union have **broken down**.

―――――――

**This song reminds me of being a teenager again.**

This song **takes you back** to being a teenager (again).

## Student B

**After five years, the army are withdrawing from the country.**

After five years, the army are **pulling out** of the country.

―――――――

**I found by chance this beautiful antique watch in a market at the weekend.**

I **came across** this beautiful antique watch in a market at the weekend.

―――――――

**I caught three kids as they were illegally entering my car.**

You caught three kids as they were **breaking into** your car.

―――――――

**I have to get a new car. My old Ford just keeps going wrong.**

You have to get a new car. My old Ford just keeps **breaking down**.

―――――――

**I feel regret and didn't mean what I said.**

You should **take back** what you said.

―――――――

**The company are introducing their latest computer onto the market tomorrow.**

The company are **bringing out** their latest computer tomorrow.

―――――――

**He wants to stay at my house for a couple of days.**

He wants you to **put him up** for a couple of days.

―――――――

**Thousands of fans attended in order to welcome their team home from the World Cup.**

Thousands of fans **turned out** to welcome their team home from the World Cup.

| GAME 1 | GAME 2 | GAME 3 | GAME 4 | GAME 5 | GAME 6 |
|---|---|---|---|---|---|
| 1 **a few** | 1 **every** | 1 **each** | 1 **several** | 1 **a few** | 1 **both** |
| 2 **hardly any** | 2 **neither** | 2 **a few** | 2 **great deal of** | 2 **every** | 2 **quite a lot of** |
| 3 **none** | 3 **a little** | 3 **plenty of** | 3 **hardly any** | 3 **neither** | 3 **lots of** |
| 4 **a great deal of** | 4 **few** | 4 **quite a lot of** | 4 **a little** | 4 **quite a few** | 4 **few** |
| 5 **all** | 5 **quite a few** | 5 **little** | 5 **all** | 5 **little** | 5 **both** |
| 6 **several** | 6 **lots of** | 6 **both** | 6 **none** | 6 **plenty of** | 6 **a little** |
| **Topics**<br>Advice<br>Friends<br>The media<br>The news<br>Information<br>Population | **Topics**<br>Weather<br>Nature<br>Time<br>Towns/cities<br>Accommodation<br>Families | **Topics**<br>Government<br>Information<br>People<br>Clothes<br>Food<br>The police | **Topics**<br>Advice<br>Population<br>Money<br>Health<br>Politics<br>Weather | **Topics**<br>The news<br>Equipment<br>Habits<br>Food<br>People<br>Transport | **Topics**<br>Scenery<br>Children<br>Clothes<br>Time<br>Accommodation<br>Nature |

## Student A
### Record company Executive Assistant

You are an assistant for a record company executive at AGM Records. AWOL is your most important band but its lead singer, Vinnie, recently disappeared moments before the start of the first concert of their world tour.

The company has no idea where he is. The tour has been cancelled and your boss is absolutely furious and really anxious to know the situation, especially when the band can resume the tour.

Your boss has sent you to have a meeting with the band manager. You've made notes on the things your boss has said and wants to find out. You are going to report these to the band manager and find out some answers.

Try and sort out the situation so both sides are happy.

## Your boss said:

'The cancelled tour will cost $25m and might bankrupt the company.'

'The tour absolutely must go ahead.'

'When is AWOL going to resume the tour?'

'Is it possible for the guitarist to sing instead? He told me yesterday he would.'

'We'll sue the band and terminate its contract at the end of the year, if they don't tour.'

'Can I see Vinnie in person or can he phone me immediately?'

'Why didn't he didn't speak to the manager or the band if he had a problem about something?'

'What's Vinnie's mental state? Is he going to kill himself?'

## Student B
### AWOL's Manager

You are the manager of a famous band called AWOL. The lead singer, Vinnie, recently disappeared moments before the start of the first concert of their world tour. The tour has been cancelled and the record company are absolutely furious. The band is also upset about Vinnie's behaviour and you are worried about his mental state. You also know that if the band split up you lose your job.

You spoke to Vinnie yesterday, made some notes on what he said. You now have a meeting with the assistant of the record company boss to report what Vinnie said.

Try and sort out the situation so both sides are happy.

## Vinnie said:

'I don't want to leave the band – I love the guys.'

'I don't want to do the tour now – maybe in the summer.'

'I split up with my girlfriend of two years just before the concert. I couldn't face doing the show.'

'I told the band I wasn't doing the show.'

'I'm addicted to the prescription drugs I was taking for my stage fright and need some time in rehab.'

'I want to be left alone and not see anyone until next week.'

'I'm not suicidal.' (but he does seem very depressed)

'Can I get $10,000? I've spent all my money.'

'Can we remix the album? It could be so much better.'

Sherpa's cleaning up rubbish left by climbers on Mount Everest have found the camera of George Mallory, a British climber who died on the mountain in 1924. Mountaineering's biggest unsolved mystery is whether he and partner, Andrew Irving, were the first to reach the peak. Both died on the descent. Mallory's body was found in 1999 but not his camera. The perfectly preserved film seems to show the pair at the summit twenty-nine years earlier than the successful 1953 expedition.

*Black's news agency*

---

One of Italy's most famous monuments, the Leaning Tower of Pisa, has collapsed. The fifty-five-metre-tall tower had been leaning since its construction in 1173. It was reopened in 2001 after two decades of work and was declared 'stable' for another 300 years. There are reports of the ground shaking before it collapsed and some are blaming a minor earthquake. Some tourists caught the collapse on their mobiles and cameras. A spokesperson for the monument said it would be rebuilt, leaning!

*SANA's news agency*

---

A giant anaconda, over twenty metres long, has been shot in the Democratic Republic of Congo. Villagers had reported a giant snake in the river and complained it had been eating their cattle. This was ignored by the local police until they encountered it whilst looking for a missing child. It was shot, opened up but the remains of the child were not found in the stomach. She was found alive and well at a relative's house. The previous largest reliable measurement of an anaconda was about nine metres in length.

*Black's news agency*

---

Scientists have grown a baby mammoth using DNA found in a frozen mammoth in Siberia. Finding completely frozen mammoths is not unusual but the DNA is usually unuseable. However, three years ago, scientists found usable mammoth DNA in a well-preserved specimen. It was implanted into unfertilised Asian Elephant eggs, fertilised and implanted into a female. The mammoth, a male, was born two days ago, but died today. The last mammoth to die before this was 4000 years ago.

*Glock's news agency*

---

American astronomers have discovered that an asteroid, 5km in diameter, may collide with the Earth in 2028. Previously, the next big asteroid impact was expected in March 2788. It will be equivalent to ten million megatons of TNT and leave a crater ninety-five kilometres across. For comparison, the largest nuclear weapon was just fifty megatons. Scientists hope that technology will be available to destroy the asteroid before in reaches Earth and we can avoid the greatest catasthrophe in modern times.

*USN's news agency*

---

Tattoist Jed Michaels has had his whole face tattooed purple, including his ears and eyelids. Jed said he loved his new colour but having his eyelids tattoed was quite painful. Asked why he did it, he just said he liked the colour and thought it suited him. Jed has been getting tattoes done since he was fourteen. Asked if he might regret it, he said he has regretted some, his worse one is Mickey Mouse playing drums on his leg but he thinks the best one is now his face.

*USN's news agency*

You are a strict vegetarian and have been invited to your partner's parents' home for the first time. You are having dinner and you discover just before you start eating the vegetable soup that it has meat in it. Do you **follow your principles** and explain you can't eat it or say nothing?

---

You are an unemployed actor and a man selling pirate DVDs comes to your restaurant table and offers you some recent films. You know that your money will help criminal gangs and won't help the film industry but you want to see the films. Do you **go against your principles** and buy them?

---

You are a police officer and you stop a motorist driving very fast, fast enough for them to lose their licence for a year. The motorist is a top politician and they offer you $2,000 to let them drive away without punishment. Do you **stick to your principles** and not take the bribe?

---

You know your son has been involved in a bank robbery. The police are looking for the robbers. If you tell the police, your son may never speak to you again but if you don't, you could also be in trouble. It's a big dilemma. What **decision** do you **come to**?

---

You've been offered a job in a distant foreign country for three years. You don't like the country, the climate, the people or the food but you will get double your present salary. After **weighing up the pros and cons** what do you decide to do?

---

Your rich boy/girlfriend wants to marry you. If you do this, you would never worry about money again and would have a very comfortable life. However, you don't really love them. You **compare the advantages and the disadvantages**. What's your decision?

---

You've been trying to sell your house for six months and need to sell it within one week or your dream of emigrating to Australia won't happen. You have a cash offer but for twenty-five per cent less than your price. Do you **postpone the decision** to sell to this buyer or accept the offer?

---

You've just crashed your partner's new car. When you see them, they are in a really bad mood and you can't tell them but if you don't tell them soon it could makes things worse. How much longer do you **put off the decision**?

---

You made a big mistake at work which cost your company $10,000. Your boss blames your colleague and they will lose their job if you don't say something. If you say nothing, there is no way they could ever find out it was your mistake. After **examining the situation** carefully, what do you decide?

---

| TRUTH | TRUTH | LIE |
|:-----:|:-----:|:---:|
| **TRUTH** | **TRUTH** | **LIE** |
| **TRUTH** | **TRUTH** | **LIE** |

## Student A

### Situation one

You are planning to go on holiday with your old school friends. You are anxious to start booking flights etc. but you suspect one of your friends hasn't told their partner yet because their partner doesn't like you or your friends. You speak to him/her to ask about the situation.

### Situation two

You are driving with your colleague to an important meeting but have been stuck in traffic caused by road works for the last hour. You are both getting anxious about being late and are annoyed as you are commonly delayed by road works.

**a** Well, time is money. The price of the flights is going up all the time.
You need to **make up your mind** soon. ☐

**b** Fantastic! It'll be a brilliant holiday! ☐

**c** Did you see those guys 'working' on the road! Just **killing time** until they
can go home and not doing anything. Unbelievable! ☐

**d** Anyway, looks like the traffic is getting better now. We may get there just
**in the nick of time.** ☐

**e** Yeah I know. We need to **make up for lost time.** I'm going drive as fast
as I can. ☐

**f** So, have you told your partner yet about the holiday? [1]

**g** You're incredible! We only see each other as a group **once in a blue moon.**
Why the delay? ☐

## Student B

### Situation one

You are planning to go on holiday with your old school friends who your partner doesn't know very well or like. Your partner will be upset when they find out and therefore you have delayed telling them. One of your friends is anxious to start booking flights etc. and is asking you about the situation.

### Situation two

You and your colleague, who is driving, are going to an important meeting but you have been stuck in traffic caused by road works for the last hour. You are both getting anxious about being late and are annoyed as you are commonly delayed by road works.

**h** Not exactly, I'm just **biding my time**, waiting for the right moment to
say something. ☐

**i** OK, OK. I'll phone right now. ☐

**j** Those road works were terrible! We're going to be late for the meeting. [1]

**k** Tell me about it! **Time after time** I drive down this road and there are
road works but nobody working. ☐

**l** I think we will. But don't get us killed on the way! ☐

**m** I know I've been **dragging my feet** but I have to wait until he's/she's
in a good mood. ☐

**n** Good idea. We're going to be really **pressed for time.** The meeting starts
in under an hour. ☐

**1** Your son has been suspended from school for two weeks for bad behaviour.

You **consider** _____ **(send)** him to a private school. **(5)**

Tell him he **had better** _____ **(improve)** his behaviour. **(9)**

---

**2** Your son says it was the worst experience of his life and **will never** _____ **(forgive)** you. He goes back to his old school unhappier than he was before. **(1)**

---

**3** Choose a hobby:

_____ **(play)** guitar might be a nice idea for him. Buy him an electric guitar and pay for lessons. **(6)**

_____ **(attend)** art classes. He was quite good at drawing when he was younger. **(14)**

---

**4** He goes back to his old school but it's time to try something different.

**Arrange for him** _____ **(see)** a psychologist **(17)**

Try and get him **interested in** _____ **(do)** something new, help him find a hobby perhaps? **(3)**

---

**5** **Despite you not** _____ **(be)** able to afford it, he spends the next three months studying at private school. However, he **doesn't enjoy** _____ **(travel)** three hours a day.

You pay for another year of school and hope he gets used to the travelling. **(7)**

You send him to a boarding school instead. **(8)**

---

**6** This is a disaster. He never **wants** _____ **(play)** his guitar and he's rude to his guitar teacher.

You think **it's better** _____ **(sell)** the guitar and use the money for something else. Perhaps buying a set of golf clubs? **(12)**

Send him to art classes. **(14)**

---

**7** Success! He seems to be doing better at school and his teachers see an improvement in his behaviour.

You **intend** _____ **(continue)** sending him to this school. **(11)**

You send him back to his old (local) school now his behaviour is better. You can also save money! **(4)**

---

**8** OK, there isn't any travelling but he really hates boarding school and becomes really quiet and withdrawn.

You **would rather** see him _____ **(behave)** badly than being so depressed. You send him back to his old private school. **(11)**

You **expect him** _____ **(get)** used to it. **(10)**

---

**9** It doesn't improve and he gets expelled from school. No other state school is **prepared** _____ **(take)** him.

You send him to a private day school far away from your home. **(5)**

You send him to a boarding school so he **doesn't have to** _____ **(travel)**. **(8)**

---

**10** He doesn't and runs away. The police find him one week later. This was terrible, you were really worried and **promise not** _____ **(send)** him away again. He goes back to his first school. **(4)**

---

**11** Unfortunately, you lose your job and you really **can't afford** _____ **(spend)** money on private education. Send him back to his old school. **(4)**

---

**12** He's really **good at** _____ **(play)** golf and as you **used** _____ **(play)** too you can spend time with him. You buy him expensive clubs and private lessons.

You don't want to spoil him so you send him to a US camp for problem kids for one month. **(18)**

You send him to a golf camp in the US resort and hope he behaves himself. **(20)**

---

**13** **Try** _____ **(get)** him interested in culture and take him to museums, galleries and the theatre. **(15)**

Do some sport together. Try golf, you play and you never know he **might** _____ **(like)** it. **(12)**

---

**14** He really **likes** _____ **(paint)** and **enjoys** _____ **(be able to)** express himself. He also makes some new friends in the class.

You send him on a two week painting course in the summer holidays. **(16)**

You don't approve of his new friends and think he should try something else but this time with his family. **(13)**

---

**15** He's not interested and spends most of the time **complaining about** _____ **(be)** bored and talking on his mobile phone.

Either go back to **(13)**

or, try a camp in US for badly behaved children _____ **(make)** him realise how lucky he is and hopefully change him. **(18)**

---

**16** While on the course, he was arrested by the police for graffiting. You **had to** _____ **( pay)** a fine and you think it's time he did things with his family so you can keep an eye on him. **(13)**

---

**17** The psychologist thinks there is not so much wrong with your son. She **suggests** _____ **(do)** a couple of things.

Painting and you send him to art classes. **(14)**

**Spending more time** _____ **(do)** things together as a family. **(13)**

---

**18** The summer camp **is like** _____ **(be)** in the military and is very strict. Your son phones you every day pleading to come home.

Let him come home. **(2)**

**Make him** _____ **(stay)** until the end. **(19)**

---

**19** Bad decision. He gets really angry and is **accused of** _____ **(attack)** one of the organisers. He spends two months in a prison for young offenders in the USA. You send him back to his old school when he gets back. **(1)**

---

**20** Trusting your son was a good move. He didn't get into trouble. He **continues** _____ **(play)** golf and **ends up** _____ **(play)** in tournaments and being quite successful. He has a focus and is more motivated to study. You have a happy son again!

**THE END**

## Complaining students

You are studying English for six months at the International Oxford City School of English. You have spent a lot of money to study in an English speaking country and although your English has been improving, there have been some problems with the school. You and a couple of other students are going to see the Principal and their assistant to discuss these. Even though you are very frustrated, you need to be diplomatic when trying to find a satisfactory solution. You've made a list of your main points.

- Teachers are often late in the morning – this is unprofessional and a bad example for students.

- Some teachers don't seem very motivated (the late ones!). They don't seem to care.

- There are too many students of one nationality in some classes and they naturally speak their first language not English.

- Classes are sometimes cancelled and the lesson is not rescheduled or the fees refunded.

- There are only a few computers for students to use and the internet is very slow.

- The food in the canteen is expensive and not fresh. The sandwiches have hard bread and the coffee is terrible.

- The canteen is always full so students have to eat in the classrooms, which isn't allowed.

- The library is too small.

## Director and Assistant Director

You are in charge of the International Oxford City School of English, a language school in the centre of a busy city. Your school has a good reputation and is very busy but this has caused you problems. You can't find enough good teachers and the facilities are now inadequate. Some unhappy students have decided to come and see you to discuss the situation but there are some things which the students need to be reminded about, diplomatically! Do your best to keep the students happy and find a solution. You've made a list of your main points.

- Students have been using the computers in the classroom (for teachers), this isn't allowed and teachers have complained.

- Students are often late in the morning, too. The buses are unreliable and both the teachers and the students use them.

- Students are eating food in the classrooms and teachers and students have been complaining about this.

- There is a problem with some of the teachers. Some don't phone to say they are not coming in or just don't turn up. It's a nightmare!

- Good teachers are hard to find but some teachers are fed up with students not switching off their mobile phones, arriving late and speaking in their first language.

- Students leave bags on chairs in the library or use it to go to sleep.

- There are plans to replace all the student computers and add four more.

- You are thinking about getting a new company to provide the food in the canteen.

- There are plans to have no more than fifty per cent of students speaking the same first language in a class. This will take time to introduce.

You are guilty of **arson**. You set fire to your neighbour's car. Nobody was injured, but why did you do it?

---

You are guilty of **kidnapping**. You kidnapped the wife of a wealthy man. You asked for $5m ransom. Why did you do it?

---

You are guilty of **bribery**. You tried to bribe a planning officer $20,000 to let you build a modern extension to your home in the old part of the city.

---

You are guilty of **stalking**. You stalked a famous actor for two years. You sent over 500 letters in this time and the police found you in the actor's garden.

---

You are guilty of **tax evasion**. You are a builder and have paid no tax for five years. The police estimate you have earnt $1m in that time.

---

You are guilty of **vandalism**. You have sprayed graffiti on over eighty trains. The cost of cleaning them has been $50,000.

---

You are guilty of **identity theft**. You stole the identity of four people to get bank loans and credit cards. You spent $150,000.

---

You are a **mugger**. You have been found guilty of mugging fifteen people. You stole their wallets and mobiles at knifepoint but didn't physically hurt anyone.

---

You are guilty of **counterfeiting**. You have a factory which makes copies of designer handbags. You employ 40 people and made $500,000.

---

You are guilty of **shoplifting**. You were caught after you stole three pairs of jeans and a T-shirt from a high street clothes store.

---

You are a **pickpocket**. You were caught on the metro system and admitted pickpocketing five people. You stole only wallets and purses.

---

You are guilty of **hacking**. You entered military sites, which contained highly confidential and extremely sensitive information. Why did you do it?

## Game one

| | | |
|---|---|---|
| 1 I helped her with her bags and she said 'Thank you'. | 2 He said he was sorry he upset her. | 3 It was the driver's fault. He caused the accident. **(P)** |
| 4 The police think I stole the paintings. **(P)** | 5 She said I was wrong to not wear a seatbelt. | 6 I want to be a world famous chef. |
| 7 The court decided he didn't murder his colleague. **(P)** | 8 He was not allowed to drive for a year. **(P)** | 9 The residents stopped the trees from being cut down. |

> blame    clear    ban    criticise    suspect
> thank    dream    save    apologise

## Game two

| | | |
|---|---|---|
| 1 It's your fault we're lost. | 2 He was found not guilty of offering a bribe to a policeman. **(P)** | 3 The court said he can't own a dog for five years. **(P)** |
| 4 I lent him my laptop. He really appreciated this. | 5 She thinks I lied to her. | 6 The charity rescued the building. It was going to be demolished. **(P)** |
| 7 I'm sorry if I offended you. | 8 She told me I was a bad driver and drove too fast. **(P)** | 9 She wishes she lived in France. |

> thank    criticise    save    apologise    suspect
> dream    clear    ban    blame

## Game three

| | | |
|---|---|---|
| 1 Sorry. I was wrong about your mother. | 2 I think you took my phone. | 3 The dogs were going to attack but the farmer saved me. |
| 4 You are the reason we are late. | 5 I raised lots of money for a charity. They were very grateful. | 6 He said it was a big mistake for me to sell the land at this time. |
| 7 What she'd really like to do one day is start her own business. | 8 He's now free. The judge said he didn't start the fire. | 9 He mustn't leave the country or go near a football stadium. **(P)** |

> clear    ban    thank    blame    criticise
> suspect    rescue    apologise    dream

## Answers

### Game one

1 She thanked me for helping her with her bags.   2 He apologised for upsetting her.   3 The driver was blamed for causing the accident.   4 I am suspected of stealing the paintings   5 She criticised me for not wearing a seatbelt.   6 I dream of being a world famous chef.   7 He was cleared of murdering his colleague   8 He was banned from driving for a year.   9 The residents saved the trees from being cut down.

### Game two

1 I blame you for us being lost.   2 He was cleared of offering a bribe to a policeman.   3 He is banned from owning a dog for five years.   4 He thanked me for lending him my laptop.   5 She suspects me of lying to her.   6 The building was saved from being demolished (by a charity).   7 I apologise for offending you.   8 I was criticised for being a bad driver and driving too fast.   9 She dreams of living in France.

### Game three

1 I apologise for being wrong about your mother.   2 I suspect you of taking my phone.   3 The farmer rescued me from being attacked by the dogs.   4 I blame you for us being late.   5 The charity thanked me for raising lots of money.   6 He criticised me for selling the land at this time.   7 She often dreams of starting her own business.   8 He's now free. The judge cleared him of starting the fire.   9 He is banned from leaving the country or going near a football stadium.

| | | |
|---|---|---|
| **Try** | What did she do after her car broke down?<br>*She tried to find help.*<br><br>I heard she hasn't managed to give up smoking.<br>*She tried to give up, but found it too hard.* | What did he do to help him sleep?<br>*He tried drinking tea, taking sleeping pills, etc.*<br><br>She gets back ache. I think it's her high heels.<br>*She should try wearing flat shoes.* |
| **Go on** | Did she go to university after finishing school?<br>*Yes, she went on to study at university.*<br><br>Did you go anywhere after the restaurant?<br>*Yes, we went on (to go) to a club/bar.* | Did he stop talking after the play started?<br>*No, he went on talking.*<br><br>Did he give up gambling after he lost his house?<br>*No, he went on gambling?* |
| **Stop** | Did he speak to you? He looked like he was in a hurry?<br>*No, he didn't stop to speak to me.*<br><br>No more driving. I'm tired and I need a coffee.<br>*Let's stop to have a coffee.* | Does he still visit his grandmother now he lives in another town?<br>*No, he stopped visiting her.*<br><br>I heard she became a vegetarian five years ago.<br>*Yes, she stopped eating meat five years ago.* |
| **Remember** | Shall I remind you about your Mum's birthday?<br>*No, I always remember to call her/send her a card.*<br><br>You posted the letter, didn't you?<br>*Yes, I remembered to post it.* | Are you absolutely sure you posted the letter?<br>*Yes, I (clearly) remember posting it.*<br><br>I don't think I saw Ben at the party.<br>*I don't remember seeing him either.* |
| **Forget** | Do you sometimes leave your wallet or phone at home?<br>*Yes, I always/sometimes/never forget to take my wallet or phone.*<br><br>The boss said you didn't tell her the important news.<br>*(Oh dear) I forgot to tell her.* | You said the best day of your life was the day you met your partner.<br>*Yes, I'll never forget meeting him/her.*<br><br>So the first time you flew by plane was an incredible experience?<br>*Yes, I'll never forget flying for the first time.* |

**Bingo card one**

| | |
|---|---|
| **forget** | **try** |
| **remember** | **stop** |
| **go on** | **forget** |
| **stop** | **go on** |
| **try** | **remember** |

**Bingo card two**

| | |
|---|---|
| **go on** | **go on** |
| **remember** | **forget** |
| **stop** | **try** |
| **try** | **remember** |
| **forget** | **stop** |

| **❶** | **❷** | **❸** | **❹** | **❺** | **❻** |
|---|---|---|---|---|---|
| *Must + have + pp* | *Could + have + pp* | *Might + have + pp* | *Couldn't + have + pp* | *Can't + have + pp* | *Any modal + have + pp* |
| You hear a loud cheer from the local stadium. | Your parents are coming to see your new house but they are late. | You come across a friend you've not seen for two years. They look really thin. | A motorist pulls out in front of you and you crash into him. | You've eaten some chicken and now two hours later you feel really ill. | You see a man with his leg in plaster. |
| Your flatmate doesn't seem to be at home. | You see a couple with shopping bags running down the street. | You dog was in your garden this morning but now it isn't there. | A competitor completed a marathon running backwards dressed as a frog. | The match was cancelled but Greg still went to the stadium. | Your teenage son is looking really guilty. |
| Your neighbour has just bought a really expensive new car. He's usually broke. | You see your neighbour for the first time in a month. She looks tanned and relaxed. | You're a teacher and your worst student has given you some excellent homework. | You are a building inspector and the quality of the work in this building is terrible. | I shouted 'turn right' but he didn't, he went straight on. | You see an old man wearing lots of medals. |
| You see lots of people leaving the cinema crying. | Your colleague has just arrived for work out of breath. | Your neighbour's curtains are closed all day and you can't hear any noise from their house. | You're a teacher and your best student has just got terrible marks in the exam. | A motorist crashed his car. The road was empty at the time. | You see your teenage daughter looking really sad. |
| You meet a woman who tells you she got married in a castle. | There was a fire in your house while you were at work. | Your partner usually gets home at 6.30p.m. You hear them arrive at 6.00p.m. | There's a guest at the restaurant shouting angrily at the waiter. | The person in front of you at the cash point hits the wall angrily. The machine has just kept his card. | You notice the screen of your mobile is cracked. |

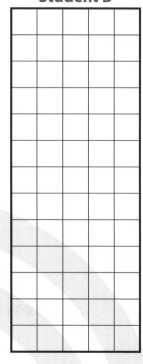

**Student A**              **Student B**

**Customers**

**Employees**

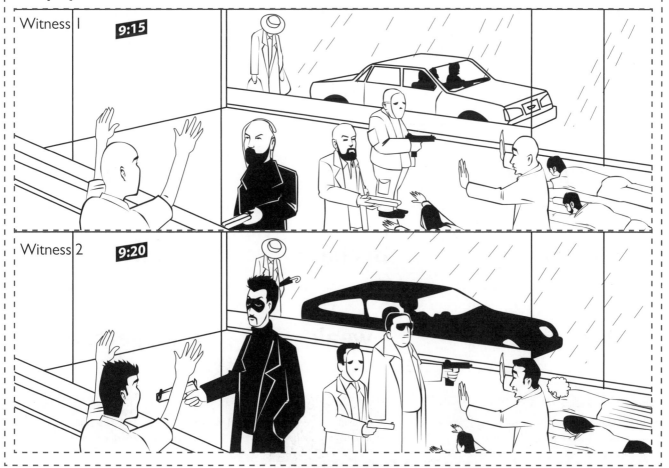

| 1 'I knew exactly how the film was going to end. It was so …' | 2 'It's about the relationship between a dying grandfather and his grandson. It's really …' | 3 'It was such a sad story. I found it very …' |
|---|---|---|
| 4 'The way that he helped his wife recover after the accident was really …' | 5 'At the end, he takes revenge by shooting everyone. It's …' | 6 'He gave an amazing performance. I thought he was absolutely …' |
| 7 'I was on the edge of my seat all the way through. It was absolutely …' | 8 'The main character is this strange old man who wears black. He's really …' | 9 'The pace was slow and not much happened. I'd describe this film as …' |
| 10 'You can't take your eyes off him. His performance was …' | 11 'The plot is really clever. You could never guess the ending. It's …' | 12 'The film was really bad. in fact I'd go so far as to say it was …' |
| 13 'It was non-stop action all the way through. I love films that are …' | 14 'He wasn't good. I'd describe his performance as a Bond villain as …' | 15 'It's just about the best film I've ever seen. It's …' |

| **predictable** | **poignant** | **moving** |
|---|---|---|
| **touching** | **chilling** | **awesome** |
| **gripping** | **creepy** | **dull** |
| **electrifying** | **brilliant** | **horrific** |
| **fast-paced** | **weak** | **unforgettable** |

**Answer sheet**

1 predictable  2 poignant/touching/moving  3 poignant/touching/moving  4 poignant/touching /moving  5 chilling
6 awesome  7 gripping  8 creepy  9 dull  10 electrifying  11 brilliant  12 horrific  13 fast-paced  14 weak
15 unforgettable

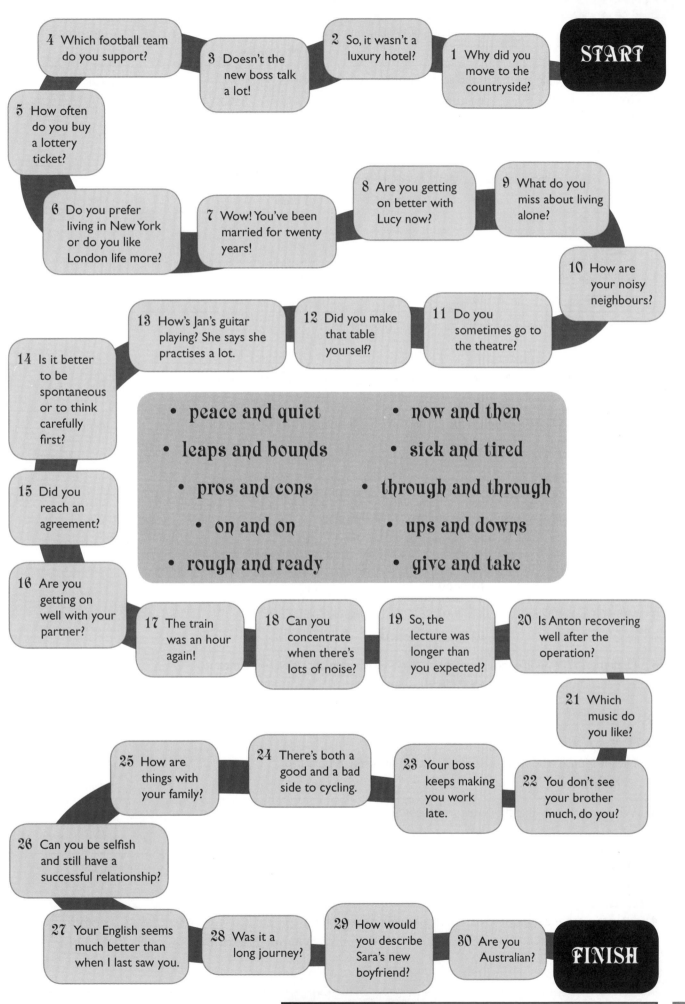

**START**

1 Why did you move to the countryside?

2 So, it wasn't a luxury hotel?

3 Doesn't the new boss talk a lot!

4 Which football team do you support?

5 How often do you buy a lottery ticket?

6 Do you prefer living in New York or do you like London life more?

7 Wow! You've been married for twenty years!

8 Are you getting on better with Lucy now?

9 What do you miss about living alone?

10 How are your noisy neighbours?

11 Do you sometimes go to the theatre?

12 Did you make that table yourself?

13 How's Jan's guitar playing? She says she practises a lot.

14 Is it better to be spontaneous or to think carefully first?

15 Did you reach an agreement?

16 Are you getting on well with your partner?

- peace and quiet
- leaps and bounds
- pros and cons
- on and on
- rough and ready
- now and then
- sick and tired
- through and through
- ups and downs
- give and take

17 The train was an hour again!

18 Can you concentrate when there's lots of noise?

19 So, the lecture was longer than you expected?

20 Is Anton recovering well after the operation?

21 Which music do you like?

22 You don't see your brother much, do you?

23 Your boss keeps making you work late.

24 There's both a good and a bad side to cycling.

25 How are things with your family?

26 Can you be selfish and still have a successful relationship?

27 Your English seems much better than when I last saw you.

28 Was it a long journey?

29 How would you describe Sara's new boyfriend?

30 Are you Australian?

**FINISH**

| | | commas |
|---|---|---|
| **I** | Ulan Bator which is in Asia is the capital of which country? a)                    b)                    **c) Mongolia** | commas |
| **2** | How many people are there who speak English as a first language? a)          **b) about 380 million**          c) | Ok |
| **3** | The marriage which lasted the longest was between a Taiwanese couple. How long did it last? **a) 86 years**          b)                    c) | Ok |
| **4** | What was Napoleon Bonaparte who was emperor of France afraid of? a)                    b)                    **c) cats** | commas |

| | | |
|---|---|---|
| **I** | Eating eggs which are 100 years old is a delicacy in which country? **a) China**          b)                    c) | Ok |
| **2** | Polar bears who live in the Arctic have what colour skin? a)          **b) black**          c) | commas |
| **3** | What is the name of the city which had the biggest population 1000 years ago? **a) Beijing**          b)                    c) | Ok |
| **4** | The Great Wall of China which the Chinese started building in 220 BC is how long? **a) 6600km**          b)                    c) | commas |

| | | |
|---|---|---|
| **I** | A Nephophobic is a person who is afraid of what things? **a) clouds**          b)                    c) | Ok |
| **2** | The man who had the most wives ever was king Mongut of Siam. How many did he have? a)          **b) 9000**          c) | Ok |
| **3** | When did the Vikings who were from Scandinavia first visit America? a)          **b) the 11th century**          c) | commas |
| **4** | Until the 1970s people thought that Kangaroo which is an aborigine word meant … a)          **b) I don't know!**          c) | comma |

| | | |
|---|---|---|
| **I** | Mickey Mouse who was created by Walt Disney used to be called? **a) Mortimer**          b)                    c) | commas |
| **2** | What was the city that Bill Gates grew up in? a)                    b)                    **c) Seattle** | Ok |
| **3** | How old was King Tutankhamen when he died? a)          **b) 18**          c) | Ok |
| **4** | How fast can the puck which is what ice-hockey players hit travel? a)                    b)                    **c) about 220kmh** | commas |

**Look at the list of statements and questions below. If possible, change them so they contain a participle clause. It is not possible in every case.**

1  In your country, is it impolite to make noise while you are eating?

2  People who were born in the last two decades would find it impossible to live without the internet.

3  It is better for companies to employ people who are experienced than employ graduates.

4  Did you always study hard when you took exams at school?

5  It is better to marry someone who you think is funny than someone rich.

6  It's depressing to see so many young people who are endangering their health by eating junk food and smoking.

7  Motorists who are still drive at seventy-five, years old should take another driving test.

8  The best nights out are the ones which are unplanned.

9  Do you listen to music while you are travelling?

10 The most beautiful places are the ones which are unchanged by mankind.

11 All the technology which has been created in the last fifteen years has not improved our lives.

12 Company employees who work from home are more productive than the ones in the office.

13 People who have children later in life make better parents.

14 When you read English, do you want to understand every word?

15 A man who holds doors open for women is old fashioned and sexist.

16 People who have dogs should pick up their dogs' mess.

17 Rail passengers who have to wait more than fifteen minutes late should not have to pay.

18 People who have been found guilty of a crime should not be allowed to vote.

19 Cars which are made in Germany are reliable but too expensive.

20 Homes which are located in the centre of cities should be cheaper for nurses, teachers and emergency service workers.

**Tour 1**

**Tour 2**

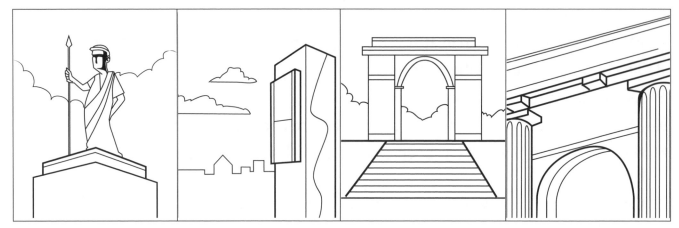

**Tour 3**

**Tour 4**

# Unit 1

## HAPPY FLATMATES

**Materials: one Student A and Student B worksheet per pair of students**

Ss work in pairs. Give each pair a copy of Student A and Student B worksheets. They have to share the information on their worksheet to name the housemates in the picture and find the two words or phrases that describe each person's personality. Student A starts by reading the first piece of information labelled 'Start'. Student B listens and looks for any information that links to it. If they have, they read it to Student A. For example, when Student A says that Sam is a *geek*, the link is Student B's information about a housemate who is *obsessed with computers*. If Student B is unable find a link with the first piece of information their partner reads, Student A can try reading out others until they do. The Ss then continue taking it in turns to read pieces of information. By sharing and matching what they have, they will gradually be able to fill in the gaps below the picture.

Encourage the Ss to read clearly and listen carefully to each other. They must not show each other their worksheets. Explain that they need to listen for words and phrases with similar meanings, e.g. *keeps to himself* and *introverted,* and use logic and their powers of deduction to complete the task.

> **Answer key**
> 1 Lucy – a good laugh, down to earth
> 2 Sam – a geek, keeps to himself
> 3 Josh, a people person, out until the early hours
> 4 Gemma – particular about the washing-up, into theatre
> 5 Sara – tight-fisted, doesn't pull her weight

## HOW DO I FEEL?

**Materials: one set of cards per group**

Ss work in groups of three or four. Cut up the cards and distribute one set per group. Ss put them face down on the table. The first student picks up a card and reads the text in **bold** to the others. They listen and have to answer the question on the card, either *How do I feel?* or *What's the feeling?* The first question requires an adjective as the answer and the second a noun. The answers are written in **bold** at the bottom of the card. The first student to give the correct answer wins the card. It is then the next student's turn. This continues until all the cards have been won. Ss need to be quick to win the card and the winner is the student with the most cards.

## GOOD COP, BAD COP

**Materials: one set of role cards per group**

Ss work in groups of three. Tell them that five valuable paintings have been stolen from a famous gallery and two detectives are going to interview the director of the gallery about the incident. Organise the students into groups of three – two are detectives and the third is the gallery director.

Explain that one of the detectives is the 'good cop' and does not want to upset the important and famous director, but the other is the 'bad cop' and doesn't care. The bad cop will lead the interview and only ask direct questions. However, in order not to upset the director, the good cop will rephrase every direct question the bad cop asks to make an indirect question, e.g. if the bad cop says *Can we see your personal emails?* then good cop will say, *We were wondering if we could see your personal emails?* The gallery director can also ask questions, e.g. *How long are you going to close the gallery?* or *Could you tell me how long you are going to close the gallery?* Distribute the role cards and give the Ss a few minutes to read them and prepare. The cops should work together and decide on the questions they are going to ask. When everyone is ready, the two cops interview the director. At the end of the activity, the cops have to say if they think the director is guilty or not.

## TALK ABOUT …

**Materials: one copy of the worksheet and a dice per group**

Ss work in groups of four. Give each group a board, enlarged to A3 if possible, a counter each and a dice. Place the counters at the **START**. The first student rolls the dice and moves the number shown. The student then has to talk to their group about the subject in the square for at least half a minute (the other Ss should keep time). If the student is successful, they remain on that square. If not, they go back to where they were. Explain that Ss are not restricted to using just the tense form in the question in their answer. On the contrary, they should use as many different tense forms as they can, e.g. for *Talk about something you've just bought.* A possible answer could begin *I bought a new phone last week. I was walking past a shop and saw that there was a special offer.* If a student lands on a FREE QUESTION square they can ask any question to another member of the group using the past simple or present perfect, e.g. *What's the funniest thing you have ever seen?* or *Did you suck your thumb as a child?* etc. During the activity, monitor for interesting ideas which students can share with the class at the end of the activity. Note any errors you hear related to the two tense forms. You can either elicit corrections for these at the end or on the spot. The winner is the first student to reach the finish.

## HOW CAN I HELP YOU?

**Materials: two role cards per student**

Ss work in pairs. Give all Student As and Student Bs their two role cards. Start by discussing Ss' experiences of telephone customer service and call centres. Focus on whether they are generally positive or negative and why. Explain that in the activity Ss will have a chance both to make and to respond to enquiries. Check the vocabulary *to clone a card, overdraft* and *overdrawn* and give the Ss time to read their role-cards and prepare what they are going to say. The role play begins with Student A phoning Student B about a power cut. Before you start, remind Ss to use the functional language from 1.3 and to always be polite. Ss continue with the second role play. At the end, discuss whether the class felt their enquiries were dealt with politely and effectively.

# Unit 2

## SCRAMBLED ISSUES
**Materials: one worksheet per pair of students**

Ss work in pairs. Give each pair a worksheet. They unscramble the social issues vocabulary and write the word or phrase in the second column. Still in pairs, students think of three ideas to help with that particular issue and write them in the spaces provided (see example on the worksheet). When they have produced as many ideas as possible, put the pairs into groups of four or six to exchange ideas and consider which they consider to be the best and most effective for each issue. The groups then report their best ideas to the whole class. Encourage the groups to challenge the ideas presented or to try to build a consensus about the best ways to deal with the issues.

> **Answer key**
> drought, divorce, homelessness, pollution, domestic violence, drunkenness and drug abuse, poverty, lack of drinking water, famine, obesity

## YOU'RE ON CAMERA
**Materials: one set of role cards per group**

Ss work in groups of four. Tell the students that they are four councillors (local government politicians) and they are responsible for governing a small town. The town has a number of problems and the possible solution to these problems could be a range of surveillance measures. Pre-teach/check *microchip* as a verb (micro-chipping dogs involves implanting a simple microchip in the dog with information about the dog and its owner). Put Ss into groups of four and distribute the role cards. They are going to have a meeting in their group of four to decide which measures, if any, they will introduce. Give them a few minutes to prepare what they are going to say and make sure they understand that although they should express and defend their views energetically, they should also be prepared to compromise in order to reach an agreement. At the end of the role-play, ask the groups to report back to the class about how they are going to deal with the problems.

## A BRIEF HISTORY OF ENERGY DRINKS
**Materials: one copy of worksheet A and worksheet B per pair of students**

Ask the class if they drink energy drinks, what brands they know and whether they think there are any health risks. Then ask the class when they think energy drinks were first made. Tell them they are going to find out more about the history of energy drinks.

Students work in pairs. Give them their worksheet. The object is to complete the gaps in their text by asking questions in the passive. For example, Student A asks '*What has Irn Bru never been marketed as?* Student B has the missing information in their text and gives the answer *'an energy drink'*. Student A writes this in the gap and then Student B asks Student A a question about the next gap. This continues until both Ss have completed all the missing information.

Before the students start the activity, give them a few minutes to prepare their questions. Make sure they understand that they must not look at each other's worksheet. At the end, discuss as a class whether or not energy drinks are dangerous and whether they should be banned.

NB: *a salaryman* is an English-sounding word for a Japanese office worker. *Genki* means healthy and full of energy.

## IT'S A PERFECT WORLD
**Material: one copy of the worksheet per group of three students**

Ss work in groups of three. Give Students A, B and C their part of the worksheet. The objective of the activity is to guess the situation in **bold** at the bottom of each box from the clues given and to make a similar present perfect simple or continuous sentence. Student A begins with the situation in the first box and reads the first clue about it, e.g. *I feel emotional and I'm crying*. Student B has the first guess. If they guess incorrectly, e.g. *You've split up with your partner*, Student C has a guess. If Student C also gets it wrong, e.g. *You've lost your dog*, then Student A reads the second clue *I love the cinema* and they continue taking it in turns to guess until one of them gets it right. It will then be Student B's turn to start, with Student C making the first guess. This continues until all the sentences in bold have been guessed. Correct guesses win a point and the winner is the student with the most points at the end. Encourage students to consider carefully whether to use present perfect simple or continuous.

## BIG ISSUES
**Materials: one copy of the board and a counter each per group of four students**

Students work in groups of four. Give each group a board, enlarged to A3 if possible, and four counters. Each student places their counter in one of the four starting positions around the board. The aim of the game is to reach the opposite side of the board. Ss can move one square at time horizontally, diagonally and vertically, but they can't move to a square which is already occupied. Pre-teach/check the vocabulary *justifiable, myth, victimless crime, terminally ill* and possibly the phrase *a country gets the government it deserves* (if a government is corrupt and brutal it is because the people are).

The first student begins by moving their counter one space onto any one of the issues in the first row. They then have to give their opinion on the issue and support it with at least two reasons and an example. The other Ss in the group decide if they have completed the task successfully, regardless of whether they agreed with the views stated, and they also have the opportunity to respond to the first student's opinion. If there is a consensus that the first student was successful, the first student moves to a new square. If not, they remain where they are. It is then the second student's turn. Encourage Ss to use the adjectives and expressions from 2.3. At the end, ask the class which issues they agreed and disagreed on most and why.

# Unit 3

## CARLO'S CAR

**Material: one copy of worksheet A and worksheet B per pair of students**

Ss work in pairs. Give them their worksheets. The objective of the activity is to put the ten sentences of the story into the correct order by reading them out to each other. Before you start, pre-teach *ultimatum*. Student A begins by reading to Student B what they think is the first line of the story (D). It is then up to Student B to find and read the second line of the story. Students take it in turns to find the lines of the story until they reach the end. Ss must not look at each other's worksheets, instead they need to listen carefully and ask each other to repeat anything which is not clear. When Ss have reached the end of the story, tell them to fold over the text of their worksheets and look at the pictures together. They then retell the story taking it in turns.

### Answer key

1 D  2 G  3 B  4 J  5 E  6 F  7 A  8 H  9 C  10 I

## TREASURE HUNT

**Materials: one set of role cards and one map per group**

Tell the Ss that you have a treasure map and they are going to take part in a treasure hunt and race to find the treasure. Organise the Ss into groups of four. Give each group a set of role cards and a treasure map, enlarged to A3 size if possible. On their role cards, Ss have pieces of information giving directions to the treasure. They have to read these to each other and decide on the correct order so they can find the treasure. There are often links between the directions and they form a logical sequence, so students must listen carefully to each other. They also need to look closely at the map itself at all times, as it shows important places and things referred to on the cards. Student A starts and reads the first card (A2) to the group, whilst the other students look at the map and their cards for links. Student C follows with (C3), the link being that Porto Nico is a big town and has an airport (and there are also no mountains to the west of Jackson Bay). No student has two consecutive cards in the sequence and Ss should agree as a group before following a direction. The directions will take them across the island to the place where the treasure is buried. The first group to mark the location of the treasure with an X on the map is the winner.

### Answer key

1 SA2   2 SC3   3 SB1   4 SD2   5 SA3   6 SD3   7 SC2
8 SB3   9 SC1  10 SB2  11 SA1  12 SD1
The treasure is on the northern island of the group of three, to the east of the palm tree.

## AM I GETTING USED TO IT?

**Materials: one copy of worksheets A, B and C per group of three students.**

Organise the students into three groups: one group of Student As, one of Student Bs and one of Student Cs. Give each individual student a worksheet, making sure that the answer section is folded over so students cannot see the answers. In the first stage of the activity, Ss work together in their groups and read the situations then complete the gaps with the correct form of *used to, would, be* or *get used to*. Tell students that the first two lines need a *used to* or *would* answer, but the third line needs a form of *be/get used to*. When students have completed the gaps, they unfold the answers and check them in their groups. Answer any questions that arise.

For the second stage of the activity, put the Ss into A, B, C groups of three. They take it in turns to read out the three sentences that they completed and the other two students have to guess the situation. Correct guesses win point and the winner is the student with the most points at the end.

## QUESTIONS OF THE FUTURE

**Materials: one copy of the board and a dice per group, a counter per student**

Students work in groups of four. Give them a board, enlarged to A3 if possible, a dice and counters (small objects such as coins can be used as counters). Students take it in turns to roll the dice and move around the board. They have to answer the questions in the squares they land on. If a student successfully answers a question according to the other students, they stay on that square. If they do not, they need to go back to the square they were on before. All the questions use future forms and the answers should usually use the same future form as the questions. However, there are some cases in which a different future form might also be acceptable e.g. The answer to *Might you live in another county one day?* could be *Definitely, I'm moving to Spain next year.* Encourage students to give details with their answers and for the other students to ask supplementary questions. The winner is the first student to reach the finish.

## THE NEW FOOTBALL

**Materials: one worksheet per group of four students**

Ss work in groups of four. Their task is to invent a new sport or game incorporating at least four of the items on the worksheet. Distribute the worksheets and check the pronunciation of any unfamiliar items in the pictures: *flippers, swing, slide, cannon, spear, pram, mallet, power-wash/hose*, etc. Ss brainstorm ideas in their groups and make notes about their decisions. They should make sure they include the name and aim of the new sport, the equipment used, the rules and procedures the players have to follow and any other important points.

When all the groups have finished developing their idea, they take it in turns to present it to the class. At the end of the presentations, Ss vote on which sport or game they like best and which one will be used in the programme. Encourage Ss to use the functional language in 3.3 when presenting their idea to the other groups, and to use mirror questions if they are unsure about anything they hear when they are listening to a presentation.

# Unit 4

## WHAT'S MY SAYING?

**Materials: one worksheet per pair of students and two pictures from the worksheet per individual student**

Students work in pairs. Distribute one worksheet per pair of students and ask them to look at the pictures and to try to remember the sayings. After you have checked the answers, give the Ss two pictures each, which they must not show to anyone, and ask them to prepare short stories or anecdotes based on the sayings in their pictures. Explain that they are going to a party where they will mingle and be able to tell their anecdotes. At the end of each story/anecdote, the student listening has to respond to the storyteller using the correct saying in a natural, conversational way, e.g.

**Student A:** *I went to Spain to last year, it's very different from my country – lots of things like the food and the weather but especially the time people eat. They eat very late, about 11p.m. This was very difficult for me. I usually eat around 6.00p.m., but I changed and started eating much later.*

**Student B:** *Ah yes that's good. When in Rome do as the Romans do!*

Student A shouldn't tell B whether or not they have guessed correctly but should listen, in turn, to B's anecdote and try to respond naturally with the correct saying. Since all the students have two anecdotes to tell, they should then exchange second anecdotes with a different partner. At the end of the activity, students try to guess which saying they thought the other students were given.

> **Answers:**
>
> 1 Every cloud has a silver lining.    2 When in Rome do as the Romans do.    3 What goes around comes around.
> 4 Where there's life there's hope.    5 Where there's smoke there's fire.    6 Nothing ventured nothing gained.
> 7 Once bitten twice shy.    8 Let's cross that bridge when we come to it.

## CHANGE IT!

**Materials: one copy of the board and verb list and one answer sheet per group**

Ss work in teams of three or five. One student has the answer sheet and acts as the referee whilst the other students play against each other using an enlarged A3 board. The competing teams take it in turns to choose a square on the board and try to reformulate the sentences using the phrasal verbs in the column on the left. If they correctly reformulate the phrase, they win that square and should initial it clearly and cross out the phrasal verb. It is then the other team's turn. If Ss don't correctly reformulate the sentence, the referee must not say what the correct answer is so both teams still have a chance to win it.

The objective of the activity is to make a line of four squares. These can be horizontal, diagonal, or vertical. The winning team is the first team to get four squares. The opposing teams must try to block each other.

## PAST CONSEQUENCES

**Materials: one copy of the worksheet per student or pair of students**

Tell Ss they are going to write a story with the title *A day to forget, a night to remember* using narrative tenses, but they are going to get some help. Ss can work in pairs or alone and are given a worksheet. Ask the Ss to read and complete the first stage of the story only, using the question on the right to guide them. They should then fold over what they have written and pass the story to the next student or pair who fill in the next stage. This continues until the story is finished. Monitor closely to make sure Ss are looking at the questions and give ideas where necessary. It is important to ensure that there isn't too much waiting. When Ss have filled in the last section of their story they can unfold it and read it. Ss must not look at what other Ss have written until then. Ss should decide which story is the funniest, most implausible etc. Look at any incorrect uses of the narrative tenses or issues about which ones to use.

## SPIRALLING REGRET

**Materials: one copy of the board and a dice per group, one counter per student**

Ss in work in groups of four. Each group has a board, enlarged to A3 if possible, a dice and a counter for each student. Ss take it turns to throw the dice and move around the board, using the cues in the boxes to express regrets and wishes, e.g. for the first box, *You missed the train and can't get home*, the student could say *I wish I'd got to the station earlier* (a regret about the past/past wish) or *I wish I was at home now* (a wish for the present). In most cases, the cue in the box relates clearly to either a past or present situation but in some cases both past and present wishes and regrets can be used (as above). Ss have the opportunity to talk about their own regrets when they land on a 'real regret you have' box. The other Ss should ask additional questions, for example, *Why do you regret doing that?* The winner is the first student to reach the end of the spiral.

## LITERARY CRITICS

**Materials: one copy of the worksheet and one set of role cards per group**

Tell Ss that they are a group of important literary critics who give an annual prize of $50,000 to the best new novel. They have read and made notes on the four shortlisted books and they are now going to meet to decide which book should win the prize. Organise the students into groups of four and give each individual the blurbs to read and one of the four role cards. Give Ss about seven minutes to understand the plots and their opinions about the books. Teach/check *twist at the end*, *torture*, *far-fetched* and any other items that you think they might find challenging. Ss then have the discussion and tell each other their opinions about the books. They should generally follow the opinion on their role card, so if it is negative they can't change it to positive. Encourage them to invent further details about the characters and scenes to make their opinions more believable. They should use *What I liked/didn't like was … or It was the … that I liked/didn't like* to talk in detail about their ideas and opinions. Each group should decide which book they are going to award the prize to. At the end, the different groups share their ideas and decide on one overall winner.

# Unit 5

## COMPOUND SNAP

**Materials: one set of cards and set of answers per group**

Ss work in small teams. Two teams compete against each other and one student is the referee. The teams have one set of cut up cards and the referee has the answers. Half the cards are compound nouns and the other half are gapped sentences that can be completed with the nouns. Ss shuffle all the cards together and distribute them equally between the two teams, so that each player has one set of cards face down in front of them. The referee has the answer card. A player from each team turns over one of their cards at the same time and places it face up on the table in a pile in front of them. When there is a matching compound noun and sentence card Ss shout *Snap!* and say the complete sentence. The referee verifies whether the answer is correct. If it is, the student wins the cards. If the student is wrong, the students carry on turning over their cards until they run out, when they shuffle them and start again. The winner is the student with the most pairs at the end.

## TALKING ADVERTISING

**Materials: one crossword A and crossword B per pair of students**

Ss work in pairs. Student A's crossword has words going across and is missing the words going down and Student B's crossword has words going down, but is missing the words going across. Ss have to complete their crosswords by asking for definitions of their missing words from the other student. They must not look each other's crossword grids. Student A starts and asks for a word, e.g. *What's one down?* Student B describes the word but must not say it. They might say: *These are things we buy. They have names we all know. Some famous ones are Coca Cola or Armani.* Student B keeps on describing until Student A guesses the word. If a student can't remember a word, they can move on and come back to it later. Ss take it in turns to ask for and give definitions until their crossword is complete.

## AHEAD OF ITS TIME

**Materials: one copy of the text per group of four students**

Show Ss a picture of a C5 and tell them it was a real product. Ask them to guess what it is, how it worked (a battery-operated electric tricycle) and whether it was successful or not. Distribute the texts and check/pre-teach *pedal, handlebar, steer* and *tricycle*. Ask Ss to read the text quickly to check their predictions. Organise the students into groups of four with two students on each team. The teams take it in turns to identify the article mistake on each line. The first team has the first guess on line one. If they are correct, they win that line and can initial the box on the right. If they are wrong, the second team can guess and try to win it. The teams take it in turns until the mistake is identified and the line is won. The second team then has the first guess with the second line. At the end, the winner is the team with the most lines.

### Answers

1 the United Kingdom  2 a handlebar  3 the driver's knees
4 The C5's  5 a driving licence  6 the media  7 the 1980s
8 serious concerns  9 low to the ground  10 cold weather
11 the motor  12 long hills  13 gentle slopes  14 millions
15 the company  16 a spectacular

## CONDITIONAL DOMINOES

**Materials: one set of cards per group**

Ss work in groups of three or four. Give out one set of cut up cards per group. Check/pre-teach *shop around, sponsor* and *endorse*. Deal out the cards. Each player has the same number of cards which they put face-up on the table in front of them. The cards contain different halves of conditional sentences. To begin, the first player puts one of their cards in the middle of the table. The next student has to add a card to make a correct conditional sentence. They can add to the beginning or the end of the sentence. If a student is unable to put down a correct card, it's the next player's turn. The winner is the first student to get rid of all their cards. When all the cards have been used, check that all the sentences are correct. Then ask the Ss to discuss the sentences and say whether or not they are true for them and/or if they agree or disagree with what they say.

## CAMPAIGN COMPETITION

**Materials: one copy of the worksheet per group**

Explain that the Ss are advertising executives and they are going to plan the launch campaign for a new energy drink. Ss work in groups of three and four and spend a few minutes reading the information on the worksheet. Check/pre-teach key vocabulary items, such as *sponsorship, endorsement, billboard, slogan, logo* and *prime-time*. Ss discuss their ideas and put together their campaign. Remind them to make notes about their decisions to help them with the presentation later. Encourage Ss to use the functional language from 5.3 when putting forward their ideas and making suggestions and to express reservations about ideas. Monitor and help them with any language they need. When the campaigns are ready, Ss present them to the rest of the class and they vote on which one is the best.

# Unit 6

## TELL THE GROUP
**Materials: one copy of the worksheet per student**

Ss have a worksheet each and work alone to complete the missing words, the first three letters of which have been given. They need to think about the correct form of the words (either verb or noun) from page 70 of the Student's Book. When they have finished, they check their answers in pairs before checking all together as a class. Then, put Ss into groups of four and give them a few minutes to collect ideas and prepare what they are going to say about the different things on the list, e.g. for the first item a student might say, *The last time I bought a gift to show my appreciation was last year. I bought my teacher some flowers at the end of my course.* When the students are ready, the discussion starts and they share their ideas. Encourage Ss to give plenty of details when speaking and to ask each other questions.

> **Answers:**
>
> 1 appreciation   2 achievement   3 pretended   4 advice
> 5 react   6 involved   7 judgement   8 obligation
> 9 impression   10 interfered   11 practice   12 preference
> 13 enjoy   14 satisfaction   15 encouragement

## COFFEE MACHINE CHAT
**Materials: one copy of the worksheet per pair of students**

Ss work in pairs. Give them their worksheet. Begin by explaining the scenario outlined at the top: Student A and B work in the same company but Student B, who is a very popular boss, is leaving the office for a better job in Spain and is going to be replaced by an unpopular colleague, Marco. Student A is talking to Student B at the coffee machine about how bad things are going to be after Student B's departure. Ss have to put the conversation in the correct order. Student A starts, Student B finds the correct response, then it's Student A's turn again and so on. Ss take it in turns until the conversation finishes. They are not allowed to look at each other's worksheets at any time. When they have finished, Ss should try to have the conversation again but this time without the prompts. They should try to still use the vocabulary in **bold**, but can invent other details and extend the conversation.

> **Answer key**
>
> 2 i   3 f   4 g   5 a   6 k   7 e   8 h   9 c   10 l   11 b   12 j   13 d

## OFF THE BEATEN TRACK
**Materials: one set of cards per group**

Ss work in groups of four. Give each person a card. The groups are adventurous travellers who are planning a trip together. Each person in the group has to research an interesting destination. Give the Ss a few minutes to read and make notes. They have to give their group as much information as possible about the destination on their card using the modals they studied on page 69. The group then vote on where they want to go. Each student should talk about:

– what they *ought/have/are supposed/need* to do and what they *don't have to* do in order to prepare for visiting this destination or in order to get around, stay safe whilst they are there, etc.

– what they *will/won't be able to* do in this destination.

– specific events in the past when certain things *had to* happen or *couldn't* happen in these destinations.

Write these points up on the board as a reference. When the preparation time is up, collect in the cards. Ss then tell their groups about the different destinations using the notes they have made. The others listen and ask further questions. Ss can invent details if necessary. Monitor and ensure that Ss are using the modals. Remind them they can use the notes on the board as prompts. At the end of the activity, ask each group which destination they want to travel to.

## FUTUROLOGIST FORUM
**Materials: one worksheet per student**

Tell Ss they are going to be futurologists – people who predict future trends in society. Distribute the worksheet and pre-teach or check any vocabulary you think might be challenging, e.g. *cashless* and *holographic*. Remind Ss that *within* in time phrases mean the same as *by*. Tell Ss to look at the predictions and questions on the worksheet. Do they think these things are likely to happen? The Ss should evaluate and respond to the predictions in the space provided using the phrases at the bottom of page 71 to help them. They also make two predictions of their own. When they have finished, put Ss into groups of four and get them to discuss their answers and opinions as well as their own predictions with the group, justifying and supporting their opinions with reasons and examples. The groups should try to agree on which predictions are *likely, possible, impossible*, etc. At the end of the lesson, the groups present their different opinions to the whole class.

## IT'S DEBATABLE
**Materials: one worksheet per student**

Give the Ss a worksheet each and explain the idea of a debate – a formal discussion of a topic. It starts with 'a motion' – something which 'the house' or the class believes. Two Ss support the motion and two oppose it. Each side argues their case for and against, starting with the side that supports the motion and then alternating speakers between the side that supports the motion and the side that opposes it. Finally, having listened to all four speakers and heard both sides of the argument, the group takes a vote to decide whether the majority is for or against the motion. Give the Ss a few minutes to read the topics on the worksheet and decide which they would most like to have a debate about. Get the class to vote on which of these will be the final topic. Working on their own, Ss then brainstorm ideas to support their views for and against the motion and write notes in the appropriate box. Monitor and help Ss with vocabulary, checking to see who supports and opposes the motion. From these, nominate stronger Ss to speak for and against it. Hold a debate, as outlined above, with the teacher as the chair. When both sides have had an equal opportunity to present their views, the class can take a vote to determine the majority view.

# Unit 7

## WHAT'S MY PROGRAMME?
**Materials: one set of cards per group**

Ss work in groups of three or four. Give each group a set of cut up cards. The cards are placed face down in the middle and the first student picks up a card. They have to elicit from the other Ss the word(s) in **bold** at the top of the card by describing it. All the words are types of TV programme. The Ss can say anything to elicit the TV programme, but they are not allowed to use the three bullet-pointed words below it in their descriptions, or any other related forms of the these words, e.g. if *investigate* is one of the words on the card, Ss are not allowed to use words like *investigation* or *investigator* in their definitions either. The first student to guess the TV programme being described wins the card. The winner is the student with the most cards at the end.

## PHRASAL VERB REFORMULATION
**Materials: one copy of worksheet A and worksheet B per pair of students**

Ss work in pairs. Give them Student A and Student B worksheets. They take it in turns to read each other their sentences, which do not contain a phrasal verb. These are the ones written in **bold**. The student who is listening has to reformulate the sentence in a natural conversational way using one of the phrasal verbs in the grid at the top of their worksheet, e.g. if Student A reads the first sentence in **bold** (*I can't stand living in this city any longer.*) Student B looks for a suitable phrasal verb and replies with something like *Oh dear, you can't put up with living in this city any longer*. Student A can check to see if Student B is right by looking at the phrasal-verb sentence under the sentence in bold. If Student B is correct, it's Student B's turn to read a sentence to Student A for reformulation and Student B can cross off *put up with* from the grid.

The phrasal verbs are only used once. If a student doesn't reformulate correctly, Ss can go back to the sentence later when there are fewer phrasal verb options.

## QUANTIFIER DICE
**Materials: one board and a dice per group of students**

Ss work in groups of three. Give each group one board and a dice. There are six games on each board, one in each vertical column and the groups should play through all six games to decide the winner, starting with game one. To play, the first student rolls the dice, e.g. four, and looks at the quantifier in square four, game one, which is *a great deal of*. The student then has to make a sentence with this and one of the topics in the box at the bottom of the column for game one, e.g. *Wikipedia contains a great deal of information*. If the other Ss agree that this is correct, the student wins the square and initials it. The topic is crossed off and can't be used again. The game continues with the next student rolling the dice and trying to win another square in game one by making a sentence combining the quantifier in the square with an available topic. If a student rolls a number for a square already won, it's the next student's turn. It will get more difficult to win squares as the game progresses. When all six squares in game one have been won, the next game starts. The overall winner is the student who wins the most games.

## AWOL
**Materials: one set of role cards per pair of students**

Explain to Ss that one of them is the assistant of a record company executive and the other is the manager of one of the label's biggest bands, AWOL. Explain the situation as outlined on the role cards and that the Ss are going to have a meeting to resolve the problem. Pre-teach or check *rehab* and *sue*. Emphasise that the situation is delicate as both parties need each other and therefore both the band manager and the record company executive are going to be polite and diplomatic. Consequently, they are more likely to backshift the tenses of what they say, however, there are situations where they might not do this because the situation is still current. Ss work in pairs and have a role card each. They spend a few minutes deciding what they are going to say and how they are going to report what they have been told. The discussion can then begin. Encourage Ss to reach a compromise. At the end Ss report to the class what they have decided to do.

## HOLD THE FRONT PAGE
**Materials: one copy of the worksheet per group of three students**

Tell Ss they are journalists for the same paper and they want their story on the front page. Organise the Ss into groups of three and give each student two different news stories from the worksheet. Tell them to choose one story to present to their group as the story that should go on the front page. Give them a few minutes to read and prepare before collecting the stories in again. Ss now have to sell their story to the group using as much emphasis as possible to make it sound dramatic and interesting. To do this, they should use ways of adding emphasis from page 86, e.g. *The amazing thing is …* Encourage the Ss who are listening to use some of the vocabulary from *Learn to make guesses* on page 87 when responding to what is being said, for example, *That's surely not possible*. Remind Ss of these phrases by putting them on the board first. When Ss have presented their stories, the group discusses which one will interest their readers the most and use it for the front page. They should also decide what the headline will be.

# Unit 8

## COLLOCATION DILEMMAS
**Materials: three situations cards and one lie and two truth cards per group**

Start by asking how you tell when someone is lying and ask the Ss if they think they are good at lying. Explain that the activity is about lying convincingly and also being able to identify a liar. Ss work in groups of three and are given three situation cards and one lie and two truth cards per group. The students with truth cards have to tell the truth, and the students with lie cards have to lie. Give the groups time to read their situation cards and make sure everyone understands the dilemmas. The first group starts by explaining their first dilemma to the other groups. The individuals in the other groups take it turns to briefly say what they would do and why, lying or telling the truth according to their cards. The students should naturally use the collocations from 8.1 when they do this since they are prompted to by the dilemma cards. When everyone has answered, the first group have to identify the liar in each of the other groups. They get a point for every one correctly identified. It is then the next group's turn to explain a dilemma. At this point everyone should exchange their lie and truth cards so the next group doesn't know who the liars are.

## TIME LINES
**Materials: one set of role cards per pair of students**

Ss work in pairs. Give them their role card. There are two short conversations relating to the two situations described on each card. However, the lines of the conversation are mixed up. Ss have to put the lines into the correct order by reading them to each other.

Ss have alternate lines. Student A starts for the first conversation and Student B for the second. There are seven lines in each conversation and students should number them as they go along. Students must not show their lines to their partner or look at their partner's lines. When students have finished, they can swap roles, turn over their handouts and have the conversations again, trying to use all the phrases and idioms but also adding extra details.

> **Answer key**
> **Situation 1 –** f, h, g, m, a, i, b
> **Situation 2 –** j, e, n, c, k, d, l

## CONDITIONAL FOX AND HOUNDS
**Materials: one copy of the board per group and a counter per student**

Ss work in groups of three. Give each group a board, enlarged to A3 if possible and a counter each. Two of the Ss are hounds and the other student is a fox. The hounds have to catch the fox by landing on the same diamond on the board. The game begins with the Ss placing their counters on their starting diamond. Both fox and hounds can only move diagonally, one diamond at a time. The fox starts and moves one space onto any one of the four diamonds next to the start. Subsequently, in order to move from one diamond to the next, both the fox and the hounds have to make conditional sentences using the picture in the diamond they are in. Depending on the shade of the diamond, the sentence has to be either in the past (black), in the present (white) or both past and present (grey). For example, if the fox lands on the picture of the bed in the grey diamond, they could say *If I hadn't come to school this morning, I'd still be in bed now.* (past clause followed by present). If they move to the picture of the police car on the black diamond, they could say *If I'd seen the police car, I would have stopped.* (two past clauses), etc. If the other Ss agree the sentence is correct, the student can stay on the diamond they have moved to. If not, the student has to go back to where they were. The two hounds chase the fox and try to catch it. Ss can then change roles and one of the hounds can become the fox.

## BAD BEHAVIOUR
**Materials: one set of cards per group**

Ss work in groups of three or four. Give each group a set of cut up cards. Explain to Ss that they are the parents of a fifteen-year-old boy who is having serious behaviour problems at school and they are going to make a series of decisions to help him. Pre-teach or check *golf clubs, boarding school, private school, expelled from school* and *suspended from school*. Tell Ss to write the numbers of the cards in marker pen on the back and lay the cards out in order, face down in five rows. Do the first card together as a class. Ss turn over card one and one student reads the situation. Ss must first decide what the correct form of the verb is – infinitive without *to*, infinitive with *to* or an *-ing* form and complete the options on the card. They can then decide which of the given options to follow. Point out that each option has a number after it. Explain that this is the number of the next card they should turn over as the cards are all linked in some way to create a decision maze. They turn over the number of the card indicated at the end of the option (and put back and turn over the card they have just read). Ss continue doing this, completing verb forms and making group decisions until they reach the end of the maze.

At the end of the activity Ss can discuss which decisions were bad and which were good.

> **Answers:**
> 1 consider sending, had better improve   2 will never forgive
> 3 playing guitar, attending art classes   4 arrange for him to see, interested in doing   5 despite you not being, doesn't enjoy travelling   6 wants to play, it's better to sell
> 7 intend to continue   8 see him behave, expect him to get
> 9 prepared to take, doesn't have to travel   10 promise not to send   11 can't afford to spend   12 good at playing, used to play   13 try to get, might like   14 like painting, enjoys being able   15 complaining about being, to make
> 16 had to pay   17 suggest doing, spending more time doing
> 18 is like being, make him stay   19 accused of attacking
> 20 continues to play/playing, ends up playing

## DON'T TAKE THIS THE WRONG WAY
**Materials: one role card per student**

Tell Ss that they are studying or working at the International Oxford City School of English. The school has recently had some problems and some dissatisfied Ss have made an appointment see the Directors to discuss the situation.
Ss work in groups of four to six. In each group there needs to be a Director and an Assistant Director – they will have the same role card. The rest of the group are complaining Ss and also have the same card. Give the Ss a few minutes to read their role and plan what they are going to say. Explain that the Ss need to be diplomatic, not confrontational and remind them to use the functional language on pages 98 and 99 for handling an awkward situation and softening a message.

When Ss are ready, they have the meeting. Both sides have a number of points they want to make, but also need to reach a solution which they are happy with. At the end of the discussion, the class compares what they have agreed in their groups.

# Unit 9

## WHAT'S MY PUNISHMENT?
**Materials: one set of cards per group**

Tell the students that the activity involves deciding the appropriate punishments for different types of crime. Revise the different types of punishments and put these up on the board: *a caution (warning), a fine, a ban, community service, imprisonment, a suspended sentence, capital punishment* (though not for these crimes!).

Put the Ss into groups of six. Give each student two crime cards and a few minutes to think about why and in what circumstances they committed those two crimes. When they are ready, the Ss take it in turns to confess one of their crimes to the group. They should add details and give a justification or reason why they did it. The other Ss listen and ask further questions. They then discuss what the appropriate punishment is. Finally, if everyone can come to an agreement, the group sentences the student. It is then the next student's turn to confess. When everyone has confessed their first crime, they confess their second. At the end, compare the punishments different groups gave for the same crime. Do Ss think any of the punishments are especially harsh/severe or too lenient?

## NOUGHTS AND CROSSES
**Materials: one copy of the grid and one answer key per group of three**

Check Ss knowledge of the rules of noughts and crosses and demonstrate how to play on the board if necessary. Ss work in groups of three and have one grid, enlarged to A3 if possible, and a copy of the answers. There are three games and two Ss play each other in a game with the third student acting as referee. The students should change referee after every game. The players take it in turns to reformulate the sentences in the grid using the appropriate verb from the box at the bottom with the correct dependent preposition. If the sentence in the grid has the letter 'P' in brackets next to it, this indicates that the reformulated sentence has to be passive. All the other sentences are active. The referee checks and confirms the answers (looking at the answers for the game in progress only). If the answer is not correct, the referee must not reveal what the correct answer is so the box can still be won fairly. If the sentence is correct, the student crosses out the verb used and draws either a nought or a cross the grid. The object of the game is to get either three noughts or crosses in a horizontal, diagonal or vertical line. When the game is finished, Ss can look at any boxes which were not won and guess what the answers are. They then swap roles and start the second game.

## VERB FORM BINGO
**Material: one prompt sheet and one set of bingo cards per group**

The Ss work in groups of three or five. There is one question master and two teams of either one or two Ss. The question master has the large prompt sheet with the example sentences and the teams have a bingo card each. The first team starts by calling out one of the verbs on their bingo card, e.g. *stop*. The question master then reads one of the prompts for that verb, e.g. *I heard she became a vegetarian five years ago.* The team has to produce a sentence with the same meaning using the verb on the bingo card with the correct form after it (infinitive or -ing), e.g. *She stopped eating meat five years ago.* If the answer

uses the correct form and is similar in meaning to the prompt (it doesn't have to have exactly the same wording) the team can cross out that word on their bingo card and it is the other team's turn. If the answer is wrong, the team can't cross out the verb and may be given the same prompt or a different one later by the question master. The winner is the first team to cross out all their words. When they do this they shout 'Bingo!'

## DEDUCTION BLOCKS
**Materials: one copy of the board and grids and a dice per group**

Students work in groups of four, with two on each team. Enlarge the board and grids to A3 if possible. The first team begins play by rolling the dice. Each number on the dice corresponds to a modal verb and also to a pattern, as shown at the top of the board, e.g. I = must + have + pp and the pattern is '□'. The team has to choose a situation from the boxes under the modal (it can be any box in the column) and make a deduction using that modal. For example, for the situation in the first box *You hear a loud cheer from the local stadium,* the deduction might be *The home team must have scored a goal.* If the other team agree the deduction is correct, the first team has 'won' the pattern and can draw it in their grid. The situation is crossed out on the board and cannot be used again. It is then the other team's turn to play. To win the game, the teams need to use patterns they win to fill in their grid. The idea is to make horizontal lines without gaps. Each pattern has to 'fall' to the bottom of the grid or until it lands on top of another part of a pattern. (the rules are similar to Tetras-type computer games). Each complete line wins a point and the winner is the team with the most complete lines at the end of the game.

## TELL ME WHAT YOU SAW
**Materials: one set of cards per group**

Tell Ss they have all witnessed a bank robbery and are going to discuss what they saw in order to help the police catch the robbers. They will also decide who the most reliable witness is. Ss work in groups of four: two Ss are bank customers and two are bank employees. Distribute the cards and give Ss a few minutes to look at their card and think about how they are going to describe what they saw. Elicit ideas for the kinds of questions it might be useful to ask the witness of a crime e.g. the time, what exactly happened in what order, description of people, anything unusual noticed, etc and put ideas up on the board. The bank employees and the bank customers then take it in turns to take to interview each other about what they saw. There are two objectives: the first is to build up a picture of events and to see whether the Ss reach the conclusion that the robbery was an inside job (the cashier is winking to one of the robbers who appears to be his brother/close relative). The second is for Ss to decide who the most reliable witness was. While Ss are interviewing each other, they need to identify witness descriptions that are the same. If two witnesses describe something identically, it means the witness account is reliable. At the end, Ss look at each other's pictures and can see, if they have not already guessed, that it was an inside job.

# Unit 10

## I WOULDN'T RECOMMEND IT!
**Materials: one set of cards and an answer sheet per group**

Explain to Ss that they are going to read some comments about films and that they will have to complete them with the appropriate adjective. Ss work in groups of four and have one set of cards and answer sheet. The cards are divided into two piles – sentences and adjectives – and spread out, face down. The Ss take turns to try and turn over matching pairs of a sentence card and an adjective card. If the student turns up a matching pair, they win the cards and have another turn. If the pair doesn't match they simply turn the cards back over in the same position and it's the next student's turn. The answer sheet should be kept face down on the table and used to check answers. With some sentences there is more than one correct answer, but only the options given on the answer sheet can be accepted since they are the strongest collocations or the most likely answers. The winner is the student with the most pairs of cards at the end.

## TWO-PART PHRASE GAME
**Materials: one copy of the board and a dice per group**

Ss work in groups of three. Give each group a board, enlarged to A3 size if possible, a dice and a counter each. The Ss all place their counters on the 'Start' square. The first student rolls the dice and moves the number of places shown. They have to respond to the prompt in the square they land on using one of the two-part phrases listed on the board, e.g. *Why did you move to the countryside?* could be met with the response *Because I wanted peace and quiet* or *Because I was sick and tired of living in a noisy city*. If the student gives an appropriate response, they can stay in that square. If not, they have to go back to where they were before. The other Ss decide whether the response is possible or not, referring to the teacher if there are disputes. If two students land on the same square, they can't give exactly the same response – the second student has to find something different to say with a two-part phrase. The first student to reach the 'Finish' square is the winner.

## RELATIVE CLAUSE QUIZ
**Materials: one card per group**

Ss work in four groups. Give each group a set of cards, but make sure that the final column is folded over. Ss look at the questions and decide if the relative clause in the question is defining or non-defining. If it is a non-defining clause, then they should add the necessary commas. After completing all five sentences, Ss can unfold the final column to check their answers. They then work with their group to think of two incorrect answers for each of the five questions and write these onto the card. Explain that they should make these as believable as possible as later they are going to use them for a quiz. When all the groups are ready, the quiz starts and the groups take it in turns to read questions to the other groups. The other teams have to guess which of the three given alternatives is the correct answer. A correct guess wins a point. Keep score and the team with the most points at the end is the winner.

## CHANGE AND DISCUSS
**Materials: one worksheet per pair of students**

Ss work in pairs. Give each pair a worksheet. For the first stage of the activity, Ss have to change the statements or questions so that they contain a participle clause, e.g. *In your country, is it impolite to make noise while you are eating?* can become *In your country, is it impolite to make noise while eating?* In some cases, the statement can't be changed and in most cases the change involves removing the relative pronoun. Check the answers with the class. Then put Ss into groups of four or five to discuss the statements and questions. Monitor and listen for the more interesting ideas or controversial opinions. At the end ask Ss to share these with the other groups.

### Answer key

1 while eating   2 People born   3 can't be changed
4 when taking exams   5 can't be changed, but 'who' can be omitted   6 people endangering   7 Motorists still driving
8 the ones unplanned   9 while travelling?   10 the ones unchanged   11 All the technology created
12 Company employees working   13 People having
14 When reading English   15 A man holding   16 can't be changed   17 Rail passengers having to   18 People found guilty   19 Cars made   20 Homes located

## TOP TOURS
**Materials: one set of tours per group of four**

Ss work in groups of four. Give each Student in the group a tour. Tell them that they are tour guides who work on an open-top double-decker bus for a company called Top Tours and they are going to prepare a tour in an imaginary city. The tourist bus will visit the places on each tour in the order shown on the tour cards and the Ss need to prepare what they are going to say for each place. Tell them to invent names for the places and buildings and facts and stories about them. Make sure you give them plenty of time to prepare this information and make notes. Then, arrange chairs into a row, like the seats on a bus, and the Ss take it in turns to be the tour guide and stand at front to give their tour, showing the 'tourists' the picture of the places as they talk about them. The tourists have to ask questions about what they are being shown including at least one question about dimensions, e.g. *What is the height of the tower?* At the end of activity ask Ss which tour they enjoyed the most and what was the most interesting thing they saw.

# Tests index

## LISTENING

**1** ▶ 43 **Listen to six speakers. Are the statements true (T) or false (F)?**

1  The woman has always enjoyed dancing.                        _F_

2  The man gets on well with his flatmate.             ____

3  The woman wishes she hadn't turned down a
   good job overseas.                                 ____

4  The woman enjoys contemporary novels.              ____

5  The man prefers independent travel.                ____

6  The woman now uses her mobile phone regularly.     ____

| | 10 |

**2** ▶ 44 **What are they talking about? Listen and tick the correct answer: a), b) or c).**

1  a) website forum ✓
   b) manga ____
   c) e-book ____

2  a) pollution ____
   b) drought ____
   c) famine ____

3  a) speed cameras ____
   b) phone cameras ____
   c) CCTV cameras ____

4  a) a geek ____
   b) a people person ____
   c) a good laugh ____

5  a) an advertising slogan ____
   b) an advertising jingle ____
   c) an advertising campaign ____

6  a) being frustrated ____
   b) being adventurous ____
   c) being anxious ____

| | 10 |

## PRONUNCIATION

**3** ▶ 45 **Listen and underline the stressed syllables in sentences 1–6.**

1  How ___long___ have you been ___wor___king
   ___here___ ?

2  What've you been doing? You look exhausted!

3  Their photos might be sent to the newspapers.

4  Dan was feeling sad because his holiday was coming to an
   end.

5  If only I hadn't refused to help.

6  I'm not a big fan of autobiographies.

| | 5 |

## GRAMMAR AND VOCABULARY

**4** **Underline the correct alternative.**

1  I'm very particular ___about___ / *for* hygiene.

2  I've really got *over* / *into* salsa dancing.

3  We were brought *on* / *up* in a village.

4  I have finished my report. Now I can hand *over* / *up* the
   project to my colleague.

5  I take care *for* / *of* her when she's ill.

6  The Grants turned *up* / *in* late as usual so they missed the
   meal.

7  I always put *off* / *on* filling in my tax return until the very
   last minute.

8  We'll have to take *over* / *on* more staff if we want to
   expand.

9  Dan lives *on* / *in* the edge of a forest.

10 *At* / *With* hindsight I'd have done a lot of things very
   differently.

11 Let's cross that bridge when we come *to* / *over* it.

| | 5 |

**5** **Complete the sentences. Use the correct form of the word in capitals.**

1  Stephen's _generosity_ is almost too much sometimes.
   GENEROUS

2  His behaviour at the party was totally _____.
   OUTRAGE

3  Rising unemployment can result in more problems with
   _____. HOME

4  I could see John's _____ as he heard that he'd come
   second. DISAPPOINT

5  The internet has _____ the way we communicate.
   REVOLUTION

6  '_____ guaranteed', that's what it says on the packet!
   SATISFY

| | 5 |

**6** **Complete the text with one word in each gap.**

I've never been interested ¹ _in_ having the latest
gadgets, but Mark is just ² _____ opposite. He's a
³ _____ of a geek and has recently ⁴ _____ to
playing the *Warcraft* game with all his online friends.
He doesn't take ⁵ _____ notice of me. He disappears
for ⁶ _____ on end and only comes downstairs to
eat! I'll have to get used to ⁷ _____ more time on
my own, but I could kick ⁸ _____ for having bought
him ⁹ _____ new laptop for his birthday. Mind you,
I've taken ¹⁰ _____ ballroom dancing and have met
lots of 'real' people so I ¹¹ _____ you could say that
every cloud has a silver lining.

| | 5 |

**7** Correct <u>two</u> mistakes in each sentence.

1  I'm ___*very*___ exhausted after all ___*an*___ excitement of today.
   ___*absolutely*___             ___*the*___

2  The news last night were extremely disturbed.
   _____      _____

3  Paul was never pulled his heaviness around the house.
   _____      _____

4  Let's build that bridge when we get to it.
   _____      _____

5  I would pay for the meal as often as you make the reservation.
   _____      _____

6  Tony Blair had written about his time as Prime Minister in his biography.
   _____      _____

| | 5 |
|---|---|

**8** Choose the correct answer: a), b), c) or d).

1  Pay attention __*c*__ this announcement.
   a) on      b) for      (c) to      d) at

2  The concert was called off because too few tickets ____ sold beforehand.
   a) had been      b) have been
   c) were being      d) are

3  ____ goes around comes around.
   a) With      b) Why      c) Which      d) What

4  Chris and Ken have recently ____ up a web design company.
   a) got      b) put      c) set      d) turned

5  ____ calling is an invasion of privacy in my opinion.
   a) Cool      b) Cold      c) Warm      d) Hot

6  Simon is really ____-fisted and never pays for anything when we go out.
   a) tight      b) hard      c) light      d) tough

7  Mark always gets to work late ____ he leaves before the rush hour begins.
   a) as long as    b) providing   c) if      d) unless

8  The train is my favourite ____ of transport.
   a) mean      b) modes      c) means      d) way

9  After graduating Jo went ____ to do an MA.
   a) up      b) on      c) over      d) in

10 I really don't think Maria ____ go travelling next year.
   a) will      b) might      c) is going      d) is likely

11 We ____ live in a small cottage by the sea before we moved to the city.
   a) would           b) were used to
   c) got used to     d) used to

| | 5 |
|---|---|

**9** Complete the second sentence so that it means the same as the first. Use the word in capitals.

1  Peter ignored the crowds of reporters outside his house. TOOK
   *Peter took no notice of the crowds of reporters outside his*
   *house* _____ .

2  I've been working for five years. AGO
   I _____ .

3  When will the current director resign? STEP
   When _____ ?

4  Judy doesn't mix much with others. HERSELF
   Judy _____ .

5  There isn't any more milk. RUN
   We've _____ .

6  I'll never recover from the death of my dog. OVER
   I'll never _____ .

| | 5 |
|---|---|

**10** Complete the words.

1  If o__*n*__ __*l*__ __*y*__ I hadn't said anything!

2  It's ten kilometres to town as the c _ _ _ flies.

3  I really enjoy reading b _ _ _ _ _ _ _ _ _ of the old Hollywood stars.

4  Ben's having s _ _ _ _ _ thoughts about applying for promotion as he's not sure about his new boss.

5  Where there's life, there's h _ _ _.

6  I've never been able to make out the l _ _ _ _ _ of most heavy metal songs.

7  Tokyo is an incredibly d _ _ _ _ _ _ populated city.

8  Before you start messing around with your new keyboard, I think you should read the m _ _ _ _ _.

9  The main d _ _ _ _ _ _ _ to working from home is the sense of isolation which can be quite depressing.

10 It's a p _ _ _ you can't make it this evening, but hopefully we'll get together soon.

11 Everyone is praying for rain after the longest d _ _ _ _ _ _ in living memory.

| | 5 |
|---|---|

## READING

**11** Match gaps 1–6 in the text with a)–g). There is one extra sentence you do not need.

---

Hi Annie

Thanks so much for your newsy email – I'm glad you're enjoying your new job. I know how you were rather dreading it, but I think it's always hard to start again especially when you have to move as well. And what about accommodation – did you decide to find something on your own or are you sharing? ¹ _c_

Quite a lot's happened here as well since I last wrote to you. I finally moved last month. You know I'd been looking to move out of the city centre, well, I found a lovely little house half way between where I had been living and the coast. ² ____ And dark too as there are no street lights – so you can see the stars. I haven't quite got used to it yet, having always been a city girl!

Everyone has been very friendly though. You know, before I moved everyone was saying that I was crazy because villagers tend to keep themselves to themselves and don't welcome outsiders, but I can't tell you how kind everyone has been. ³ ____ I'm living in a terraced house so have neighbours on either side. Both sets are friendly, but not too friendly, if you know what I mean. In any case, it's certainly good to know that there are people there if I need help.

⁴ ____ You know what it's like in the city – everyone's in a rush all the time and it's hard not to join in somehow. Here, however, everything is much slower. I really like it. It usually takes me an hour or so to go to the post office by the time I've stopped a few times to chat to people!

Things are going well on the work front as well. I wasn't sure how this would work out at first. My boss was happy to let me work from home so that's what I'm doing at the moment. ⁵ ____ I bet some of my colleagues think I'm not really doing anything down here but in fact, I think I get far more done at home as I'm not constantly being disturbed by colleagues. It's amazing how much you can get through in an hour when there's no one else there.

It's early days yet I know, but I really do feel very happy and settled here. Long may it last! ⁶ ____ You can give me some tips on the garden. It's not very big but there's enough room for a small vegetable patch.

Let me know how you're getting on. And send me some photos if you get the chance. I want to see what your new haircut looks like!

Love

Hannah x

---

a) I still have to go into the office once a week for meetings but it's a good balance (and a chance to catch up on office gossip!).

b) It's been a very stressful time for me recently with all the problems at work and problems with my health.

c) ~~I guess it must be quite expensive if you want to be in town so you might not have much choice.~~

d) Of course I was the hot topic of conversation for the first week or so but I guess that's to be expected in a small community, so I didn't feel bad about it.

e) I hope you can get some time off soon to come and visit as I know you'll love it too, and it will do you good.

f) The hardest thing for me to adjust to has been the change of pace in life here – I've found it difficult to slow down.

g) It's on the edge of the village so it's really peaceful and very quiet, especially at night.

|  | 10 |
|---|---|

## SPEAKING

**12** Rewrite the sentences using the prompts in brackets.

1 Where's the nearest bank?
(Could / tell)
_Could you tell me where the nearest bank is_ ?

2 Help me with my luggage.
(Would / mind)
_____ ?

3 Send me another copy of the latest contract.
(I / grateful)
_____ .

4 Tell me about the council's plans for the city centre.
(like / enquire)
_____ .

5 When did the language courses for foreign students start?
(Can / tell)
_____ .

6 Can I make a reservation for this evening?
(wondering / possible)
_____ .

|  | 5 |
|---|---|

**13** Complete the conversation with the words in the box.

| convinced | point | ~~favour~~ | suppose | sure | way |

A: I'm all in ¹ _favour_ of lowering the voting age.

B: Hmm, I'm not so ²_____. After all, a lot of teenagers are quite immature, aren't they?

A: You've got a ³_____ there, but only those who are really interested would bother to vote.

B: I ⁴_____ so, but how would you encourage them?

A: Well, the ⁵_____ I see it, kids need to learn about politics and current affairs at school.

B: I'm still not ⁶_____, but why don't we see what Jan thinks?

☐ 5

**14** Put the words into the correct order to make sentences.

1 into / science / John / really / fiction / isn't
   _John really isn't into science fiction_____.

2 I'm / short / of / big / a / stories / fan
   _____

3 stand / I / punctuation / of / couldn't / lack / the
   _____

4 thing / the / writing / The / love / his / I / about / is / humour
   _____

5 I / What / their / main / was / characters / liked / the / about / relationship
   _____

6 couldn't / I / into / mood / get / the / just / right
   _____

☐ 5

## WRITING

**15** Underline the mistakes using the correction code. Then write the corrections.

1 (sp) Dad is such an _embarrasment_ on the dance floor.
   _embarrassment_

2 (p) If you knew you were going to be late why didn't you call?
   _____

3 (wo) I feel as though I'll never get this cold over.
   _____

4 (ww) I thought the documentary was really interested.
   _____

5 (v) We lived in the same house since 2005.
   _____

6 (gr) I'll never get used to drive on the left.
   _____

☐ 5

**16** You have just started a new job in a new town. Write an informal email to tell your friends how everything is going. Write 140–180 words.

_____
_____
_____
_____
_____
_____
_____
_____
_____
_____
_____
_____
_____
_____
_____
_____
_____
_____
_____
_____
_____
_____
_____
_____
_____
_____
_____
_____
_____
_____
_____
_____
_____
_____
_____

☐ 10

| Total: | 100 |

## LISTENING

**1** ▶ **43 Listen to six speakers. Are the statements true (T) or false (F)?**

1   The woman has always enjoyed dancing.          _F_
2   The man's flatmate is quite reserved.          ___
3   The woman wishes she hadn't stayed in Australia.   ___
4   The woman has read Jane Eyre several times.     ___
5   The man prefers organised holidays.            ___
6   The woman now uses her mobile phone all the time. ___

| | 10 |

**2** ▶ **44 What are they talking about? Listen and tick the correct answer: a), b) or c).**

1   a)  website forum  ✓
    b)  manga ____
    c)  e-book ____
2   a)  pollution ____
    b)  famine ____
    c)  drought ____
3   a)  CCTV cameras ____
    b)  phone cameras ____
    c)  speed cameras ____
4   a)  a people person ____
    b)  a geek ____
    c)  a good laugh ____
5   a)  an advertising campaign ____
    b)  an advertising slogan ____
    c)  an advertising jingle ____
6   a)  being adventurous ____
    b)  being frustrated ____
    c)  being anxious ____

| | 10 |

## PRONUNCIATION

**3** ▶ **45 Listen and underline the stressed syllables in sentences 1–6.**

1   How __long__ have you been ____wor____king __here__?
2   What've you been doing? You look exhausted!
3   Their photos might be sent to the newspapers.
4   Dan was feeling sad because his holiday was coming to an end.
5   If only I hadn't refused to help.
6   I'm not a big fan of autobiographies.

| | 5 |

## GRAMMAR AND VOCABULARY

**4   Underline the correct alternative.**

1   I'm very particular ___about___ / *for* hygiene.
2   Jack never got *into* / *over* technology.
3   I grew *on* / *up* in a small village.
4   Martin thanked Lucy *on* / *for* her interesting presentation.
5   I looked *for* / *after* her when she was ill.
6   I always put *off* / *on* filling in my tax return until the very last minute.
7   We'll have to take *over* / *on* more staff soon.
8   *At* / *With* hindsight I'd have done a lot of things very differently.
9   I'll cross that bridge when I come *to* / *over* it.
10  Our neighbours turned *up* / *in* late as usual so they missed the speech.
11  Dan lives *on* / *in* the edge of an estate.

| | 5 |

**5   Complete the sentences. Use the correct form of the word in capitals.**

1   Stephen's _generosity_ is almost too much sometimes. GENEROUS
2   I could see the _____ in his face.  DISAPPOINT
3   Ian's _____ at meetings makes me feel very uncomfortable.  AWKWARD
4   Rising unemployment can result in more problems with _____.  HOME
5   '_____ guaranteed', that's what it says on the packet! SATISFY
6   The mobile phone has _____ the way we communicate.  REVOLUTION

| | 5 |

**6   Complete the text with one word in each gap.**

I've never been interested ¹_in_ having ²_____ latest gadgets, but Mark is just the opposite. He's ³_____ bit of a geek and ⁴_____ recently taken to playing the *Warcraft* game with his online friends. He doesn't ⁵_____ any notice of me. He disappears for hours ⁶_____ end and only comes downstairs to eat! I'll have to ⁷_____ used to spending more time ⁸_____ my own, but I could kick myself ⁹_____ having bought him a new laptop for his birthday. I've taken ¹⁰_____ salsa dancing and I've met lots of 'real' people, so you could ¹¹_____ every cloud has a silver lining.

| | 5 |

## 7 Correct two mistakes in each sentence.

1 I'm _____very_____ exhausted after all _an_ excitement of
today.
  _absolutely_          _the_

2 We would live in an old house at close proximity to a
lake.
_____          _____

3 Let's build that bridge when we get to it.
_____          _____

4 Paul was never pulled his heaviness around the house.
He's just too lazy.
_____          _____

5 I won't pay for the meal as often as you make the
reservation.
_____          _____

6 Tony Blair has been written about his time as Prime
Minister in his biography.
_____          _____

[    | 5 ]

## 8 Choose the correct answer: a), b), c) or d).

1 Pay attention _c_ this announcement.
  a) on        b) for        c) to        d) at

2 The concert was called off because ____ tickets had been
sold beforehand.
  a) a few      b) too few    c) many      d) little

3 ____ calling is an invasion of privacy in my opinion.
  a) Cool       b) Cold       c) Warm      d) Hot

4 After passing his test, Tom went ____ to apply for another
job.
  a) up         b) on         c) over      d) in

5 This is my favourite ____ of transport.
  a) means      b) modes      c) mean      d) way

6 ____ goes around comes around.
  a) With       b) Why        c) Which     d) What

7 I don't think Maria ____ go travelling next year.
  a) will       b) might      c) is going  d) is likely

8 Chris and Ken recently ____ up a web design company.
  a) got        b) put        c) set       d) turned

9 Karen is really tight-____ and never pays for anything
when we go out.
  a) handed     b) nosed      c) fingered  d) fisted

10 Mark never gets to work on time ____ he leaves before
the rush hour begins.
  a) as long as  b) providing  c) if        d) unless

11 We ____ have a big dog at home before we moved to the
city.
  a) would            b) were used to
  c) used to          d) got used to

[    | 5 ]

## 9 Complete the second sentence so that it means the same as the first. Use the word in capitals.

1 Peter ignored the crowds of reporters outside his house.
TOOK
  _Peter took no notice of the crowds of reporters outside his_
  _house_____.

2 Paul might be late because it's rush hour now.  LIKELY
  Paul _____.

3 Judy doesn't mix much with others.  HERSELF
  Judy _____.

4 When will the current director resign?  DOWN
  When _____?

5 Claudia will be upset if you don't go to her party.
UNLESS
  Claudia will be upset _____.

6 There isn't any more sugar.  OUT
  We've _____.

[    | 5 ]

## 10 Complete the words.

1 If o_n_ _l_ _y_ I hadn't said anything!

2 The p _ _ _ _ _ _ _ _ in the city centre is so bad in the
winter that it's hard to breathe.

3 Ben's having second t _ _ _ _ _ _ _ about applying
for promotion as he's not sure that he wants the extra
responsibility.

4 Everyone is praying for rain after the longest
d _ _ _ _ _ _ in living memory.

5 I've just finished reading an excellent
b _ _ _ _ _ _ _ _ of Bill Clinton.

6 Where there's l _ _ _, there's hope.

7 I've never been able to make out the l _ _ _ _ _ of most
pop songs.

8 Phil is such a g _ _ _! All he talks about is computer
games.

9 Before you start messing around with your new keyboard,
I think you should read the m _ _ _ _ _.

10 What's going on in the news these days? I haven't been
keeping t _ _ _ _ of developments at all.

11 It's a p _ _ _ you can't make it to my party, but hopefully
we'll meet up soon.

[    | 5 ]

## READING

**11** Match gaps 1–6 in the text with a)–g). There is one extra sentence you do not need.

Hi Annie

Thanks so much for your newsy email – I'm glad you're enjoying your new job. I know how you were rather dreading it, but I think it's always hard to start again especially when you have to move as well. And what about accommodation – did you decide to find something on your own or are you sharing? ¹ _c_

Quite a lot's happened here as well since I last wrote to you. I finally moved last month. You know I'd been looking to move out of the city centre, well, I found a lovely little house half way between where I had been living and the coast. It's on the edge of the village so it's really quiet, especially at night. ² ___ I haven't quite got used to it yet, having always been a city girl!

Everyone has been very friendly though. You know, before I moved everyone was saying that I was crazy because villagers tend to keep themselves to themselves and don't welcome outsiders, but I can't tell you how kind everyone has been. Of course I was the hot topic of conversation for the first week or so but I guess that's to be expected in a small community. I'm living in a terraced house so have neighbours on either side. ³ ___ In any case, it's certainly good to know that there are people there if I need help.

The hardest thing for me to adjust to has been the change of pace in life here – I've found it difficult to slow down. You know what it's like in the city – everyone's in a rush all the time and it's hard not to join in somehow. Here, however, everything is much slower. I really like it. ⁴ ___

Things are going well on the work front as well. I wasn't sure how this would work out at first. ⁵ ___ I still have to go into the office once a week for meetings, but it's a good balance (and a chance to catch up on office gossip!). I bet some of my colleagues think I'm not really doing anything down here but in fact, I think I get far more done at home as I'm not constantly being disturbed by colleagues. It's amazing how much you can get through in an hour when there's no one else there.

It's early days yet I know, but I really do feel very happy and settled here. Long may it last! I hope you can get some time off soon to come and visit as I know you'll love it too. ⁶ ___ It's not very big, but there's enough room for a small vegetable patch.

Let me know how you're getting on. And send me some photos if you get the chance. I want to see what your new haircut looks like!

Love

Hannah x

a) And it's incredibly dark too as there are no street lights – so you can see the stars.

b) My boss was happy to let me work from home, so that's what I'm doing at the moment.

c) ~~I guess it must be quite expensive if you want to be in town so you might not have much choice.~~

d) It usually takes me an hour or so to go to the post office by the time I've stopped a few times to chat to people!

e) It's been a very stressful time for me recently with all the problems at work and problems with my health.

f) You can give me some tips on the garden.

g) Both sets are friendly, but not too friendly, if you know what I mean.

```
          10
```

## SPEAKING

**12** Rewrite the sentences using the prompts in brackets.

1 Where's the nearest bank?
(Could / tell)
_Could you tell me where the nearest bank is_ ?

2 When did the new course start?
(Can / tell)
_____ ?

3 Help me fill in this application form for a new job.
(Would / mind)
_____ ?

4 Send me another copy of your travel brochure.
(I / grateful)
_____ .

5 Can I make a reservation for this evening?
(wondering / possible)
_____ ?

6 Tell me about the council's plans for the industrial estate.
(like / enquire)
_____ .

```
          5
```

**13** Complete the conversation with the words in the box.

| convinced | point | ~~favour~~ | suppose | sure | way |

A: I'm all in ¹ _favour_ of lowering the voting age.

B: Hmm, I'm not so ²_____. After all, a lot of teenagers are quite immature, aren't they?

A: You've got a ³_____ there, but only those who are really interested would bother to vote.

B: I ⁴_____ so, but how would you encourage them?

A: Well, the ⁵_____ I see it, kids need to learn about politics and current affairs at school.

B: I'm still not ⁶_____, but why don't we see what Jan thinks?

☐ **5**

**14** Put the words into the correct order to make sentences.

1 into / science / John / really / fiction / isn't
_John really isn't into science fiction_ _____.

2 I'm / the / of / big / a / not / classics / fan
_____.

3 stand / I / spelling / just / couldn't / poor / the
_____.

4 thing / the / writing / The / enjoy / the / I / about / is / humour / most
_____.

5 I / What / their / main / was / characters / liked / the / about / relationship
_____.

6 couldn't / I / into / mood / get / the / just / right
_____.

☐ **5**

## WRITING

**15** Underline the mistakes using the correction code. Then write the corrections.

1 **(sp)** Dad is such an _embarrasment_ on the dance floor.
_embarrassment_

2 **(p)** I'm not feeling very well which is unusual for me.
_____

3 **(wo)** Do you think you'll ever get your first great love over?
_____

4 **(ww)** I haven't finished my homework already.
_____

5 **(v)** Jeff worked in the same company since 2005.
_____

6 **(gr)** I'll never get used to speak English all day.
_____

☐ **5**

**16** You have just started a new job in a new town. Write an informal email to tell your friends how everything is going. Write 140–180 words.

_____
_____
_____
_____
_____
_____
_____
_____
_____
_____
_____
_____
_____
_____
_____
_____
_____
_____
_____
_____
_____
_____
_____
_____
_____
_____
_____
_____
_____
_____
_____
_____
_____
_____
_____

☐ **10**

**Total:** ☐ **100**

## LISTENING

**1** ▶ 39 **Listen to six speakers. Are the statements true (T) or false (F)?**

1 The woman is aggressive towards Ben. _____F_
2 The woman likes factual programmes. _____
3 The man is older than his colleagues. _____
4 The woman thinks the exhibition reflected the critics' views. _____
5 The man is embarrassed about enjoying gossip. _____
6 The man looks forward to getting up every day. _____

| | 10 |

**2** ▶ 40 **What are they talking about? Listen and tick the correct answer: a), b) or c).**

1 a) kidnapping _____
  b) stalking ✓
  c) mugging _____
2 a) mugging _____
  b) shoplifting _____
  c) pickpocketing _____
3 a) hacking _____
  b) tax evasion _____
  c) identity theft _____
4 a) shoplifting _____
  b) vandalism _____
  c) pickpocketing _____
5 a) kidnapping _____
  b) mugging _____
  c) bribery _____
6 a) arson _____
  b) vandalism _____
  c) counterfeiting _____

| | 10 |

## PRONUNCIATION

**3** ▶ 41 **Underline the main stress in the words.**

1 appreciate
2 obligation
3 advice
4 oblige
5 prefer
6 interference
7 appreciation
8 practise
9 encouragement
10 achievement
11 preference

| | 5 |

## GRAMMAR AND VOCABULARY

**4** **Underline the correct alternative.**

1 I saw the train pull *off* / _out_ of the station.
2 Ian insisted *on* / *for* paying for the meal.
3 I was falsely accused *for* / *of* shoplifting.
4 Jo looks very young *for* / *in* her age.
5 We're campaigning to save our village hall *against* / *from* property developers.
6 He blames me *about* / *for* his mistakes.
7 I can't believe you fell *for* / *in* that old trick – you're so gullible.
8 I'm never really *on* / *over* the ball in the morning. I need coffee to wake me up.
9 It's important to look *at* / *on* the bright side especially when life is tough.
10 I thought Mike came *across* / *down* very well at the meeting.
11 Our neighbours' house was broken *into* / *in* again last week.

| | 5 |

**5** **Complete the sentences. Use the correct form of the word in capitals.**

1 What's the ___width___ of your table? WIDE
2 I always enjoy reading the _____ pages of the Sunday papers. EDIT
3 I'm very impressed by Susan's _____. She's really grown up now. MATURE
4 What is the _____ of your most popular newspaper? READ
5 You're under no _____, but I would really appreciate your help. OBLIGE
6 You choose. I really don't have a _____. PREFER

| | 5 |

**6** **Correct two mistakes in each sentence.**

1 It's hard to come _on_ a decision as I can see all the _prose_ and cons so easily.
   _to_          _pros_
2 The policeman tried arresting the burglar, what was a dangerous thing to do.
   _____     _____
3 I will be leaving the country by the time you are reading my letter.
   _____     _____
4 Julia Roberts, whose my favourite actress, got raving reviews for her film.
   _____     _____
5 As a child I was only let to stay up late once on a blue moon.
   _____     _____
6 I wouldn't live in Australia now if I had got a visa.
   _____     _____

| | 5 |

**7** Complete the second sentence so that it means the same as the first. Use the word in capitals.

1 Were you able to get tickets for the World Cup Final?
MANGE
*Did you manage to get tickets* for the World Cup Final?

2 I'm sure you didn't see John yesterday because he's abroad at the moment. HAVE
You _____ he's abroad at the moment.

3 I'm really tired because I stayed up late last night. IF
I wouldn't be so tired _____ late last night.

4 'I'm sorry I let you down Maria,' said Lucy.
APOLOGISED
Lucy _____ her down.

5 Emily isn't allowed to watch horror films by her parents.
LET
Emily's parents _____ horror films.

6 Can I stay at your place tonight? PUT
Can you _____ tonight?

| | 5 |
|---|---|

**8** Complete the text with <u>one</u> word in each gap.

I've never been ¹ _able_ to understand why so
² _____ people are obsessed with the ageing
process. Whenever you ³ _____ on the television or
flick through ⁴ _____ magazine, you'll see loads of
advertisements ⁵ _____ beauty products claiming
to ⁶ _____ years off you. Of course it's great to look
young ⁷ _____ your age, but I believe that when
you feel good on the ⁸ _____, you look good on the
outside. I'd say that I'm ⁹ _____ my prime now.
I wake up every morning feeling focused and I look
¹⁰ _____ to getting up and going to work. The last
thing I feel ¹¹ _____ doing is retiring as there are still
so many things to do.

| | 5 |
|---|---|

**9** Choose the correct answer: a), b), c) or d).

1 I'm sorry I didn't mean what I just said. I _b_ it all back.
   a) give    b) take    c) put    d) pull

2 I'm really looking forward ____ you later.
   a) to see    b) seeing    c) to seeing    d) see

3 That sales assistant was so ____ – in fact she was downright rude.
   a) diplomatic    b) tactful
   c) helpless    d) unhelpful

4 Please ____ papers now and correct your partner's answers.
   a) swap    b) grab    c) divert    d) scam

5 We'll have to cut the meeting ____ as something urgent has come up.
   a) down    b) off    c) up    d) short

6 We'll ____ sun, sand and sea this time next week.
   a) be enjoying    b) have been enjoying
   c) have enjoyed    d) enjoy

7 Steve ____ have lost his way as he's never late.
   a) can't    b) must    c) mustn't    d) can

8 My grandmother ____ me eat everything on my plate even if I didn't want to.
   a) let    b) allowed    c) made    d) forced

9 I'm so busy these days that there's ____ time to relax.
   a) a little    b) enough    c) few    d) little

10 I can't really remember the house ____ I grew up in.
   a) where    b) that    c) what    d) whose

11 If Sam had enough money, he ____ his car last week.
   a) wouldn't have sold    b) would have sold
   c) wouldn't sell    d) would sell

| | 5 |
|---|---|

**10** Match 1–11 with a)–k).

| | | | | |
|---|---|---|---|---|
| 1 | pros and | _i_ | a) | on |
| 2 | peace and | ___ | b) | ready |
| 3 | leaps and | ___ | c) | downs |
| 4 | on and | ___ | d) | then |
| 5 | rough and | ___ | e) | through |
| 6 | now and | ___ | f) | breezy |
| 7 | sick and | ___ | g) | bounds |
| 8 | ups and | ___ | h) | take |
| 9 | through and | ___ | i) | ~~cons~~ |
| 10 | give and | ___ | j) | quiet |
| 11 | bright and | ___ | k) | tired |

| | 5 |
|---|---|

**11** Read the article and write true (T) or false (F) next to the statements 1–11.

# Live long, keep healthy

Thanks to developments in medical research it is no longer unusual for people to live well into their eighties and nineties, but this longevity can come at a price and there are few who would wish to have a long life if they knew that they were going to end their days suffering from ill health or loneliness.

Here at *Healthy Ageing*, we believe that humour and a positive outlook play a big part in keeping us young so we hope you will enjoy our humorous guide to growing old.

## Forget numbers

Don't worry about numbers. Most of them are not important. Don't think about numbers connected to age, weight and height. Let the doctors worry about those. After all, that's what we pay them for, isn't it?

## Be a student

Continue to learn. Keep abreast of what's going on in the world. If you don't have one already, get a computer and teach yourself how to use it. Take up new hobbies. Get out into the garden. Join the local history society. Whatever it is, make sure you use your brain because if you don't, your brain will just give up on you.

## Spend time with happy people

Be careful about the company you keep. Avoid negative people. They bring you down and make you feel depressed.

## Laugh

Laughter works in more ways than you can imagine. Did you know that laughter dissolves tension, stress, anxiety, irritation, anger, grief and depression? Laughter boosts the immune system as well as releasing endorphins so make sure you start seeing the funny side.

## Remember simple pleasures

Take time to listen to the birds. Sit back and watch the clouds. Go to a café and just simply watch the world go by.

## Accept times of sadness

Everyone goes through difficult times, no one's denying that. It's how you deal with them that counts: cry if you need to and move on.

## Surround yourself with things you love

Whatever that might be: family, pets, keepsakes, music, plants. Your home is your refuge.

## Take care of your health

If it is good, preserve it. If it is unstable, improve it. If you can't improve it by yourself, be sure to ask for professional help.

## Don't feel guilty

Enjoy your pleasures, and don't reproach yourself. Go shopping, go abroad. If you have the money, enjoy it.

## And most important of all …

Tell the people you love that you love them, at every opportunity. It's good for you, it's good for them.

We hope that you've enjoyed reading these tips. Please write in and let us know what keeps you young at heart and we'll print your ideas in next month's edition.

According to the writer:

1 we are living longer than we used to. _T_
2 old people can feel lonely. ____
3 it doesn't matter if we have a pessimistic outlook on life. ____
4 you should pay your doctor to worry about you. ____
5 your brain needs stimulation. ____
6 you shouldn't be with people who are negative. ____
7 laughter improves your health. ____
8 you must go outdoors every day. ____
9 it is bad for you to cry. ____
10 you should have a pet. ____
11 your health is your responsibility. ____

| 10 |

## SPEAKING

**12** Complete the conversation by adding the missing words from the box to the phrases in bold.

| shouldn't | obvious | ~~you~~ | can | surely | is |
|---|---|---|---|---|---|

A: [1]**Don't** _you_ **agree that** voting should be compulsory like it is in Australia?

B: [2]**But** it should be up to the individual.

A: Why? [3]**Anyone see that** politics affects our daily lives.

B: [4]**But** we just let politicians get on with governing the country?

A: [5]**So what you're saying that** we as individuals have no power?

B: [6]**But isn't it that** we don't?

A: Well clearly we'll have to agree to disagree.

[  ] **5**

**13** There is <u>one</u> extra word in each sentence. Cross out the extra word.

1  Tom is such a ~~so~~ helpful person, don't you think?
2  Why on the earth didn't you listen to me?
3  I so do know the answer to the question if you don't mind!
4  My neighbours are the ones who they looked after my house while I was away.
5  It's very completely insane to spend so much money on clothes.
6  There's no the way you could have met Paul before.

[  ] **5**

**14** Complete the sentences with the correct form of the words in the box.

| happen | ~~catch~~ | realise | occur | go | remind |
|---|---|---|---|---|---|

1  I'm afraid I didn't ___catch___ the make of car. It could have been a Renault.
2  It _____ to me that the young man was acting suspiciously.
3  My mind just _____ blank and I couldn't remember anything.
4  It all _____ so fast that I just froze.
5  She _____ me of my sister as they're both tall and blonde.
6  It was only later that I _____ the danger I'd been in.

[  ] **5**

## WRITING

**15** Rewrite the two sentences as one sentence. Use the word in brackets.

1  Some teenagers watch too much television. Others prefer to do sport.  (While)
   _While some teenagers watch too much television, others_
   _prefer to do sport._

2  Max started going to the gym every day. He hoped to impress his colleagues.  (in order to)
   _____
   _____

3  My brother is very ambitious. He doesn't work hard. (Although)
   _____
   _____

4  Julia wrote out a new CV. She wanted to apply for another job.  (because)
   _____
   _____

5  Sally was exhausted. She still went to Jodie's wedding. (Despite)
   _____
   _____

6  Ben took a week off. He wanted to go to his sister's wedding in Canada.  (for)
   _____
   _____

[  ] **5**

**16** Write a leaflet giving advice about using public transport in your town/country. Write 140–180 words on a separate sheet of paper.

[  ] **10**

| Total: | 100 |
|---|---|

## LISTENING

**1** ▶ 39 Listen to six speakers. Are the statements true (T) or false (F)?

1 The woman is aggressive towards Ben.  _F_
2 The woman doesn't like television much.  ____
3 The man is losing his job because of his age.  ____
4 The woman didn't enjoy the exhibition.  ____
5 The man only reads serious news.  ____
6 The man used to be on the ball in the mornings.  ____

**10**

**2** ▶ 40 What are they talking about? Listen and tick the correct answer: a), b) or c).

1 a) kidnapping
  b) stalking ✓
  c) mugging ____
2 a) mugging ____
  b) pickpocketing ____
  c) shoplifting ____
3 a) identity theft ____
  b) tax evasion ____
  c) hacking ____
4 a) vandalism ____
  b) shoplifting ____
  c) pickpocketing ____
5 a) kidnapping ____
  b) bribery ____
  c) mugging ____
6 a) arson ____
  b) vandalism ____
  c) counterfeiting ____

**10**

## PRONUNCIATION

**3** ▶ 41 Underline the main stress in the words.

1 appreciate
2 obligation
3 advice
4 oblige
5 prefer
6 interference
7 appreciation
8 practise
9 encouragement
10 achievement
11 preference

**5**

## GRAMMAR AND VOCABULARY

**4** Underline the correct alternative.

1 I saw the train pull off / _out_ of the station.
2 My car broke down / up in the middle of town. It was so embarrassing.
3 He was accused of / for shoplifting.
4 Did you fall for / into that old trick – you're so gullible.
5 George looks rather old for / in his age.
6 We're campaigning to save our village hall against / from property developers.
7 He blames me about / for his mistakes.
8 I'm never really on / over the ball in the morning. I'm much more of a night owl.
9 When things aren't going well, it's important to look at / on the bright side.
10 He came across / down well at the meeting.
11 My shed was broken into / in last week.

**5**

**5** Complete the sentences. Use the correct form of the word in capitals.

1 What's the ___width___ of your table? WIDE
2 I'm tired of Sue's _____. Why can't she mind her own business? INTERFERE
3 Jack seems incredibly _____. After all, he's in his twenties now. MATURE
4 Look at the _____ of that tree. It's magnificent! HIGH
5 You're under no _____ to help, but I'd certainly appreciate your advice. OBLIGE
6 I'd like to have these photos _____ so we can frame them. LARGE

**5**

**6** Correct two mistakes in each sentence.

1 It's hard to come _on_ a decision as I can see all the _prose_ and cons so easily.
  _to_  _pros_
2 I remember to see a man outside, but I didn't suspect him for doing anything bad.
  _____  _____
3 Julia Roberts, whose my favourite actress, got rave critics for her last film.
  _____  _____
4 My parents only allowed me stay up late once in a green moon.
  _____  _____
5 I wouldn't live in Australia now if I had got a visa.
  _____  _____
6 You mustn't have seen Jason at the gym as he's been banned of that place.
  _____  _____

**5**

**7** Complete the second sentence so that it means the same as the first. Use the word in capitals.

1 Were you able to get tickets for the World Cup Final? MANAGE

   _Did you manage to get tickets_ for the World Cup Final?

2 Jane started eating less because she wanted to lose weight. ORDER

   Jane started eating less _____.

3 I'm really tired because I stayed up late last night. IF

   _____, I wouldn't be so tired.

4 'I'm sorry I let you down Maria,' said Lucy. APOLOGISED

   Lucy _____ her down.

5 Can I stay in your spare room tonight? PUT

   Can you _____ tonight?

6 Although she's very intelligent, Debs is also very modest. DESPITE

   Debs is very modest _____.

[ ] **5**

**8** Complete the text with <u>one</u> word in each gap.

I've never been ¹__able__ to understand why so many people ²_____ obsessed with the ageing process. Whenever you turn ³_____ the television or flick through a magazine, ⁴_____ 'll see loads of advertisements ⁵_____ beauty products claiming to ⁶_____ years off you. Of course it's great to look young for your ⁷_____, but I believe that when you feel good on the inside, you look good on the ⁸_____. I'd say that I'm in my prime now. I wake ⁹_____ every morning feeling focused and I look forward to ¹⁰_____ up and going to work. The last thing I feel like ¹¹_____ is retiring as there are still so many things I can do in my job.

[ ] **5**

**9** Choose the correct answer: a), b), c) or d).

1 I'm sorry, I didn't mean what I just said. I _b_ it all back.
   a) give   b) take (circled)   c) put   d) pull
2 I'm really looking forward ____ you later.
   a) to see   b) seeing   c) to seeing   d) see
3 That sales assistant was completely ____ – in fact she had no idea what to do.
   a) diplomatic   b) tactful   c) helpless   d) unhelpful
4 Please ____ papers now and correct your partner's answers.
   a) scam   b) grab   c) divert   d) swap
5 We'll have to ____ the meeting short as something urgent has come up.
   a) cut   b) break   c) put   d) get
6 We'll ____ a week of sun, sand and sea by this time next week.
   a) be enjoying   b) have been enjoying   c) have enjoyed   d) enjoy
7 Steve ____ have lost his way as he's never late.
   a) can't   b) must   c) mustn't   d) can
8 My grandmother never ____ me eat everything on my plate thank goodness.
   a) let   b) allowed   c) made   d) forced
9 I'm so busy these days that there's ____ time to relax.
   a) a little   b) enough   c) few   d) little
10 I can't really remember the house ____ I grew up.
   a) where   b) that   c) what   d) whose
11 If Sam had enough money, he ____ his car last week.
   a) wouldn't have sold   b) would have sold   c) wouldn't sell   d) would sell

[ ] **5**

**10** Match 1–11 with a)–k).

1 pros and ___ _i_
2 peace and ___
3 leaps and ___
4 on and ___
5 rough and ___
6 now and ___
7 sick and ___
8 ups and ___
9 through and ___
10 give and ___
11 bright and ___

a) on
b) take
c) downs
d) then
e) tired
f) breezy
g) bounds
h) ready
i) ~~cons~~
j) through
k) quiet

[ ] **5**

## READING

**11** Read the article and write true (T) or false (F) next to the statements 1–11.

# Live long, keep healthy

Thanks to developments in medical research it is no longer unusual for people to live well into their eighties and nineties, but this longevity can come at a price and there are few who would wish to have a long life if they knew that they were going to end their days suffering from ill health or loneliness.

Here at *Healthy Ageing*, we believe that humour and a positive outlook play a big part in keeping us young so we hope you will enjoy our humorous guide to growing old.

### Forget numbers

Don't worry about numbers. Most of them are not important. Don't think about numbers connected to age, weight and height. Let the doctors worry about those. After all, that's what we pay them for, isn't it?

### Be a student

Continue to learn. Keep abreast of what's going on in the world. If you don't have one already, get a computer and teach yourself how to use it. Take up new hobbies. Get out into the garden. Join the local history society. Whatever it is, make sure you use your brain because if you don't, your brain will just give up on you.

### Spend time with happy people

Be careful about the company you keep. Avoid negative people. They bring you down and make you feel depressed.

### Laugh

Laughter works in more ways than you can imagine. Did you know that laughter dissolves tension, stress, anxiety, irritation, anger, grief and depression? Laughter boosts the immune system as well as releasing endorphins so make sure you start seeing the funny side.

### Remember simple pleasures

Take time to listen to the birds. Sit back and watch the clouds. Go to a café and just simply watch the world go by.

### Accept times of sadness

Everyone goes through difficult times, no one's denying that. It's how you deal with them that counts: cry if you need to and move on.

### Surround yourself with things you love

Whatever that might be: family, pets, keepsakes, music, plants. Your home is your refuge.

### Take care of your health

If it is good, preserve it. If it is unstable, improve it. If you can't improve it by yourself, be sure to ask for professional help.

### Don't feel guilty

Enjoy your pleasures, and don't reproach yourself. Go shopping, go abroad. If you have the money, enjoy it.

### And most important of all ...

Tell the people you love that you love them, at every opportunity. It's good for you, it's good for them.

We hope that you've enjoyed reading these tips. Please write in and let us know what keeps you young at heart and we'll print your ideas in next month's edition.

According to the writer:

1 we are living longer than we used to. _T_

2 old people can get ill and lonely. ____

3 it is important to be optimistic. ____

4 you should pay your doctor to worry about you. ____

5 your brain will stop working if it is not stimulated. ____

6 you should try to avoid negative people. ____

7 laughter improves both mind and body. ____

8 you must go out every day. ____

9 you should not cry. ____

10 people with pets live longer. ____

11 your health is your responsibility alone. ____

| 10 |

## SPEAKING

**12** Complete the conversation by adding the missing words from the box to the phrases in bold.

> shouldn't   it   ~~you~~   see   surely   what

A: ¹**Don't** _you_ **agree that** voting should be compulsory like it is in Australia?

B: ²**But** it should be up to the individual.

A: Why? ³**Anyone can that** politics affects our daily lives.

B: ⁴**But** we just let politicians get on with governing the country?

A: ⁵**So you're saying is that** we as individuals have no power?

B: ⁶**But isn't obvious that** we don't?

A: Well clearly we'll have to agree to disagree.

☐ 5

**13** There is <u>one</u> extra word in each sentence. Cross out the extra word.

1 Tom is such a ~~so~~ helpful person, don't you think?
2 Why on the earth didn't you listen to me?
3 I so do know the answer to the question if you don't mind!
4 My neighbours are the ones who they looked after my house while I was away.
5 It's very completely insane to spend so much money on clothes.
6 There's no the way you could have met Paul before.

☐ 5

**14** Complete the sentences with the correct form of the words in the box.

> happen   realise   occur   go   remind   ~~catch~~

1 I'm afraid I didn't __catch__ the make of car. It could have been a Renault.
2 It _____ to me that the young man was acting suspiciously.
3 It all _____ so fast that I just froze.
4 She _____ me of my sister as they're both tall and blonde.
5 It was only later that I _____ the danger I'd been in.
6 My mind just _____ blank and I couldn't remember anything.

☐ 5

## WRITING

**15** Rewrite the two sentences as one sentence. Use the word in brackets.

1 Some teenagers watch too much television. Others prefer to do sport. (While)
   _While some teenagers watch too much television, others prefer to do sport._

2 Max started going to the gym last month. He hopes to impress his children. (to)

3 My brother doesn't work hard. He is very ambitious. (Although)

4 Julia sent out lots of CVs. She wanted to find a new job. (because)

5 Sally was exhausted. She still went to Jodie's party. (Despite)

6 Ben took a break. He wanted to go to his sister's wedding. (for)

☐ 5

**16** Write a leaflet giving advice about using public transport in your town/country. Write 140–180 words on a separate sheet of paper.

☐ 10

Total: ☐ 100

## Mid-course Test A

### LISTENING

**1**

Audioscript

**1**

I'm not really one for dancing. I mean, I love listening to music and doing the odd bit of toe tapping but that's pretty much as far as it goes, or at least that's what I'd have said a year ago … but now … well! My neighbour persuaded me to go along to salsa classes at the local community centre a few months ago … she didn't want to go alone so I agreed, somewhat reluctantly I must say, but once I'd got over the initial embarrassment I just loved it. The rhythms, the moves and apart from anything, it's a really good work-out.

**2**

I started renting this apartment about two years ago and just recently decided to advertise for a flatmate. I got loads of answers to my ad as this flat's right in the city centre. Obviously I couldn't interview everyone so I narrowed it down to people I thought would fit in well with my lifestyle and I've been very lucky. Jack keeps himself to himself pretty much most of the time and certainly pulls his weight with all the household stuff which is great as I must say I'm quite particular about things.

**3**

There aren't many things I'd change if I had my time again, but if I could turn back the clock I think I'd have stayed in Australia when I had the chance. I was offered a really good job in Sydney during my gap year but decided not to take up the offer as I'd already got a place at uni for that autumn. At the time I remember thinking that I could always go back but somehow life just got in the way!

**4**

I've always loved the classics, much more than current fiction, so I'd say my favourite book has to be *Jane Eyre* by Charlotte Brontë. I first read it when I was at school and was struck by the passion in the writing. The book had everything … adventure, love, hate, despair … I guess I was probably too young to appreciate it all when I read it the first time but now that I'm an adult, it's a book I have often returned to. It's just the perfect read for a winter's afternoon curled up by the fire.

**5**

I'm not a great fan of package holidays so tend to go off the beaten track to look for the more remote, unspoilt places on our planet and Lake Baikal in Siberia is one such place! I went last winter and spent a few days on the shore of that incredible lake. I was pretty much the only person staying in the hotel as far as I could make out so it was quite eerie in some ways. The lake was starting to freeze over so the views were breathtakingly beautiful … definitely a place to go back to.

**6**

… without a doubt, the mobile phone. I can't think of anything more annoying than sitting on the train listening to everyone's inane conversations. I always sit in the 'quiet' carriage where people aren't supposed to listen to their MP3 players or use their phones but that doesn't seem to stop anyone. Mind you, even though I hate them, I have to confess I finally succumbed and bought a mobile last year but only because I was going travelling and everyone wanted me to get one in case of emergency. And now I'm back I never bother to switch it on and don't even know how to use it properly.

2T   3T   4F   5T   6F

**2**

Audioscript

**1**

I've signed up to quite a few connected with environmental issues. I try to post my comments before I start work otherwise it can all get too time-consuming. That's the drawback I guess, but used wisely, they're a great tool.

**2**

To be honest I don't think the solution is sending in loads of food. Year after year these countries suffer such terrible tragedies but in so many cases the food doesn't get delivered to the people who are starving and in any case that's just a short-term fix.

**3**

I read somewhere that during an average working day you can be caught on film up to 300 times! How is that possible? And what's the point?! There aren't enough people to go through all the footage and what evidence is there to suggest that crime figures have fallen in areas where they've been installed?

**4**

Most of my colleagues are OK but unfortunately I have to share my office with someone who must be the world's greatest bore when it comes to computers … on and on and on he goes. I'm sure I could walk out of the room and he'd still carry on!

**5**

There's a new ad on TV and I just can't get the tune out of my head. I find myself singing it to myself when I'm on the bus, walking along the road … something will set me off and that's it. Really irritating but I suppose it shows just how powerful advertising is though, ironically, I couldn't tell you what the ad is actually for.

**6**

Well, if you don't try you'll never know will you? I've always been a bit of a risk taker especially when it comes to work. I can't think of anything worse than being stuck in a dead-end job doing the same thing day in day out. There are so many interesting things to do and as they say … nothing ventured, nothing gained.

2c   3c   4a   5b   6b

### PRONUNCIATION

**3**

2   What've you been <u>doing</u>? You look ex<u>haus</u>ted!

3   Their <u>photos</u> might be <u>sent</u> to the <u>news</u>papers.

4   Dan was feeling <u>sad</u> because his <u>holi</u>day was <u>com</u>ing to an <u>end</u>.

5   If <u>only</u> I hadn't re<u>fused</u> to <u>help</u>.

6   I'm <u>not</u> a big <u>fan</u> of autobi<u>og</u>raphies.

### GRAMMAR AND VOCABULARY

**4**

2 into   3 up   4 over   5 of   6 up   7 off
8 on   9 on   10 With   11 to

**5**

2   outrageous   3 homelessness
4   disappointment   5 revolutionised
6   Satisfaction

**6**

2   the   3 bit   4 taken   5 much/any
6   hours   7 spending   8 myself   9 a
10 up   11 suppose/guess

**7**

2   ~~were~~ was, ~~disturbed~~ disturbing

3   ~~was~~ has, ~~heaviness~~ weight

4   ~~build~~ cross, ~~get~~ come

5   ~~would~~ will, ~~often~~ long

6   ~~had~~ has, ~~biography~~ autobiography

**8**

2a   3d   4c   5b   6a   7d   8c   9b   10a   11d

**9**

2   started working/work five years ago.

3   will the current director step down?

4   keeps herself to herself.

5   run out of milk.

6   get over the death of my dog.

**10**

2   crow   3 biographies   4 second   5 hope
6   lyrics   7 densely   8 manual
9   drawback   10 pity   11 drought

### READING

**11**

2g   3d   4f   5a   6e   *extra sentence = b*

### SPEAKING

**12**

2   Would you mind helping me with my luggage?

3   I'd be grateful if you would/could send me another copy of the contract.

4   I'd like to enquire about the council's plans for the city centre.

5   Can you tell me when the new language course started?